A Casebook on European Consumer Law

Edited by

REINER SCHULZE

HANS SCHULTE-NÖLKE

and

JACKIE JONES

·HART·
PUBLISHING

HART PUBLISHING

OXFORD AND PORTLAND, OREGON

2002

Published in North America (US and Canada) by
Hart Publishing
c/o International Specialized Book Services
5804 NE Hassalo Street
Portland, Oregon
97213-3644
USA

Distributed in Netherlands, Belgium and Luxembourg by
Intersentia, Churchillaan 108
B2900 Schoten
Antwerpen
Belgium

Hart Publishing is a specialist legal publisher based in Oxford, England. To order
further copies of this book or to request a list of other publications please
write to:

Hart Publishing, Salters Boatyard, Folly Bridge,
Abingdon Rd, Oxford, OX1 4LB
Telephone: +44 (0)1865 245533 Fax: 44 (0) 1865 794882
email: mail@hartpub.co.uk
WEBSITE: http//:www.hartpub.co.uk

British Library Cataloguing in Publication Data
Data Available

ISBN 1-84113-227-6 (paperback)

Typeset by SNP Best-set Typesetter Ltd., Hong Kong
Printed and bound in Great Britain
by Bell and Bain Ltd, Glasgow.

A CASEBOOK ON
EUROPEAN CONSUMER LAW

Preface

European Community law has led to a profound change in the legal systems of the Member States. The effects of European legal harmonisation are becoming ever more noticeable in the everyday life of European citizens. This applies especially to consumers. From the consumer's point of view the introduction of the Euro and market liberalisation with cross-border competition bring with it not only great opportunities but also great risks. An effective protection of the consumer demands a European consumer policy which corresponds with the realisation of a European Internal Market. In the European Community a European consumer law is being created which stands besides and actively changes the Member States' legal systems. Today, in many fields of legal practice knowledge of European consumer law has become a mandatory requirement. The new Directive on the sale of consumer goods only serves to illustrate this point.

This Casebook serves as an introduction to the case law of the European Court of Justice (ECJ) on consumer law. It forms part of a series of Casebooks on the case law of the ECJ. The aim and structure of the Casebooks are more fully described in the annex to the contents page of this volume. The subjects dealt with in the series are intended to meet the needs of legal practice. This particular Casebook is concerned with areas of private law relating to consumer contracts, advertising and European product liability. Some closely related cases concerning product safety and the labelling of goods have been included as has the Brussels Convention, reflecting the increasing importance of cross-border disputes between consumers.

The book is aimed at lawyers in general and not solely at consumer law specialists. It therefore does not concentrate on the various academic disputes and individual opinions. First and foremost the book should act as an introduction to the aims and content of European consumer law and the way it interacts with the legal systems of Member States. To this end the book illustrates step-by-step how the ECJ contributes to the formation of European consumer law and seeks to reconcile it with the sometimes conflicting aims pursued by the Internal Market. Particular attention is paid to the question surrounding the object of consumer protection illustrated by the debate concerning the ECJ's concept of the consumer and its compatibility with the domestic legal systems. This point concerns the basic question pertaining to the relationship between the autonomy of the private individual, competition and the regulation of the market by the State. Naturally, each Member State has developed its own concept of where the line demarcating the responsibilities of the individual and the State should be drawn. This demarcation is often shifted during the process of European legal harmonisation. One of the main tasks of legal academia and practice lies in noting such shifts and restructuring the domestic laws of Member States (which are, in certain areas, based on different principles), accordingly. The aim of this endeavour must not be to afford the respective legal systems the best possible protection from the threat of change presented by 'foreign' European law. In any case, European law forms part of each domestic legal system. Ultimately, it comes down to the development of a legal and economic order which reflects the new conditions of the European market and which is tailored to meet the needs of all, not least those of the consumer. This balance between freedom and limitation, between private autonomy and State intervention is admittedly a precarious one at any time. *Ius est ars boni et aequi.*

This Casebook has been produced by the Centre for European Private Law at the University of Münster in connection with the Research Network 'Common Principles of European Law', a project supported by the European Union. The following corespondents have participated in the preparation and the editing of the book: Dr *Benoît Dumollard* from Lyon, Dr *Arno Engel* from Salzburg, *Ursula Flüchter* from Münster, Dott *Alberto Musy* and Dott *Paulo Gozzo* from Turin, Dott *Paolisa Nebbia* from Southampton and Dott *Arianna Pretto* from Turin. Much of the Casebook was originally written in German and we are very grateful to *Christopher Dallimore* LLB (Cardiff), LLM (Trier) for translating these sections into English. We would also like to thank Professor Dr *Christian Kohler* (Luxemburg) and Dr *Rachel Fenton* (Bristol) for their invaluable support. Many have been involved in the organisation and editorial tasks and we would also like to thank them for their time and effort, in particular *Christoph Busch* and *Christian Vogel*. It has been very rewarding and pleasant to work with all those involved. The whole project would not have been possible without the financial support of the European Union in connection with the aforementioned Research Network 'Common Principles of European Contract Law' which has been supported from funds of the TMR Programme (Training and Mobility of Researchers) of the European Commission. The Network partners are the universities of Barcelona, Berlin (Humboldt), Lyon, Nijmegen, Oxford, Turin, together with Münster which acts as Network Co-ordinator.

Bristol and Münster   Reiner Schulze
September 2001   Hans Schulte-Nölke
                                                                    Jackie Jones

Contents

Abbreviations

AMG	Arzneimittelgesetz (Pharmaceutical Law, Austria)
ASA	Advertising Standards Authority (United Kingdom)
Brussels Convention	Brussels Convention of 27 September 1968 on the Jurisdiction and Enforcements of Judgments in Civil and Commercial Matters
COM	Commission Document
CCA	Consumer Credit Act 1974 (United Kingdom)
CPA	Consumer Protection Act 1987 (United Kingdom)
EC	European Community
ECJ	European Court of Justice
ECR	European Court Reports
edn	Edition
EEC	European Economic Community
eg	For Example
et seq	Et sequentes
GWB	Gesetz gegen Wettbewerbsbeschränkungen (Law against Restraints of Competition, Germany)
ITC	Independent Television Commission (United Kingdom)
KSchG	Konsumentenschutzgesetz (Law on Consumer Protection, Austria)
OFT	Office of Fair Trading (United Kingdom)
OJ	Official Journal
R	Regina, Rex
RSV	Reisebürosicherungsverordnung (Travel Agency Security Regulation, Austria)
resp	Respectively
Rome Convention	EC Convention of 19 June 1980 on the Law Applicable to Contractual Obligations
TKG	Telekommunikationsgesetz (Law on Telecommunication, Austria)
UCTA	Unfair Contract Terms Act 1977 (United Kingdom)
UWG	Gesetz gegen den unlauteren Wettbewerb (Law against Unfair Competition, Germany, Austria)
Vol	Volume

The Casebooks—the Structure and Aim of the Series

This new series of Casebooks serves as an introduction to the case law of the European Court of Justice (ECJ) and at the same time illustrates how this case law affects the law of the Member States. The first volume presents decisions of the ECJ which have had a profound influence on the development of private law in Europe (Vol 1: European Private Law 1999). The following volumes are devoted to the ECJ's case law and its effect on the law of the Member States concerning particular areas of law (Vol 2: European Consumer Law 1999; in preparation are European Competition Law and European Company Law). European law develops at all levels not just by building on the basic Treaties setting up the European Union and European Community or by issuing Directives and Regulations but to a large extent by the case law of the ECJ in Luxembourg. It is often the case that the provisions of the basic Treaties and pieces of European legislation are far more in need of interpretation than domestic statutes. This means that the case law of the ECJ as the court of final instance in matters of binding interpretation plays a role of great importance. Moreover, in many areas European law has emerged as 'case law' which has been created by the ECJ itself—using the market freedoms contained in the EC Treaty as a basis, for example (two publications on this subject have appeared at the same time as this Casebook: *Reiner Schulze* (ed), Auslegung europäischen Privatrechts und angeglichenen Rechts; *Hans Schulte-Nölke/Reiner Schulze* (eds), Europäische Rechtsangleichung und nationale Privatrechte; both 1999).

The Casebooks are aimed at lawyers both in education and practice who would like to familiarise themselves with the basic principles and structure of the mountainous corpus of European law. Each volume guides the reader through the leading case law of the ECJ, offers an introduction to the central topics of each legal area and simultaneously presents the arguments and style adopted by the Court. The key passages of the leading judgments in this area of law have been reproduced *verbatim*. A short commentary to each of these cases summarises the background and consequences on European law and explains further important judgments. Finally, the effects that the judgment has had in individual countries are presented. This presentation enables the reader to grasp the way in which European and domestic law intertwines. A selection of important literature and case law references from the Member States enables the reader to deepen his or her knowledge.

The Casebooks are suitable for self-study and as a basis for teaching and further education. The choice of the subjects dealt with in each Casebook is designed to meet the needs of judges and lawyers who are occupied with the relevant legal area. Although it has been necessary to limit the scope, the layout of the volumes' aim is to combine the educational concern of an introductory overview with a representative collection of the leading decisions of the ECJ. It is possible to commence reading the Casebooks at any place. The individual cases are linked by references to parallel problems found in other cases. A table of the leading legislative measures of European law and the cases dealt with additionally allow the Casebooks to be used as reference materials for a quick method of obtaining information.

The decisions of the ECJ have been reproduced using the official collection of the European Court's judgments. The ruling of the Court is placed at the beginning of each case. Following this, the facts of the case upon which the judgment is based are summarised. The information contained in the facts of the case has largely been taken from the judgment of the Court of Justice but in a partially shortened and linguistically simplified form. There then follows an extract from the judgment. As with the holding of the Court, this section is emphasised by use of a different font. In suitable cases an extract from the Opinion of the Advocate-General has been included. The extracts from the original text of the ECJ have been reproduced *verbatim*; only the references to legislation of Community law or earlier case law have been shortened and presented in a uniform fashion. The paragraph numbers with which the judgments and Opinions are presented in the official collection of judgments from the European Court of Justice appear in the Casebook as ordinals. References to Treaty articles are to the new numbering with the old in brackets, apart from the facts of the case and the judgments themselves which retain the old numbering and (for the facts) the new numbering in brackets.

The commentaries to each judgment start with a European section. There then follow short 'country reports', presented from the point of view of the relevant legal system and which are concerned with the effects that the judgment has had on the law of the relevant Member State. The country reports are in the following order: England and Wales; Germany, France, Italy and in some cases, Austria. It is planned to employ correspondents in several countries to include further countries in future series. The commentaries intend to provide an insight into the most important questions of European law and the effects they have on the legal systems of Member States. With respect to this aim of providing an introduction and guide it is not possible to provide an exhaustive account of each subject, further literature and case law references nor have we attempted to do so. In addition to authoritative books, the literature references contain a selection of discussions on the judgment from a collection published by the ECJ (*Notes-Références des notes de doctrine aux arrêts de la Cour de justice et du Tribunal de première instance des Communautés européennes*). Judgments of the Member States' courts which are related to the case law of the ECJ have been taken from sources available in Member States. As a supplement, the databank set up by the ECJ has been used (*Jurisprudence nationale en matière de droit communautaire*).

The choice of the subjects dealt with, literature and case law is naturally subjective. The correspondents upon whose reports the individual sections of the commentaries have been based are identified by initials. The publishers are responsible for the co-ordination and final revision. The presentation and the subject area have been determined by the aim of providing introductory text-books. For example, the country reports are concerned with the reaction to the judgment in academic literature and whether it the case has been cited in the courts of Member States. Occupying centre stage is the question whether the ECJ's case law has had a discernable impact on the legal systems of Member States. Above all, the country reports make clear how the mass of laws from various sources overlay and mutually influence each other. The reader is provided with a series of examples ready to hand of the areas and ways in which the 'Europeani-sation' of the legal systems of Member States is proceeding apace.

I

International Law of Procedure

INTRODUCTION

With the completion of the Internal Market the possibility of cross-border legal disputes in the field of consumer law is increasing. At the same time the consumer's fear of having fewer rights or rights which are only enforceable with difficulty itself presents an obstacle to competition between domestic and foreign commercial undertakings. An increase in consumer mobility in the Internal Market therefore additionally includes, next to an harmonisation of substantive legal status, measures to improve the enforceability of consumer rights. The consumer's access to justice is one of the major themes dominating the European Union's policy relating to the consumer in recent times. The ECJ is concerned with questions of procedural consumer protection mainly in the interpretation of specific rules on consumer matters in Articles 13 *et al* of the Brussels Convention of 27 September 1968 on the Jurisdiction and Enforcements of Judgments in Civil and Commercial Matters. The decisions, *Bertrand* and *Benincasa*, which follow have been reproduced and commented upon. Both cases illustrate the concept of the consumer which the ECJ has developed for the application of the Convention. Further decisions of the ECJ relating to consumer protection aspects of the Brussels Convention are referred to in the case law displayed. Meanwhile the Council has enacted Regulation 44/2001 on the jurisdiction and recognition and enforcement of judgments in civil and commercial matters (OJ 2001, L12/1). This Regulation will enter into force on 1 March 2002 and will replace the Brussels Convention. The definition of the 'consumer' in Article 13 of the Brussels Convention has not been changed and can be found in Article 15 of the new Regulation 44/2001.

LITERATURE REFERENCES

M Bogdan (ed) *The Brussels Jurisdiction and Enforcement Convention—an EC Court Casebook* (1996); Th Bourgoignie 'L'accès des consommateurs au droit de la justice' (1992) *Revue européenne de droit de la consommation* 119; P de Bra *Verbraucherschutz durch Gerichtsstandsregelungen im deutschen und europäischen Zivilprozeßrecht* (1992) 119; H Gaudemet-Tallon *Les Conventions de Bruxelles et de Lugano* (2nd edn 1996); C Joustra *De internationale consumentenovereenkomst* (1997); H Koch *Verbraucherprozeßrecht* (1990); J Kropholler *Europäisches Zivilprozeßrecht, Kommentar zu EuGVÜ und Lugano-Übereinkommen* (6th edn 1998).

CASE NO. 1 — *Bertrand* C–150/77

Société Bertrand v Paul Ott KG
[1978] ECR 1431

A. Judgment of the ECJ of 21 June 1978

1. Held

The concept of the sale of goods on instalment credit terms within the meaning of Article 13 of the Brussels Convention of 27 September 1968 is not to be understood to extend to the sale of a machine which one party agrees to make with another on the basis of a price to be paid by way of bills of exchange spread over a period.

2. Facts of the Case

The French *Cour de Cassation* made a reference to the ECJ concerning the interpretation of Articles 13, 14 and 28 of the Convention of 27 September 1968 on Jurisdiction and Enforcement of Judgments in Civil and Commercial Matters (the 'Brussels Convention'). This question arose in a suit between two companies which had their registered offices in Germany and France respectively. The case concerned a contract for the sale of a machine tool which had been concluded in 1972. The price of the machine was agreed at DM 74,205 and was to be paid by two equal bills of exchange payable at 60 and 90 days. These bills of exchange were only partly paid. In its absence, the *Landgericht* (Regional Court) Stuttgart ordered the French company to pay DM 7,319, excluding interest. This judgment was declared to be enforceable first by order of the *Tribunal de Grande Instance* Le Mans, and subsequently by a confirmatory judgment of the *Cour d'Appel* Angers. The French company appealed on a point of law against that judgment to the *Cour de Cassation* (First Civil Chamber). The *Cour de Cassation* held that the judgment:

> would be valid under the third paragraph of Article 28 of the Brussels Convention, by virtue of which the jurisdiction of the courts of the state in which the judgment was given may not be reviewed by the court before which enforcement is sought unless the sale can be held to be a sale of goods on instalment credit terms within the meaning of Article 13 of the Convention, in which case, under the second paragraph of Article 14 and the first paragraph of Article 28, proceedings may be brought only in the courts of the state in which the respondent company is domiciled, namely, the courts of France, and execution must be withheld from the decision of a German court.

The *Cour de Cassation*, finding that the solution to the problem thus posed depended on the classification of the contract, referred the following question to the Court for a preliminary ruling:

> Whether the sale of a machine which one company agrees to make with another company on the basis of a price to be paid by way of two equal bills of exchange payable at 60 and 90 days can be held to be sale of goods on instalment credit terms within the meaning of Article 14 of the Brussels Convention?

3. *Extract from the Grounds of the ECJ's Judgment*

8/11. In relation to the sale of goods on instalment credit terms, the second paragraph of Article 14 of the Convention provides that 'proceedings may be brought by a seller against a buyer . . . Only in the courts of the state in which the defendant is domiciled'. In consequence of that imperative rule of jurisdiction the Landgericht Stuttgart, the court in which the original judgment was given, the Tribunal de Grande Instance 'Le Mans' and the Cour d'Appel, Angers, the courts in which enforcement was sought, refused, whether by implication or expressly, in defining their jurisdiction, to classify the contract of sale in question as a contract for the sale of goods on instalment credit terms. The reservations of the Cour de Cassation regarding the precise status of the said contract persuaded it to refer the above-mentioned question to the Court of Justice. By that question the court is asked whether a contract of sale such as that described is entitled to the privileged position with regard to jurisdiction created by the second paragraph of Article 14 of the Convention.

12/16. The concept of a contract of sale on instalment credit terms varies from one Member State to another, in accordance with the objectives pursued by their respective laws. Although all of those laws incorporate the idea of protection for the buyer 'on instalments' because, in general, he is the weaker party in economic terms in comparison with the seller, certain of them are also based on considerations of economic, monetary and savings policy, which are intended to control the practice of sales on instalment credit terms, in particular in relation to consumer durable goods (cars, household electrical and audio-visual equipment, etc). Most often by the indirect expedient of provisions relating to minimum deposits or to the maximum duration of credit or by laying down minimum or maximum values for the total sale price. Since these various objectives have led to the creation of different rules in the various Member States it is necessary, for the purpose of eliminating obstacles to legal relations and to the settlement of disputes in the context of intra-community relations in matters of the sale of goods on instalment credit terms, to consider that concept as being independent and therefore common to all the Member States. In fact, it would not be possible to guarantee the harmonious operation of Article 13 *et seq* of the Convention if the expression in question were given different meanings in the various Member States according to the court first seized of a dispute concerning a contract for the sale of goods on instalment credit terms or the court having jurisdiction to order enforcement. It is therefore indispensable, for the coherence of the provisions of Section 4 of the Convention, to give that expression a uniform substantive content allied to the community order.

17/18. To this finding must be added the fact that the compulsory jurisdiction provided for in the second paragraph of Article 14 of the Convention must, because it derogates from the general principles of the system laid down by the Convention in matters of contract, such as may be derived in particular from Articles 2 and 5 (1), be strictly limited to the objectives proper to Section 4 of the said Convention. Those objectives, as enshrined in Articles 13 and 14 of the Convention, were inspired solely by a desire to protect certain categories of buyers who, having been parties to contracts for the 'sale of goods on instalment credit terms', may be sued by the seller only in the courts of the state in the territory of which the said buyers are domiciled, whereas sellers domiciled in the territory of a contracting state may be sued either in the courts of that state or in the courts of the contracting state in which the buyer is domiciled.

19/22. In order to reply to the question referred to the court an attempt must be made to elaborate an independent concept of the contract of sale on instalment credit terms in view of the general principles which are apparent in this field from the body of laws of the Member States and bearing in mind the objective of the protection of a certain category of buyers. It is clear from the rules common to the laws of the Member States that the sale of goods on instalment credit terms is to be understood as a transaction in which the price is discharged by way of several payments or which is linked to a financing contract. A restrictive interpretation of the second paragraph of Article 14, in conformity with the objectives pursued by Section 4, entails the restriction of the jurisdictional advantage described above to buyers who are in need of protection, their economic position being one of weakness in comparison with sellers by reason of the fact that they are private final consumers and are not engaged, when buying the product acquired on instalment credit terms, in trade or professional activities. The answer to be given to the national court should therefore be that the concept of the sale of goods on instalment credit terms within the meaning of Article 13 of the Brussels Convention of 27 September 1968 is not to be understood to extend to the sale of a machine which one company agrees to make to another company on the basis of a price to be paid by way of bills of exchange spread over a period.

4. *Extract from the Opinion of the Advocate-General*

4. I referred above to the importance of having recourse to the general principles which may be derived from the various laws of the Member States in order to determine independently the meaning of the expressions adopted within the Convention. It must therefore be asked whether such general principles exist in relation to the subject-matter with which we are concerned and, if so, what they provide.

It cannot be said that the phenomenon of sale on instalment credit terms is regulated in a uniform manner in the Member States. It is clear that the national legislatures have considered that phenomenon from three different points of view: sometimes in the context of the ordinary rules relating to contract (as has occurred in Italy and in the Netherlands), at others in special laws adopted for the purpose of protecting persons buying on instalment credit terms (such laws are present in force in nearly all Member States), and, finally, more rarely in the context of avoiding the inflationary consequences which the device of payment on instalment credit terms may entail (such is the case in France, in Belgium, in the United Kingdom and, during a certain period, in Italy). It is clear that, as the point of view changes, the description of the phenomenon may also change; this is one reason why a uniform concept of sale on instalment credit terms does not exist in the laws of the Member States.

By way of a first approximation we may say that at one extreme there is the very broad concept, according to which it is necessary and sufficient that the purchase price of a good, which passes immediately into the possession of the purchaser, is paid in two or more successive instalments; at the opposite extreme there are various restrictive concepts, the criteria for the definition of which are either subjective factors (status of the contracting parties) or objective factors (type, value and intended use of the Article) or factors inherent in the price (minimum or maximum number of instalments, the total amount of the price, the maximum period of payment), or, finally, factors relating to the transfer of possession (clause relating to the retention of possession until the total price has been paid). Of course, beyond the field which may be traced by one or other of those factors there is, purely and simply, the sale by deferred payment in two or more instalments, which is not subject to any special rules: this type of commercial transaction is encountered very frequently, as was rightly noted by the undertaking Ott, in international trade, without its being identified without more ado—whether in practice or at law—with the sale on instalment credit terms.

In a situation which displays such wide divergencies, it may appear pointless to seek principles which are common to the Member States. However, a common tendency may be identified in the field of laws adopted for the protection of buyers on instalment credit terms; and I would emphasise that it is logical and appropriate to approach the matter from this angle, since Article 13 to 15 of the Brussels Convention are themselves, as we saw above, provisions whose objective is to redress the balance in favour of the buyer on instalment credit terms. The common tendency of which I am speaking consists in the exclusion of certain categories of buyers from the protective system in relation to sales on instalment credit terms. This may occur either directly, where that system is stated to be inapplicable where the purchase is made by traders, entrepreneurs or legal persons, or indirectly, with reference to purchases of industrial plant and purchases which are connected with the buyer's professional activity. This course is common to the laws of nearly all the Member States, with the exception of Denmark and Italy.

I shall now turn to the problem which has to be resolved in this dispute. It seems to me that the above-mentioned tendency indicated by national laws, although it cannot be confused with the existence of common principles properly so-called, provides definite confirmation of the conclusions previously drawn by way of a systematic interpretation of the Convention. In short, as long as the buyer on instalment credit terms is a private consumer and the object of the purchase is a consumer good, special rules regarding sales on instalment credit terms are justified since in that situation one of the contracting parties is weaker and deserves special protection. Outside that context, there is no reason to extend the 'protective' rules relating to sales on instalment credit terms, and therefore the *nomen juris* itself of 'sale on instalment credit terms', within the meaning of Article 13 of the Convention, ceases to be applicable.

5. Mention should be made of two further circumstances, which indicate how written Community law has been developing in the direction indicated. The first, and most important, is the following: the ad hoc Working Party on Adjustments to the Conventions under Article 220 of the EEC Treaty, in drafting the amendments to the Brussels Convention which were to accompany the accession of the United Kingdom, Ireland and Denmark, proposed modifications to Articles 13 to 15, and suggested, inter alia, that the sphere of application of Article 13 should be restricted to contracts entered into by a person for a purpose which could be considered extraneous to his professional or trade activity, thereafter to be referred to as the consumer. In consequence, in Article 14 and 15 reference would no longer be made to the buyer or the borrower, but to the 'consumer' (working document no 5 revised version; Article 9a of the Accession Convention). It is clear that draft cannot influence the interpretation of Article 13 which must now be provided; however, it seems to me interesting to be able to say that the solution suggested by myself coincides in this matter with the foreseeable course of development of the Brussels Convention. In the second place, I would recall that the draft proposal for a Directive on consumer credit, drawn up by the Commission, places contracts for the sale of goods on deferred payment terms within the category of 'consumer credit agreements' and defines the consumer as a natural person who is not acting in pursuance of a commercial or professional activity. That means that Community action for the protection of the consumer impinges on the field of sales on instalment credit terms from an angle which coincides with the conception of that phenomenon accepted by the Brussels Convention.

B. Commentary

1. European Law

The judgment in *Bertrand* broke new ground in consumer law and made advances in European law. At the same time the case serves as an example of the method of interpretation employed by the ECJ in its case law. The subject of this reference was the provisions of the Brussels Convention of 1968 on Jurisdiction and Enforcement of Judgments in Civil and Commercial Matters which had been concluded by the then Member States as a contract of international law (OJ 1972, L299/32). In its original version, Article 13 of the Convention set out the following provision:

> In matters relating to the sale of goods on instalment credit terms, or to loans expressly made to finance the sale of goods and repayable by instalments, jurisdiction shall be determined by this Section, . . .

The original version of Article 14(1) then applicable stated:

> A seller or lender who is domiciled in a Contracting State may be sued either in the court of that State or in the courts of the Contracting State in which the buyer or borrower is domiciled. Proceedings may be brought by a seller against a buyer or by a lender against a borrower only in the courts of the State in which the defendant is domiciled. (concerning subsequent amendments of Articles 13 und 14 see the European Law Commentary to *Benincasa*: Case no 2 in this Casebook)

The compulsory jurisdictional venue which was granted therefore applied in a literal sense to 'proceedings in relation to the sale of goods on instalment credit terms', without limitation, regardless of whether the transaction took place amongst traders themselves or as between a trader and consumer. The original versions of Articles 13 and 14 make no mention of the (now standard) rule that contracts must have been made between traders and consumers before EU consumer law can be invoked. This is explained by the fact that the Brussels Convention was in force before the European Community had an effective consumer protection policy.

It was first decided to expand the European Community's consumer protection policy at the 1972 summit in Paris. The First Programme of the European Economic Community on a policy for the protection and education of the consumer was presented in 1975 (OJ 1975, C92/1). In 1978 the ECJ was presented with the question whether a contract concluded between two companies concerning the sale of tool machines which was to be paid in two instalments came under the definition 'sale of movable goods on instalment credit terms'. The judgment is divided into three parts (the same as the Advocate-General's Opinion): first, the ECJ carried out an extensive comparison of the laws in the Member States and in so doing established that the term 'sale of goods on instalment credit terms' varied in meaning in accordance with the objectives pursued by the respective laws of each Member State. The ECJ concluded from its findings that it was essential to the effectiveness of the Convention that the term 'instalment credit terms' had to be given a substantive content which was uniform, independent of the Member States and allied to the European Community legal order (paragraphs 12/16). The ECJ's interpretation is therefore independent and was applied by the Court in the second part of its judgment. It examined the objective of the provision in the Convention which was to be interpreted. The exceptions in Articles 13 and 14 of the Convention which—in derogation from the general system of law laid down by the Convention—grant the buyer of goods on instalment credit terms the venue of jurisdiction have as their objective the protection of only certain categories of buyers (paragraphs 17/18).

The buyers who were to be protected were the subject of the third part of the judgment. Here the ECJ employed the 'general principles which are apparent in this field from the body of laws of the Member States' (paragraphs 19/22). During the course of its investigations the ECJ established that a general principle which applied in most Member States was that certain buyers were considered to be especially deserving of protection. These were consumers whose economic position was characterised by their weakness in relation to the seller. This group of vulnerable buyers was defined by the ECJ as 'private final consumers', who are 'not engaged, when buying the product acquired on instalment credit terms, in trade or professional activities.'

In this way, the ECJ introduced a definition of the term 'consumer' into its case law which has become a fundamental concept of Community law. This further development took place in reliance only on the common principles derived from the legal systems of the Member States, and despite the fact that the Brussels Convention itself did not offer any jurisdictional basis.

At the time of the *Bertrand* judgment, negotiations were under way to allow Denmark, Ireland and the United Kingdom to join the Brussels Convention. In the course of these negotiations the proposal was put forward to limit the application of Article 13 of the Brussels Convention to contracts which a person had concluded in pursuit of an aim which was unconnected with the professional or trading activity of that person (on the further development of the Brussels and Rome Conventions which were being negotiated at the same time (see the European Commentary *Benincasa*: Case no 2 in this Casebook). In addition, a proposal for the later Directive 87/102 (Consumer Credit, OJ 1987, L42/48) had been presented which contained a similar definition. The *Bertrand* case meant the adaptation into European law of the Brussels Convention before it was amended.

ECJ CASE LAW REFERENCES

Shearson Lehman Hutton [1993] ECR I–139; *Brenner* [1994] ECR I–4275; *Benincasa* [1997] ECR I–3767 (Case no 2 in this Casebook); *Mietz* [1999] ECR I–2277.

LITERATURE REFERENCES

Th Bourgoignie (ed) 'L'accès des consommateurs au droit de la justice' (1992) *Revue européenne de droit de la consommation* 119; T Hartley (1979) *European Law Review* 47; (Casenote on *Bertrand*); E Mezger (1979) *Revue critique de droit international privé* 123 (Casenote on *Bertrand*); N Reich *Europäisches Verbraucherrecht* (3rd edn 1996) 512.

HS-N/JJ

2. *England, Wales & Scotland*

The UK government made written observations in the *Bertrand* case. It submitted that underlying Article 4 of the Convention is a desire to protect the buyer similar to that which exists in the legislation of several Member States. Such protection, however, is reserved to those buyers who may be classified as 'consumers', ie buyers who are not engaged in commercial activities or who buy goods for private consumption and not for the purposes of the exercise of a business or trade (according to the same reasoning (at the time of the *Bertrand* case) protection for buyers on credit terms in the UK was limited to small transactions of less than £2,000). In the case at issue, the true test of a sale on instalment credit terms was not the number of instalments, but lay in the relationship between the parties and the nature of the transaction: only if the latter fell into the category of consumer transaction should Article 13 be applied.

The *Bertrand* ruling has recently been given a wide interpretation (perhaps exceedingly wide in the light of the *Di Pinto* judgment) by a Scottish court in the case *Chris Hart (Business Sales) Ltd. v Niven*. A firm specialising in the marketing of hotels and licensed premises raised an action in the Glasgow Sheriff Court for payment of sums claimed under a contract with the owners of licensed premises for the marketing of the premises. The owners were domiciled outside the jurisdiction of the Court. The Sheriff Court refused to grant a decree on the grounds of lack of jurisdiction. The pursuer appealed to the Sheriff Principal, relying, inter alia, on the cases of *Bertrand* and *Di Pinto*. The Sheriff principal, in refusing the appeal, disregarded the *Di Pinto* judgment and argued that in the *Bertrand* case the European Court had adopted a purposive interpretation of the relevant rules by looking at whether the buyers were in a weaker position than the sellers. In the case at issue, the traders were selling liqueurs: their business was certainly not that of selling licensed premises. Accordingly, the defendants were acting privately when contracting with the appellant. Additionally they were economically in a weaker position. This led the Sheriff to the conclusion that the defendants were in need of the protection afforded by the Convention and were therefore entitled to be sued in the jurisdiction where they were domiciled.

CASE LAW REFERENCES

Chris Hart (Business Sales) Ltd. v Niven judgment of 12 February 1992, *Scots Law Times* (1992, Sherriff Court), 53.

LITERATURE REFERENCES

L Collins *Dicey and Morris on the Conflict of Laws* (2000) 11–319/321; 33–004/007; Miller *Product Liability and Safety Encyclopedia* (1999) VI 609.

PN

3. Germany

The position taken by the German government in these proceedings is worthy of mention. It argued that a sale of goods on instalment credit terms between traders should also fall under Articles 13 and 14 of the Convention (in its original version). Indeed, the German government had seen that in most legal systems of the Member States a common principle existed according to which the provisions on the sale of goods on instalment credit terms did not apply for the benefit of traders. However, the Convention, which was to be interpreted independently of any other provision, did not have a limitation to this effect. The main reason for the Federal government's attitude appears to have lain in the difficulties presented by the demarcation between those deserving of protection and those who are not. It can be seen from the German government's opinion just how alien the concepts of the consumer protection movement were at the end of the seventies. Solely due to the difficulties presented by demarcation was it considered not possible to attain a norm which was correct per se. In adopting this stance the German government also contradicted its own law to a certain extent. The then applicable Law on Instalment Payments (*Abzahlungsgesetz*) which in § 6a contained a jurisdictional rule in favour of the purchaser on instalments, did not apply to traders entered on the commercial register (*Reichsgesetzblatt* 1894, 450; insertion of § 6a, *Bundesgesetzblatt* 1969, 1541).

The judgment in *Bertrand* has not elicited much interest in Germany. It has rarely appeared in print. It has hardly ever been mentioned in the case law dealing with the definition of the consumer in the Brussels Convention (see eg *Bundesgerichtshof* (Federal Court of Justice), judgments of 13 July 1987, 20 April 1993, 22 November 1994; rulings of 29 January 1991, 25 May 1993; *Oberlandesgericht* Köln (Higher Regional Court), judgment of 18 May 1992; *Oberlandesgericht* Düsseldorf, judgment of 8 March 1996). However, in a reference for a preliminary ruling made recently, the *Bundesgerichtshof* cited the judgment in *Bertrand* (amongst others) as supporting the rule of independent interpretation of the terms of the Brussels Convention (decision of 29 February 1996; Case C–99/96 *Mietz* [1999] ECR I–2277). The connection between the judgment in *Bertrand* (the beginning of European consumer protection policy) and the definition of a consumer have gone largely unnoticed in Germany.

However the effects of the European definition of the consumer are to be seen in many fields of German law. The regulation of transactions involving instalment credit has recently been incorporated into the German Law on Consumer Credit (*Verbraucherkreditgesetz, Bundesgesetzblatt* I 1990, 2840, amended in *Bundesgesetzblatt* 2000 941) which was passed in order to implement Directive 87/102 (Consumer Credit, OJ 1987 L42/48). The application of the Law on Consumer Credit (*Verbraucherkreditgesetz*) to persons is narrower than that of the Law on Credit Instalments (*Abzahlungsgesetz*). It is guided by the European definition of a consumer as developed by the judgment in *Bertrand* and expressed in Directive

87/102. The area of protection of the German Law on Credit Instalments was thereby re-defined in reliance on European concepts. Going beyond the minimum standard provided for by European law, the German Law on Credit Instalments also covers (within certain limits) the so-called Founder Credit used to start a self-employed business (see the German Commentary to *Benincasa*: Case no 2 in this Casebook). Paragraph 1(1) of the Law on Instalment Credit states:

Anwendungsbereich

Dieses Gesetz gilt für Kreditverträge und Kreditvermittlungsverträge zwischen einem Unternehmer, der einen Kredit gewährt (Kreditgeber) oder vermittelt oder nach-weist (Kreditvermittler), und einem Verbraucher. Als Verbraucher gelten auch alle anderen natürlichen Personen, es sei denn, daß der Kredit nach dem Inhalt des Vertrages für ihre bereits ausgeübte gewerbliche oder selbständige berufliche Tätigkeit bestimmt ist.

The Law on Instalment Credit no longer has a rule relating to compulsory juris-diction. The old § 6a of the Law was repealed. There is, however, a special juris-dictional venue for consumers in § 7(1) of the Law on Doorstep Selling (*Haustürwiderrufsgesetz, Bundesgesetzblatt* I 1986, 122). The definitions of 'consumer' (*Verbraucher*) and 'entrepreneur' (*Unternehmer*) are now contained in §§ 13 and 14(1) of the German Civil Code (*Bürgerliches Gesetzbuch*, amended by *Bundesgesetzblatt* I 2000, 897), which provide:

§ 13:

Verbraucher

Verbraucher ist jede natürliche Person, die ein Rechtsgeschäft zu einem Zweck abschließt, der weder ihrer gewerblichen noch ihrer selbständigen beruflichen Tätigkeit zugerechnet werden kann.

§ 14(1):

Unternehmer

Unternehmer ist eine natürliche oder juristische Person oder eine rechtsfähige Personengesellschaft, die bei Abschluss eines Rechtsgeschäfts in Ausübung ihrer gewerblichen oder selbständigen beruflichen Tätigkeit handelt.

CASE LAW REFERENCES

Bundesgerichtshof judgment of 13 July 1987 (1987) *Neue Juristische Wochenschrift* 3081; Bundesgerichtshof judgment of 29 January 1991 (1991) *Wertpapiermitteilungen* 360; Oberlandesgericht Köln judgment of 18 May 1992 (1992) *NJW-Rechtsprechungsreport Zivilrecht* 1457; Bundesgerichtshof judgment of 20 April 1993 (1993) *Neue Juristische Wochenschrift* 2683; Bundesgerichtshof judgment of 25 May 1993 (1993) *Europäische Zeitschrift für Wirtschaftsrecht* 518; Bundesgerichtshof judgment of 22 November 1994 (1995) *Neue Juristische Wochenschrift* 1225; Bundesgerichtshof judgment of 29 February

1996 (1997) *Neue Juristische Wochenschrift* 2685; Oberlandesgericht Düsseldorf judgment of 8 March 1996 (1996) *Recht der Internationalen Wirtschaft* 681.

LITERATURE REFERENCES

P Hommelhoff 'Zivilrecht unter dem Einfluß europäischer Rechtsangleichung' (1992) *Archiv für die civilistische Praxis 192* 71 86 (for the application of the Law on Consumer Credit); E Mezger (1979) *Revue critique de droit international privé* 123 (Casenote on *Bertrand*).

HS-N

4. France

The *Bertrand* case has aroused some interest in French legal journals not least because this was the first reference of the *Cour de Cassation* concerning the Brussels Convention. The French government did not put forward its observations in the proceedings. Having received the ECJ's answer, the *Cour de Cassation* decided against the Société Bertrand (judgment of 23 January 1979). French law already had a principle that provisions protecting buyers on instalment credit should mainly operate to the benefit of those who deal in a private capacity. The earlier rule on the area of application of consumer credit law in Article 3 of the Law no 78–22 *sur la protection et l'information du consommateur* of 10 January 1978 has since been incorporated into the *Code de la Consommation*. Article L 311–3 states:

> Sont exclus du champ d'application du présent chapitre: (. . .)
>
> 3° Ceux qui sont destinés à financer les besoins d'une activité professionnelle, ainsi que les prêts aux personnes morales de droit public; (. . .)

With the *Bertrand* case the area of application of the rules in the Brussels Convention on instalment credit terms were assimilated to the legal position in France. The following sentence from a discussion in the *Recueil Dalloz* can be seen as characteristic of the French response to the judgment in *Bertrand*: '*La convention de 1968 a subi le grand vent qui souffle au profit des consommateurs*' (*Vasseur*). Examples of the application of provisions on consumer protection are the judgments of the *Tribunal de Grande Instance* Dunkerque of 19 February 1986 or for sales on instalment credit terms the *Cour d'Appel* Douai of 9 February 1989.

CASE LAW REFERENCES

Cour de Cassation, 1ère chambre civile judgment of 23 January 1979, *Bulletin des arrêts de la Cour de Cassation* chambres civiles 1979 I no 28: *Juris-classeur périodique—La Semaine juridique* édition générale 1979 IV 105; Tribunal de Grande Instance de Dunkerque, judgment of 19 February 1986 *Journal du droit international,* 1986 713; Cour d'Appel de Douai judgment of 9 February 1989 *Journal du droit international* 1991, 160 (Casenote by A Huet).

LITERATURE REFERENCES

H Gaudemet-Tallon *Les Conventions de Bruxelles et de Lugano* (2nd ed 1996); P Gulphe (1979) *Revue trimestrielle de droit européen* 182 (Casenote on *Bertrand*); I Fadlallah (1979) *Journal du droit international* 375 (Casenote on *Bertrand*); F Jeantet *Juris-classeur périodique—La semaine juridique* (édition générale 1979) II 19051 (Casenote on *Bertrand*); Y Loussouarn/P Bourel (1979) *Revue trimestrielle de droit commercial* 170 (Casenote on *Bertrand*); M Vasseur *Recueil Dalloz Sirey* (1980, Informations rapides) 16 (Casenote on *Bertrand*).

BD

5. Italy

The judgment in *Bertrand* has aroused some attention in Italy. It is regarded as agreeing with private law principles and objectives of the Brussels Convention. At the same time it is seen as 'creative interpretation' which limits the actual scope of application of Articles 13 to 15 of the Brussels Convention (for example, *Carporti* at a conference in Pavia, 1983). With this decision the Court is seen as anticipating the later amendment (see above under B1) to the Convention (*Toriello,* see also *Pocar*).

Italian law regulates the part-payment of movable goods in a subsection of the *Codice civile* '*Della vendita con riserva della proprieta*' (Articles 1523–1526) as well as in some rules of Insolvency law and in *Legge* 132 no 1332 of 28 November 1965 on '*Vendita di macchine utensili*' in the case of special materials.

The general provision in the *Codice civile* provides relatively advantageous terms for the consumer in the case of part-payment. An example is Article 1523 according to which the transfer of property takes place only after the last payment has been made, whereas the risk is transferred on delivery. Article 1526 states that the seller has a claim for compensation for use and damage where the contract has been breached by the buyer. However, there are also provisions relating to consumer protection. For example Article 1525 according to which an outstanding re-payment equivalent in amount to no more than one-eighth of the total price does not constitute a right of the seller to withdraw from the transaction. The buyer has some time remaining to make the next payment. Irrespective of the regulation of part-payment, Italian law apportions the risk principally to the buyer. These provisions do not require that the buyer also be the end consumer, but are to be applied generally. Therefore the notion of part-payment in Italian law differed from the notion of Article 13 of the Brussels Convention which the ECJ formulated in *Bertrand.* With the implementation of Directive 87/102 by

Legge no 142 of 19 February 1992, a special measure in the field of consumer credit was introduced into Italian law. As with the Directive this is applicable only in the case where a relationship exists between the businessman and consumer. The provisions in Article 18 no 1 of this Law on the scope of application comply with the Directive:

> Ai fini della presente sezione, si definisce credito al consumo la concessione nell' esercizio di una attività commerciale o professionale di credito sotto forma di dilazione di pagamento o di prestito o di analoga facilitazione finanziaria (finanziamento) a favore di una persona fisica (consumatore) che agisce, in tale rispetto, per scopi estranei all'attività imprenditoriale o professionale eventualmente svolta.

CASE LAW REFERENCES

Corte di Cassatione, judgment of 14 January 2000, n 372, (2000) *Il Foro italiano* I, 1638.

LITERATURE REFERENCES

G Alpa (1995) *Il diritto dei consumatori* 58; F Capotorti 'L'interpretazione uniforme della Convenzione di Bruxelles del 1968 nella giurisprudenza della Corte di giustizia comunitaria' (1985) *La Convenzione giudiziaria of Bruxelles del 1968 e la riforma del processo civile italiano* 34; F Pocar *La convenzione di Bruxelles sulla giurisdizione e l'esecuzione delle sentenze* (1986); F Toriello 'Contratti dei consumatori e convenzione di Bruxelles del 1968 sula giurisdizione' (1996) *Nuova Giurisprudenza Civile Commentata* I 300 (Casenote on ECJ *Brenner* [1994] ECR I–4275).

AM

CASE NO. 2 — *Benincasa* C–269/95

Francesco Beninzcasa v Dentalkit Srl
[1997] ECR I–3767

A. Judgment of the ECJ of 3 July 1997

1. *Held*

1) The first paragraph of Article 13 and the first paragraph of Article 14 of the Convention of 27 September 1968 on jurisdiction and the enforcement of judgments in civil and commercial matters, as amended by the Convention of 9 October 1978 on the accession of the Kingdom of Denmark, Ireland and the United Kingdom of Great Britain and Northern Ireland, must be interpreted as meaning that a plaintiff who has concluded a contract with a view to pursuing a trade or profession, not at the present time but in the future, may not be regarded as a consumer.

2) The courts of a Contracting State which have been designated in a jurisdiction clause validly concluded under the first paragraph of Article 17 of the Convention of 27 September 1968 also have exclusive jurisdiction where the action seeks in particular a declaration that the contract containing that clause is void.

2. Facts of the Case

The *Oberlandesgericht* (Higher Regional Court) Munich referred three questions to the ECJ on the interpretation of the first paragraph of Article 13, the first paragraph of Article 14 and the first paragraph of Article 17 of the Convention of 27 September 1968 on the Jurisdiction and Enforcement of Judgments in Civil and Commercial Matters (OJ 1978 L304/36), as amended by the Convention of 9 October 1978 on the accession of the Kingdom of Denmark, Ireland and the United Kingdom of Great Britain and Northern Ireland (OJ 1978, L304/1; hereinafter 'the Brussels Convention'). Those questions were raised in proceedings between Dentalkit Srl ('Dentalkit'), and Mr Benincasa, an Italian national, relating to the validity of a franchising contract concluded between them. In 1987 Dentalkit developed a chain of franchised shops in Italy specializing in the sale of dental hygiene products. In 1992 Mr Benincasa concluded a franchising contract with Dentalkit with a view to setting up and operating a shop in Munich. In that contract Dentalkit authorised Mr Benincasa to exploit the exclusive right to use the Dentalkit trademark within a particular geographical area. Dentalkit further undertook to supply goods bearing that trademark, to support him in various spheres, to carry out the requisite training and promotion and advertising activities and not to open any shop within the geographical area covered by the exclusive right. For his part, Mr Benincasa undertook to equip business premises at his own cost, to stock exclusively Dentalkit's products, not to disclose any information or documents concerning Dentalkit and to pay it a sum of LIT 8 million as payment for the cost of technical and commercial assistance provided when opening the shop and 3 per cent of his annual turnover. By reference to Articles 1341 and 1342 of the Italian Civil Code, the parties specifically approved a clause of the contract stating:

> The courts at Florence shall have jurisdiction to entertain any dispute relating to the interpretation, performance or other aspects of the present contract.

Mr Benincasa set up his shop, paid the initial sum of LIT 8 million and made several purchases, for which, however, he never paid. In the meantime, he had ceased trading altogether. Mr Benincasa brought proceedings in the *Landgericht*

(Regional Court) Munich I, where he sought to have the franchising contract declared void on the ground that the contract as a whole was void under German law. He also claimed that the sales contracts concluded subsequently pursuant to the basic franchising contract were void. Mr Benincasa argued that the *Landgericht* Munich I had jurisdiction as the court for the place of performance of the obligation in question within the meaning of Article 5(1) of the Convention. He argued that the clause of the franchising contract conferring jurisdiction on the courts at Florence did not have the effect of derogating from Article 5(1) as regards his action to avoid the contract because that action sought to have the whole franchising agreement declared void and, therefore, also the jurisdiction clause. Mr Benincasa further argued that, since he had not yet started trading, he should be regarded as a consumer within the meaning of the first paragraph of Article 13 and the first paragraph of Article 14 of the Convention. The relevant provisions of the Convention read as follows:

Article 13

In proceedings concerning a contract concluded by a person for a purpose which can be regarded as being outside his trade or profession, hereinafter called 'the consumer', jurisdiction shall be determined by this section, without prejudice to the provisions of point 5 of Articles 4 and 5, if it is:

1. a contract for the sale of goods on instalment credit terms.

Article 14

A consumer may bring proceedings against the other party to a contract either in the courts of the Contracting State in which that party is domiciled or in the courts of the Contracting State in which he is himself domiciled.

The *Landgericht* Munich I declined jurisdiction on the ground that the jurisdiction clause contained in the franchising contract was valid and that the contract was not a contract concluded by a consumer. Mr Benincasa appealed against that decision to the *Oberlandesgericht* Munich, which stayed proceedings and referred the following questions to the Court for a preliminary ruling:

1) Is a plaintiff to be regarded as a consumer within the meaning of the first paragraph of Article 13 and the first paragraph of Article 14 of the Convention even if his action relates to a contract which he concluded not for the purpose of a trade which he was already pursuing but a trade to be taken up only at a future date (here: a franchising agreement concluded for the purpose of setting up a business)?

2) If Question 1 is to be answered in the affirmative: Does point 1 of the first paragraph of Article 13 of the Convention (contract for the sale of goods on instalment credit terms) cover a franchising agreement which obliges the plaintiff to buy from the other party to the agreement, over a period of several

(three) years, the articles and goods required to equip and operate a business (without instalment credit terms having been agreed) and to pay an initial fee and, as from the second year of the business, a licence fee of 3 per cent of turnover?

3) Does the court of a Member State specified in an agreement conferring jurisdiction have exclusive jurisdiction pursuant to the first paragraph of Article 17 of the Convention even when the action is inter alia for a declaration of the invalidity of a franchising agreement containing the jurisdiction clause itself, which is worded 'The courts at Florence shall have jurisdiction to entertain any dispute relating to the interpretation, performance or other aspects of the present contract', that clause having been specifically approved within the meaning of Articles 1341 and 1342 of the Italian Civil Code?

3. Extract from the Grounds of the ECJ's Judgment

The first question

11. The point sought to be clarified by the national court's first question is whether the first paragraph of Article 13 and the first paragraph of Article 14 of the Convention must be interpreted as meaning that a plaintiff who has concluded a contract with a view to pursuing a trade or profession, not at the present time but in the future, may be regarded as a consumer.

12. In this connection, regard should be had to the principle laid down by the case-law (see, in particular, Case 150/77 *Bertrand* [1978] ECR 1431, paragraphs 14, 15, 16 and 19, and Case C–89/91 *Shearson Lehman Hutton* [1993] ECR I–139, paragraph 13) according to which the concepts used in the Convention, which may have a different content depending on the national law of the Contracting States, must be interpreted independently, by reference principally to the system and objectives of the Convention, in order to ensure that the Convention is uniformly applied in all the Contracting States. This must apply in particular to the concept of 'consumer' within the meaning of Article 13 *et seq* of the Convention, in so far as it determines the rules governing jurisdiction.

13. It must next be observed that, as the Court has consistently held, under the system of the Convention the general principle is that the courts of the Contracting State in which the defendant is domiciled are to have jurisdiction and that it is only by way of derogation from that principle that the Convention provides for cases, which are exhaustively listed, in which the defendant may or must, depending on the case, be sued in the courts of another Contracting State. Consequently, the rules of jurisdiction which derogate from that general principle cannot give rise to an interpretation going beyond the cases envisaged by the Convention (*Shearson Lehman Hutton*, paragraphs 14, 15 and 16).

14. Such an interpretation must apply *a fortiori* with respect to a rule of jurisdiction, such as that contained in Article 14 of the Convention, which allows a consumer, within the meaning of Article 13 of the Convention, to sue the defendant in the courts of the Contracting State in which the plaintiff is domiciled. Apart from the cases expressly provided for, the Convention appears hostile towards the attribution of jurisdiction to the courts of the plaintiff's domicile (see Case C–220/88 *Dumez France and Tracoba* [1990] ECR I–49, paragraphs 16 and 19, and *Shearson Lehman Hutton* paragraph 17).

15. As far as the concept of consumer is concerned, the first paragraph of Article 13 of the Convention defines a consumer as 'a person acting for a purpose which can be regarded as being outside his trade or profession'. According to settled case-law, it follows from the wording and the function of that provision that it affects only a private final consumer, not engaged in trade or professional activities (*Shearson Lehman Hutton* paragraphs 20 and 22).

16. It follows from the foregoing that, in order to determine whether a person has the capacity of a consumer, a concept which must be strictly construed, reference must be made to the position of the person concerned in a particular contract, having regard to the nature and aim of that contract, and not to the subjective situation of the person concerned. As the Advocate-General rightly observed in point 38 of his Opinion, the self-same person may be regarded as a consumer in relation to certain transactions and as an economic operator in relation to others.

17. Consequently, only contracts concluded for the purpose of satisfying an individual's own needs in terms of private consumption come under the provisions designed to protect the consumer as the party deemed to be the weaker party economically. The specific protection sought to be afforded by those provisions is unwarranted in the case of contracts for the purpose of trade or professional activity, even if that activity is only planned for the future, since the fact that an activity is in the nature of a future activity does not divest it in any way of its trade or professional character.

18. Accordingly, it is consistent with the wording, the spirit and the aim of the provisions concerned to consider that the specific protective rules enshrined in them apply only to contracts concluded outside and independently of any trade or professional activity or purpose, whether present or future.

19. The answer to the national court's first question must therefore be that the first paragraph of Article 13 and the first paragraph of Article 14 of the Convention must be interpreted as meaning that a plaintiff who has concluded a contract with a view to pursuing a trade or profession, not at the present time but in the future, may not be regarded as a consumer.

The second question

20. In view of the answer given to the first question, there is no need to answer the second.

4. *Extract from the Opinion of the Advocate-General*

38. The status of consumer referred to by Article 13 is not determined by a pre-existing subjective situation: the same natural person may be a consumer for certain purposes and an entrepreneur for others. The decisive factor is, therefore, not the personal circumstances of the individual but rather his position under a particular contract, having regard to its scope and purpose.

39. Where contracts such as franchise agreements are concerned, which are clearly of a commercial nature and necessarily relate to a trade or profession of the parties, the latter's personal circumstances before the formation of the contract are irrelevant for the purpose of Article 13.

40. Contrary to the appellant's view—which was expounded at greater length during the oral procedure—I certainly do not consider that the Court should disregard or water down the traditional principle of autonomous interpretation of the terms, including 'consumer', used in the Brussels Convention.

41. In my opinion, the autonomous interpretation of 'consumer' to which I referred in connection with the *Shearson Lehman Hutton* judgment is preferable to an interpretation which relies on national law, and there are two reasons for that view:

(a) national legislation need not coincide from one State to another and may differ slightly in certain respects, depending on the particular case. To rely on one body of legislation rather than another (and what would be the criterion for making the choice?) would prejudice the legal certainty which the Brussels Convention aims to ensure.

(b) the same national legislation may contain different definitions of 'consumer', depending on the field of law in which they occur.

42. In the opinion of counsel for the appellant, the Court should give primacy to the German definition of 'consumer' deriving from the German Law on consumer credit (*Verbraucherkreditgesetz*), which confers the status of consumers upon persons applying for credit in order to pursue an activity which they had not previously taken up.

43. I do not agree with that argument: it is also opposed by the German Government itself which, in its written observations, points out that that wider definition of 'consumer' was expressly and intentionally formulated by the national legislature to go beyond the minimum standard laid down by the Directive which the Law on consumer credit was intended to implement so as to offer consumers a higher level of protection than that provided for by the Community measure.

44. According to the German Government, the Community definition of 'consumer' in the Directive on Consumer Credit excludes not only persons who are parties to contracts relating to a trade or profession 'already taken up' (in the actual words of the Law on consumer credit), but also generally persons who are parties to contracts which are concluded for the purpose of a trade or profession.

45. In the same observations, the German Government adds that in its legal system a narrower definition of 'consumer' is used in other consumer protection measures: for example, the Law on the Cancellation of Doorstep Sales (*Haustürwiderrufsgesetz*).

46. All this merely confirms the necessity to adhere to the autonomous interpretation of the definition of 'consumer' in Article 13 of the Brussels Convention, which need not be linked to the definitions used in individual cases in the respective national legal systems.

47. Finally, the view I have just put forward is not contradicted by the inclusion in the EC Treaty of a new Title XI on consumer protection, in which Article 129a lays down 'a high level of consumer protection' as an objective of the Community. First, the legal scope of that provision is limited and, secondly, Article 129a(3) expressly permits Member States to maintain or introduce more stringent protective measures. It follows logically that the Community level of protection need not be identified with the level obtaining in one or more of the Member States.

48. To sum up, it is in my view necessary to uphold the autonomous interpretation of the term 'consumer' used in the Brussels Convention, as the Court did in the *Shearson Lehman Hutton* judgment, which means that the term must be limited to private final consumers not acting in the capacity of parties to contracts concerning their trade or professional activities.

49. Sometimes, no doubt, franchisees do not have previous business experience, but this does not justify describing the activity covered by the franchise agreement as being outside a trade or profession. It is precisely the activity in question—and not, I emphasise, the existing personal circumstances of the party to the agreement—which was the factor taken into account when special rules of jurisdiction in relation to certain contracts were laid down in Article 13 of the Convention.

50. Therefore, the wording of Article 13 does not permit it to be extended to cover any contract, irrespective of its subject-matter and purpose, in which an economically weaker party is faced by a party in a position which is objectively superior or superior by reason of the circumstances.

51. Contracting parties are not normally in a position of equality in the area of business relationships, but that does not mean that contracts of that kind, including standard-form contracts, entered into by businessmen benefit from the special rule in Article 13. Although that provision aims to protect the weaker party in a contractual relationship, its scope is limited to contracts in which one party is acting for purposes unrelated to a business activity, that is to say as a 'private final consumer, not engaged in trade or professional activities'.

52. In other words, the mere fact that one of the parties to a contract concluded with a view to the pursuit of a trade or professional activity or in the course of such activities is in an inferior position, as in the case of franchise agreements, is not regarded by the Brussels Convention as requiring special protection in relation to the attribution of jurisdiction.

53. Therefore I consider that the Court's reply to the first question should be that Article 13 of the Brussels Convention does not apply to a contract such as that in the present case.

B. Commentary

1. European Law

The ECJ is responsible for applying the Brussels Convention of 27 September 1968 on jurisdiction and the enforcement of judgments in civil and commercial matters pursuant to a protocol of the Member States (OJ 1975 L204/28) and the Court ensures that its provisions are applied uniformly. In *Benincasa*, the ECJ applied the concept of the consumer which, since 1978, has been used in relation to Article 13 of the Brussels Convention (The text of Article 13 is reprinted above in the facts of the case under A2; concerning the history see the European law Commentary to *Bertrand*: Case no 1 in this Casebook). The Convention adopted this provision following the accession of Denmark, Ireland and the United Kingdom (OJ 1978 L304/1) to the Convention. At the same time, negotiations were taking place to amend the Rome Convention in relation to contractual obligations which contained the same definition in Article 5 (OJ 1980 L266/1). At the negotiations concerning Article 13 of the Brussels Convention and Article 5 of the Rome Convention, the participants 'influenced by the proceedings before the ECJ, acknowledged the interpretation of the term "transactions on instalment credit terms"' (*Bertrand*, quoted from the so-called *Schlosser* Report OJ 1979 C59/71 paragraph 153). This clearly demonstrates the immediate influence of the ECJ case law on the development of the Convention, which in turn played a leading role in the development of Community secondary legislation. The agreements implementing the accession of the latest States to the Convention (Austria, Finland and Sweden) have not changed the text of Article 13. Meanwhile the Council has enacted Regulation 44/2001 on jurisdiction and the recognition and enforcement of judgements in civil and commercial matters (OJ 2001 L12/1). This Regulation which will enter into force on 1 March 2002 will replace the Brussels Convention. In Article 15 the definition of 'consumer' is the same as in Article 13 of the Brussels Convention. The notion of 'consumer' within the procedural law of the European Union appears therefore to be established.

The Brussels Convention provides that the compulsory jurisdictional venue for consumer-related matters lies with the State in which the consumer is domiciled. According to Article 13(1) of the Convention special provisions apply in an action which arises from a:

> (. . .) contract concluded by a person for a purpose which can be regarded as being outside his trade or profession, hereinafter called 'the consumer'.

The definition of this term largely corresponds with the case law developed by the ECJ in the case of *Bertrand* [1978] ECR 1431 (Case no 1 in this Casebook) relating to Article 13 of the Convention in the 1968 version which applied at the time. The definition of the consumer in the Convention is mainly characterised by the subjective link to one of the aims pursued by one of the parties to the contract: only the party who pursues an aim which may not be attributed to his professional or commercial activity is a consumer. Most of the Directives which have been issued since 1985 have adopted this concept of the consumer almost *verbatim* (see the European law Commentary to ECJ, *Di Pinto*: Case no 10 in this Casebook). The Convention and Community law have, therefore, shown a tendency towards a uniform formulation of the concept of the consumer. Article 13 of the Convention, however, derogates from the Directives on consumer protection in that it does not require that one of the contracting parties be a trader. Article 13 of the Brussels Convention, therefore, also applies to legal transactions in which both parties are consumers. Should the ECJ ever get the opportunity to decide this question it is to be expected that it would follow its current case law and decline to apply Article 13 to a contract concluded between consumers.

The judgment in *Benincasa* follows that in *Shearson Lehman Hutton* [1993] ECR I–139. In this case the ECJ followed its decision in *Bertrand* and confirmed that Article 13 was an exception to the general rule regulating to jurisdictional venue. It was to be interpreted narrowly and in accordance with its wording and purpose only protected 'a private final consumer, not engaged in trade or professional activities' (ECJ *Shearson Lehman Hutton*, paragraph 22). This protection only applies to consumers who appear in person as claimants or defendants to the proceedings and does not apply to parties acting in a trading capacity such as the claimant in the case *Shearson Lehman Hutton*, who had brought a private claim and sued as an assignee.

The judgment in *Benincasa* consistently continues this narrow interpretation of Article 13 of the Brussels Convention in the case where the contract is concluded for the purpose of taking up a professional or trading occupation in the future. The relativism of the concept of the consumer as developed by the ECJ can be seen particularly clearly from the Advocate-General's repeated formulations made in the judgment: one and the same person may be regarded as a consumer in relation to certain transactions and as an economic operator in relation to others (ECJ *Benincasa* paragraph 16, see also the Opinion of the Advocate-General, paragraph 38, reprinted under A4). According to the Convention, the compulsory jurisdictional venue only becomes relevant in contracts concluded 'for the purpose of satisfying an individual's own needs in terms of private consumption' (ECJ *Benincasa*, paragraph 17).

Even if some aspects of the Convention's concept of the consumer become clearer in light of the cases mentioned, many questions nevertheless remain unanswered by the ECJ which declined to give an opinion. For example, it is unclear whether a contract concluded for a purpose which could be attributed to a professional activity of a person acting as a dependent employee can also be regarded as a consumer contract (for an opposing opinion see *Faber*). Similarly it is unclear how the so-called 'dual use' in which a contract is concluded in respect of an object which is used both for private and business purposes may be resolved. The evidence presented by preparatory materials to the similarly worded definition of the consumer in Article 5 of the Rome Convention proceed on the assumption that a contract can only be regarded as having been concluded between consumers if a party to the contract 'to a significant extent acts outside his professional or trading activity' (see report of *Giuliano/Lagarde* OJ 1980 C282/1 23; for different opinion see *Joustra*). It also remains uncertain whether the concept of the consumer developed for the Convention is to be regarded as being identical to the concept of the consumer adopted in the Directives relating to contract law (see for example, the ECJ judgments in *Di Pinto* [1991] ECR I–1189, and *Dietzinger* [1998] ECR I–1199: Cases nos 10 and 14 in this Casebook). Certainly, opinion is divided on whether the Convention actually forms part of Community law. Regardless of this question, the close connection between the two suggests that both should be considered in matters of interpretation. In its judgments relating to the Convention, the ECJ has up to now (as far as ascertainable) avoided citing its decisions relating to the concept of the consumer contained in the Directives. Similarly in its case law to the Convention, the ECJ does not rely on the concept of the consumer which it has formulated in its judgments relating to other areas of Community law. The grounds to its judgments on the Convention are largely guided by the exceptional character of Articles 13 and 14 within the system laid down by the Convention in order to justify their narrow interpretation. This precondition is not present in the Directives relating to consumer protection in contractual relations. Nevertheless, the ECJ judgments demonstrate the efforts made to create a uniform concept of the consumer.

ECJ CASE LAW REFERENCES

Bertrand [1978] ECR 1431: Case no 1 in this Casebook; *Di Pinto* [1991] ECR I–1189: Case no 10 in this Casebook; *Shearson Lehman Hutton* [1993] ECR I–139; *Dietzinger* [1998] ECR I–1199: Case no 14 in this Casebook.

LITERATURE REFERENCES

M Ekelmans (1997) *Journal des Tribunaux* 685 (Casenote on *Benincasa*); W Faber 'Elemente verschiedener Verbraucherbegriffe in EG-Richtlinien, zwischenstaatlichen Übereinkommen und nationalem Zivil-und Kollisionsrecht' (1998) *Zeitschrift für Europäisches Privatrecht* 854; J Harris 'Jurisdictions Clauses and Void Contracts' (1998) *European Law Review* 279 (Casenote on *Benincasa*); C Joustra *De internationale consumentenovereenkomst* (1997) 47–55; P Mankowski (1998) *Juristenzeitung* 898 (Casenote on *Benincasa*).

HS-N/JJ

2. England & Wales

The Brussels Convention was implemented in the UK by the Civil Jurisdiction and Judgments Act 1982. Provisions concerning jurisdiction within the UK are contained in Schedule 4 of the Act which contains Title II of the Convention (as modified). English academics did not fail to notice that the notion of 'consumer contract' introduced in the 1978 amendment to the Convention closely resembled the one provided by the British Unfair Contract Terms Act 1977 (UCTA). According to section 12:

(1) A party to a contract, deals as 'consumer' in relation to another party if

(a) he neither makes the contract in the course of a business nor holds himself out as doing so; and

(b) the other party does make the contract in the course of a business; and

(c) in the case of a contract governed by the law of sale of goods or hire-purchase, or by section 7 of this Act, the goods passing under or in pursuance of the contract are of a type ordinarily supplied for private use or consumption.

A number of decisions on UCTA have clarified the notion of what is done 'in the course of a business'. In the well-known *R & B Customs Brokers Ltd. v United Dominions Trust Ltd.* case, for example, the Court of Appeal held that where an activity is merely incidental to the carrying on of a business a degree of regularity has to be established before it can be said that the activity is an integral part of the business, and therefore 'carried on in the course of the business'. A similar ruling was also given by the Queen's Bench Division in 1981.

The more recent case of *Stevenson & Anor v Rogers*, however, gives a separate interpretation of the same formula 'in the course of business' rooted in the Sale of Goods Act 1979 and offers an interesting example of the use of the 'mischief' rule of interpretation with regard to statutory changes. The issue was whether certain provisions of the Act (section 14(2)), applicable only if the seller was acting 'in the course of a business', would apply to the sale by a fisherman of his own fishing vessel. The Court of Appeal focused on the change in statutory wording from the previous 1893 Act which clearly covered only situations where the seller was a dealer in the type of goods sold. On the other hand, the intention underlying the new legislation was to impose on every business seller, whether or not habitually dealing in goods of the type sold, certain conditions, and to remove the requirement for regularity of dealing, or of any dealing, in the goods. It would therefore be out of place to re-introduce some implied qualifications, difficult to define, in order to narrow what appeared to be the wide scope and purpose of the words. Accordingly, the case had to be distinguished from the precedents interpreting the same formula in other legislative contexts, and the sale at issue was held to have been made 'in the course of a business'.

In addition, *Benincasa* has been mentioned in the recent High Court case (Queen's Bench Division) *Standard Bank London Ltd. v Dimitrios and Styliani Apostolakis*. One of the points at issue was whether the contracts entered into by the Greek couple (an engineer and a lawyer) with the London bank were consumer contracts for the purposes of the Convention and of the Unfair Terms in Consumer Contract Regulations 1994/1999. The couple entered into a foreign exchange agreement according to which the bank would make forward purchases of ECUs on their behalf in exchange for drachmas. When litigation arose, the bank sought to rely on *Dentalkit* in order to claim that only contracts concluded for the purposes of satisfying an individual's own needs in terms of his private consumption could be classified as consumer contracts, and that *Dentalkit* implied that 'consumption' should mean that something is 'literally consumed' so as to be destroyed. The judge refused to accept such an interpretation and stated that 'consuming' simply means using or enjoying the relevant product. In addition, the fact that the couple was using their income in what they hoped would be a profitable manner, did not justify the claim that they should be considered as acting within their trade or profession.

CASE LAW REFERENCES

Standard Bank London Ltd. v Apostolakis (QBD (Comm Ct)), judgment of 19 January 2000 n.y.r.; *Stevenson & Anor v Rogers* [1999] QB 1028; *R & B Customs Brokers Ltd. v United Dominions Trust Ltd.* [1988] 1 WLR 321; *Symmon v Cook* (1981) *New Law Journal* 758 [1998] CA TLR of 31 March 1998 (QBD (Comm Ct)), judgment of 19 January 2000 n.y.r.

LITERATURE REFERENCES

J Harris 'Jurisdiction Clauses and Void Contracts' (Casenote), (1998) *European Law Review* 279; A Waldron 'Contracts' (Casenote) (1998) *International Trade Law Quarterly* 114; on the *Stevenson & Anor* case, see Commercial reporter: sales in the course of business (1999) *Solicitor's Journal* 64.

PN

3. Germany

In contrast to *Bertrand* ([1978] ECR 1431: Case no 1 in this Casebook) the *Benincasa* judgment has received some attention in German legal journals. Not surprisingly the case arose because of a reference by a German court (*Oberlandesgericht* Munich ruling of 5 May 1995). The concept of the consumer is defined differently in various German laws. Paragraph 1(2) of the Law on Consumer Credit (*Verbraucherkreditgesetz, Bundesgesetzblatt* I 1990 2840, *Bundesgesetzblatt* 2000 941) states:

> Als Verbraucher gelten auch alle anderen natürlichen Personen, es sei denn, daß der Kredit nach dem Inhalt des Vertrages für ihre bereits ausgeübte gewerbliche oder selbständige berufliche Tätigkeit bestimmt ist.

The requirement that the business or professional occupation should already have been engaged in (*bereits ausgeübt*), makes clear that credit arrangements for the purpose of taking up such an activity also fall within the law (see the German commentary to *Bertrand*: Case no 1 in this Casebook). The German Law on Consumer Credit also protects, within certain limits, borrowers acting in a commercial capacity if the credit is to be used to start a business in a self-employed capacity (so-called Founder Credit). Mr Benincasa who had not been self-employed before the conclusion of the franchise contract, claimed the protection offered by this law. Moreover, he had argued that the Court should interpret the concept of the consumer contained in the Convention using the German Law on Consumer Credit.

In its written observations before the ECJ, the German government objected to the plaintiff's claim (Opinion of the Advocate-General, paragraphs 44 and 45: reprinted above under A4). The concept of a consumer contained in the Law on Consumer Credit was deliberately expanded by the national legislator in order to incorporate the minimum standards provided for in Directive 87/102 (Consumer Credit OJ 1987 L42/48). In addition, all other German laws relating to the protection of the consumer use a narrower concept of the consumer, as now stated in the general definition of this term provided by § 13 of the Civil Code (*Bürgerliches Gesetzbuch*, amended in *Bundesgesetzblatt* 2000 897), which provides:

> Verbraucher ist jede natürliche Person, die ein Rechtsgeschäft zu einem Zweck abschließt, der weder ihrer gewerblichen noch ihrer selbständigen beruflichen Tätigkeit zugerechnet werden kann.

The German case law does not answer the question as to whether the definition which had similar forerunners in several other statutes can also operate consistently to the benefit of business founders (see the German commentary to *Di Pinto*: Case no 10 in this Casebook). The differences which exist even within the

German legal system illustrate that only an independent or autonomous interpretation of the concept of the consumer contained in the Convention can lead to uniformity throughout the Community. This independence from the Member States, however, does not exclude modelling the Convention's concept of the consumer according to that developed for Community law (see the European law Commentary to this case above under B1).

CASE LAW REFERENCES

Oberlandesgericht Munich, ruling of 5 May 1995 (1995) *Die deutsche Rechtsprechung auf dem Gebiete des Internationalen Privatrechts* no 144.

LITERATURE REFERENCES

P Mankowski (1998) *Juristenzeitung* 898 (Casenote on *Benincasa*).

HS-N

4. France

French Law does not have a general definition of the concept '*consommateur*'. A proposal for the French Code on Consumer Law, the *Code de la Consommation* of 1993 contained the following definition of the concept which was not enacted:

> Les consommateurs sont les personnes physiques ou morales de droit privé qui se procurent ou qui utilisent des biens ou des services pour un usage non professionnel. (*Calais-Auloy*, Propositions pour un code de la consommation, Article 3)

There is considerable difference in opinion and uncertainty as to the extent to which the laws relating to consumer protection should apply to traders (see the French commentary to *Di Pinto*: ECJ, Case no 10 in this Casebook). This fundamental problem encapsulated by the *Benincasa* case is also a feature of French law. The discussion does not expressly concern transactions which have as their purpose a trading activity in the future, but above all transactions concluded by traders who act outside their professional capacity (*professionnels agissant en dehors de leur compétence*). The case law of the *Cour de Cassation* concerning this question is divided, but tends historically towards a wide interpretation to the benefit of traders. For example, laws relating to consumer protection have been applied to the benefit of a farmer who had requested an expert report on fire damage to his business (*Cour de Cassation* judgment of 15 April 1982), and to the benefit of a trader who had purchased an alarm for his premises (*Cour de Cassation* judgment of 25 May 1992; further examples can be found in *Cornet* und *Paisant*).

The wording used in the law describing the area of application of the provisions on consumer protection vary. Thus, the provisions on consumer credit arrangements according to Article L 311–3 no 3 *Code de la Consommation* do not apply in the case of loans which are intended to finance the needs of a professional or commercial activity. According to Articles L 132–1 of the *Code de la Consommation* the provisions apply to contracts which have been concluded between traders on the one hand and non-traders on the other (*contrats conclus entre professionnels et non-professionnels ou consommateurs*). The area of application of the provisions on Doorstep Sales and business activities of a similar nature has been amended several times. Article 8(1)(e) of the original Law no 72–1137 of 22 December 1972 *relative à la protection des consommateurs en matière de démarchage et de vente à domicile* excluded from its area of application:

> les ventes, locations ou locations-ventes de marchandises ou d'objets ou les prestations de services lorsqu'elles sont proposées pour les besoins d'une exploitation agricole, industrielle ou commerciale ou d'une activité professionnelle.

The currently applicable version contained in Article L 121–22 (2) no 4 *Code de la Consommation* is considerably broader in scope. According to this version the laws regulating doorstep sales are not applicable only where such transactions are made in direct connection (*rapport direct*) with a commercial activity:

> Ne sont pas soumis aux dispositions des Articles L 121–23 à L 121–28:
>
> 4° Les ventes, locations ou locations-ventes de biens ou les prestations de services lorsqu'elles ont un rapport direct avec les activités exercées dans le cadre d'une exploitation agricole, industrielle, commerciale ou artisanale ou de toute autre profession.

The narrow interpretation of the concept *consommateur* in the Brussels Convention which the ECJ adopted in the case *Benincasa* is therefore somewhat at odds with the rather broader concept of the consumer contained in the French *Code de la Consommation*. Nevertheless the view appears to be gaining ground in France that commercial activities even if they take place outside the individual's professional area of activity, should basically not fall within the scope of consumer protection law (*Calais-Auloy/Steinmetz*). The criteria demarcating the direct connection (*rapport direct*) of a transaction with a commercial activity is being increasingly used by the *Cour de Cassation* in order to exclude traders from the scope of consumer protection (eg the judgments of 3 and 30 January 1996). The case law no longer clings to the professional capacity but at the transaction aimed at. However, two cases decided in 1999 illustrate the different approaches encountered among judges on the requirement of a *rapport direct* with a business activity (in order to qualify a transaction as professional).

The judgment in *Benincasa* could serve to strengthen this restrictive tendency. It is nevertheless too soon to see wide-reaching effects. The first reactions in French legal literature appear to be favourable (*Bischoff*).

CASE LAW REFERENCES

Cour de Cassation 1ère chambre civile judgment of 15 April 1982 *Bulletin des arrêts de la Cour de Cassation* chambres civiles 1982 I no 133: *Recueil Dalloz Sirey* (1984) Jurisprudence 439; Cour de Cassation 1ère chambre civile judgment of 25 May 1992 *Recueil Dalloz Sirey* (1992) *Sommaires* 401; Cour de Cassation 1ère chambre civile judgments of 3 and 30 January 1996 *Recueil Dalloz Sirey* (1996) *Jurisprudence* 228, Cour d'Appel de Paris 17 September 1999, *Lexis* no 024863 and Cour d'Appel de Grenoble 27 September 1999, no 102501.

LITERATURE REFERENCES

J Bischoff (1998) *Journal du droit international* 581 (Casenote on *Benincasa*); J Calais-Auloy 'Propositions pour un code de la consommation' *La Documentation française* (1990); J Calais-Auloy/F Steinmetz *Droit de la consommation* (4th edn 1996) 4, 8, 93; I Cornet (1998) *Revue de droit commercial belge* 388 (Casenote on *Benincasa*); J Mayali 'La notion de consommateur' I Thèse Montpellier 1993 (Microfiche); G Paisant 'Essai sur la notion de consommateur en droit positif', *Juris-classeur périodique—La semaine juridique* (édition générale, 1993) I, 3655; C Cathelineau 'La notion de consommateur en droit interne: à propos d'une derive . . .' *Contrats, Concurrence, Consommation* (1999) Chronique 13.

BD

5. Italy

Italian writers regard two aspects of the judgment in *Benincasa* as vitally impor-tant. One is the implementation of the concept of the consumer, not only with respect to the Brussels Convention, but also to Italian law; the other is the clari-fication that exclusive jurisdiction chosen by the parties pursuant to Article 17 of the Convention cannot simply be set aside (*Giacalone*, see also *Ballarino*).

Italy has implemented the concept of consumer in Article 1469 *Code civile*:

il consumatore è la persona fisica che agisce per scopi estranei all'attività imprenditori-ale o professionale eventualmente svolta.

This provision poses some basic problems: Who is a consumer? Can a legal person be a consumer from a legal point of view or not? What is the real meaning of '*scopi estranei all'attività imprenditoriale o professionale eventualmente svolta*'? Do courts have to take into account the reasons and intentions of the consumer in buying goods or services or must they employ objective criteria? What are 'objec-tive criteria'?

With respect to the first problem the *Corte Costituzionale* has been called upon to decide the constitutionality of Article 1469 in light of Articles 3, 35, 41 of the Constitution. It does not recognise that a consumer can also be a legal person (*Corte Costizionale* 3 June 1999 n 282).

Regarding the concept of the consumer and the notion of 'scopi estranei all'attività imprenditoriale e professionale eventualmente svolta', the Tribunale di Roma recently stated that:

> E' consumatore il soggetto che acquista un bene o un servizio da utilizzare nell'ambito della propria attività imprenditoriale o professionale, purchè non rientri nel quadro di tale attività la conclusione di contratti dello stesso genere di quello stipulato. Infatti, al fine di stabilire se il contraente abbia agito 'per scopi estranei all'attività imprenditoriale o professionale eventualmente svolta' occorre verificare se la conclusione di tale contratto sia o non un atto della professione di chi acquista il bene o il servizio, come lo è per la sua controparte (nella specie è stato ritenuto consumatore uno scultore professionista che aveva stipulato un contratto di trasporto di un'opera d'arte per la patecipazione ad un concorso, non rientrando la conclusione di un atto du tal genenre nel quadro della sua attivitàdi scultore). (*Tribunale di Roma*, 20 October 1999).

CASE LAW REFERENCES

Pretura di Milano judgment of 30 January 1997 (1997) *Foro Padano* I 168, n Luongo; Tribunale di Roma judgment of 20 October 1999 (2000) *Giustizia Civile* I 2117, n Correa; Corte Costitiuzione, judgment of 3 June 1999, n 282, (1999) *Il Foro italiano* I 3118, n Palmieri.

LITERATURE REFERENCES

T Ballarino *Diritto internazionale privato* (2nd ed 1996) 141; G Giacalone 'Valida la clausola abusiva attributiva di competenza anche se si agisce per la nullità del contratto' *Guida al Diritto*, no 35 of 20 September 1997 85; G Chinè 'Il consumatore', in N Lipari *Diritto Privato Europeo* (1997); S Tonolo Sacco 'La nozione di consumatore ai fini della convenzione di Bruxelles concernente la competenza giurisdizionale e l'esecuzione delle decisioni in materia civile e commerciale' (1999) *Studium iuris* 438; U Corea 'Sulla nozione di 'consumatore': il problema dei contratti stipulati a scopi professionali' (Casenote on *Benincasa*), (1999) *Giustitia civile* I, 13; A Gratani 'La nozione di 'consumatore' nella convenzione di Bruxelles' (Casenote on *Benincasa*) (1997) *Diritto communitario e degli scambi internazionali* 510; A Zanoletti 'Protezione del consumatore e disciplina della giurisdizione nella CEE', *Giurisdizione e legge applicabile ai contratti nella CEE, a cura di Jayme e Picchio Forlati* (1990); L Gatt 'L'ambito soggettivo di applicazione della normativa sulle clausole vessatorie' (1998) *Giustizia Civile* I 2341; Palmieri, 'L'ibrida definizione di consumatore e I beneficiari (talvolta pretermessi) degli strumenti di riequilibrio contrattuale' (1999) *Il Foro italiano* I, 3118.

II

The Free Movement of Goods and Freedom to Provide Services

INTRODUCTION

The ECJ mainly influences the law of Member States by its decisions on the fundamental freedoms guaranteed in the EC Treaty, such as the free movement of goods laid down in Article 28 (ex Article 30) and the freedom to provide services laid down in Article 49 (ex Article 59). The influence that the ECJ has had on consumer protection is clearly discernable from its decisions relating to competition law. Here, the ECJ is confronted with the difficult task of harmonising not only the Member States' different methods of protecting competition and the consumer but also a variety of economic interests. Of the numerous cases decided in this area, only very few serve to highlight the progressive development of consumer protection. Further decisions concerning competition law are examined in the commentaries: *Aragonesa de Publicidad Exterior*, *Nissan*, *Yves Rocher* and *Mars*, as well as *Keck* and *Hünermund*, which have heralded a change in the ECJ's case law on the free movement of goods. Foremost amongst these decisions is the famous *Cassis de Dijon* judgment. In this case the ECJ reiterated the fundamental principles of Community law and established the protection of the consumer as an objective of Community law. Further decisions concerning competition law are examined in the commentaries.

LITERATURE REFERENCES

M Dauses 'Die Rechtsprechung des EuGH zum Verbraucherschutz und zur Werbefreiheit im Binnenmarkt' (1995) *Europäische Zeitschrift für Wirtschaftsrecht* 425; M Jarvis *The Application of EC Law by National Courts, The Free Movement of Goods* (1998); I Klauer *Die Europäisierung des Privatrechts, Der ECJ als Zivilrichter* (1998); P Oliver *Free Movement of Goods in the European Community* (3rd edn 1996).

CASE NO. 3 — Cassis de Dijon C–120/78

REWE-Zentral-AG v Bundesmonopolverwaltung für Branntwein
[1979] ECR 649

A. Judgment of the ECJ of 20 February 1979

1. Held

The concept of 'Measures having an effect equivalent to quantitative restrictions on imports' contained in Article 30 of the EEC Treaty is to be understood to mean that the fixing of a minimum alcohol content for alcoholic beverages intended for human consumption by the legislation of a Member State also falls within the prohibition laid down in that provision where the importation of alcoholic beverages lawfully produced and marketed in another Member State is concerned.

2. Facts of the Case

The *Hessisches Finanzgericht* (Germany) made two references to the ECJ concerning the interpretation of Articles 30 and 37 (new Articles 28 and 31) EC Treaty in order to determine whether a provision of German law on the marketing of alcoholic beverages was in accordance with Community law. The plaintiff in the main proceedings before the *Hessisches Finanzgericht* wished to import a consignment of Cassis de Dijon of French origin and market it in the Federal Republic of Germany. The plaintiff applied to the *Bundesmonopolverwaltung für Branntwein* (Federal Monopoly Administration for Spirits) for authorisation to import the product in question. The *Bundesmonopolverwaltung* informed the plaintiff that the product was not suitable to be marketed in Germany because of its insufficient alcoholic strength. It based its decision on Article 100 of the German Law on Monopoly in Spirits (*Branntweinmonopolgesetz, Reichsgesetzblatt* 1922, 335, amended by, inter alia, *Bundesgesetzblatt* 1976, 1145) together with the rules drawn up pursuant to that provision, the effect of which were to fix the minimum alcohol content of specified categories of liqueurs and other potable spirits (*Verordnung über den Mindestweingeistgehalt von Trinkbranntweinen* of 28 February 1958, *Bundesanzeiger* no 48 of 11 March 1958). Those provisions stated that the marketing of fruit liqueurs, such as Cassis de Dijon, was conditional upon attaining a minimum alcohol content of 25 per cent. The alcohol content of the product in question was between 15 and 20 per cent and was freely marketed as such in France.

The plaintiff took the view that the fixing by the German rules of a minimum alcohol content led to the result that well-known spirit products from other Member States of the Community could not be sold in the Federal Republic of Germany and that the said provision therefore constituted a restriction on the free movement of goods between Member States which exceeded the bounds of the trade rules reserved to the latter. In its view it was a measure having an effect equivalent to a quantitative restriction on imports contrary to Article 30 (new Article 28) EC Treaty. Since, furthermore, it was a measure adopted within the context of the management of the spirits monopoly, the plaintiff considered that there was also an infringement of Article 37 (new Article 31), according to which Member States would progressively adjust any state monopolies of a commercial character so as to ensure that when the transitional period had ended no discrimination regarding the conditions under which goods were procured or marketed existed between nationals of Member States. In order to reach a decision in this dispute the *Hessisches Finanzgericht* referred two questions to the ECJ:

1. Must the concept of 'measures having an effect equivalent to quantitative restrictions on imports' contained in Article 30 (new Article 28) of the EC Treaty be understood as meaning that the fixing of a minimum wine-spirit content for potable spirits laid down in the German *Branntwein-monopolgesetz*, the result of which is that traditional products of other Member States whose wine-spirit content is below the fixed limit cannot be put into circulation in the Federal Republic of Germany, also comes within this concept?

2. May the fixing of such a minimum wine-spirit content come within the concept of 'discrimination regarding the conditions under which goods are procured and marketed . . . Between nationals of Member States' contained in Article 37 (new Article 31) of the EC Treaty?

3. Extract from the Grounds of the ECJ's Judgment

6. The national court is thereby asking for assistance in the matter of interpretation in order to enable it to assess whether the requirement of a minimum alcohol content may be covered either by the prohibition on all measures having an effect equivalent to quantitative restrictions in trade between Member States contained in Article 30 of the Treaty or by the prohibition on all discrimination regarding the conditions under which goods are procured and marketed between nationals of Member States within the meaning of Article 37.

7. It should be noted in this connexion that Article 37 relates specifically to state monopolies of a commercial character. That provision is therefore irrelevant with regard to national provisions which do not concern the exercise by a public monop-oly of its specific function—namely, its exclusive right—but apply in a general manner to the production and marketing of alcoholic beverages, whether or not the latter are covered by the monopoly in question. That being the case, the effect on intra-Community trade of the measure referred to by the national court must be examined solely in relation to the requirements under Article 30, as referred to by the first question.

8. In the absence of common rules relating to the production and marketing of alcohol—a proposal for a regulation submitted to the Council by the Commission on 7 December 1976 (OJ C309/2) not yet having received the Council's approval—it is for the Member States to regulate all matters relating to the production and mar-keting of alcohol and alcoholic beverages on their own territory. Obstacles to move-ment within the community resulting from disparities between the national laws relating to the marketing of the products in question must be accepted in so far as those provisions may be recognised as being necessary in order to satisfy mandatory requirements relating in particular to the effectiveness of fiscal supervision, the pro-tection of public health, the fairness of commercial transactions and the defence of the consumer.

9. The government of the Federal Republic of Germany, intervening in the proceed-ings, put forward various arguments which, in its view, justify the application of provisions relating to the minimum alcohol content of alcoholic beverages, adduc-ing considerations relating on the one hand to the protection of public health and on the other to the protection of the consumer against unfair commercial practices.

10. As regards the protection of public health the German government states that the purpose of the fixing of minimum alcohol contents by national legislation is to avoid the proliferation of alcoholic beverages on the national market, in particular alcoholic beverages with a low alcohol content, since, in its view, such prod-ucts may more easily induce a tolerance towards alcohol than more highly alcoholic beverages.

11. Such considerations are not decisive since the consumer can obtain on the market an extremely wide range of weakly or moderately alcoholic prod-ucts and furthermore a large proportion of alcoholic beverages with a high alcohol content freely sold on the German market is generally consumed in a diluted form.

12. The German government also claims that the fixing of a lower limit for the alcohol content of certain liqueurs is designed to protect the consumer against unfair prac-tices on the part of producers and distributors of alcoholic beverages. This argument is based on the consideration that the lowering of the alcohol content secures a competitive advantage in relation to beverages with a higher alcohol content, since alcohol constitutes by far the most expensive constituent of beverages by reason of the high rate of tax to which it is subject. Furthermore, according to the German government, to allow alcoholic products into free circulation wherever, as regards their alcohol content, they comply with the rules laid down in the country of production would have the effect of imposing as a common standard within the Community the lowest alcohol content permitted in any of the Member States, and even of rendering any requirements in this field inoperative since a lower limit of this nature is foreign to the rules of several Member States.

13. As the Commission rightly observed, the fixing of limits in relation to the alcohol content of beverages may lead to the standardisation of products placed on the market and of their designations, in the interests of a greater transparency of commercial transactions and offers for sale to the public. However, this line of argument cannot be taken so far as to regard the mandatory fixing of minimum alcohol contents as being an essential guarantee of the fairness of commercial transactions, since it is a simple matter to ensure that suitable information is conveyed to the purchaser by requiring the display of an indication of origin and of the alcohol content on the packaging of products.

14. It is clear from the foregoing that the requirements relating to the minimum alcohol content of alcoholic beverages do not serve a purpose which is in the general interest and such as to take precedence over the requirements of the free movement of goods, which constitutes one of the fundamental rules of the Community. In practice, the principle effect of requirements of this nature is to promote alcoholic beverages having a high alcohol content by excluding from the national market products of other Member States which do not answer that description. It therefore appears that the unilateral requirement imposed by the rules of a Member State of a minimum alcohol content for the purposes of the sale of alcoholic beverages constitutes an obstacle to trade which is incompatible with the provisions of Article 30 of the Treaty. There is therefore no valid reason why, provided that they have been lawfully produced and marketed in one of the Member States, alcoholic beverages should not be introduced into any other Member State; the sale of such products may not be subject to a legal prohibition on the marketing of beverages with an alcohol content lower than the limit set by the national rules.

15. Consequently, the first question should be answered to the effect that the concept of 'measures having an effect equivalent to quantitative restrictions on imports' contained in Article 30 of the Treaty is to be understood to mean that the fixing of a minimum alcohol content for alcoholic beverages intended for human consumption by the legislation of a Member State also falls within the prohibition laid down in that provision where the importation of alcoholic beverages lawfully produced and marketed in another Member State is concerned.

B. Commentary

1. European Law

The formula developed by the ECJ in this case has formed a lasting basis for the determination of whether the laws of Member States are acceptable under the fundamental freedoms laid down by the EC Treaty. The ECJ also uses this formula as a basis for controlling the laws of Member States relating to consumer protection. The most important part of the judgment states:

> Obstacles to movement within the Community resulting from disparities between the national laws relating to the marketing of a product must be accepted in so far as those provisions may be recognized as being necessary in order to satisfy mandatory requirements relating in particular to the effectiveness of fiscal supervision, the protection of public health, the fairness of commercial transactions and the defence of the consumer (paragraph 8).

This formula provides a standard against which the compatibility of national provisions with the free movement of goods are measured. Article 28 (ex Article 30) EC Treaty briefly states that:

> Quantitative restrictions on imports and all measures having equivalent effect shall [. . .] be prohibited between Member States.

A large part of the ECJ's case law which concerns this Article deals with the meaning of the phrase 'measures having equivalent effect'. Even before its judgment in *Cassis de Dijon* the ECJ had adopted a wide interpretation of this phrase in *Dassonville*. The so-called '*Dassonville* formula' defines a measure having equivalent effect as:

> all trading rules enacted by Member States which are capable of hindering, directly or indirectly, actually or potentially, intra-Community trade (ECJ, *Dassonville* [1974] ECR 837, paragraph 5).

The decision in *Cassis de Dijon* identifies the circumstances under which the Member States may enact 'measures having equivalent effect' pursuant to the *Dassonville* case without infringing Article 28 (ex Article 30) EC Treaty. Community law tolerates such measures provided they are 'necessary in order to satisfy mandatory requirements'. The ECJ has provided a catalogue of mandatory requirements legitimising obstacles to free movement within the Community: fiscal supervision, the fairness of commercial transactions, the protection of public health and the defence of the consumer.

Consumer protection has been included in the catalogue of mandatory requirements as a ground to justify an obstacle to trade. In so doing the ECJ has raised the policy of consumer protection to an objective of Community law. Its importance in European law may be seen above all by the fact that it can justify a restriction on the free movement of goods, one of the 'fundamental principles' of the Community (ECJ *Cassis de Dijon* paragraph 14). The acknowledgement that consumer protection has equal importance to the fundamental freedoms went far beyond the state of Community law at the time. The EC Treaty itself made only cursory mention of the consumer. Before the judgment in *Cassis de Dijon*, restrictions on the free movement of goods in the interests of consumer protection could only be justified on the basis of Article 30 (ex Article 36) EC Treaty (text reproduced in the European law Commentary to *Aragonesa de Publicidad Exterior.* Case no 4 in this Casebook), in so far as such restrictions served to protect the health or the life of the consumer. The broadening of this protection to include economic interests of the consumer was first introduced by the Court's decision in *Cassis de Dijon.* By granting consumer protection this status, the ECJ gave effect to the 'Preliminary Programme of the European Economic Community for a Consumer Protection and Information Policy' of 14 April 1975 (OJ 1975 C92/1). In this programme the Commission and the Council formulated rights available to the consumer (inspired by American law) including the consumer's right to the protection of his economic interests and his right to information.

The ECJ's decision in *Cassis de Dijon* developed Community law along these lines long before the first Directives protecting the economic interests of the consumer had been passed and long before consumer protection had found its way into the EC Treaty as an express objective of Community law in the course of achieving the aims of the programme. The formula laid down by *Cassis de Dijon* illustrates under which circumstances national measures protecting the consumer may justify a restriction of the fundamental freedoms; 'in so far as those provisions may be recognized as being necessary in order to satisfy mandatory requirements'. The judgment provides an example of what is meant by 'mandatory requirements'. A statutory provision regulating the minimum content of alcohol can contribute towards consumer protection by providing greater transparency in commercial transactions. However, this objective may be just as effectively achieved by requiring the properties of the product to be displayed on its packaging. Prohibiting the marketing of Cassis de Dijon therefore proved disproportionate. It was possible to adequately protect the consumer by way of the more reasonable requirement of labelling in order to inform the consumer. This 'labelling doctrine' which was developed in *Cassis de Dijon* revealed the model of the European consumer adopted by the ECJ. Only those who actually observe the information displayed on the label or otherwise are capable of benefiting therefrom when making decisions relating to their legal transactions are to be protected. Thus Community law is beneficial to the consumer who is both critical and actively looking for information which provides him with a wide range of offers and better information about the products (for further annotations on the ECJ's notion of the consumer, see the European law Commentary to *Gut Springenheide.* Case no 17 in this Casebook).

The Commission summarised the effects of this judgment in a report to the Member States, the Council and the Parliament (OJ 1980 C256/2) stating that the *Cassis de Dijon* judgment prevents national consumer habits becoming entrenched. The jurisprudence gives the consumer access to goods which he could otherwise only buy abroad. A continuous stream of decisions from the ECJ in the light of this case illustrates the improvement of the market for consumer goods. For example, in Belgian shops one can buy margarine which is packaged differently from the normal cubic form (ECJ *Rau* [1982] ECR 3961); German consumers are able to purchase beer which has been brewed according to a foreign methods (ECJ *Commission v Germany* [1987] ECR 1227); one may buy noodles in Italy which have been made according to German recipes (ECJ *Drei Glocken* [1988] ECR 4233); or, in a recently decided case, it was held that pressed ham manufactured in the Netherlands could be imported into Germany (ECJ *van der Laan* [1999] ECR I–731).

The ECJ forthwith extended the case law based on the free movement of goods to the freedom to provide services (eg for national lotteries see ECJ *Schindler* [1994] ECR I–1039; see also ECJ *Familiapress* [1997] ECR I–1039). At present it is not possible to determine conclusively whether any gaps in consumer protection may arise from the deregulatory effect of this case law.

The importance of the decision in *Cassis de Dijon* goes beyond the question of how to interpret the fundamental freedoms laid down in the EC Treaty. The Court's formula in *Cassis de Dijon* established the relationship between Community law and the domestic law of Member States as well as the interplay between the EC Treaty and secondary legislation. The first condition for a Common Market is the abolition of restrictions to trade which contravene the fundamental freedoms. The ECJ implements such 'negative harmonisation' by interpreting the EC Treaty. A 'positive harmonisation' by Community legislation is then necessary if national provisions which present an obstacle to trade prove admissible pursuant to the *Cassis de Dijon* formula (this is also the case in relation to consumer protection). The doctrine laid down in *Cassis de Dijon* establishes areas of domestic competences which may restrict the free movement of goods, while at the same time leaving certain areas to be harmonised by the Community in order to complete the Internal Market (Article 94 (ex Article 100) and Article 95 (ex Article 100a) EC Treaty). The pressure on Member States to harmonise laws comes from two sources. Negative harmonisation removes provisions which create obstacles to the market without replacing them. In those areas where obstacles to trade have proved admissible, increasing Community legislation—for example in the case of consumer protection—leads to a co-existence of and an interaction between domestic and Community law. This 'logic of integration' (*Micklitz*) in *Cassis de Dijon* also allocates responsibility among the institutions of the European Union. Ultimately, the final decision on where the boundary lies between the extent of the fundamental freedoms and the competencies reserved to both the national and the Community legislator remains with the ECJ. The Court has thereby reserved to itself a key role and at the same time promoted market integration by means of legal harmonisation. Nevertheless it remains to be seen the extent to which the ECJ in the *Keck* judgment has shifted power back to the Member States (see the European law Commentary to ECJ *Keck*: Case no 7 in this Casebook).

ECJ CASE LAW REFERENCES

Dassonville [1974] ECR 837; *Rau* [1982] ECR 3961; *Oosthoek's Uitgeversmaatschappij* [1982] ECR 4575; *Commission v Germany* [1987] ECR 1227; *Drei Glocken* [1988] ECR 4233; *GB–INNO* [1990] ECR I–667; *SARPP* [1990] ECR I–4695: Case no 15 in this Casebook; *Aragonesa de Publicidad Exterior* [1991] ECR I–4151: Case no 4 in this Casebook; *Nissan* [1992] ECR I–131: Case no 5 in this Casebook; *Yves Rocher* [1993] ECR I–2361: Case no 6 in this Casebook; *Keck* [1993] ECR I–6097: Case no 7 in this Casebook; *Hünermund* [1993] ECR I–6787: Case no 8 in this Casebook; *Clinique* [1994] ECR I–317; *Schindler* [1994] ECR I–1039; *Mars* [1995] ECR I–1923: Case no 9 in this Casebook; *De Agostini* [1997] ECR I–3483; *Familiapress* [1997] ECR I–3689; *van der Laan* [1999] ECR I–731.

LITERATURE REFERENCES

A Bleckmann 'Zur Problematik der Cassis de Dijon-Rechtsprechung des Europäischen Gerichtshofs' (1986) *Gewerblicher Rechtsschutz und Urheberrecht-Internationaler Teil* 172; L Gormley (1981) *European Law Review* 454 (Casenote on *Cassis de Dijon*); A Mattera 'L'arrêt "Cassis de Dijon": une nouvelle approche pour la réalisation et le bon fonctionnement du marché intérieur' (1980) *Revue du marché commun* 505; H Micklitz 'Perspektiven eines Europäischen Privatrechts' (1998) *Zeitschrift für Europäisches Privatrecht* 253; P Verloren van Themaat, 'La libre ciculation de marchandises depuis l'arrêt "Cassis de Dijon"' (1982) *Cahier de droit européen* 123; D Wyatt (1981) *European Law Review* 185 (Casenote on *Cassis de Dijon*).

HS-N/JJ

2. *England & Wales*

Confusion as to the circumstances under which a national measure would be justified by the use of one of the mandatory requirements led one English judge to state:

> I confess I find some of the decisions as to whether a measure is outside Article 30 altogether or within it but justified by mandatory requirements perplexing. I am not alone. For instance the learned authors of Halsbury describe the court in *Oebel* and *Blesgen* as 'less than convincing in its approach', and suggest the cases can be justified under the mandatory requirement exception. That may be so, but I have to deal with what the court itself said. Prof. Arnull goes on to say . . . that: 'it is widely acknowledged that the Court's case law on Article 30 is in disarray'.

The case (*South Pembrokeshire District Council v Wendy Fair Markets Ltd* [1994] 1 CMLR 213), concerning a fourteenth-century monopoly right to hold a market in Tenby, was decided in 1994—some sixteen years after *Cassis de Dijon*. Certainly he is correct in stating that the case law of the Court is unclear with regard to the mandatory requirements. It was not until 1991, for example, that the Court clarified the use of the protection of health in *Cassis* and Article 30 (ex Article 36) EC Treaty (*Aragonesa de Publicidad Exterior SA v Departamento de Sanidad y Seguridad Social de la Generalitat de Cataluña*). The source of confusion is, therefore, hardly surprising, considering that, as one commentator pointed out:

> *Cassis* produced a change to the institutional context for the initiation of rule-making by requiring a higher level of justification for the adaptation of Community rules. In short, where trade barriers arise from disparities between national regulations Community rule-making should only be initiated where mutual recognition cannot successfully remove the barrier. (*Armstrong*)

In *SA Magnavision NV v General Optical Council (No. 1)* the Divisional Court had to interpret part of the *Dassonville* formula. It decided that section 21 of the Opticians Act 1958 which required reading glasses to be sold only after supervision by either a doctor or optician did not 'actually or potentially hinder trade'. In referring to the *Cassis* ruling specifically it stated:

> It is true that the *Cassis de Dijon* case shows that national measures can infringe Article 30 even though they apply to both imported and domestic products, subject to justification by reference to the mandatory requirement under examination . . . But *Cassis de Dijon* involved effectively a direct ban upon the sale of the low alcohol beverage and thus upon its import to Germany. So that the measures were plainly discriminatory and protectionist in their effect.

This reasoning does not reflect any understanding on the part of the Welsh court of, on the one hand, the fact that indistinctly applicable measures are capable of breaching Article 28 (ex Article 30) EC Treaty, and on the other, that it had completely misunderstood the rest of the ruling in the case. This is not an isolated incident in British or any other national court.

In *Wellingborough* and *Kettering* (*Wellingborough Borough Council v Payless DIY plc* and *Kettering Borough Council v WH Smith Do-It-All Ltd*) the Crown Court had to decide whether section 47 of the Shops Act fell into the category of 'national or regional socio-cultural characteristics'. The Court stated the importance:

> is the preservation of the special and traditional character of Sunday in England and Wales as a day of rest, relaxation, socialising and, for a significant part of the population, worship . . . One part of the population entitled to benefit from the distinctiveness of Sundays is shop workers; they can enjoy a day of rest on the same day as their relatives and friends and when weekend activities are available.

And thus allowed the injunction. It clearly felt that shops should not open on Sundays because of national cultural reasons. This decision following on the heals of *Torfaen* (Case C–145/88 *Torfaen Borough Council v B & Q* [1989] ECR 3851), where the Court had held that the issue should be determined by national courts. This policy led to divergent interpretations of domestic law, not least in the Sunday trading cases. This certainly did not aid consumers.

CASE LAW REFERENCES

High Court, Queen's Bench Division, *S A Magnavision N V v General Optical Council (No 1)*, (1987) *Common Market Law Reports* 1, 887; High Court, Chancery Division, *Wychavon District Council v Midland Enterprises (Special Event) Ltd* (1988) *Common Market Law Reports* 1, 397; High Court, Chancery Division, *London Borough of Waltham Forest v Scott Markets Ltd Common Market Law Reports*, 1988, 3, 773; High Court, Queen's Bench Divisional Court, *W H Smith Do-it-all Ltd and Payless DIY Ltd v Peterborough City Council*, (1990) *Common Market Law Reports* 2, 577; High Court, Chancery Division, *Stoke-on-Trent City Council v B & Q plc*, (1990) *Common Market Law Reports* 3, 31; East Gwent Magistrates, *Torfaen Borough Council v B & Q plc*, (1990) *Common Market Law Reports* 3, 455; Shrewsbury Crown Court, *B & Q Ltd v Shrewsbury and Atcham Borough Council*, (1990) *Common Market Law Reports* 3, 535.

LITERATURE REFERENCES

K Armstrong 'Regulating the free movement of Goods: institutions and institutional change', in J Shaw/G More *New Legal Dynamics of European Integration* (1995); R Barents 'New Developments in Measures having equivalent effect' (1981) *Common Market Law Review* 271; L Gormley 'Cassis de Dijon and the Communication from the Commission' (1981) *European Law Review* 454; M Jarvis *The Application of EC Law by National Courts* (1998) 53–88, 96–101, 201–30; P Oliver *Free Movement of Goods in the EC* (1996).

JJ

3. Germany

In the *Cassis de Dijon* proceedings those accused, the *Bundesmonopolverwaltung für Branntwein* and the German government, submitted some very dubious arguments to the ECJ in defence of the controversial prohibition on spirits. The protection of the consumer against deception, the protection of public health and protection from unfair commercial practices were cited as justifying this prohibition (Opinion of the Advocate-General [1979] ECR 655 671). In his Opinion the Advocate-General stated that these arguments were both untenable and somewhat absurd. Concerning the protection of public health he noted that a special preparation of the Cassis de Dijon liqueur was available on the market, which had a higher alcohol content due to the requirements proscribed in the *Branntwein-monopolgesetz*. The concluding rhetorical question speaks for itself:

Would it not be better for public health if consumers who are partial to a liqueur with a blackcurrant flavour had the possibility of consuming less alcohol, quite independently of the satisfaction of drinking the original product? ([1979] ECR at 673).

The Advocate-General drew attention to the real reason at issue with comparable clarity:

These doubts lead me to say that the real motive for the measure in question must be sought elsewhere; it is to be found in a market tradition to which national producers have long conformed and to which, therefore, the tastes of consumers have grown accustomed, such that there is reason to fear an invasion of foreign products having a lower alcohol content. ([1979] ECR at 674)

The protectionist effect of the *Branntweinmonopolgesetz* had also been the subject of infringement proceedings instigated by the Commission. As a result of these proceedings the rules governing minimum alcohol content were altered, if only partially (see [1979] ECR 652) as early as 1976. *Cassis de Dijon* serves as an example of the resistance put up by a Member State's legal and economic system against enforced market liberalisation and legal harmonisation by Community law. A reliance on consumer protection and competition is characteristic of arguments for maintaining obstacles to trade which infringe Community law. Following *Cassis de Dijon*, the provisions relating to the minimum alcohol content for imported products were lifted (statutory instrument of 10 March 1983, *Bundesanzeiger* no 58 of 28 March 1983). Once the ECJ had given judgment, the parties to the main proceedings before the *Hessisches Finanzgericht* settled the case. The court ordered costs against the defendant *Bundesmonopolverwaltung für Branntwein (Hessisches Finanzgericht*, ruling of 8 August 1979).

The *Cassis de Dijon* judgment is one of the most well-known ECJ decisions in Germany. There have been a series of judgments from German courts in which the case has either been directly quoted or where it has had an influence (for example shortly after the case, *Landgericht* Hamburg (Regional Court), judgment of 16 December 1982; *Bundesgerichtshof* (Federal Court of Justice) in the same case, judgment of 28 February 1985; further examples in *Roth*). Another example is the recent decision of the *Oberlandesgericht* Karlsruhe (Higher Regional Court) relating to competition law (judgment of 13 March 1996) on the advertising of automobiles imported from other Member States. The *Oberlandesgericht* applied the formula developed by the ECJ in *Cassis de Dijon* in relation to Article 28 (ex Article 30) EC Treaty. It held that terms contained in the German Law against Unfair Competition (*Gesetz gegen den unlauteren Wettbewerb* (hereafter '*UWG*'), *Reichsgesetzblatt* 1909, 499, amended by *Bundesgesetzblatt* I 1969, 633 amongst others) must be interpreted in accordance with the spirit of the EC Treaty since otherwise it would constitute an unjustified restriction on trade (for more on this see German commentary to *Nissan* [1992] ECR I–131: Case no 5 in this Casebook). The *Oberverwaltungsgericht* Lüneburg (Higher Administrative Court) in a case concerning waste disposal regulations (judgment of 3 May 1993) relied on

Cassis de Dijon, holding that laws enacted by Member States to protect the environment may restrict the free movement of goods in accordance with the settled case law of the ECJ. Such restrictions are only permissible if their genuine purpose is to protect the environment. They must not pursue other aims using the protection of the environment as a pretext nor must they either procedurally or substantially favour domestic goods or manufacturers over those from other Member States. In addition, such restrictions must only go so far as it enables the Member State to achieve its objective. The fundamental principle espoused in *Cassis de Dijon* is clearly recognisable in the wording (concerning the addition of the protection of the environment to the catalogue of 'mandatory requirements' see ECJ *Commission v Denmark* [1988] ECR 4627). The German *Bundesverwaltungsgericht* in its judgment of 23 January 1992 recognised the influence the ECJ case law had on German laws relating to the labelling of foodstuffs. In interpreting these laws it referred to decisions of the ECJ on consumer protection beginning with *Cassis de Dijon* (more details under the German commentary to *SARPP* [1990] ECR I–4695: Case no 15 in this Casebook). These examples alone provide sufficient evidence that the principles of *Cassis de Dijon* have influenced German case law. However, it is not possible to conclusively assess the extent of this influence.

CASE LAW REFERENCES

Hessisches Finanzgericht ruling of 8 August 1979 (1979) *Recht der Internationalen Wirtschaft* 699; Landgericht Hamburg judgment of 16 December 1982 (1982) *Recht der Internationalen Wirtschaft* 348; Bundesgerichtshof *Cocktail-Getränk* judgment of 28 February 1985 (1985) *Gewerblicher Rechtsschutz und Urheberrecht* 886; Bundesverwaltungsgericht judgment of 23 January 1992, *Entscheidungen des Bundesverwaltungsgerichts* Vol 89, 320: (1992) *Neue Zeitschrift für Verwaltungsrecht* 781; Oberverwaltungsgericht Lüneburg judgment of 3 May 1993, (1994) *Neue Zeitschrift für Verwaltungsrecht* 508; Oberlandesgericht Karlsruhe judgment of 13 March 1996, (1996) *Neue Juristische Wochenschrift* 2313.

LITERATURE REFERENCES

M Dauses 'Die Rechtsprechung des EuGH zum Verbraucherschutz und zur Warenverkehrsfreiheit im Binnenmarkt' (1995) *Europäische Zeitschrift für Wirtschaftsrecht* 425; E Millarg (1979) *Europarecht* 420 (Casenote on *Cassis de Dijon*); W Roth 'The Application of Community Law in West Germany 1980–1990' (1991) *Common Market Law Review* 137; R Sack 'Staatliche Werbebeschränkungen und die Art 30 und 59 EG-Vertrag' (1998) *Wettbewerb in Recht und Praxis* 103.

HS-N

4. France

The French government did not give its opinion in the proceedings to *Cassis de Dijon*, despite the fact that a French product was affected (this was not the case with the Danish government which drew attention to the fact that German law restricted imports of Danish cherry brandy; [1979] ECR 658). The French reticence could have been due to the fact that in France prohibitions on the advertising of alcohol were in force at the time which crassly discriminated against foreign products. Due to these prohibitions the Commission instigated proceedings for a breach of the Treaty which was later upheld (ECJ *Commission v France* [1980] ECR 229; see the French commentary to *Aragonesa de Publicidad Exterior* [1991] ECR I–4151: Case no 4 in this Casebook).

The ECJ case law on the free movement of goods owes much to the imaginative domestic obstacles to trade, particularly for alcoholic beverages (apart from the cases mentioned see also ECJ *Fietje* [1980] ECR 3839; *Bocksbeutel* [1984] ECR 1299; *Miro* [1985] ECR 3731; *Commission v Germany* [1987] ECR 1227).

The influence of even *Cassis de Dijon* on French case law is difficult to discern. The typically cursory *ratio decidendi* occasionally indicate, however, that the proportionality of 'measures having equivalent affect' has been reviewed by the courts: for example, where it protects the consumer. An example of this is the judgment of the *Conseil d'État* of 19 November 1986 (*Smanor*). In this case, a law prohibiting the selling of deep frozen yoghurt under the description 'Yoghurt' was not considered to have constituted a breach of Article 28 (ex Article 30) EC Treaty. The core of the reasoning was as follows:

> Considérant (. . .) que (. . .) lesdites dispositions qui ne comportent par elles-mêmes aucune restriction quantitative aux importations ont pour seul objet, dans l'intérêt des consommateurs, de réserver à des produits présentant certaines caractéristiques la dénomination de 'yaourts' et ne sauraient être regardées comme ayant un effet équivalent à de telles restrictions.

In this sentence the question was posed whether the provision constituted a 'measure having equivalent effect' for the purposes of Article 28 (ex Article 30) EC Treaty overlapped with a possible justification on the basis of 'mandatory requirements' of which consumer protection is one. This judgment which is not unique (see *Jarvis* and *Conseil d'État*, judgment of 18 December 1981) came in for a great deal of criticism both from legal writers and the Community institutions. In a report to the European Parliament concerning the application of Community law the Commission criticised the *Conseil d'État* for an interpretation and construction 'which taking into account the settled case law of the Court in relation to Article 28 (ex Article 30) EC Treaty is questionable at the very least' (OJ 1987 C338 33, 34). The ECJ held in parallel proceedings concerning the permissibility of marketing deep frozen yoghurt under this description that the French provisions infringed Article 28 (ex Article 30) EC Treaty (ECJ *Smanor* [1988] ECR 4489).

There are also decisions which contain arguments reminiscent of those put forward in *Cassis de Dijon* without actually quoting them. One example is a case heard by the *Tribunal de Grande Instance* Créteil (judgment of 5 May 1987) concerning the permissibility of importing Italian salami which infringed French provisions on moisture content. The Tribunal justified its decision (based on Article 28 (ex Article 30) EC Treaty) by reference to the fact that salami bears a label which allows the consumer to establish the origin of the product. Since the salami complies with the relevant Italian laws, it followed that its marketing must also be permitted in France. One will look in vain however for any reference to the case law of the ECJ. In a more recent decision of the *Cour de Cassation* (judgment of 17 October 1994) explicit reference was made to the ECJ's decision in *Parfumerie-Fabrik 4711* ([1989] ECR 3891) that domestic measures which restrict the import of cosmetic products cannot be justified as a mandatory requirement because this area is conclusively regulated by a Directive. The *Cour de Cassation* therefore considered applying the *Cassis de Dijon* formula but decided against doing so, in accordance with the case law of the ECJ.

CASE LAW REFERENCES

Conseil d'État judgment of 18 December 1981 (1982) *Revue trimestrielle de droit européen* 201; Conseil d'État *Smanor*, judgment of 19 November 1986 *Juris-classeur périodique—La semaine juridique*, édition générale 1987 II 20822; Tribunal de Grande Instance Créteil, judgment of 5 May 1987 *Juris-classeur périodique—La semaine juridique*, édition enterprise 1987 II, 15041; Cour de Cassation, chambre criminelle judgment of 17 October 1994 *Bulletin des arrêts de la Cour de Cassation* chambre criminelle 1995 no 332.

LITERATURE REFERENCES:

V Constantinesco (1988) *Revue trimestrielle de droit européen* 113 (Casenote on the judgment of the Conseil d'État of 19 November 1986—*Smanor*); M Jarvis *The Application of EC Law by National Courts, The Free Movement of Goods* (1998) 187–191; R Kovar (1981) *Journal du droit international* 106 (Casenote on *Cassis de Dijon*); J Masclet 'Les articles 30, 36 et 100 du traité C.E.E. à la lumière de l'arrêt "Cassis de Dijon"' (1980) *Revue trimestrielle de droit européen* 611.

BD

5. Italy

Cassis de Dijon aroused a great deal of interest in Italian jurisprudence, both with regard to the European Community itself (*Scannicchio*) and also for Italian contract law (*Barenghi*). An especially important theme in Italian law concerned the enforceability of contracts. In order for a contract to be enforceable, it is necessary for the subject of the contract (*oggetto del contratto*) to be of a legal nature (*lecito*). Article 1346 of the *Codice civile* states:

L'oggetto del contratto deve essere possibile, lecito, determinato o determinabile.

An Italian court can therefore hold that a contract of sale is invalid if the subject of the transaction is illegal in nature or if the acquisition of such goods amounts to a criminal act. Following the judgment in *Cassis de Dijon* the nature of what amounted to illegal transactions had to be given a narrower interpretation in Italian law due to the fact that interfering with the free movement of goods was not justifiable on the basis of illegality (*Barenghi*). Hitherto, however, there have not been any cases brought before the Italian courts which demonstrate such an influence.

The *Cassis de Dijon* judgment also entailed a liberalisation of the market concerning foreign products with an accompanying increase in the choice of goods available. One example from Italian case law is the now legal importation of noodles (*Drei Glocken* [1988] ECR 4233) and vinegar (*Aceto* [1981] ECR 3019; [1985] ECR 3397), which have not been produced according to traditional Italian methods.

A different example of the influence of the *Cassis De Dijon* case is the marketability of dietary goods. These are considered medical goods by Italian administrative authorities. This contrasts with the practices in other Member States. Italian administrative courts stated two things in these cases: first, on the preliminary statement that measures adopted by Member States interfering with free movement of goods are measures having the equivalent effect to import restrictions; second, the public authority denial of the marketing of dietary goods was in contrast with other Member States' decisions and scientific studies as illegal (*Tribunale Regionale Amministrativo Emilia Romagna* Parma 18 June 1997 no 235).

CASE LAW REFERENCES

Corte Costituzionale, judgment of 2 February 1988 *Il Foro Italiano* Repertorio 1989, see *Alimenti e Bevande*, no 147; Corte Costituzionale judgment of 18 April 1991 *Il Foro Italiano* Repertorio 1991 see *Alimenti e Bevande* no 170; Corte Costituzionale judgment of 10 February 1994 (1995) *Il Foro Italiano* I 1713; Tribunale Regionale Amministrativo Emilia Romagna Parma, 18 June 1997 no 235.

LITERATURE REFERENCES

A Barenghi 'L'oggetto del contratto' in N Lipari (ed) *Diritto Privato Europeo* (1997) 604; F Capelli 'E' legittima la "discriminazione alla rovescia" imposta per tutelare la qualità della pasta alimentare italiana' no 27, (1994) *Diritto Comunitario degli Scambi Internazionali* 421 (Casenote on the judgment of the Corte Costituzionale of 26 January 1994); G Cavani/G Ghidini 'Una sentenza pilota (*Cassis de Dijon*) in tema di ostacolo alla libera circolazione delle merci' (1981) *Rivista di Diritto Commerciale* I 197; N Scannicchio 'Dal diritto comunitario al diritto privato europeo nella Giurisprudenza della Corte di Giustizia' in N Lipari (ed) *Diritto Privato Europeo* (1997) 58; R Perchinunno 'L'architettura dei contratti di profilo europeo fondata sul principio della "libera circolazione" in relazione ai soggetti e alle attività' in N Lipari (ed) *Diritto Privato Europeo* (1997) 58.

AM

CASE NO. 4 — *Aragonesa de Publicidad Exterior*
Joined Cases C–1/90 & 176/90

*Aragonesa de Publicidad Exterior SA and Publivía SAE v
Departamento de Sanidad y Seguridad Social de la Generalitat
de Cataluña*
[1991] ECR I–4151

A. Judgment of the ECJ of 25 July 1991

1. Held

Articles 30 and 36 of the EC Treaty, viewed together, do not preclude legislation such as the law at issue in the main proceedings which, in part of the territory of a Member State, prohibits the advertising of beverages having an alcoholic strength of more than 23 degrees in the media, on streets and highways (with the exception of signs indicating centres of production and sale) in cinemas and on public transport where that legislation, even if it constitutes a measure having equivalent effect within the meaning of Article 30 of the EC Treaty, can be justified under Article 36 of the Treaty on grounds of the protection of public health, and where, in view of its characteristics and the circumstances set out in the documents before the Court, it does not appear to be a means of protecting certain local products.

2. Facts of the Case

The *Tribunal Superior de Justicia* Cataluña (High Court of Catalonia) referred three questions on the interpretation of Articles 30 and 36 (new Articles 28 and 30) EC Treaty to the Court for a preliminary ruling under Article 177 (new Article 234) EC Treaty. Those questions were raised in the course of proceedings between, on the one hand, Aragonesa de Publicidad Exterior and Publivía SAE, which operate advertising hoardings and the Departamento de Sanidad y Seguridad

Social (Department of Health and Social Security) of the Autonomous Community of Catalonia.

Administrative fines were imposed on those companies for infringing the provisions of Law no 20/85 enacted on 25 July 1985 by the Parliament of the Autonomous Community of Catalonia on prevention and assistance with regard to substances likely to lead to dependency, which prohibit the advertising of beverages having an alcoholic strength of more than 23 degrees in the media, on the streets and highways (except to indicate centres of production and sale) and in cinemas and on public transport. Aragonesa de Publicidad Exterior and Publivía SAE appealed against those fines to the *Tribunal Superior de Justicia* Cataluña. Before that court they contended in particular that the Catalan law on which the decision was based was contrary to Article 30 (new Article 28) EC Treaty, inasmuch as by virtue of the advertising restrictions which it imposed, it affected marketing opportunities for beverages originating in other Member States. The *Tribunal Superior de Justicia* decided to stay the proceedings until the Court had given a preliminary ruling on the following questions:

1. Does the law of a Member State (or in this case, of the Parliament of an autonomous community of a Member State with powers, under domestic legislation, to legislate on particular matters) which prohibits, within the territory under its jurisdiction, the advertising of beverages having an alcoholic strength of more than 23 degrees in (a) the mass media (b) streets and highways, with the exception of signs indicating centres of production and sale (c) cinemas (d) public transport, constitute a measure having an effect equivalent to a quantitative restriction on exports within the meaning of Article 30 EC Treaty?

2. If the answer is in the affirmative, must the first sentence of Article 36 of the EC Treaty be interpreted as meaning that a Member State may lawfully impose a partial prohibition of the advertising of beverages having an alcoholic strength of more than 23 degrees for the protection of the health of humans in accordance with domestic law?

3. May a prohibition on grounds of public health as described above constitute a means of arbitrary discrimination or a disguised restriction on trade between the Member States?

3. Extract from the Grounds of the ECJ's Judgment

7. With these three questions, which must be examined together, the national court is seeking to ascertain whether Articles 30 and 36 of the EEC Treaty preclude rules, such as those contained in the law at issue in the main proceedings, which in the cases therein specified prohibit the advertising of beverages having an alcoholic strength of more than 23 degrees.

8. It should first be pointed out that Article 30 of the Treaty may apply to measures adopted by all the authorities of the Member States, be they the central authorities, the authorities of a federal State, or other territorial authorities.

9. Under Article 30 of the Treaty 'quantitative restrictions on imports and all measures having equivalent effect shall . . . be prohibited between Member States'. In accordance with the settled case-law of the Court, any measure capable of hindering, directly or indirectly, actually or potentially, intra-Community trade is to be deemed to be a measure having equivalent effect.

10. As the Court held, inter alia, in its judgment in Case C–362/88 *GB–INNO–BM v Confederation du Commerce Luxembourgoise* [1990] ECR 667 paragraph 7, legislation which restricts or prohibits certain forms of advertising and certain means of sales promotion may, although it does not directly affect trade, be such as to restrict the volume of trade because it affects marketing opportunities.

11. Accordingly, national legislation such as that at issue in the main proceedings, which prohibits the advertising in certain places of beverages having an alcoholic strength of more than 23 degrees may constitute a hindrance to imports from other Member States and, therefore must in principle be regarded as a measure having equivalent effect within the meaning of Article 30.

12. However, in its observations to the Court, the Commission argues that such legislation, which applies without distinction to domestic and imported products, must be upheld by reference to Article 30 alone without its being necessary to have recourse, as the national court does, to Article 36, because that legislation is justified by an imperative requirement, namely the protection of public health.

13. That form of reasoning cannot be accepted. The protection of public health is expressly mentioned amongst the grounds of public interest which are set out in Article 36 and enable a restriction on imports to escape the prohibition laid down in Article 30. In those circumstances, since Article 36 also applies where the contested measure restricts only imports, whereas according to the Court's case-law the question of imperative requirement for the purposes of the interpretation of Article 30 cannot arise unless the measure in question applies without distinction to both national and imported products, it is not necessary to consider whether the protection of public health might also be in the nature of an imperative requirement for the purposes of the application of Article 30.

14. In those circumstances it is first of all necessary to ascertain whether the legislation at issue is of such a nature as to protect public health and, secondly, is proportionate to the objective to be attained.

15. On the first point it is sufficient to observe, as the Court pointed out in its judgment in Case 152/78 *Commission v France* [1980] ECR 2299 paragraph 17, that advertising acts as an encouragement to consumption and the existence of rules restricting the advertising of alcoholic beverages in order to combat alcoholism reflects public health concerns.

16. On the second point it must be stated that in the present state of Community law, in which there are no common or harmonised rules governing in a general manner the advertising of alcoholic beverages, it is for the Member States to decide on the degree of protection which they wish to afford to public health and on the way in which that protection is to be achieved. They may do so, however, only within the limits set by the Treaty and must, in particular, comply with the principle of proportionality.

17. A national measure such as that at issue restricts freedom of trade only to a limited extent since it concerns only beverages having an alcoholic strength of more than 23 degrees. In principle, the latter criterion does not appear to be manifestly unreasonable as part of a campaign against alcoholism.

18. On the other hand, the measure at issue does not prohibit all advertising of such beverages but merely prohibits it in specified places some of which, such as public highways and cinemas, are particularly frequented by motorists and young persons, two categories of the population in regard to which the campaign against alcoholism is of quite special importance. It thus cannot in any event be criticized for being disproportionate to its stated objective.

19. Secondly, in order to benefit from the derogation provided for in Article 36, a national provision must not constitute a means of arbitrary discrimination or a disguised restriction on trade between Member States, to use the precise terms of the second sentence of that Article.

20. As the Court held in Case 34/79 *Regina v Henn and Darby* [1979] ECR 3795 paragraph 21, the function of the second sentence of Article 36 is to prevent restrictions on trade based on the grounds mentioned in the first sentence from being diverted from their proper purpose and used in such a way as to create discrimination in respect of goods originating in other Member States or indirectly to protect certain national products.

21. In that connection, Aragonesa de Publicidad Exterior and Publivía argue that, in assessing the discriminatory and protective nature of the measure, it is necessary to take more into account than the fact that the Catalan law makes no formal distinction between the domestic or foreign origin of the beverages in question. It should be borne in mind that that law applies only within the territorial jurisdiction of the parliament of Catalonia.

22. According to the applicants in the main proceedings, what should be compared, therefore, is not the situation of imported products with that of products from Spain as a whole but the situation of imported products with that of Catalan products. Since the majority of Catalan-produced alcoholic beverages have an alcohol content of less than 23 degrees, the measure at issue should be regarded as discriminatory and protective in nature, inasmuch as it seeks to discourage the consumption of beverages with a high alcohol content and thus places at a disadvantage beverages originating outside Catalonia, and inasmuch, on the other hand, as it does not restrict the advertising of beverages with a lower alcohol content, thus protecting locally-produced beverages.

23. Those arguments cannot be upheld.

24. It is true that, when a national measure has limited territorial scope because it applies only to a part of the national territory, it cannot escape being characterized as discriminatory or protective for the purposes of the rules on the free movement of goods on the ground that it affects both the sale of products from other parts of the national territory and the sale of products imported from other Member States. For such a measure to be characterised as discriminatory or protective, it is not necessary for it to have the effect of favouring national products as a whole or of placing only imported products at a disadvantage and not national products.

25. However, national legislation such as that in question in the main proceedings does not constitute arbitrary discrimination or a disguised restriction on intra-Community trade. On the one hand, it is clear from the documents before the Court that such legislation does not distinguish between products according to their origin. The restrictions which it imposes do not apply to beverages having an alcoholic strength of less than 23 degrees and therefore do not restrict imports of such beverages from other Member States. In regard to beverages having an alcoholic strength of more than 23 degrees, those restrictions affect both products, in not inconsiderable quantities, originating in the part of the national territory to which they apply and products imported from other Member States. On the other hand, the fact that that part of the national territory produces more beverages having an alcoholic strength of less than 23 degrees than beverages with a higher alcohol content is not in itself sufficient to cause such legislation to be regarded as liable to give rise to arbitrary discrimination or a disguised restriction on intra-Community trade.

26. Accordingly, the reply to be given to the questions submitted for a preliminary ruling should be that Articles 30 and 36 of the EEC Treaty, viewed together, do not preclude legislation such as the law at issue in the main proceedings which, in part of the territory of a Member State, prohibits the advertising of beverages having an alcoholic strength of more than 23 degrees, in the media, on streets and highways (with the exception of signs indicating centres of production and of sale) in cinemas and on public transport, where that legislation, even if it constitutes a measure having equivalent effect within the meaning of Article 30 of the EEC Treaty, can be justified under Article 36 of that Treaty on grounds of the protection of public health, and where, in view of its characteristics and the circumstances set out in the documents before the Court, it does not appear to be a means, even an indirect means, of protecting certain local products.

B. Commentary

1. European Law

Before its judgment in *Keck* (Case no 7 in this Casebook), the case law of the ECJ had shown that the Court consistently viewed provisions which prohibit or restrict certain forms of advertising as potential restrictions on the free movement of goods which are prohibited according to Article 28 (ex Article 30) EC Treaty provided that the provisions could not be justified under Community law. The ECJ had in *Aragonesa de Publicidad Exterior* accordingly held that the prohibition on advertising beverages which have an alcoholic strength of more than 23 degrees contravened Article 28 (ex Article 30) EC Treaty without any further justification (paragraphs 9–11). On this point the judgment could therefore be out of date, since a prohibition on advertising of this kind which is applicable to imported or domestic products without distinction may be a mere 'selling arrangement' in accordance with the decision in *Keck*. Nevertheless, the decision in *Aragonesa de Publicidad Exterior* continues to be good law, as the ECJ in its judgment of 1991 regarded the restriction on the freedom of goods as justified on the ground of protection of public health under Article 30 (ex Article 36) EC Treaty. Such a law is therefore compatible with Community law regardless of whether one considers Article 28 (ex Article 30) EC Treaty as being applicable or not.

The decision contains some other important points. One is the use of Article 30 (ex Article 36) EC Treaty as opposed to the judge-made 'mandatory requirements' developed in the case *Cassis de Dijon* which allow a restriction of the free movement of goods (see the European law commentary to *Cassis de Dijon* [1979] ECR 649: Case no 3 in this Casebook). The Court forcibly emphasised that only Article 30 (ex Article 36) EC Treaty was to be used in determining whether a prohibition on advertising is permitted. An investigation as to whether the prohibition on advertising may be justified as a 'mandatory requirement' is therefore unnecessary (paragraph 13). One reason for the 'either-or' relationship between these two justifications on the restriction of the free movement of goods is the difference in the legal consequences. Article 30 (ex Article 36) EC Treaty states:

> The provisions of Articles 28 and 29 shall not preclude prohibitions or restrictions on imports, exports or goods in transit justified on the grounds of public morality, public policy or public security; the protection of health and life of humans, animals or plants; the protection of national treasures possessing artistic, historic or archaeological value; or the protection of industrial and commercial property. Such prohibitions or restrictions shall not, however, constitute a means of arbitrary discrimination or a disguised restriction on trade between Member States.

This provision permits very wide-ranging restrictions on the free movement of goods, in particular a prohibition or restriction on the importation of foreign goods, whilst a justification on the grounds of 'mandatory requirements' only applies to indistinctly applicable measures (paragraph 13). Due to the more radical legal consequences of Article 30 (ex Article 36) EC Treaty, however, its scope of application is to be interpreted narrowly whilst the list of 'mandatory requirements', which may justify measures which apply without distinction has been left open by the ECJ. There are therefore two different grounds on which Member States may rely in order to restrict trade for the protection of the consumer. Measures protecting the consumer which pursue one of the aims laid down in Article 30 (ex Article 36) EC Treaty: in particular measures relating to the protection of health may expressly discriminate against imported products (eg the import ban imposed on dangerous foodstuffs such as beef). In any event other consumer protection aims, such as the securing of the consumers' economic interests justify restrictions on trade which affect indistinctly applicable measures. From the interplay between Articles 28 and 30 (ex Articles 30 and 36) EC Treaty there arises a hierarchy of the aims relating to consumer protection in Community law. The Member States may also discriminate against foreign products in order to protect the life and health of humans. Such discrimination cannot be justified solely on the basis of the economic interests of the consumer. Recent developments suggest that this relationship between the grounds of justification for a restriction on the basic freedoms could be changing. The judgments in *De Agostini* (ECJ [1997] ECR I–3843), *Aher-Waggon* (ECJ [1998] ECR I–4473) and *TK-Heimdienst* (ECJ [2000] ECR I–151) are seen as evidence that the ECJ would also apply the grounds of justification laid down in *Cassis de Dijon* to national laws which are discriminatory in nature (*Roth, Sack*).

Further regard should be had to the ECJ's clarification that a regional restriction on trade which applied to only part of the national territory may also be directly held to be an infringement of the free movement of goods (paragraph 24). The protectionist nature of such a provision may not therefore be rebutted by the argument that the law affects the sale of products originating from other national areas to the same extent as the sale of goods which are imported from abroad. By relying on the factually indeterminate situation, the ECJ was nevertheless able to evade the interesting legal question presented by this case as to whether the limited prohibition on advertising in Catalonia is in fact a disguised restriction on trade pursuant to Article 30 (ex Article 36) EC Treaty. The parties had represented the argument that predominantly beverages with an alcoholic strength of less than 23 degrees were produced in Catalonia. Therefore mainly those beverages which do not originate in Catalonia are placed at a disadvantage (paragraph 22). The Court countered this argument, stating that beverages of greater alcoholic strength are produced in Catalonia 'in not inconsiderable quantities' and that there was accordingly insufficient evidence for the assumption that a disguised restriction on intra-Community trade was intended.

This judgment reveals a facet in the ECJ's case law in its concept of the consumer which diverges somewhat from the image attributed to Community law of the prudent/circumspect consumer who makes decisions independently (on this subject see the European law Commentaries to cases *Benincasa:* Case no 2; *Mars:* Case no 9; *Di Pinto:* Case no 10; and *Gut Springenheide:* Case no 17 in this Casebook). The consumer is seen as vulnerable to the dangers of addiction which justifies his being protected against enticing advertising such as that for alcohol, even if this protection leads to a restriction of the free movement of goods. The ECJ grants Member States freedom to enact independent measures relating to the protection of public health provided that there are no Community rules on the same subject (see *Commission v France* [1980] ECR 2299 paragraph 17). The measures protecting consumers against the dangers of addiction take precedence over the free movement of goods. This shows that the policies and legal system of the European Union pursue aims of a protective nature which transcend the establishment of an Internal Market orientated around the suppliers of products. This jurisprudence has been clarified by the judgment in the *Tobacco Advertising* case. Here the ECJ on the one hand annulled Directive 98/43 on Tobacco Advertising for reasons connected with its legal base but on the other hand the court confirmed that public health protection is a constituent part of the Community policies. It highlighted that a prohibition of certain forms of tobacco advertising could be adopted under Article 95 (ex Article 100a) EC Treaty (ECJ judgment of 5 October 2000 Case C–376/98 paragraphs 88 and 98). In its recent decision *Konsumentombudsmannen* (judgment of 8 March 2001 Case C–405/98) the ECJ confirmed this position.

ECJ CASE LAW REFERENCES

Cassis de Dijon [1979] ECR 649: Case no 3 in this Casebook;_*Commission v France* [1980] ECR 2299; *Di Pinto* [1991] ECR I–1189: Case no 10 in this Casebook; *Keck* [1993] ECR I–6097: Case no 7 in this Casebook; *Mars* [1995] ECR I–1923: Case no 9 in this Casebook; *Benincasa* [1997] ECR I–3767: Case no 2 in this Casebook; *De Agostini* [1997] ECR I–3842; *Gut Springenheide* [1998] ECR I–4657: Case no 17 in this Casebook; *Aher-Waggon* [1998] ECR I–4473; *TK-Heimdienst* [2000] ECR I–151; *Tobacco Advertising,* judgment of 5 October 2000, Case C–376/98 n.y.r. in the ECR; *Konsumentombudsmannen* Case C–405/98 n.y.r. in ECR.

LITERATURE REFERENCES

C Berr (1992) *Journal du droit international* 435 (Casenote on *Aragonesa de Publicidad Exterior*); M Dauses 'Information der Verbraucher in der Rechtsprechung des EuGH' (1998) *Recht der Internationalen Wirtschaft* 750; G Lange (1992) *European Food Law Review* 59 (Casenote on *Aragonesa de Publicidad Exterior*); A Leupold/A Nachbaur 'Werbebeschränkungen und Warenverkehrsfreiheit nach Art 30 EWG-Vertrag' (1991) *Juristenzeitung* 1110; M Mok (1993) *TVVS Maandblad voor Ondernemingsrecht en Rechtspersonen* 213 (Casenote on *Aragonesa de Publicidad Exterior*); W Roth 'Diskriminierende Regelungen des Warenverkehrs und Rechtfertigung durch die 'zwingenden Erfordernisse' des Allgemeininteresses' (2000) *Wettbewerb in Recht und Praxis* 979; R Sack 'Staatliche

Werbebeschränkungen und die Art 30 und 59 EG-Vertrag' (1998) *Wettbewerb in Recht und Praxis* 103.

HS-N/JJ

2. England & Wales

The United Kingdom submitted written observations to the European Court of Justice concerning two issues which were raised in the case. First, the UK highlighted the power of advertising and its influence as an adjunct to the process of trade, and urged the Court to recognise that prohibitions on advertising could be important factors in restricting trade in breach of Article 28 (ex Article 30) EC Treaty and the *Dassonville* formula. Secondly, the UK pointed out that control of alcoholism is a question of public health. A measure intended to restrict the use of alcoholic beverages 'might' be justified under Article 30 (ex Article 36) EC Treaty. However the risk to public health must be assessed according to objective factors which take into account the risk posed by all beverages. A prohibition on advertising alcoholic drinks exceeding 23 degrees might therefore constitute a means of arbitrary discrimination or a disguised restriction on trade. The actual assessment should be subject to an evaluation of the drinks market and the facts of the case in question.

In the UK, the legal framework for advertising is to be found at a different level to that of State law: in fact, advertising is largely regulated by Codes of Practice endorsed by the Director General of Fair Trading (see Fair Trading Act 1973, section 124(3)). The Advertising Standard Authority (ASA) administers the control of the print, cinema and poster media. In addition to the ASA, two further organisations are involved in the control of advertising on radio and TV, the Independent Television Commission (ITC) and Radio Authority. The ASA, ITC and Radio Authority Codes of Practice all contain very similar measures and are all intended to be enforced through action by the media: on a recommendation of the relevant organisation, advertising space may be denied to or trading privileges withdrawn from those who contravene the Codes.

The tenth edition of the ASA Advertising and Sales Promotion Codes (established in 1975), came into force on 1 October 1999. They lay down several requirements advertisers should comply with. All advertisement should be legal, decent, honest and truthful; they should be prepared with a sense of responsibility to consumers and society, and should respect the principles of fair competition. As to alcoholic drinks (those above 1.2 per cent alcohol by volume), the restrictions imposed on advertisers are not as strict as the ones at issue in the *Aragonesa* case. Sections 46(1) to 46(12) require the advertisers to accept responsibility for ensuring that their advertisements do not lead people to 'risky' drinking habits; they underline the sense of social responsibility, especially with regard to the most vulnerable public (the young, the immature, the 'mentally weaker'). They prohibit presenting alcohol as a means of improving attractiveness and social skills.

For drinks that contain only between 0.5 per cent and 1.2 per cent alcohol, section 46(13) provides only that advertisers should ensure that the drinks are not promoted in a way that encourages their inappropriate consumption and that they do not depict activities that require complete excess.

The control of advertising was subject to scrutiny in the 1980s. A proposal was put forward to give the Codes of Practice statutory force: the Director General of Fair Trading, however, declared that there was no need to create a statutory regulatory system.

LITERATURE REFERENCES

C Scott/J Black *Cranston's Consumers and the Law* (2000) 51–68; ASA Advertising and Sales Promotion Codes, available on the Internet at: http://www.asa.org.uk.

PN

3. Germany

German law only followed the international development to restrict advertising for alcohol after some hesitation. Until then there existed only a system of self-regulation on the basis of the professional codes of conduct issued by the German Advertising Council on the advertising of alcoholic beverages. However these rules are of little relevance in legal practice. The problem as to whether such laws were compatible with the basic freedoms enshrined in the Treaty therefore did not arise.

Nevertheless, the judgment in *Aragonesa de Publicidad Exterior* aroused a relatively large degree of interest in Germany. According to some authors this case (together with the judgment in *Keck:* Case no 7 in this Casebook) is claimed to be of fundamental importance to the law on advertising. From the ECJ's express reference to the specified application of the prohibition on advertising particularly to those areas frequented by young persons and car drivers (paragraph 18 of the judgment) it has been argued that imposing a general, blanket prohibition on advertising for a specified group of tradable products without regard having been paid to the advertising media and the target group of consumers was disproportionate (*Dauses*).

LITERATURE REFERENCES

M Dauses 'Information der Verbraucher in der Rechtsprechung des EuGH' (1998) *Recht der Internationalen Wirtschaft* 750; A Leupold/A Nachbaur 'Werbebeschränkungen und

Warenverkehrsfreiheit nach Art 30 EWG-Vertrag' (1991) *Juristenzeitung* 1110 (Casenote on *Aragonesa de Publicidad Exterior*).

HS-N

4. France

For a long time French law had severely restricted the advertising of alcoholic beverages. An earlier version of this law had already formed the subject of proceedings before the ECJ (*Commission v France* [1980] ECR 2299). The French law in force at that time infringed Article 28 (ex Article 30) EC Treaty due to the fact that the restrictions on advertising clearly placed imported alcoholic products at a disadvantage. The justification for the law in force at the time put forward by the French government is an example of the attempt to tie in protectionist laws with measures protecting public health or the consumer in order to avoid a conflict with Community law. Such arguments have little chance of success before the ECJ—as the proceedings against France demonstrate—since both local and imported beverages present equal dangers to the health of the consumer.

Since then, a drastic restriction on the advertising of alcoholic products has been applied in France, which affects both domestic and imported products to the same degree. The central provision, Article L 17 *Code des débits de boisson* in the version of Law no 91–32 of 10 January 1991 and Law no 94–679 of 8 August 1994 (Article 77) states:

La propagande ou la publicité, directe ou indirecte, en faveur des boissons alcooliques dont la fabrication et la vente ne sont pas interdites sont autorisées exclusivement:

1° Dans la presse écrite à l'exclusion des publications destinées à la jeunesse, définies au premier alinéa de la loi n° 49–956 du 16 juillet 1949 sur les publications destinées à la jeunesse;

2° Par voie de radiodiffusion sonore pour les catégories de radios et dans les tranches horaires déterminées par décret en Conseil d'État;

3° Sous forme d'affiches et d'enseignes; sous forme d'affichettes et d'objets à l'intérieur des lieux de vente à caractère spécialisé, dans des conditions définies par décret en Conseil d'État;

Toute opération de parrainage est interdite lorsqu'elle a pour objet ou pour effet la propagande ou la publicité, directe ou indirecte, en faveur des boissons alcooliques.

Despite this background, the judgment in *Aragonesa de Publicidad Exterior* does not appear to have met with much interest. In the few instances where the case has been discussed, French writers choose to confine themselves to the aspects of the case which relate to Community law.

LITERATURE REFERENCES

C Berr (1992) *Journal du droit international* 435 (Casenote on *Aragonesa de Publicidad Exterior*); J Calais-Auloy/F Steinmetz *Droit de la consommation* (4th edn 1996) 125; A Decocq 'Les nouvelles restrictions à la publicité en faveur des boissons alcooliques' *Juris-classeur périodique—La semaine juridique* édition générale 1991 I 3501; G Raymond 'Publicité commerciale et protection des consommateurs' *Juris-classeur Concurrence Consommation* Fascicule 900 1998.

BD

5. Italy

The *Aragonesa* case has not yet been discussed by Italian legal writers. There are moves to control the advertising of alcohol by statute. As yet, however, no measures to this effect have been introduced. More interesting from the point of view of the Italian courts is the restriction on advertising in the field of pharmaceutical and/or dietary products. Recently, Italian courts, and especially the Antitrust Authority (*Autorità Garante per la concorrenza*), developed an interesting case law in this area.

CASE LAW REFERENCES

Corte di Cassatione judgment of 18 February 2000 no 1862, *Massimario Guistizia Civile* 2000.

AM

CASE NO. 5 — *Nissan* C–373/90

Criminal Proceedings against X
[1992] ECR I–131

A. Judgment of the ECJ of 16 January 1992

1. Held

Council Directive relating to the approximation of the laws, regulations and administrative provisions of the Member States concerning misleading advertising (OJ 1984 L250/17) must be interpreted as meaning that it does not preclude vehicles from being advertised as new, less expensive and guaranteed by the manufacturer when the vehicles concerned are registered solely for the purpose of importation, have never been on the road, and are sold in a Member State at a price lower than that charged by dealers established in that Member State because they are equipped with fewer accessories.

2. Facts of the Case

The Examining Magistrate attached to the *Tribunal de Grande Instance* Bergerac made a reference to the Court for a preliminary ruling on the interpretation of Article 2(2) of Council Directive 84/450 of 10 September 1984 relating to the approximation of the laws, regulations and administrative provisions of the Member States concerning misleading advertising (OJ 1984 L250/17). The question arose in the context of a complaint lodged against X, together with a claim for civil indemnity, by the Chairman of the Board of Directors of the Societé Richard-Nissan, which enjoys an exclusive importation contract for Nissan vehicles on French territory. The complaint was brought under Article 44 of French Law no 73–1193 of 27 December 1973 on the Orientation of Business and Crafts (*Loi Royer*), and alleged untruthful and unlawful advertising. The complaint concerned a garage in Bergerac which placed display advertisements in the press with the words 'buy your new vehicle cheaper', followed by the words 'one year manufacturer's guarantee'. The advertising referred to vehicles imported from Belgium which were registered for import purposes but had never been driven. They were sold in France below local dealers' prices. However, Belgian basic models had fewer accessories than the basic models sold in France.

   The Examining Magistrate dealing with the dispute at the *Tribunal de Grande Instance* Bergerac decided to stay the proceedings pending a preliminary ruling from the Court of Justice on the question 'whether such a marketing practice is in compliance with the European rules currently in force'.

3. *Extract from the Grounds of the ECJ's Judgment*

7. It should be recalled at the outset that, by a line of authority now well-established by the Court, the Member States' obligation arising from a Directive to achieve the result envisaged by the Directive and their duty under Article 5 of the Treaty to take all appropriate measures, whether general or particular, to ensure the fulfilment of that obligation is binding on all the authorities of Member States including, for matters within their jurisdiction, the courts, and that, in applying national law, the national court is therefore required to interpret it in the light of the wording and purpose of the Directive in order to achieve the result pursued by the latter and thereby comply with the third paragraph of Article 189 of the Treaty (see Case 14/83 *Von Colson and Kamann* [1984] ECR 1891 paragraph 26, and Case C–106/89 *Marleasing* [1990] ECR I–4135 paragraph 8).

8. The national court's question must therefore be understood as asking whether or not the Council Directive relating to the approximation of the laws, regulations and administrative provisions of the Member States concerning misleading advertising (OJ 1984 L250/17), precludes advertising of the type at issue in the main proceedings.

9. As is clear from the preamble, this Directive, adopted under Article 100 of the Treaty, aims to improve consumer protection and to put an end to distortions of competition and hindrances to the free movement of goods and services arising from disparities between the Member States' laws against misleading advertising. With those objectives in mind, it seeks to establish minimum and objective criteria as a basis for determining whether advertising is misleading.

10. Article 2(2) of the Directive defines 'misleading advertising' as:

> any advertising which in any way, including its presentation, deceives or is likely to deceive the persons to whom it is addressed or whom it reaches and which, by reason of its deceptive nature, is likely to affect their economic behaviour or which, for those reasons, injures or is likely to injure a competitor.

11. In interpreting this provision in relation to the features of advertising such as that at issue in the main proceedings, one must consider in turn the three claims made in the advertising, namely that the cars in question are new, that they are cheaper, and that they are guaranteed by the manufacturer.

12. Before embarking on such an examination, it should be emphasised that these aspects of the advertising are of great practical importance for the business of parallel car importers, and that, as the Advocate-General has pointed out in paragraphs 5 and 6 of his Opinion, parallel imports enjoy a certain amount of protection in Community law because they encourage trade and help reinforce competition.

13. On the first point, concerning the claim that the cars in question are new, it should be noted that such advertising cannot be considered misleading within the meaning of Article 2 just because the cars were registered before importation.

14. It is when a car is first driven on the public highway, and not when it is registered, that it loses its character as a new car. Moreover, as the Commission has pointed out, registration before importation makes parallel import operations considerably easier.

15. It is for the national court, however, to ascertain in the circumstances of the particular case and bearing in mind the consumers to which the advertising is addressed, whether the latter could be misleading in so far as, on the one hand, it seeks to conceal the fact that the cars advertised as new were registered before importation and, on the other hand, that fact would have deterred a significant number of consumers from making a purchase, had they known it.

16. On the second point, concerning the claim that the cars are cheaper, such a claim can only be held misleading if it is established that the decision to buy on the part of a significant number of consumers to whom the advertising in question is addressed was made in ignorance of the fact that the lower price of the vehicles was matched by a smaller number of accessories on the cars sold by the parallel importer.

17. Thirdly and finally, regarding the claim about the manufacturer's guarantee, it should be pointed out that such information cannot be regarded as misleading advertising if it is true.

18. It should be remembered in this respect that in *ETA v DK Investment* [1985] ECR 3933 (paragraph 14) the Court held that a guarantee scheme under which a supplier of goods restricts the guarantee to customers of his exclusive distributor places the latter and the retailers to whom he sells in a privileged position as against parallel importers and distributors and must therefore be regarded as having the object or effect of restricting competition within the meaning of Article 85(1) of the Treaty.

19. In answer to the question referred to the Court for a preliminary ruling it must therefore be held that Council Directive relating to the approximation of the laws, regulations and administrative provisions of the Member States concerning misleading advertising (OJ 1984 L250/17) must be interpreted as meaning that it does not preclude vehicles from being advertised as new, less expensive and guaranteed by the manufacturer when the vehicles concerned are registered solely for the purpose of importation, have never been on the road, and are sold in a Member State at a price lower than that charged by dealers established in that Member State because they are equipped with fewer accessories.

B. Commentary

1. European Law

The *Nissan* judgment demonstrates the scope of the Community's prohibition on misleading advertising as part of the law of consumer protection. At the same time the judgment illustrates the concept of the consumer upon which this prohibition is based. In this case the ECJ submitted (using the so-called 'parallel imports' as an example) that aspects of consumer protection and the possible adverse interests of the free movement of goods are capable of being satisfactorily reconciled. The directly effective law in this case was not Article 28 (ex Article 30) EC Treaty but rather a provision of secondary Community law, Directive 84/450 relating to misleading and comparative advertising (OJ 1984 L250/17 amended by Directive 97/55 OJ 1997 L290/18). This Directive defines 'misleading advertising' in Article 2(2) as follows:

For the purposes of this Directive (. . .):

2. 'misleading advertising' means any advertising which in any way, including its presentation, deceives or is likely to deceive the persons to whom it is addressed or whom it reaches and which, by reason of its deceptive nature, is likely to affect their economic behaviour or which, for those reasons, injures or is likely to injure a competitor.

According to Article 4(1) the Member States must provide adequate and effective methods of combating misleading advertising. As pointed out by the Court, the Directive pursues two aims (paragraph 9). On the one hand, it aims to improve consumer protection and on the other, to put an end to distortions of competition and hindrances to the free movement of goods arising from the disparities in Member States' laws. The ambivalence in the restrictions to trade for the purpose of protecting the consumer is clearly illustrated in this case. Characteristically, the proceedings arose from a complaint which was made by an agent of an exclusive importer of Nissan cars against a garage in Bergerac which carried on parallel imports and displayed advertisements for that purpose. The prohibition on misleading advertising was therefore to be used as a means of preventing unwanted competition. Measures protecting the consumer are capable of damaging market conditions to the disadvantage of the consumer if these measures interfere with the free movement of goods or competition. Both the Advocate-General and the Court have emphasised the great practical significance of parallel imports in the development of the Internal Market (paragraph 12 of the judgment, paragraph 4 of the Opinion of the Advocate-General).

In its judgment the Court first emphasised the obligation on Member States to interpret domestic laws in the light of the wording and purpose of the Directive (paragraph 7). It is worth noting here that the applicable French Law no. 73-1193 of 27 December 1973, the so-called *Loi Royer*, which prohibits misleading advertising (with criminal sanctions), pre-dates the relevant Directive. The ECJ has again made clear in this case that even older provisions of national law must be interpreted in the light of the wording and purpose of Directives (see *Marleasing* [1990] ECR I–4135). In its interpretation of the prohibition on misleading advertising in Article 2(2) of Directive 84/450 the Court did not expressly address the question of which concept of the consumer the provision was based upon. The Opinion of the Advocate-General speaks more clearly about the 'average consumer' who is 'not wholly undiscerning'. This consumer is seen as somebody who makes 'a careful comparison of the prices on offer and to enquire of the seller, sometimes very meticulously, about the accessories with which the vehicle is equipped'. The Advocate-General's plea for a concept of an independent consumer culminated in his reference to the saying '*vigilantibus non dormientibus iura succurrunt*' (paragraph 9 of the Opinion). The ECJ's arguments reveal (less pointedly perhaps, yet still clearly recognisable) a similar concept of the consumer. It emphasised twice that the advertising in question must mislead 'a considerable number of consumers' and influence their decision to purchase goods (paragraphs 15 and 16). The Community therefore tolerates a certain not 'considerable' number of deceived consumers. It therefore protects (to use the words of the Advocate-General) only the vigilant and not the absent-minded.

In a similar vein the judgment also established that information cannot be regarded as misleading advertising if it is true (paragraph 17). This stance assumes that accurate information, even if it is contained in advertising statements, will serve to protect rather than endanger the consumer. The ECJ's concept of the consumer is dominated by an 'information dogma': the main task of Community law is to provide the consumer with access to the information necessary in order to conclude a contract (see ECJ, *GB-INNO* [1990] ECR I–667, ECJ, *Yves Rocher* [1993] ECR I–2361: Case no 6 in this Casebook).

The decision in *Nissan* also elucidates the question as to how to determine whether advertising is misleading. If it is clear that an advertising statement is truthful, the ECJ will itself decide without any further investigation that the advertising is not misleading (paragraphs 17 and 18). To the extent that the expectations and behaviour of consumers is decisive the ECJ leaves the decision to the domestic courts. It is unclear, however, whether domestic courts are to establish the decisive expectations of the consumer by applying certain normative standards or by means of market research. The definitions in the judgment of a 'significant number' of misled consumers which has to be 'proved' (paragraph 16), leads to the conclusion that market research may be necessary (*Wytinck*). In more recent decisions relating to labelling laws the ECJ was more reserved in its answer to this question (ECJ, *Gut Springenheide* [1998] ECR I–4657: Case no 17 in this Casebook). In its decision in *Lifting-Crème* ([2000] ECR I–117) the ECJ gave national courts discretion to order a survey of public opinion or an expert opinion for the purpose of clarifying whether or not the advertisement was misleading.

ECJ CASE LAW REFERENCES

GB-INNO [1990] ECR I–667; *Marleasing* [1990] ECR I–4135; *Yves Rocher* [1993] ECR I–2361: Case no 6 in this Casebook; *CMC Motorradcenter* (*Yamaha*) [1993] ECR I–5009; *Gut Springenheide* [1998] ECR I–4657: Case no 17 in this Casebook; *Lifting-Crème* [2000] ECR I–117.

LITERATURE REFERENCES

M Dauses 'Die Rechtsprechung des EuGH zum Verbraucherschutz und zur Werbe-freiheit im Binnenmarkt' (1995) *Europäische Zeitschrift für Wirtschaftsrecht* 425; H Micklitz 'Verbraucherrecht und EG-Binnenmarkt—Vertrag, Werbung und Öffnung der Rechtswege' (1993) *Verbraucher und Recht* 2; N Reich *Europäisches Verbraucherrecht* (3rd ed., 1996) 314.

HS-N/JJ

2. *England & Wales*

Advertising in the UK was mainly regulated by Codes of Practice until the implementation of Directive 84/450. On 20 June 1988 the Control of Misleading Advertisements Regulations 1988 (statutory instrument 1988/915) were enacted. These were recently amended by the Control of Misleading Advertisements (Amendment) Regulations 2000 (statutory instrument 2000/914) implementing Directive 97/55 on Comparative Advertising.

Regulation 2(2) defines an advertisement as 'misleading' if

> in any way, including its presentation, it deceives or it is likely to deceive the persons to whom it is addressed or whom it reaches and if, by reasons of its deceptive nature, it is likely to affect their economic behaviour or, for those reasons, injures or is likely to injure a competitor of the person whose interest the advertisement seeks to promote.

Complaints that an advertisement is misleading should be addressed to the Director of Fair Trading, who may then consider bringing an injunction against any person concerned with the publication of the advertisement (Regulation 4).

The issue of advertising cars which have already been registered as new, less expensive and guaranteed by the manufacturers has not been addressed by English judges in the light of the Regulations. However, a similar issue arose in the Court of Appeal (*R v Anderson*) before the implementation of the Directive and was decided on the grounds of the Trade Description Act 1968. A motorcar dealer registered in the name of his company certain Nissan cars in order to inflate the manufacturer's sales figures. Three months later he sold the cars as 'new': each car had no registration number plate affixed, was in mint condition and registered only very low delivery mileage. The dealer was charged and found guilty of contravening section 1(1)(a) and (b) of the Trade Description Act 1968. The dealer appealed against conviction to the Court of Appeal. The Court, dismissing the appeal, held that the word 'new' was susceptible of a variety of interpretations depending on the context in which it was used. In this case, there was affirmative evidence from the purchasers that for them the word carried the implication that the car had never before been registered. *Per curiam*, the court held that the practice of registering vehicles in the name of dealers in order to inflate manufacturer's sales (which would avoid the risk of manufacturers losing their import quota in future allocations) may have disadvantageous results for customers.

If the Court of Appeal had to decide a similar case today, in the light of the Misleading Advertisements Regulations, it is not clear whether it would be under a duty to follow the definition of 'misleading' as defined in the *Nissan* case or whether it could maintain an interpretation more favourable to the consumer by relying on the minimum harmonisation formula included in the Directive. In its decision, the ECJ did not explicitly deal with the problem of stricter laws or interpretations at national level. The ECJ and the Advocate-General concerned themselves with the interpretation of a general definition given by the Directive, rather than the question of specific measures aimed at ensuring more extensive protection for the consumer. The existence of a minimum harmonisation formula might be irrelevant, and the Court of Appeal, in determining what is 'misleading', might have to comply with the guidelines given by the ECJ.

CASE LAW REFERENCES

C–266 & 267/87 *R v Royal Pharmaceutical Society of Great Britain & Anor, ex parte Association of Pharmaceutical Importers* (1987) *Common Market Law Report* 504 (1987) *Common Market Law Report* 951 (1989) *Common Market Law Report* 751; *R v Anderson* (1988) *Road Traffic Reports* 260.

LITERATURE REFERENCES

I Klauer 'General Clauses in European Private Law and Stricter National Standards: the Unfair Terms Directive' (2000) *European Review of Private Law* 187.

PN

3. Germany

In Germany Directive 84/450 on misleading advertising did not lead to any change in the law. Among the laws which remained in force was § 3 of the Law against Unfair Competition (*Gesetz gegen den unlauteren Wettbewerb*, hereafter '*UWG*', *Reichsgesetzblatt* 1909, 499, amended by *Bundesgesetzblatt* I 1969, 633, 2000, 1374), which states:

> Wer im geschäftlichen Verkehr zu Zwecken des Wettbewerbs über geschäftliche Verhältnisse, insbesondere über die Beschaffenheit, den Ursprung, den Herstellungsort oder die Preisbemessung einzelner Waren oder gewerblicher Leistungen oder des gesamten Angebots, über Preislisten, über die Art des Bezugs oder den Zweck des Verkaufs oder über die Menge der Vorräte irreführende Angaben macht, kann auf Unterlassung der Angaben in Anspruch genommen werden. Angaben über geschäftliche Verhältnisse im Sinne des Satzes 1 sind auch Angaben im Rahmen vergleichender Werbung.

Despite the fact that the words used are the same, the concept of 'misleading' (*irreführend*) under § 3 *UWG* departs in some respects from Community law's definition of misleading which was developed by the ECJ in *Nissan* under Article 2(2) of the Directive. German courts have developed strict standards in the application of § 3 *UWG*. It used to be enough to deceive a 'not inconsiderable portion of the consumer group addressed' which was the case if a deception quota was 15–20 per cent or sometimes merely 10 per cent (*Bundesgerichtshof*, judgment of 6 April 1979). The model used in this concept of misleading is the so-called 'casual observer' (*flüchtiger Verbraucher*) who only in passing glances at adverts. This concept of the consumer forms the basis of the decisions on § 3 *UWG* so far but has recently begun to shift under the influence of the ECJ's decisions. The long list of decisions emanating from the ECJ on the misleading of consumers, together with the *Nissan* case presented here, can be seen as settled case law. Many of these cases have a direct effect on German law (eg *Pall* [1990] ECR I–4827; *Clinique* [1994] ECR I–317; *Mars* [1995] ECR I–1923: Case no 9 in this Casebook; *Gut Springenheide* [1998] ECR I–4657: Case no 17 in this Casebook; *Lifting-Crème* [2000] ECR I–1177). However, this is not to say that the German concept of 'misleading' in § 3 *UWG* is contrary to Community law. Directive 84/450 is expressly designed to be a minimum harmonisation measure. Article 7 of the Directive states:

> 1. This Directive shall not preclude Member States from retaining or adopting provisions with a view to ensuring more extensive protection, with regard to misleading advertising, for consumers, persons carrying on a trade, business, craft or profession, and the general public.

To a certain degree therefore German law may offer more extensive protection to the consumer against misrepresentation. However, according to a controversial argument, this ability is limited by Article 28 (ex Article 30) EC Treaty (for current opinion see *Sack*). This relationship becomes clear in a decision of the *Oberlandesgericht* Karlsruhe (Higher Regional Court) of 10 November 1993. The court, referring to the decision in *Nissan*, held that the ECJ's interpretation of what constituted 'misleading' was at odds with German decisions relating to § 3 of the *UWG*. However, this interpretation related to Article 2(2) of Directive 84/450, not Article 7. The court conclusively investigated the circumstances under which a more extensive protection of the consumer provided by autonomous German law was capable of breaching Article 28 (ex Article 30) EC Treaty. In conclusion, it held that the case at hand did not breach Article 28 (ex Article 30) EC Treaty.

A decision of the *Oberlandesgericht* Karlsruhe of 13 March 1996, influenced by the decisions of the ECJ, clearly indicates a relaxation of the definition of 'misleading' in German law. The case concerned a case of parallel imports similar to the *Nissan* case decided by the ECJ (see the German commentary to *Cassis de Dijon*: Case no. 3 in this Casebook). The plaintiff imported cars from Europe. At the time of the sale the vehicles no longer offered the manufacturer's one year guarantee since the guarantee period had started to run from the time the vehicles were exported. At the trial the issue turned on the question to what extent and in which way the plaintiff had to draw attention to the shorter period of guarantee. The plaintiff had advertised the vehicles using catch phrases such as 'New EC Vehicles with Guarantee'. The *Oberlandesgericht* Karlsruhe, relying expressly on the ECJ's judgment in *Nissan*, held that extensive obligations of information in advertising would interfere considerably with the parallel imports of vehicles. As a result, it was necessary to tolerate, under certain circumstances, the possibility that the consumer could be attracted to the offer advertised on the basis of an incorrect notion in the interests of the free movement of goods provided that a comprehensive explanation is provided before the contract is concluded. Nevertheless the *Oberlandesgericht* Dresden on 21 January 1997 delivered a judgment which was more in line with the traditional German view of what constituted 'misleading'. In a similar case of parallel imports with a shortened guarantee period it held an advertisement with the statement 'Standard new vehicle guarantee with EC vehicles' to be misleading despite the fact that the advertisement also displayed the reference 'Guarantee runs from date of import or initial registration'.

Recently the *Bundesgerichtshof* (Federal Court of Justice) has explicitly decided to what extent the seller of parallel imported cars has to provide information in his advertisements (judgments of 15 July and 19 August 1999). This new jurisprudence is expressly based on the ECJ's judgment in *Nissan*. The *Bundesgerichtshof* held that the seller has only to inform the consumer about the shortened guarantee period if more than two weeks have already expired at the time when the advertisement is published. As to differences in the equipment of parallel imported cars, the *Bundesgerichtshof* ruling was less strict. If the cars are advertised as 'EC-vehicles' there is generally no need to include information about minor differences in equipment.

The *Nissan* decision invited a great deal of criticism because it was feared that it would lead to a reduction in the protection of the consumer. The extent to which the decision of the ECJ has compelled a different view to be taken of § 3 *UWG* (see *Deutsch, Köhler, Sack* for current opinion) has yet to be clarified. The *Bundesgerichtshof* seems to adapt more and more the German law of misleading advertising to the model shaped by the Community Law (see recent ruling of 20 October 1999). It is doubtful whether a relaxation of the German model of the 'casual' consumer would lead to a substantial restriction in consumer protection. Using parallel imports as an example it can be demonstrated that the opening up of the market and accompanying liberalisation of competition law brings with it considerable advantages for the consumer.

CASE LAW REFERENCES

Bundesgerichtshof, *Kontinent Möbel*, judgment of 6 April 1979 (1979) *Gewerblicher Rechtsschutz und Urheberrecht* 716; Oberlandesgericht Karlsruhe, judgment of 10 November 1993 (1994) *NJW-Rechtsprechungsreport Zivilrecht* 817; Oberlandesgericht Karlsruhe, judgment of 13 März 1996 (1996) *Neue Juristische Wochenschrift* 2313; Oberlandesgericht Dresden, judgment of 21 January 1997 (1997) *Entscheidungen zum Wirtschaftsrecht* 217; Bundesgerichtshof, *EG-Neuwagen I, EG-Neuwagen II*, judgments of 15 July 1999 and 19 August 1999 (2000) *Wettbewerb in Recht und Praxis*, 1151, 1155; Bundesgerichtshof, *Orient-Teppichmuster*, ruling of 20 October 1999 (2000) *Wettbewerb in Recht und Praxis* 517.

LITERATURE REFERENCES

V Deutsch 'Der Einfluß des europäischen Rechts auf den Irreführungstatbestand des § 3 UWG' (1996) *Gewerblicher Rechtsschutz und Urheberrecht* 541; K Heinemann (1992) *Zeitschrift für Wirtschaftsrecht* 720 (Casenote on *Nissan*); H Köhler 'Irreführungs-Richtlinie und deutsches Wettbewerbsrecht' (1996) *Gewerblicher Rechtsschutz und Urheberrecht—Internationaler Teil* 396; R Sack 'Die Bedeutung der EG-Richtlinien 84/450/EWG und 97/55/EG über irreführende und vergleichende Werbung für das deutsche Wettbewerbsrecht' (1998) *Gewerblicher Rechtsschutz und Urheberrecht—Internationaler Teil* 263; R Sack 'Die Beurteilung irreführender Werbung für Importfahtzeuge aus EG-Staaten nach EG-Recht' (2000) *Wettbewerb in Recht und Praxis* 23.

HS-N

4. *France*

French law considered misleading advertising to be a criminal offence and dealt with it accordingly in the earlier Law no 73–193 of 27 December 1973, the so-called *Loi Royer*. The relevant provisions are now part of the *Code de la Consommation* (Article L 121–1 to L 121–7). Article L 121–1 states:

> Est interdite toute publicité comportant, sous quelque forme que ce soit, des allégations, indications ou présentations fausses ou de nature à induire en erreur lorsque celles-ci portent sur un ou plusieurs des éléments ci-après; existence, nature, composition, qualités substantielles, teneur en principes utiles, espèce, origine, quantité, mode et date de fabrication, propriétés, prix et conditions de vente de biens ou services qui font l'objet de la publicité, conditions de leur utilisation, résultats qui peuvent être attendus de leur utilisation, motifs ou procédés de la vente ou de la prestation de services, portée des engagements pris par l'annonceur, identité, qualités ou aptitudes du fabricant, des revendeurs, des promoteurs ou des prestataires.

Concerning the question as to which concept of the consumer is decisive for the assessment of the misrepresentation, French law has appeared to follow the '*consommateur moyen*' (*Calais-Auloy/Steinmetz*). There does not appear to be a profound difference between this and the 'average consumer' concept employed by the ECJ. In the actual application, however, differences could arise. The *Cour de Cassation* held shortly before the judgment of the ECJ in *Nissan* that a vehicle may only be promoted as new if it has neither been driven nor imported (judgment of 18 April 1989). The ECJ apparently decided this question differently (paragraph 13) but ultimately left the decision to the French court. The Examining Magistrate in Bergerac applied the interpretation given by the ECJ in his preliminary proceedings and came to the conclusion that the advertising was not misleading (*Tribunal de Grande Instance* Bergerac, *Ordonnance* of 29 June 1992, unreported).

To the extent that French law protects the consumer more extensively than provided for in the Directive, it does not as a rule breach Community law because the Directive was designed to be a minimum harmonisation measure (*Cour de Cassation*, judgment of 27 March 1996).

An example of a French case relating to advertising of parallel imports of vehicles is the decision of the *Cour d'Appel* Grenoble of 8 July 1992. This case concerned the question whether the following insert in a car magazine amounted to 'misleading' pursuant to the *Loi Royer*:

> Voitures neuves moins chères. Exemples: −12% S/R 21 Turbo D, −14% S/Patrol 2,8 TD court, livraison possible dans toute la France, credit-leasing IMPEXPORT 10, rue Duploye 38100 GRENOBLE tel / 76.43.19.02.

The company, IMPEXPORT, thereby advertised its services as agent in the acquisition of vehicles from dealers in other Member States. The *Cour d'Appel* was of the opinion that the brevity of the insert could lead the reader to make a mistake concerning the conditions of the purchase, the role of the advertisers as well as their quality and their abilities. Above all it had not been made clear that IMPEXPORT was only acting as agent whereas the insert could give the impression that it was acting as the vendor. The judgment of the ECJ was mentioned in the court's *ratio decidendi.* However, the *Cour d'Appel* clearly accepted that the judgment did not relate to misrepresentation pertaining to the advertisers' quality of dealership.

CASE LAW REFERENCES

Cour de Cassation, chambre criminelle, judgment of 18 April 1989, *Bulletin des arrêts de la Cour de Cassation,* chambre criminelle 1989, no 159; Tribunal de Grande Instance Bergerac, Ordonnance of 29 June 1992, unreported, documented in the database of the ECJ; Cour d'Appel Grenoble, judgment of 8 July 1992, no 438/92, *Lexis;* Cour de Cassation, chambre criminelle, judgment of 27 March 1996, *Bulletin des arrêts de la Cour de Cassation,* chambre criminelle 1996, no 139.

LITERATURE REFERENCES

J Calais-Auloy, F Steinmetz *Droit de la consommation* (4th ed., 1996) 109–118; A Giudicelli 'Infractions contre l'ordre économique et financier' (1997) *Revue de science criminelle et de droit pénal comparé* 122; Soulard, Ch. (1992) *Revue de science criminelle et de droit pénal compare* 645 (Casenote on *Nissan*); P Storner 'La revente hors réseau de véhicules neufs à l'épreuve du droit de la concurrence déloyale' *Lamy Droit Economique,* February 1999, no. 114, 1.

BD

5. Italy

Italian writers have not yet discussed the *Nissan* case. The question surrounding parallel imports, especially in the case of cars, is clearly an issue which preoccupies Italian jurisprudence. In various proceedings an infringement of Article 28 (ex Article 30) EC Treaty had been detected (eg *Commission v Italy* [1985] ECR 1753). On occasion, Italian administrative tribunals appear to seek ways of protecting official distributors from parallel imports (*Tribunale Amministrativo Regionale* Lazio, judgment of 28 October 1991). A large part of the Italian case law on parallel imports is connected with trademark regulations. Most of the Italian case law in the field of parallel imports and misleading advertising is developed not only by ordinary tribunals but by the Antitrust Authority (*Autorità Garante per la concorrenza*).

In any case, Italian civil tribunals, influenced by the ECJ, stated that the conditions necessary to consider parallel imports are: first, that the import originate from one Member State to another Member State and, secondly, that the trademark owner is the one who distributes the goods into the Internal Market or gives his consent for someone else to do so.

Italian misleading advertising provisions are contained in several acts. In particular, the *Legge* of 6 August 1990, no 223 *Disciplina del sistema radiotelevisivo pubblico e privato;* *Decreto Legislativo* of 25 January 1992, no 74 and *Codice di autodisciplina pubblicitaria. Legge* of 6 August 1990, no 223 concentrates on the way in which information is presented in advertising. The notion of misleading advertising, strictly connected with the unfair competition, is regulated by Article 2(b) *Decreto Legislativo* 74/92. It provides:

> E' pubblicità ingannevole quella che, in qualunque modo, compresa la sua presentazione, induca o possa indurre in errore le persone fisiche o giuridiche alle quali è rivolta o che essa raggiunge e che, a causa del suo carattere ingannevole, possa pregiudicare il loro comportamento economico ovvero che, per questo motivo, leda o possa ledere un concorrente.

The above-mentioned article has led Italian courts to develop a notion of misleading advertisement in any situation in which it is possible for a consumer to misunderstand or be induced by misleading information or labelling (*Rossello*). One commentator observed that it makes no difference under *Decreto Legislativo* 74/92, which is different to Article 1469 *Codice Civile*, if the consumer, victim of a misleading advertising, is a natural or legal person, because both are protected under Article 2(b).

CASE LAW REFERENCES

Tribunale Amministrativo Regionale del Lazio, sezione III, judgment of 28 October 1991 (1992) *Il Foro Amministrativo* 2372; Tribunale di Milano, 9 April 1998 (1998) *Rivista di Diritto Industriale* II, 415; Tribunale di Bologna 27 June 1997 (1998) *Diritto Industriale* 18; Autorità Garante per la concorrenza, judgment of 18 March 1998, no 5790 (1998) *Rassegna di Diritto Farmacentico* 784; Autorità Garante per la concorrenza, judgment of 11 June 1998, no 6111 (1998) *Rassegna di Diritto Farmacentico* 1125; Tribunale di Napoli, judgment of 26 October 1999 (2000) *Giurprudenza napoletana* 55; Autorità Garante per la concorrenza, judgment of 7 October 1999, no 7587 (2000) *Giustizia civile* I, 1891; Autorità Garante per la concorrenza, judgment of 25 August 1999, no 7498 (2000) *Giustizia civile* I, 1243.

LITERATURE REFERENCES

L Rubini 'Le stranezza della giurisprudenza della Corte di giustizia tra importazioni parallele da Paesi terzi, tra esurimento del marchio e norme sulla concorrenza' (2000) *Diritto communitario e degli internazionali* 67; G Cesarini 'Importazioni parallele: giurisprudenza italiana e giurisprudenza communitaria a confronto' (1998) *Rivista di Diritto Industriale* II, 415; S Mancuso 'Contraffazione di marchio mediante importazioni parallele ed abuso della personalità giuridica' (1998) *Rivista di Diritto Industriale* 18; N Francione 'La nozione di 'operatore pubblicitario' ai sensi del d.lgs. n 74 del 1992. I destinatari della tutela offerta dalla normativa' (2000) *Giustizia Civile* I, 1243; C Rossello 'Pubblicità ingannevole' (1995) *Contratto e Impresa* 137.

CASE NO. 6 — *Yves Rocher* C–126/91

Schutzverband gegen Unwesen in der Wirtschaft v Yves Rocher GmbH
[1993] ECR I–2361

A. Judgment of the ECJ of 18 May 1993

1. Held

Article 30 of the EEC Treaty is to be interpreted as precluding the application of a rule of Member State A which prohibits an undertaking established in that State, carrying on mail order sales by catalogue or sales brochure of goods imported from Member State B, from using advertisements relating to prices in which the new price is displayed so as to catch the eye and reference is made to a higher price shown in a previous catalogue or brochure.

2. Facts of the Case

The *Bundesgerichtshof* (German Federal Court of Justice) made a preliminary reference to the ECJ with the question of interpretation of Articles 30 and 36 (new Articles 28 and 30) EC Treaty in order to decide whether a national regulation concerning commercial advertising was compatible with these provisions. This question had arisen in a case between the Schutzverband gegen Unwesen in der Wirtschaft ('Trade Protection Society against Bad Commercial Practice'), a registered society based in Munich (hereafter 'the plaintiff'), and Yves Rocher GmbH, a subsidiary of the French company Laboratoires de Biologie Végétale Yves Rocher (hereafter 'the defendant') concerning advertisements circulated by the defendant comparing the old and new prices of its products.

Before 1986, advertising in Germany by means of comparing prices charged by one and the same undertaking had been lawful provided that it was not unfair or liable to mislead consumers. Following pressure by certain retailers, the German legislature inserted § 6e into the Law against Unfair Competition (*Gesetz gegen den unlauteren Wettbewerb*, hereafter '*UWG*') prohibiting advertisements making use of individual price comparisons. This law was aimed at protecting consumers and competitors from advertising price comparisons. Paragraph 6e *UWG* does not, however, contain an absolute prohibition, but provides an exception in the case of price comparisons which are not 'eye-catching' (§ 6e(2)(1) *UWG*) and advertising in catalogues (§ 6e(2)(2) *UWG*).

The defendant sold cosmetics by mail order in Germany supplied from its parent company and mostly manufactured in France. The advertising for these products was circulated in catalogues and sales brochures to a standard design established by the parent company for the various Member States. As part of its sales activities, the defendant distributed a brochure in which the title 'save up to 50 per cent and more on 99 of your favourite Yves Rocher products' was stated with the old price crossed out and the new lower price printed alongside it in large red characters.

The plaintiff brought an action against the defendant in the *Landgericht* Munich I (Regional Court), since in his opinion this type of advertisement infringed § 6e(2)(1) *UWG*. The court issued an injunction preventing the defendant from distributing advertising of this kind as the court thought that the provision of the *UWG* in question outlawed price comparisons between old and new prices insofar that they were eye-catching. On appeal by the defendant, the *Oberlandesgericht* Munich (Higher Regional Court) reversed the judgment. It based its decision on § 6e(2)(2) *UWG*. The plaintiff lodged an appeal against this decision on a point of law. The *Bundesgerichtshof* was of the opinion that the use of § 6e(1) *UWG* turned on a question of interpretation of Community Law and therefore suspended the proceedings and referred the following question to the Court of Justice for a preliminary ruling:

> Must Article 30 of the EEC Treaty be interpreted as precluding the application of a rule of law of Member State A prohibiting an undertaking established in that State, carrying on mail order sales by catalogue or sales brochure of goods imported from Member State B, from using advertisements relating to prices in which there is an eye-catching display of the new price and reference is made to a higher price shown in an earlier catalogue or sales brochure?

3. Extract from the Grounds of the ECJ's Judgment

9. Under Article 30 of the Treaty, quantitative restrictions on imports and all measures having equivalent effect are prohibited between Member States. It is settled law that all trading rules enacted by Member States which are capable of hindering, directly or indirectly, actually or potentially, intra-Community trade constitute measures having an effect equivalent to quantitative restrictions (judgment in Case 8/74 *Dassonville* [1974] ECR 837, paragraph 5).

10. The Court has also held that national legislation which restricts or prohibits certain forms of advertising or certain means of sales promotion may, although it does not directly affect imports, be such as to restrict their volume because it affects marketing opportunities for the imported products. To compel an economic operator either to adopt advertising or sale promotion schemes which differ from one Member State to another or to discontinue a scheme which he considers to be particularly effective may constitute an obstacle to imports even if the legislation in question applies to domestic products and imported products without distinction (see the judgments in Case 286/81 *Oosthoek's Uitgeversmaatschappij* [1982] ECR 4575, paragraph 15; Case 382/87 *Buet* [1989] ECR 1235, paragraph 7; Case C–362/88 *GB-INNO-BM* [1990] ECR I–667, paragraph 7; and Joined Cases C–1/90 and C–176/90 *Aragonesa de Publicidad Exterior* [1991] ECR I–4151, paragraph 10: Case no 4 in this Casebook).

11. A prohibition of the kind at issue in the main proceedings is thus capable of restricting imports of products from one Member State into another and therefore constitutes, in that respect, a measure having equivalent effect to a quantitative restriction within the meaning of Article 30 of the Treaty.

12. However, the Court has consistently held that in the absence of common rules relating to marketing, obstacles to the free movement of goods within the Community resulting from disparities between national laws must be accepted in so far as such rules, applicable to domestic and imported products without distinction, may be justified as being necessary in order to satisfy mandatory requirements relating *inter alia* to consumer protection or fair trading (see, in particular, *GB-INNO-BM* cited above, paragraph 10). These rules must, however, as the Court has repeatedly held (see, in particular, Case 382/87 *Buet* [1989] ECR 1235 paragraph 11), be proportionate to the goals pursued.

13. It is undisputed that a prohibition of the kind at issue in the main proceedings applies both to domestic products and imported products.

14. Moreover, the German Government has stated that the prohibition in paragraph 6e of the UWG is intended to protect consumers against the special lure of advertising containing price comparisons, which is frequently liable to mislead. First, it is particularly easy to deceive consumers, since they are generally not in a position to verify the comparison between the old and the new prices. Second, advertising by means of price comparisons may suggest a level of prices which is favourable as a whole, without that being true for the entire range of products.

15. Since the protection of consumers against misleading advertising is a legitimate objective from the point of view of Community Law, the Court must examine, in accordance with the settled case-law whether the national provisions are suitable for attaining the aim pursued and do not go beyond what is necessary for that purpose.

16. It should be observed, first, that a prohibition of the kind at issue in the main proceedings applies where price comparisons catch the eye, whether or not they are correct. The prohibition does not apply to price comparisons which are not eye-catching. In the present case the advertising is prohibited not because it is alleged to be incorrect, but because it is eye-catching. It follows that any eye-catching advertising making use of price comparisons is prohibited, whether it is true or false.

17/19. Moreover, the prohibition in question goes beyond the requirements of the objectives pursued, in that it affects advertising which is not at all misleading and contains comparisons of prices actually charged, which can be of considerable use in that it enables the consumer to make his choice in full knowledge of the facts. Furthermore, a comparative examination of the laws of the Member States shows that information and protection of the consumer can be ensured by measures which are less restrictive of intra-Community trade than those at issue in the main proceedings (see paragraph 52 of the Opinion of the Advocate-General). It follows that a prohibition of the kind at issue in the main proceedings is not proportionate to the aim pursued.

20. The German Government argues further that the prohibition in question cannot be incompatible with Article 30 of the Treaty in that it causes only a marginal restriction of the free movement of goods.

21. On this point, leaving aside rules having only hypothetical effect on intra-Community trade it has been consistently held that Article 30 of the Treaty does not make a distinction between measures which can be described as having an equivalent effect to a quantitative restriction according to the magnitude of the effects they have on trade within the Community.

22. As for the protection of fair trading, and hence of competition, it is important to note that correct price comparisons, prohibited by rule of law of the kind at issue, cannot in any way distort the conditions of competition. On the other hand however, a rule which has the effect of prohibiting such comparisons may restrict competition.

23. Accordingly, the answer to the national court's question must be that Article 30 of the Treaty is to be interpreted as precluding the application of a rule of law of Member State A which prohibits an undertaking established in that State, carrying on mail order sales by catalogue or sales brochure of goods imported by Member State B, from using advertisements relating to prices in which the new price is displayed so as to catch the eye and reference is made to a higher price shown in an previous catalogue or brochure.

4. *Extract from the Opinion of the Advocate-General*

51. Besides, the aim pursued can be achieved by other less radical means.

52. If one examines the regulations for this type of advertising in other Member States, one finds that certain information requirements with regard to:

1. the time in which the compared price is promoted; and

2. the statement of the new and old price

harmonise the instruction and protection of the consumer. Such is the case in the United Kingdom with the Consumer Protection (Code of Practice for Traders on Price Indications) Approval Order of 1988 issued by the Secretary of State (Statutory Instrument 1988, no 2078). Similarly, the Belgian law of 14 July 1991 on Trade Practices and Instruction and Protection of the Consumers, provides that all advertising which refers to a price reduction, must state the price charged 'previously and usually for similar products' and correspond to actual reductions, which must be provable particularly in regard to the prices compared (see Article 43 of the aforementioned law, Moniteur belge 29 August 1991). In Portugal, decree no 253/86 of 25 August 1986 regulating the sale of goods reduced in price (Diario da Republica no 194 from the 25 August 1986), requires the 'previously charged price' to be stated. This is defined as the lowest price for the relevant product, which was charged at the same point of sale during the last 30 days before the reduction was demanded. It is for the seller to prove the price previously charged. In French law, the choice of the comparative price in advertising by the advertiser (see Article 3 of Regulation no 77–105 P of the 2 September 1977, BOSP of the 3 December 1977) is very strictly regulated. This ensures this price is correct and prohibits the trader from raising the comparative price just before the announcement of a price reduction. The fortification of the consumer protection is therefore attained by increasing and not restricting his information.

B. Commentary

1. European Law

Yves Rocher serves as a clear example from a whole range of decisions on marketing and advertisement strategies where the disparities in national laws has hindered the progress towards uniformity (see paragraph 10 of the judgment, and further ECJ, *Keck* [1993] ECR I–6097, Case no 7 in this Casebook; *Clinique* [1994] ECR I–317; *Mars* [1995] ECR I–1923, Case no 9 in this Casebook; *Österreichische Unilever GmbH* [1999] ECR I–431; *Lifting-Crème* [2000] ECR I–117). According to the formula established by the ECJ in *Dassonville* ([1974] ECR 837), all trading rules enacted by Member States can breach the free movement of goods laid down in Article 28 (ex Article 30) EC Treaty if they are capable of hindering, directly or indirectly, actually or potentially, intra-Community trade (paragraph 9). The magnitude of the trade restriction is irrelevant (paragraph 21). The ECJ strengthens this position in the *Yves Rocher* case in that even national regulations which restrict certain forms of advertising or certain forms of long-distance selling have the effect of restricting the importation of marketed goods. They are then capable of breaching Article 28 (ex Article 30) EC Treaty. The protection offered by the free movement of goods also extends to intra-Community marketing strategies. The *Dassonville* formula has nevertheless been restricted by the change in precedent on Article 28 (ex Article 30) EC Treaty introduced by the decision in *Keck*. Therefore, it is claimed that the principles established in the *Yves Rocher* judgment have been superseded by the *Keck* judgment (see European law commentary *Keck*: Case no 7 in this Casebook). It can still be argued, however, that even after *Keck* such intra-European product marketing standardisation (as in *Yves Rocher*) is covered by Article 28 (ex Article 30) EC Treaty (*Howells/Wilhelmsson*).

The decisive criterion in *Yves Rocher* is the test whether the German prohibition on 'eye-catching' price comparisons in § 6e of the *UWG* was 'proportionate to the goals pursued' (paragraphs 12 and 14). This proportionality test works against the German prohibition and in favour of the free movement of goods. The ECJ in principle recognises the consumer protection intended by the German provision. However, it did not believe that the offending provisions in § 6e *UWG* were 'proportionate to achieve the goal pursued' and the claim that they did 'not exceed the limits of what is necessary' (paragraph 15). The explanations in the *ratio decidendi* show the importance the ECJ attaches to consumer information. The judgment was mainly based on the fact that the offending provision prohibited all 'eye-catching' advertising regardless of whether it was correct or not. The ECJ considered a comparison of prices actually charged as 'of considerable use' in enabling the consumer to make a choice in full knowledge of the facts. Prohibiting 'eye-catching' price comparisons breached Article 28 (ex Article 30) EC Treaty in that it also suppressed correct information. Consequently the free movement of goods allows suppliers to inform consumers about everything, provided only that the information given is correct. The basis was therefore the ideal of an active and vigilant consumer for whom correct information is always advantageous. The Community offers no protection against the special lure of (correct) price comparisons nor does it allow a general prohibition against price comparisons in order to prevent incorrect price information.

The ECJ was helped in its decision by a comparison of the legal systems of other Member States. This was put forward in the Opinion of the Advocate-General Darmon (excerpt reprinted above). He compared the laws of the United Kingdom, Belgium, Portugal and France which attempt to prevent improper use of sales methods by means other than a prohibition on price comparisons.

The decision in *Yves Rocher* had been preceded by the judgment in *GB-INNO* ([1990] ECR I–667). This case concerned a Belgian supermarket's advertising by means of a sales brochure which contained price comparisons and limited special offers. Although this advertising was permitted under Belgian law, it nevertheless breached Luxembourg regulations. The ECJ believed the Luxembourg prohibition to be an unjustified restriction on trade prohibited by Article 28 (ex Article 30) EC Treaty. In its decision, the ECJ also expressed the view that consumer information is one of the leading principles of European consumer policy:

It has been shown that Community law considers informing the consumer to be one of the basic requirements of consumer protection. Article 30 cannot therefore be interpreted in such a way that national laws, which deny the consumer access to certain information, can be justified on the basis of mandatory requirements of consumer protection. (*GB-INNO*, paragraph 18).

The cases of *Yves Rocher* and *GB-INNO* also demonstrate the interaction of legislation and case law in the development of Community law. Directive 84/450 regarding misleading advertising already provided in its draft for, *inter alia*, a liberalisation of comparative advertising (OJ 1978 C70/4; 1979 C193/3). This law failed due to the great discrepancies between the European legal systems. By its decisions in *GB-INNO* and *Yves Rocher* the ECJ has taken the first steps towards harmonisation, despite years of legislative procrastination. Finally, the Union has also laid down legislative foundations in the field of advertising law with the enactment of the Directive on comparative advertising (OJ 1997 L290/18).

ECJ CASE LAW REFERENCES

Dassonville [1974] ECR 837; *GB-INNO* [1990] ECR I–667; *Keck* [1993] ECR I–6097: Case no 7 in this Casebook; *Clinique* [1994] ECR I–317; *Mars* [1995] ECR I–1923: Case no 9 in this Casebook; *Österreichische Unilever GmbH* [1999] ECR I–431; *Lifting-Crème* [2000] ECR I–117.

LITERATURE REFERENCES

A Beater 'Zur Europarechtswidrigkeit von § 6e des Gesetzes gegen den Unlauteren Wettbewerb (UWG)' (1994) *Zeitschrift für Europäisches Privatrecht* 506; M Dauses, 'Die Rechtsprechung des EuGH zum Verbraucherschutz und zur Werbefreiheit im Binnenmarkt' (1995) *Europäische Zeitschrift für Wirtschaftsrecht* 425; G Howells, T Wilhelmsson *EC Consumer Law* (1997) 130, 132; N Reich *Europäisches Verbraucherrecht* (3rd edn, 1996) 83, 93; N Reich *Verbraucher und Recht* (1993) 251 (Casenote on *Yves Rocher*); S Weatherill *EC Consumer Law and Policy* (1997) 53.

HS-N/JJ

2. England & Wales

The central issue of the *Yves Rocher* case of the provision of information to the consumer concerning price is governed by the Consumer Protection (Code of Practice for Traders on Price Indications) Approval Order 1988 (statutory instrument 2078/1988). It came into force on 1 March 1989. The legal basis for this Code is to be found in Section 25 of the Consumer Protection Act 1987. It provides that the Secretary of State may by order exercised by statutory instrument approve any codes of practice which can give practical guidance and assistance on the interpretation of Section 20 of the Act. Section 20 states:

Section 20. Offence of giving misleading indication.

(1) Subject to the following provisions of this Part, a person shall be guilty of an offence if, in the course of any business of his, he gives (by any means whatever) to any consumers an indication which is misleading as to the price at which any goods, services, accommodation or facilities are available (whether generally or from particular persons).

(2) Subject as aforesaid, a person shall be guilty of an offence if–

(a) in the course of any business of his, he has given an indication to any consumer which, after it was given, has become misleading as mentioned in subsection (1) above; and

(b) some or all of those consumers might reasonably be expected to rely on the indication at a time after it has become misleading; and

(c) he fails to take all such steps as are reasonable to prevent those consumers from relying on the indication.

(. . .)

(4) A person guilty of an offence under subsection(1) or (2) above shall be liable–

(a) on conviction on indictment, to a fine;

(b) on summary conviction, to a fine not exceeding the statutory maximum.

(. . .)

In addition, the Code sets out 'what is good practice to follow in giving price indications in a wide range of different circumstances, so as to avoid giving misleading indications' (paragraph 2). Price comparisons with the trader's own previous price is addressed by Part 1.2 of the Code. A number of rules, none of which is comparable to the German one, impose requirements mainly aimed at ensuring that the price reduction is real: so, for example, the previous price should be the last price at which the product was available to consumers in the previous six months and the product should have been available at the old price for at least twenty-eight consecutive days in the last six months. With regard to products sold through mail orders, ie a catalogue, advertisement or leaflet, the only specific requirement is that any comparison with a previous price is made with the price in the last catalogue, advertisement or leaflet.

A contravention of the Code will not in itself give rise to any civil or criminal liability. However, in proceedings for an offence under section 20 of the Consumer Protection Act, any contravention of the Code by the defendant may be taken into account in establishing that he committed an offence. Compliance with the Code may also be relied upon as evidence of a defence (section 25(2)).

Even though rules on price information are not as strict as in Germany, academics agree that the *Yves Rocher* judgment has certainly confirmed the feeling that the ECJ 'has significantly curtailed the competence of States to suppress the development of integrated cross-border advertising campaigns'.

LITERATURE REFERENCES

CJ Miller, B Harvey D Parry *Consumer and Trading Law* (1998) 673–707; B Harvey, D Parry *The Law of Consumer Protection and Fair Trading* (1996) 382–394; 'Significance of decision that German law prohibiting comparative price advertising is unlawful for UK companies' (Casenote) (1993) *Consumer Law Today* 16(8), i–ii; S Weatherill, 'Free Movement of Goods (EC Law-recent developments)' (1994) *International and Comparative Law Quarterly* 207.

PN

3. Germany

Whilst German competition law tends to prohibit or restrict numerous marketing strategies, above all in the area of comparative advertising, other Member States are considerably more liberal. Since differences in competition can hinder trade, the traditionally strict German rules on fair trading are now under pressure to conform. *Yves Rocher* was a case concerning the prohibition of eye-catching price comparisons. This prohibition was only inserted into the Law against Unfair Competition (*UWG*) in 1986 and since then has always proved controversial (see *Keßler, Sack*). This amendment had come about, as the ECJ sensitively pointed out, 'due to the pressure from certain groups of retailers' (paragraph 3 of the judgment). Besides consumer protection, the regulation was also clearly aimed at protecting medium-sized trade against the selling practices of large retail chains. This policy suggested a certain hostility towards the EC's Internal Market; it is obvious that the promotion of medium sized trade which is often only active in the domestic market, can operate to the detriment of large retail trade, which is also active abroad.

The consumer protection aim of § 6e *UWG* did convince the ECJ to allow a restriction on the free movement of goods. The German government argued that price comparisons presented a high risk of misrepresentation and abuse. Behind this argument was the belief that it was better to withhold correct and possibly important information from the consumer than to leave him open to the risk of incorrect or misleading information about price developments. Prohibiting price comparisons protects the gullible consumer whereas the vigilant consumer is more likely to profit from their use. Therefore, this is another case which reveals the protective attitude of German law towards the consumer which has been accused by foreign observers as employing the 'ideal of an absolutely incapable, almost pathologically stupid and negligently inattentive average consumer' (according to the admittedly exaggerated but nevertheless typical opinion of one party before the ECJ ([1984] ECR 1306)). In German legal journals the decision has met with mixed response, although the predominant impression is one of agreement (for example, *Sack* is very critical whereas *Keler* and *Schricker* agree).

Yves Rocher also illustrates the interlocking of case law and legislation in adapting German law to the European standard. The *Bundesgerichtshof*, which at the time at any rate, was reluctant to intervene, did just that in light of the decision in *GB-INNO*. It made a submission to the ECJ regarding the present case as well. After the *Yves Rocher* judgment, the *Bundesgerichtshof* dismissed the action at a preliminary hearing citing the supremacy of European law (*Bundesgerichtshof* judgment of 14 October 1993). Since Article 28 (ex Article 30) EC Treaty only applies to intra-Community trade, the offending prohibition in § 6e *UWG* remained applicable to purely domestic cases. However, in order to avoid discrimination in domestic cases and the associated competitive disadvantage, the German legislature felt obliged to repeal the provision altogether (*Bundesgesetzblatt* I 1994 1738).

The permissibility of advertising containing price comparisons is now once again determined according to general law and in particular the clause contained in § 3 *UWG*. It prohibits misleading information in the price indexes of goods (the text of § 3 *UWG* is reprinted in the commentary to *Nissan*: Case no 5 in this Casebook). According to the comprehensive case law on § 3 *UWG*, an advert with price reductions is misleading if, for example, the previous price had not in fact been charged or if it had not been charged with serious intent, recently or for a long time (see *Baumbach/Hefermehl* for case law on this subject). Since Directive 97/55 on comparative advertising was enacted (OJ 1997 L290/18) and a decisive judgment by the *Bundesgerichtshof* of 5 February 1998, German courts have held that price and product comparisons between competitors is, in principle, allowed. Before this judgment such price comparisons were thought to be unconscionable (eg *Bundesgerichtshof* judgment of 2 May 1996 referring however to the impending Directive). The *Bundesgerichtshof* has in the meantime affirmed this interpretation in its judgment of 15 October 1998. *Yves Rocher* marks an important stage in the Europeanisation of German competition law, regardless of whether certain aspects have been superseded by *Keck*. Meanwhile, Germany has implemented Directive 97/55 by an amendment to §§ 2–4 *UWG* (*Bundesgesetzblatt* I 2000 1374).

CASE LAW REFERENCES

Bundesgerichtshof judgment of 14 October 1993 (1993) *Zeitschrift für Wirtschaftsrecht* 1725; Bundesgerichtshof *Preistest* judgment of 2 May 1996 (1996) *Betriebs-Berater* 2012; Bundesgerichtshof *Testpreis-Angebot* judgment of 5 February 1998 (1998) *Neue Juristische Wochenschrift* 2208; Bundesgerichtshof *Designer-Modeschmuck* judgment of 15 October 1998 (1999) *Neue Juristische Wochenschrift* 948; for German decisions on the question whether *Yves Rocher* has been superseded by *Keck* see commentary on *Keck*: Case no 7 in this Casebook.

LITERATURE REFERENCES

A Baumbach/W Hefermehl *Wettbewerbsrecht* (22nd edn 2001) § 3 UWG; J Keler 'Wettbewerbsrechtliches Irreführungsverbot und Verbraucherinformation' (1993) *Wettbewerb in*

Recht und Praxis 571; S Neu 'Die vergleichende Werbung in Frankreich und Deutschland im Lichte der EG-Richtlinie 97/55' (1999) *Zeitschrift für Europäisches Privatrecht* 123; R Sack 'Die Auswirkungen des Art 30 EG-Vertrag auf das Verbot von Eigenpreisvergleichen (§ 6e UWG)' (1994) *Betriebsberater* 225; G Schricker (1993) *Wettbewerb in Recht und Praxis* 617 (Casenote on *Yves Rocher*).

HS-N

4. France

A comparable prohibition on price comparisons such as that at issue in *Yves Rocher* has never existed in France. French law attempts to control the advertising of price reductions in such a way that the consumer is provided with accurate information on price trends. The main legislation for this purpose is the *Arrêté* no 77–105 P *rélatif à la publication des prix à l'égard du consommateur* of 2 September 1977 to which the Advocate-General made reference in his submissions. Article 3 of the *Arrêté* states:

> Le prix de référence visé par le présent arrêté ne peut excéder le prix le plus bas effectivement pratiqué par l'annonceur pour un article ou une prestation similaire, dans le même établissement de vente au détail, au cours des trente derniers jours précédant le début de la publicité.
>
> (. . .)
>
> L'annonceur peut également utiliser comme prix de référence le prix conseillé par le fabricant ou l'importateur du produit ou le prix maximum résultant d'une disposition de la réglementation économique fixant un prix limite de vente au détail en valeur absolue soit directement, soit par fixation de prix limites en valeur absolue aux différents stades de la production ou de la distribution.
>
> Il doit dans ce cas, être à même de justifier de la réalité de ces références et du fait que ces prix sont couramment pratiqués par les autres distributeurs du même produit.

Therefore advertising featuring price comparisons is only permitted when the higher comparative price has been in force for at least 30 days before the commencement of the advertising campaign. The advertiser bears the burden of proving that the comparative price was actually requested during the 30-day period. An infringement of these provisions is punishable with a fine. Additionally, to the extent that the advertising is misleading, which will often be the case in an infringement of the *Arrêté*, a criminal prosecution may be commenced pursuant to Article L 121–1 *Code de la Consommation* (see the French Commentary to *Nissan*: Case no 5 in this Casebook). French law therefore offers an example of a less draconian means of protecting the consumer from the dangers of price comparisons than the German prohibition which the ECJ held to be disproportionate. The ECJ's judgment therefore necessitated no amendment to the *Arrêté* and other provisions. French writers nevertheless see a danger that the various laws of the Member States relating to advertising containing details of price reductions could constitute an indirect obstacle to trade and demand a Directive to be enacted in order to harmonise this field (*Calais-Auloy/Steinmetz*). In contrast to Germany, the comparative advertising of competitors' prices and products has generally been permitted for quite some time (see for example, *Cour de Cassation* judgment of 18 June 1996).

CASE LAW REFERENCES

Cour de Cassation chambre commerciale judgment of 18 June 1996, *Bulletin des arrêts de la Cour de Cassation* chambres civiles 1996 IV no 185.

LITERATURE REFERENCES

C Berr (1994) *Journal du droit international* 487 (Casenote on *Yves Rocher*); J Calais-Auloy/F Steinmetz *Droit de la consommation* (4th ed 1996) 130; S Neu 'Die vergleichende Werbung in Frankreich und Deutschland im Lichte der EG-Richtlinie 97/55' (1999) *Zeitschrift für Europäisches Privatrecht* 123.

BD

5. Italy

Italian law does not contain any specific provisions regulating price comparisons in advertising or on products. In instances of abuse, general laws are applicable, such as the *Decreto Legislativo* no 74 of 25 January 1992 on misleading advertising and *Decreto Legge* no 109 of 27 January 1992 (see the Italian commentary to the ECJ *Gut Springenheide*: Case no 17 in this Casebook).

Italian writers consider the judgment in *Yves Rocher* as an example of how far the principle of proportionality has permeated Community law. This can be seen from the fact that legal thinking in Member States is becoming increasingly harmonised (*Galetta*). The principle of proportionality is one of the general principles of law which the ECJ has extracted from the legal systems of the Member States, although in this case the German legal system ought to have hung its head in shame. It is likely that the principle of proportionality, aided by Community law, will have various repercussions on Italian law, as has been the case with other Member States.

CASE LAW REFERENCES

Tribunale di Roma sez. I 2 February 1999 (2000) *Giustizia civile* I 1190; Giurì Codice Autodisciplina pubblicitaria 13 July 1999 n 214 *soc. polaroid Italia v Soc. Fuji Film Italia* (2000) *Diritto Industriale* 59.

LITERATURE REFERENCES

D Galetta 'Il Principio di Proporzionalità nella giurisprudenza Comunitaria' (1993) *Rivista italiana di diritto pubblico comunitario* 837 (Casenote on *Yves Rocher*); (1994) *Il Foro Italiano* IV 412 (Casenote on *Yves Rocher*); A Formichetti 'Note in tema di concorrenza sleale, pubblicità ingannevole e pubblicità comparativa denigratoria' (2000) *Giustizia civile* I, 1190; G Paciullo 'La pubblicità comparativa nell'ordinamento italiano' (2000) *Diritto Informazione e Informatica* 113.

AM

CASE NO. 7 — *Keck* Joined Cases C–267/91 and C–268/91

Criminal proceedings against Bernard Keck and Daniel Mithouard
[1993] ECR I–6097

A. Judgment of the ECJ of 24 November 1993

1. Held

Article 30 of the EEC Treaty is to be interpreted as not applying to legislation of a Member State imposing a general prohibition on resale at a loss.

2. Facts of the Case

The *Tribunal de Grande Instance* Strasbourg referred two questions to the Court for a preliminary ruling under Article 177 (new Article 234) EC Treaty on the interpretation of the rules of the Treaty concerning competition and freedom of movement within the Community. Those questions were raised in connection with criminal proceedings brought against Bernard Keck and Daniel Mithouard, who were being prosecuted for reselling products in an unaltered state at prices lower than their actual purchase price ('resale at a loss'), contrary to Article 1 of French Law no 63–628 of 2 July 1963, as amended by Article 32 of Order no 86–1243 of 1 December 1986.

In their defence Keck and Mithouard contended that a general prohibition on resale at a loss, as laid down by those provisions, was incompatible with Article 30 (new Article 28) of the Treaty and with the principles of the free movement of persons, services, capital and free competition within the Community. The

Tribunal de Grande Instance Strasburg took the view that it required an interpretation of certain provisions of Community law. It therefore stayed both sets of proceedings and referred the following question to the Court for a preliminary ruling:

Is the prohibition in France of resale at a loss under Article 32 of Order no. 86–1243 of 1 December 1986 compatible with the principles of the free movement of goods, services and capital, free competition in the Common Market and non-discrimination on grounds of nationality laid down in the Treaty of 25 March 1957 establishing the EEC, and more particularly in Articles 3 and 7 thereof, since the French legislation is liable to distort competition:

(a) firstly, because it makes only resale at a loss an offence and exempts from the scope of the prohibition the manufacturer, who is free to sell on the market the product which he manufactures, processes or improves, even very slightly, at a price lower than his cost price;

(b) secondly, in that it distorts competition, especially in frontier zones, between the various traders on the basis of their nationality and place of establishment?

3. *Extract from the Grounds of the ECJ's Judgment*

6. It should be noted at the outset that the provisions of the Treaty relating to free movement of persons, services and capital within the Community have no bearing on a general prohibition of resale at a loss, which is concerned with the marketing of goods. Those provisions are therefore of no relevance to the issue in the main proceedings.

7. Next, as regards the principle of non-discrimination laid down in Article 7 of the Treaty, it appears from the orders for reference that the national court questions the compatibility with that provision of the prohibition of resale at a loss, in that undertakings subject to it may be placed at a disadvantage vis-à-vis competitors in Member States where resale at a loss is permitted.

8. However, the fact that undertakings selling in different Member States are subject to different legislative provisions, some prohibiting and some permitting resale at a loss, does not constitute discrimination for the purposes of Article 7 of the Treaty. The national legislation at issue in the main proceedings applies to any sales activity carried out within the national territory, regardless of the nationality of those engaged in it (see the judgment in *Ministère Public v Lambert* [1988] ECR 4369).

9. Finally, it appears from the question submitted for a preliminary ruling that the national court seeks guidance as to the possible anti-competitive effects of the rules in question by reference exclusively to the foundations of the Community set out in Article 3 of the Treaty, without however making specific reference to any of the implementing rules of the Treaty in the field of competition.

10. In these circumstances, having regard to the written and oral argument presented to the Court, and with a view to giving a useful reply to the referring court, the appropriate course is to look at the prohibition of resale at a loss from the perspective of the free movement of goods.

11. By virtue of Article 30, quantitative restrictions on imports and all measures having equivalent effect are prohibited between Member States. The Court has consistently held that any measure which is capable of directly or indirectly, actually or potentially, hindering intra-Community trade constitutes a measure having equivalent effect to a quantitative restriction.

12. National legislation imposing a general prohibition on resale at a loss is not designed to regulate trade in goods between Member States.

13. Such legislation may, admittedly, restrict the volume of sales, and hence the volume of sales of products from other Member States, in so far as it deprives traders of a method of sales promotion. But the question remains whether such a possibility is sufficient to characterise the legislation in question as a measure having equivalent effect to a quantitative restriction on imports.

14. In view of the increasing tendency of traders to invoke Article 30 of the Treaty as a means of challenging any rules whose effect is to limit their commercial freedom even where such rules are not aimed at products from other Member States, the Court considers it necessary to re-examine and clarify its case-law on this matter.

15. It is established by the case-law beginning with *Cassis de Dijon* ([1979] ECR 649) that, in the absence of harmonisation of legislation, obstacles to free movement of goods which are the consequence of applying, to goods coming from other Member States where they are lawfully manufactured and marketed, rules that lay down requirements to be met by such goods (such as those relating to designation, form, size, weight, composition, presentation, labelling, packaging) constitute measures of equivalent effect prohibited by Article 30. This is so even if those rules apply without distinction to all products unless their application can be justified by a public-interest objective taking precedence over the free movement of goods.

16. By contrast, contrary to what has previously been decided, the application to products from other Member States of national provisions restricting or prohibiting certain selling arrangements is not such as to hinder directly or indirectly, actually or potentially, trade between Member States within the meaning of *Dassonville* ([1974] ECR 837), so long as those provisions apply to all relevant traders operating within the national territory and so long as they affect in the same manner, in law and in fact, the marketing of domestic products and of those from other Member States.

17. Provided that those conditions are fulfilled, the application of such rules to the sale of products from another Member State meeting the requirements laid down by that State is not by nature such as to prevent their access to the market or to impede access any more than it impedes the access of domestic products. Such rules therefore fall outside the scope of Article 30 of the Treaty.

18. Accordingly, the reply to be given to the national court is that Article 30 of the EEC Treaty is to be interpreted as not applying to legislation of a Member State imposing a general prohibition on resale at a loss.

B. Commentary

1. European Law

With the important judgment in *Keck* the ECJ modified its case law on the free movement of goods (Article 28, ex Article 30 EC Treaty) which had hitherto been governed by the principles laid down in the judgments in *Dassonville* (ECJ [1974] ECR 837) and *Cassis de Dijon* (ECJ [1979] ECR 649: Case no 3 in this Casebook). According to the *Dassonville* formula, Article 28 (ex Article 30) EC Treaty applies to all trading rules enacted by Member States which are capable of hindering, directly or indirectly, actually or potentially, intra-Community trade (ECJ, *Dassonville*, paragraph 5). According to the decision in *Cassis de Dijon* such national measures are permissible only if they are justified by mandatory requirements which take precedence over the requirements of the free movement of goods. Consumer protection is one purpose which justifies a restriction on the free movement of goods (see the European law commentary to the ECJ *Cassis de Dijon*: Case no 3 in this Casebook). The decision in *Keck* modified this interplay between the free movement of goods and other legislative purposes to the extent that certain domestic measures now no longer fall within the ambit of Article 28 (ex Article 30) EC Treaty and therefore no longer require special justification. The most important paragraph of the judgment states:

> By contrast, contrary to what has previously been decided, the application to products from other Member States of national provisions restricting or prohibiting certain selling arrangements is not such as to hinder directly or indirectly, actually or potentially, trade between Member States within the meaning of the *Dassonville* judgment (Case 8/74 [1974] ECR 837), so long as those provisions apply to all relevant traders operating within the national territory and so long as they affect in the same manner, in law and in fact, the marketing of domestic products and of those from other Member States (ECJ *Keck* paragraph 16).

Domestic provisions that restrict or prohibit only 'certain selling arrangements' no longer fall under Article 28 (ex Article 30) EC Treaty. They do not interfere with the free movement of goods:

> so long as those provisions apply to all relevant traders operating within the national territory,
>
> so long as they affect the same manner, in law and in fact, the marketing of domestic products and of those from other Member States.

According to the ECJ, restrictions on the free movement of goods not designated as 'certain selling arrangements' continue to fall under Article 28 (ex Article 30) EC Treaty and the principles laid down in *Cassis de Dijon*:

> It is established by the case law beginning with '*Cassis de Dijon*' that, in the absence of harmonization of legislation, obstacles to free movement of goods which are the consequence of applying, to goods coming from other Member States where they are lawfully manufactured and marketed, rules that lay down requirements to be met by such goods (such as those relating to designation, form, size, weight, composition, presentation, labelling, packaging) constitute measures of equivalent effect prohibited by Article 30. This is so even if those rules apply without distinction to all products unless their application can be justified by a public-interest objective taking precedence over the free movement of goods (paragraph 15).

The scope of this 'clarification' which the ECJ expressly stated to be a modification of its case law up to that point (paragraph 14) has hitherto remained unclear. The first indications have appeared in a number of decisions relating to Article 28 (ex Article 30) EC Treaty. A German provision prohibiting advertising outside chemists for so-called 'normal pharmaceutical goods' (non-medical products) sold on the premises was held to constitute a mere selling arrangement within the meaning of *Keck* (ECJ *Hünermund* [1993] ECR I–6787: Case no 8 in this Casebook). The same applies to a French prohibition on television advertising in the distribution sector (ECJ *Leclerc-Siplec* [1995] ECR I–179). Alternatively there are cases such as *Clinique* (ECJ [1994] ECR I–317). This case concerned a German provision prohibiting the marketing of cosmetic products under this name because consumers could mistakenly assume that the product had medicinal properties. A similar situation arose in the case of *Mars* (ECJ [1995] ECR I–1923: Case no 9 in this Casebook). Here one corner of the packaging of an ice-cream bar was highlighted in colour with the statement '+10 per cent'. This corner was however larger than 10 per cent. The ECJ applied Article 28 (ex Article 30) EC Treaty to the case. Measures which relate to the product itself, its labelling, its packaging etc. apparently continue to be regarded as restricting the free movement of goods and therefore need to be justified under Article 30 (ex Article 36) EC Treaty (*Commission v Belgium—Nutrients* judgment of 16 November 2001 Case C–217/99). This also applies to cases such as *Familiapress* ([1997] ECR

I–3689) and *Konsummentombudsmannen* (judgment of 8 March 2001 Case C–405/98) concerning the content and advertisement in periodicals or the cases on the geographical indications and designations of origin of products (*Montagne* [1997] ECR I–2343). Mere marketing arrangements which do not relate to the product itself lie outside the scope of Article 28 (ex Article 30) EC Treaty. Nevertheless, there are also decisions emanating from the ECJ in which marketing arrangements which do not relate to products or services will contravene Articles 28 or 49 (ex Articles 30 or 59). One example is *Alpine Investments* (prohibition of telephone contact without prior agreement in the marketing of financial services [1995] ECR I–1141) or *De Agostini* (prohibition of television advertising in broadcasts which are aimed at minors, [1997] ECR I–3843).

The effects this modification could have on decisions relating to consumer protection could be regarded as a double-edged sword. On the one hand, the *Keck* judgment bestows on Member States a greater manoeuvrability in the field of consumer protection measures which now no longer fall under Article 28 (ex Article 30) EC Treaty (*Howells/Wilhelmsson*, 133). On the other hand, the ECJ has confined its options to a deregulation of those areas where domestic provisions worsen rather than improve the legal position of the consumer. This can already be seen from the facts of *Keck*; French consumers are still denied the opportunity of profiting from special offers which undercut the selling price. And yet those consumers which could be endangered by the unique alluring and tempting effect of these lowest price offers continue to enjoy protection in France.

ECJ CASE LAW REFERENCES

Dassonville [1974] ECR 837; *Cassis de Dijon* [1979] ECR 649: Case no 3 in this Casebook; *Hünermund* [1993] ECR I–6787: Case no 8 in this Casebook; *Clinique* [1994] ECR I–317; *Commission v Germany (Verfalldatum)* [1994] ECR I–2039; *Punto Casa* [1994] ECR I–2355; *Ortscheit* [1994] ECR I–5243; *Leclerc-Siplec* [1995] ECR I–179; *Alpine Investments* [1995] ECR I–1141; *Mars* [1995] ECR I–1923: Case no 9 in this Casebook; *Belgapom* [1995] ECR I–2467; *Banchero* [1995] ECR I–4663; *Bosman* [1995] ECR I–4921; *Semerano Casa Uno Srl* [1996] ECR I–2975; *Montagne* [1997] ECR I–2343; *Familiapress* [1997] ECR I–3689; *De Agostini* [1997] ECR I–3843; *Commission v Belgium (Nutrients)*, judgment of 16 November 2000, Case C–217/99, n.y.r. in ECR; *Konsumentombudsmannen*, judgment of 8 March 2001, n.y.r in ECR.

LITERATURE REFERENCES

G Howells/T Wilhemsson *EC Consumer Law* (1997) 131–34; R Joliet 'Der freie Warenverkehr: Das Urteil Keck und Mithouard und die Neuorientierung der Rechtsprechung', (1994) *Gewerblicher Rechtsschutz und Urheberrecht—Internationaler Teil* 979; C Lenz 'Ein undeutlicher Ton', (1994) *Neue Juristische Wochenschrift* 1633; A Mattera 'De l'arrêt Dassonville à l'arrêt Keck, l'obscure clarté d'une jurisprudence riche en principes novateurs et en contradictions', (1994) *Revue du Marché Unique Européen* 117; N Reich 'The "November Revolution" of the European Court of Justice: *Keck*, *Meng* and *Audi* Revisited',

(1994) *Common Market Law Review* 459; S Weatherill 'After Keck: Some Thoughts on How to Clarify the Clarification', (1996) *Common Market Law Review* 885.

HS-N/JJ

2. England & Wales

The courts in England and Wales have applied the new approach to Article 28 (ex Article 30) EC Treaty in a haphazard way. In a series of challenges to the product requirements of licensing of taxis, the courts were inconsistent in their approach to Article 28 (ex Article 30) EC Treaty. According to the Local Government (Miscellaneous Provisions) Act 1976, the local authorities had the power to force taxis to be of distinguishing appearance and design. Certain London boroughs therefore required licensed taxis to be 'Black Cabs'—traditional London taxis. After complaints from the Home Office, the authorities changed the requirements to technical specifications, including the size of doors and the shape of the taxi. In reality, these requirements mirrored a traditional London taxi. These types of vehicles were only produced by two British companies. The technical requirements were challenged by way of judicial review. It was argued that they amounted to product requirements which had the effect of restricting access to the British market of taxis manufactured in other Member States; other manufacturers would have to alter their production procedures in order to meet the technical specifications—a clear breach of Article 28 (ex Article 30) EC Treaty. This argument was unsuccessful in all of the cases. In *R v Metropolitan Borough Council of Wirral, ex parte The Wirral Licensed Taxi Owners Association* one of the grounds cited for the failure of Article 28 (ex Article 30) EC Treaty was that any continental manufacturer could, if he so desired, make such a taxi. In other words, the fact that the legislation did not discriminate against foreign manufacturers took it outside of Article 28 (ex Article 30). This was equally evident in *R v Luton Borough Council, ex parte Mirza, R v Doncaster Metropolitan Borough Council, ex parte Kelly* and *Hodgkinson v Nottingham City Council*. In *Mirza*, Brooke J in the High Court and Leggatt LJ in the Court of Appeal both drew on the decision in *Keck* in order to hold that Article 28 (ex Article 30) EC Treaty had not been breached. Leggatt thought that the technical specifications were in fact 'selling arrangements' which did not discriminate against foreign producers and were therefore outside Article 28 (ex Article 30). As *Jarvis* pointed out:

> This judgment confirms all the worst fears expressed by commentators concerning the *Keck* judgment. It is, with the greatest respect, submitted that the national regulations at issue in this case could not, and should not, have been considered to be 'selling arrangements' within the *Keck* case law. Regulations setting down type and design requirements for licensed taxis are 'product requirements' *par excellence.*

The English and Welsh courts appear not to understand that indistinctly applicable measures are also caught by Article 30. And that these technical specifications for taxis did breach Article 30 'since they restricted access to the market for licensed taxi vehicles manufactured in other Member States because, in order to get access, these manufacturers would be put to the considerable expense of developing a vehicle which meets these specifications'.

CASE LAW REFERENCES

High Court, Queen's Bench Division, *R v Metropolitan Borough Council of Wirral, ex parte The Wirral Licensed Taxi Owners Association*, (1983) *Common Market Law Reports* 3, 150; High Court, Chancery Division, *South Pembrokeshire District Council v Wendy Fair Markets Ltd*, (1994) *Common Market Law Reports* 1, 213; Court of Appeal, *Stedman v Hogg Robinson Travel Agents* (judgment of 27 October 1994, *Lexis*); High Court, *R v Doncaster Metropolitan Borough Council, ex parte Kelly* (judgment of 20 October 1994, *Lexis*); High Court, Queen's Bench Division, Court of Appeal, *R v Luton Borough Council, ex parte Mirza* (judgments of 4 November 1994, 5 February 1995, *Lexis*).

LITERATURE REFERENCES

A Arnull 'Anyone for Tripe' (1993) *European Law Review* 314; D Chalmers 'Repackaging the Internal Market—The Ramifications of the *Keck* Judgment' (1994) *European Law Review* 385; M Jarvis *The Application of EC Law by National Courts* (1998) 125–127; S Weatherill 'After Keck: Some Thoughts on How to Clarify the Clarification' (1996) *Common Market Law Review* 885.

JJ

3. Germany

German competition law (unlike France) does not have an express prohibition on sales below the cost price. Such selling arrangements are generally permitted provided that sales at a loss do not simultaneously mislead the consumer (*Baumbach/Hefermehl*). The *Keck* decision therefore did not directly affect German law but has nevertheless struck a chord with German legal writers (see *Lenz* for an overview). It has also been swiftly applied by the courts (for example, the *Bundesgerichtshof* (Federal Court of Justice) openly quoted from the case in its judgment of 16 November 1993). The analysis of the consequences from the *Keck* decision has in many respects provoked controversy. Opinions differ as to whether it has overruled the much approved decisions in *GB-INNO* (ECJ [1993] ECR I–2361: Case no 6 in this Casebook) and above all, *Yves Rocher* (ECJ [1993] ECR I–2361: Case no 6 in this Casebook—see *Sacks* for an overview of current opinions). The *Bundesgerichtshof* (Federal Constitutional Court) appears to

assume that the principles laid down by *Yves Rocher* have become null and void
as a result of *Keck* (for example, its judgments of 16 November 1995 and 4 July
1996). The *Bundesverfassungsgericht* in a cursory ruling has let it be known that
it has no objection to this view (ruling of 4 June 1998). On this controversial issue
the higher courts in Germany tend to prefer a view which allows German courts
a greater autonomy *vis-à-vis* Community law. The judgment in *Keck* appears to
be eagerly quoted since it justifies the non-application of Community law. Administrative tribunals have relied on the *Keck* judgment in answering the question as
to whether a local tax on packaging is capable of infringing Article 28 (ex Article
30) EC Treaty, claiming such taxes amount to 'selling arrangements' (*Bundesverwaltungsgericht* (Federal Administrative Court) ruling of 14 June 1996). There are,
however, decisions in which Article 28 (ex Article 30) EC Treaty has been applied
to advertising statements which display no reference to a particular product (for
example, *Oberlandesgericht* Karlsruhe (Higher Regional Court), judgment of 13
March 1996; see also the German commentary to the ECJ, *Nissan* [1992] ECR
I–131: Case no 5 in this Casebook).

   The initial concern that the change in the case law introduced by *Keck* could
lead to Community law restricting consumer protection has apparently been put
to rest (noticeable, for example, from the two contributions by *Reich*). From a
German point of view, the main effect of *Keck* may lie in its relaxing of the pressure to harmonise law imposed by previous decisions of the ECJ on Article 28 (ex
Article 30) EC Treaty. The decision in *Keck* reduces the deregulatory effect of
Community law. Now that the area of application of Article 28 (ex Article 30) EC
Treaty has been curtailed, Germany can retain its rules on unfair trade which
appear unusually strict in a European context. Moreover, Germany can retain its
concept of the 'casual' consumer in the re-nationalised field of 'selling arrangements'. The disadvantage is that there are less possibilities of the ECJ remedying
deficiencies in domestic legal policy. The first example is apparent from the
Discount Law (*Rabattgesetz, Reichsgesetzblatt* I 1933, 1011), according to which
traders were prohibited from offering a discount of more than 3 per cent. The
Commission dropped proceedings against Germany for a breach of Article 28 (ex
Article 30) due to an infringement of the Discount Law. This was an immediate
response to the decision in *Keck*; there was now little chance of success (see
Basedow, Möschel). The *Bundesgerichtshof*, expressly relying on the ECJ's decision
in *Keck*, held in a judgment of the 23 March 1995 that the Discount Law was compatible with Article 28 (ex Article 30) EC Treaty. The same conclusion was also
drawn by the *Oberlandesgericht* Nürnberg in its judgment of 18 August 1994 after
a thorough examination of the ECJ's case law on the subject. The Commission
again commenced proceedings against the Discount Law but with no success
(press release of Commission of 16 June 1998 IP/98/653). Following the recent
adaptation of the E-Commerce Directive (OJ 2000 L178/1) the German government has taken steps to abolish the Discount Law and a statutory instrument on
free gifts (*Zugabeverordnung, Reichsgesetzblatt* I 1932 121, *Bundesgesetztblatt* I
2001 1661). German traders feared that they could be disadvantaged because

German law prohibited discounts and free gifts which are very common in other Member States (eg 'buy one, get one free').

CASE LAW REFERENCES

Bundesgerichtshof judgment of 16 December 1993 (1994) *Europäische Zeitschrift für Wirtschaftsrecht* 413; Oberlandesgericht Nürnberg judgment of 18 August 1994 (1995) *Europäisches Wirtschafts-und Steuerrecht* 53; Bundesgerichtshof judgment of 23 March 1995 (1995) *Gewerblicher Rechtsschutz und Urheberrecht* 515; Bundesgerichtshof judgment of 16 November 1995 (1996) *Zeitschrift für Wirtschaftsrecht* 472; Oberlandesgericht Karlsruhe judgment of 13 March 1996 (1996) *Neue Juristische Wochenschrift* 2313; Bundesverwaltungsgericht ruling of 14 June 1996; (1997) *NVwZ-Rechtsprechungs-Report Verwaltungsrecht* 111; Bundesgerichtshof judgment of 4 July 1996 (1996) *NJW Entscheidungsdienst Wettbewerbsrecht* 266; Bundesverfassungsgericht ruling of 4 June 1998 (1998) *Wertpapiermitteilungen* 1554.

LITERATURE REFERENCES

J Basedow 'Fällt das Rabattgesetz?' (1994) *Zeitschrift für Europäisches Privatrecht* 201; A Baumbach/W Hefermehl commentary on § 1 UWG, 256–59 (on the sale at a loss in German law), *Wettbewerbsrecht* (22nd edn 2001); K Fezer 'Europäisierung des Wettbewerbsrechts' (1994) *Juristenzeitung* 317; P Heermann 'Rabattgesetz und Zugabeverordnung ade!' (2001) *Wettbewerb in Recht und Praxis* 855; C Lenz 'Ein undeutlicher Ton', (1994) *Neue Juristische Wochenschrift* 1633; W Möschel 'Kehrtwende in der Rechtsprechung des EuGH zur Warenverkehrsfreiheit', (1994) *Neue Juristische Wochenschrift* 429; N Reich 'The "November Revolution" of the European Court of Justice: *Keck, Meng* and *Audi* Revisited', (1994) *Common Market Law Review* 459; N Reich *Europäisches Verbraucherrecht*, 83–7, 92–4; O Remien 'Grenzen der gerichtlichen Privatrechtsangleichung mittels der Grundfreiheiten des EG-Vertrages' (1994) *Juristenzeitung* 349; R Sack 'Staatliche Werbebeschränkungen und die Art 30 und 59 EG-Vertrag' (1998) *Wettbewerb in Recht und Praxis* 103.

HS-N

4. France

Initially, the criminal prohibition of selling at a loss which had not been criticised by the ECJ continued in France unchanged. The French government defended the provision as being a measure which was designed both to combat unfair advertising practices and protect the consumer (Opinion of the Advocate-General, paragraph 7 [1993] ECR I–6114). In his Opinion, the Advocate-General initially rejected this reason as unconvincing. He argued that there was no justification for a general prohibition on sales at a loss. Moreover, other alternatives were conceivable which would have had a less damaging effect on the free movement of goods (paragraph 10). However, this was no longer decisive, for during the course of the proceedings the Advocate-General and the Court both decided that Article 28 (ex Article 30) EC Treaty did not apply. Even French writers doubt whether the prohibition serves the interests of consumer protection. Indeed, it has been argued that it protects the manufacturers and the smaller sole traders (*Calais-Auloy/ Steinmetz*). Due to the fact that its effects were deemed altogether inadequate, the provisions have been amended by Law no 96–588 of 1 July 1996. With the help of this amendment, sales at a loss as well as at ridiculously low prices should now be tackled more effectively. Instead of deregulation therefore France has seen an intensification of market intervention as a direct consequence of the judgment in *Keck*.

The *Keck* decision is seen by writers as having a limited effect on the protection of the consumer. The leading textbook on consumer protection only mentions the decision in a footnote (*Calais-Auloy/Steinmetz* 132 footnote 2). Most of the contributions relating to *Keck* in French legal journals concern themselves with the European law aspects of the decision (summarised in *Picod*; for more details of the French prohibition on the *revente à perte* see *Voinot*).

The French courts, on the other hand, have clearly been affected by the judgment in *Keck*, despite the fact that it has not often been expressly quoted. Examples include the decisions on the compatibility of the apothecary monopoly (Article L 511 and L 512 *Code de la santé publique*) on the sale of pharmaceutical products with Article 28 (ex Article 30) EC Treaty. This monopoly appears to be a frequent cause of legal disputes. In French law a number of products fall under the term 'pharmaceutical products' which are freely available in other Members States (eg Vitamin C tablets). The ECJ had also dealt with this monopoly on a number of occasions and had held, before the decision in *Keck*, that it was a restriction on the free movement of goods which was justified on the basis of Article 30 (ex Article 36) EC Treaty (*Delattre* [1991] ECR I–1487; *Ministère public v Monteil* [1991] ECR I–1547). In the decisions of the *Conseil d'État* (eg judgment of 7 July 1995) concerning the apothecary monopoly, the court cited from the judgment in *Keck* in order to justify the non-application of Article 28 (ex Article 30) EC Treaty. It is clear from the Opinion of the *Commissaire du gouvernement* to this judgment that the *Conseil d'État* expressly followed the changes introduced by the judgment in *Keck*. The *Cour de Cassation* in its judgment of 30 October 1996 referred to the compatibility of the apothecary monopoly with Article 28 (ex Article 30) EC Treaty. In so doing the court came to the conclusion that the monopoly did not fall within the ambit of Article 28 (ex Article 30); as a result there was no need for justification under Article 30 (ex Article 36) EC Treaty or on the basis of consumer protection. This judgment clearly showed the influence of the *Keck* judgment without actually mentioning it. It also contradicts the previous case law of the *Cour de Cassation*. Again the decisions of the *Cour de Cassation* of 24 January and 9 July 1996 held that the apothecary monopoly was justified on the basis of Article 30 (ex Article 36) EC Treaty. It thereby expressly cited in one of the cases the pre-*Keck* case law. The date on which the effect of the judgment in *Keck* came into force in France can therefore be dated back to the second half of 1996: two and a half years after it was decided by the ECJ. This occurred in the decision of the *Cour d'Appel* Versailles, where it reviewed the compatibility of the apothecary monopoly for Vitamin C with Article 28 (ex Article 30) EC Treaty. In the long judgment the court openly disagreed with case law of the ECJ, including *Delattre, Keck* und *Commission v Greece* ([1995] ECR I–1621). It classified the apothecary monopoly under the term 'selling arrangements' as defined in *Keck* and held that Article 28 (ex Article 30) EC Treaty was inapplicable.

CASE LAW REFERENCES

Conseil d'État judgment of 7 July 1995 (1995) *Recueil des décisions du Conseil d'État* 287; Cour d'Appel Versailles judgment of 22 January 1996 *Gazette du Palais*, 1996, Sommaire 32 (full text avaibale on *Lexis*); Cour de Cassation chambre criminelle judgment of 24 January 1996 95–80.902, judgment no 506, *Lexis*; Cour de Cassation chambre criminelle decision of 9 July 1996 *Bulletin des arrêts de la Cour de Cassation,* chambre criminelle 1996, no 288: *Juris-classeur périodique—La semaine juridique,* édition générale 1996 IV 2423 (extract); Cour de Cassation chambre criminelle judgment of 30 October 1996 *Recueil Dalloz Sirey,* 1997, Informations rapides, 47.

LITERATURE REFERENCES

A Brunet 'Publicité comparative, concurrence et consommation', *Gazette du Palais*, no 351, 1999, 6; J Calais-Auloy/F Steinmetz *Droit de la consommation* (4th edn 1996) 132; J Franck 'Publicité comparative at publicité pour les produits du tabac, la legislation française, example ou contre-exemple?', *Revue Européenne de Droit de la Consommation*, no 2, 1998, 85; M Jarvis *The Application of EC Law by National Courts, The Free Movement of Goods* (1998) 122–25; F Picod 'La nouvelle approche de la Cour de justice en matière d'entraves aux échanges' (1998) *Revue trimestrielle de droit européen* 169; D Voinot *Recueil Dalloz Sirey*, 1994, Jurisprudence, 187 (Casenote on *Keck*).

BD

5. *Italy*

Italian writers consider this case and that of *Hünermund* as a turning point in the ECJ's case law relating to the term 'measures having equivalent effect' in Article 28 (ex Article 30) EC Treaty (*De Vita*). Both decisions have been welcomed as an attempt to clarify the nonsensical case law. The novelty of these judgments is the fact that the mere possibility of a limitation on imports by itself is no longer sufficient to constitute a breach of Article 28 (ex Article 30) EC Treaty (*Scannicchio*). Numerous general rules relating to business activities are no longer to be regarded as restricting the Internal Market. These rules are created in the course of integrating national markets and thereby fall outside Article 28 (ex Article 30) EC Treaty.

LITERATURE REFERENCES

N Scannicchio 'Dal diritto comunitario al diritto privato europeo nella Giurisprudenza della Corte di Giustizia' in N Lipari (ed) *Diritto Privato Europeo* (1997) 58; M De Vita *Il Foro Italiano*, 1994 IV 329 (Casenotes on *Keck* and *Hünermund*).

AM

6. Austria

Even before Austria joined the European Union in 1995 the *Oberster Gerichtshof* (Supreme Court) had by its own volition adopted the decision in *Keck* (pursuant to Article 11 of the European Economic Area Agreement which corresponds literally to Article 28 (ex Article 30) EC Treaty. The reason for this was the existing case law concerning § 1 of the Law against Unfair Competition (*UWG Bundesgesetzblatt* 1984 no 448). It stated that an enterprise which advertises its products or services by telephone (so-called 'cold calling') may be barred from carrying on this practice if considered to be acting in bad faith. Paragraph 1 *UWG* states:

> Wer im geschäftlichen Verkehr zu Zwecken des Wettbewerbs Handlungen vornimmt, die gegen die guten Sitten verstoßen, kann auf Unterlassung und Schadenersatz in Anspruch genommen werden.

This prohibition on telephone advertising does not stem from an express statutory prohibition, but rather from the interpretation given to a general clause by the highest court.

In the facts of the case decided by the *Oberster Gerichtshof* on 18 October 1994, an Austrian company had offered computer courses in Austria and for this purpose had carried out a telephone advertising campaign. The company had procured the teaching materials (software) from Italy. It formed part of the course package sold to the course participants. In its defence it submitted that the case law of the *Oberster Gerichtshof* infringed the free movement of goods and was no longer tenable after the European Economic Area had come into force. The *Oberster Gerichtshof*, however, held that in the case of 'cold calling' the issue concerned the regulation of a selling arrangement. This, according to *Keck*, was not affected by the European Economic Area (*Computerkurse I*).

The general statement that the blanket prohibition on telephone advertising (without prior agreement of the addressee) amounted to a selling arrangement pursuant to *Keck* appeared questionable. This would have been particularly unclear in those case scenarios where the telephone advertising had referred to a cross-border service that was to be performed. That is to say, it was not clear at this time whether the *Keck* decision was also to be applied in the field of freedom to provide services.

Six months later the ECJ decided *Alpine Investments* (ECJ [1995] ECR I–1141). It dealt with a national prohibition on 'cold calling'. Alpine Investments, a firm situated in the Netherlands, appealed against a prohibition on 'cold calling' which had been imposed on it by the Dutch Finance Minister. This prohibition also prevented the company from advertising by means of telephone in other Member States for the financial services which it offered. According to the ECJ this prohibition was not a selling arrangement according to *Keck* and was therefore to be governed by Article 49 (ex Article 59) EC Treaty. The Court held that the prohibition could be justified in the special case that there were reasons in the public interest for advertising financial services—above all with respect to protecting the trust of those investing capital in the domestic financial markets.

The contradiction between the grounds of the ECJ and those of the *Oberster Gerichtshof* is superficial. The prohibition of the Dutch Finance Ministry in *Alpine Investments* was subject to the control of Article 49 (ex Article 59) EC Treaty because it also prohibited the company from advertising in Member States where 'cold calling' was permitted. In this way, the prohibition presented an obstacle to Alpine Investments' entry into the markets of other Member States; this was not the case for the companies in these States. Even though this was a rare case of a limitation on exports, it was capable of limiting cross-border trade and did not fall under *Keck* or Articles 28 and 49 (ex Articles 30 and 59) EC Treaty (paragraphs 15–17 of the *Keck* case).

In contrast, Austria's prohibition on telephone advertising applies exclusively to the domestic market. The *Oberster Gerichtshof* therefore saw no reason to depart from *Computerkurse I* and, following Austria's accession to the EU, once again followed its earlier decision (judgment of 7 November 1995, *Computerkurse II*). Nevertheless it worded its judgment somewhat more cautiously and noted that in the preceding case it was of no consequence that 'the prohibition on telephone advertising is in any case likely to restrict the freedom to supply goods or services', since the telephone calls in question were national calls only.

The fundamental uncertainty surrounding the compatibility of a blanket ban on telephone advertising with the EC Treaty therefore remained. The fact that the ECJ in *Alpine Investments* nonetheless reviewed whether a law demonstrated a marketing arrangement as defined in *Keck* leads to the conclusion that these principles could also apply to the provision of services. However, it is unclear whether they are also to be applied in the same way (*Knobl*). It is equally uncertain whether a blanket prohibition on unsolicited telephone advertising could still be considered to be a regulation of a marketing arrangement in every case. This becomes especially evident if a company's business is the provision of telesales and it intends to pursue this as a cross-border business. In relation to this the prohibition on telephone advertising would not constitute a marketing arrangement but a product-related or 'service-related' law. It would then have been necessary to review whether the prohibition was justified due to reasons of public interest. This could have been doubtful in the case of a blanket ban of every kind of telephone advertising.

Recently the European and Austrian legislators have reviewed this debate—in any rate as far as the prohibition on 'cold calling' is concerned. Directive 97/66 concerning the processing of personal data and the protection of privacy in the field of telecommunication was passed on 15 December 1997 (OJ 1998 L24/1). Article 12, entitled 'Unsolicited Telephone Calls', states:

> (1) Die Verwendung von Kommunikation mit Automaten als Gesprächspartner (Voice-Mail-System) oder Fernkopien (Telefax) für Zwecke des Direktmarketings darf nur bei vorheriger Einwilligung der Teilnehmer gestattet werden.

> (2) Die Mitgliedstaaten ergreifen geeignete Maßnahmen, um gebührenfrei sicherzustellen, daß mit Ausnahme der in Absatz 1 genannten Anrufe unerbetene Anrufe zum Zweck des Direktmarketings, die entweder ohne die Einwilligung der betreffenden Teilnehmer erfolgen oder an Teilnehmer gerichtet sind, die keine solchen Anrufe erhalten möchten, nicht gestattet sind; welche dieser Optionen gewählt wird, ist im innerstaatlichen Recht zu regeln.

> (. . .)

The Member States are now bound by Article 12(2) of the Directive. They can either prohibit 'cold calling' (and to make it dependant on the consent of those concerned) or at the very least, ensure that the participants who do not wish to receive telephone calls for the purposes of direct marketing are protected from them. There is therefore no longer any doubt that the decisions of the *Oberster Gerichtshof* relating to §1 *UWG* conform to Community law. The Austrian legislator has taken this as an opportunity to expressly embody the prohibition on telephone advertising without prior consent of the participant in §101 of the new Telecommunication Law (*TKG, Bundesgesetzblatt* 1997–I no 100, as amended by *Bundesgesetzblatt* 1999–I no 188):

> § 101 (Unerbetene Anrufe): Anrufe—einschließlich das Senden von Fernkopien—zu Werbezwecken ohne vorherige Einwilligung des Teilnehmers sind unzulässig. Der Einwilligung des Teilnehmers steht die Einwilligung einer Person, die vom Teilnehmer zur Benutzung seines Anschlusses ermächtigt wurde, gleich. Die erteilte Einwilligung kann jederzeit widerrufen werden; der Widerruf der Einwilligung hat auf ein Vertragsverhältnis mit dem Adressaten der Einwilligung keinen Einfluß. Die Zusendung einer elektronischen Post als Massensendung oder zu Werbezwecken bedarf der vorherigen—jederzeit widerruflichen—Zustimmung des Empfängers.

Infringement of this provision renders it ultra vires and is punishable with a fine of up to 500,000 schilling (approximately 35,000 Euro) (§ 104(3)(22) *TKG*). The *Oberster Gerichtshof* has recently emphasised the need to interpret § 101 *TKG* in light of the Data Protection and Telecommunication Directive (judgment of 18 May 1999, *Telefonwerbung II*).

CASE LAW REFERENCES

Oberster Gerichtshof *Telefonwerbung I* judgment of 8 November 1983 (1984) *Österreichische Blätter für gewerblichen Rechtsschutz und Urheberrecht* 13; Oberster Gerichtshof *Computerkurse I* judgment of 18 October 1994 (1995) *Österreichische Blätter für gewerblichen Rechtsschutz und Urheberrecht* 12; Oberster Gerichtshof *Computerkurse II* judgment of 7 November 1995 (1996) *Österreichische Blätter für gewerblichen Rechtsschutz und Urheberrecht* 84; Oberster Gerichtshof *Telefonwerbung II* judgment of 18 May 1999 (2000) *Österreichische Blätter für gewerblichen Rechtsschutz und Urheberrecht* 68.

LITERATURE REFERENCES

K Hammer *Handbuch zum freien Warenverkehr* (1998); P Knobl 'Ein Meilenstein im Europarecht der Bank—und Wertpapierdienstleistungen sowie im Anwendungsbereich der Dienstleistungsfreiheit', (1995) *Wirtschaftsrechtliche Blätter* 309; F Rüffler 'Der Einfluß des Europarechts auf das österreichische UWG', in H Koppensteiner (ed) *Österreichisches und Europäisches Wirtschaftsprivatrecht* (1996) Teil 6/2, 391.

AE

CASE NO. 8 — *Hünermund* C–292/92

Ruth Hünermund ao v Landesapothekerkammer Baden-Württemberg
[1993] ECR I–6787

A. Judgment of the ECJ of 15 December 1993

1. Held

Article 30 of the EEC Treaty is to be interpreted as not applying to a rule of professional conduct, laid down by the pharmacists' professional body in a Member State, which prohibits pharmacists from advertising quasi-pharmaceutical products outside the pharmacy.

2. Facts of the Case

The *Verwaltungsgerichtshof* Baden-Württemberg (Higher Administrative Court, Baden-Württemberg, Germany) referred a question on the interpretation of Articles 30 and 36 (new Articles 28 and 30) EC Treaty to the ECJ to enable it to determine whether a rule of professional conduct laid down by the *Landesapothekerkammer* Baden-Württemberg (the pharmacists' professional association for the Land Baden-Württemberg, hereinafter 'the Professional Association') which prohibits pharmacists practising in that Land from advertising outside the pharmacy quasi-pharmaceutical products which they are permitted to sell is compatible with those provisions. That question was raised in proceedings between several pharmacists from Baden-Württemberg and the Professional Association.

Paragraph 10(15) of the Code of Conduct of the Professional Association (*Berufsordnung*) prohibits 'excessive advertising' for the non-medicinal products which, under §§ 2(4) and 25 of the Rules Governing the Operation of Pharmacies (*Apothekenbetriebsordnung*), may be sold in a pharmacy provided that the sales do not affect the proper operation of the dispensary. It is common ground that in practice that provision of the *Berufsordnung* prohibits all forms of advertising outside pharmacies for quasi-pharmaceutical products. The applicants in the main proceedings, all owners of pharmacies in the Land Baden-Württemberg selling quasi-pharmaceutical products which they wanted to advertise outside the pharmacy, brought an action before the *Verwaltungsgerichtshof* Baden-Württemberg against the Professional Association seeking a declaration that the prohibition of advertising was invalid. Before that court the applicants' main submission was that § 10(15) of the *Berufsordnung* was incompatible with Articles 30 and 36 (new Articles 28 and 30) EC Treaty. In those circumstances the *Verwaltungsgerichtshof* Baden-Württemberg stayed the proceedings in order to refer the following question to the Court:

> Is Article 36, in conjunction with Article 30, of the EEC Treaty to be interpreted to the effect that the provisions of a *Berufsordnung* (Professional Code) by which a *Landesapothekerkammer* prohibits pharmacists within its area of competence from advertising outside their pharmacies, even for the purpose of marketing goods commonly sold in pharmacies within the meaning of § 25 of the *Apothekenbetriebsordnung* (Rules Governing the Operation of Pharmacies), justified?

3. Extract from the Grounds of the ECJ's Judgment

12. Article 30 prohibits quantitative restrictions on imports, and all measures having equivalent effect, between Member States.

13. The Professional Association submitted first that the professional conduct rule at issue before the national court could not be a 'measure' within the meaning of Article 30 of the Treaty since under German law pharmacists' professional associations had no power to strike off as a disciplinary sanction; that sanction could be applied only by the competent authorities of the relevant Land.

14. It is apparent from the order for reference that under German law the Professional Association is a public law body which has legal personality and is regulated by the State; membership is compulsory for all pharmacists practising in the Land Baden-Wuerttemberg. The Professional Association also lays down rules of professional conduct applicable to pharmacists and monitors compliance by its members with their professional obligations. Finally, professional conduct committees, which are part of and whose members are nominated by the Professional Association, may impose disciplinary measures such as fines, disqualification as a member of bodies of the Association or withdrawal of the right to vote or be elected to those bodies on pharmacists who have infringed professional conduct rules.

15. The Court has already held (see the judgment in Joined Cases 266/87 and 267/87 *The Queen v Royal Pharmaceutical Society of Great Britain, ex parte Association of Pharmaceutical Importers* [1989] ECR 1295 paragraph 15) that measures adopted by a professional body on which national legislation has conferred powers of that nature constitute, if they are capable of affecting trade between Member States, "measures" within the 'meaning' of Article 30 of the Treaty.

16. That ruling is not in any way called in question by the fact that, unlike the professional body to which that judgment relates, the Professional Association concerned in this case is not empowered to revoke the authorisation needed by its members to practise.

17. The Professional Association next submitted that the prohibition on advertising challenged before the national court was not a measure having an effect equivalent to a quantitative restriction within the meaning of Article 30 of the Treaty since it was not capable of impeding intra-Community trade in quasi-pharmaceutical goods.

18. It is settled case-law that any measure which is capable of hindering, directly or indirectly, actually or potentially, intra-Community trade constitutes a measure having an effect equivalent to a quantitative restriction (judgment in Case 8/74 *Procureur du Roi v Dassonville* [1974] ECR 837 paragraph 5).

19. It is not the purpose of a rule of professional conduct prohibiting pharmacists from advertising quasi-pharmaceutical products outside the pharmacy, drawn up by a professional association, to regulate trade in goods between Member States. Moreover, the prohibition does not affect the right of traders other than pharmacists to advertise those products.

20. Such a rule may, admittedly, restrict the volume of sales, and hence the volume of sales of quasi-pharmaceutical products from other Member States, in so far as it deprives the pharmacists concerned of a method of promoting the sales of such products. But the question remains whether such a possibility is sufficient to characterise the rule in question as a measure having equivalent effect to a quantitative restriction on imports within the meaning of Article 30 of the Treaty.

21. The application to products from other Member States of national provisions restricting or prohibiting certain selling arrangements is not such as to hinder directly or indirectly, actually or potentially, trade between Member States within the meaning of the *Dassonville* judgment (cited above), so long as those provisions apply to all relevant traders operating within the national territory and so long as they affect in the same manner, in law and in fact, the marketing of domestic products and of those from other Member States. Provided that those conditions are fulfilled, the application of such rules to the sale of products from another Member State meeting the requirements laid down by that State is not by nature such as to prevent their access to the market or to impede access any more than it impedes the access of domestic products. Such rules therefore fall outside the scope of Article 30 of the Treaty (Joined Cases C–267 and C–268/91 *Keck and Mithouard* [1993] ECR I–6097 paragraphs 16 and 17).

22. In the case of a rule such as that at issue in this case, those conditions are satisfied in relation to the application of a rule of professional conduct, laid down by a professional body in a Member State, which prohibits pharmacists within the area over which it has jurisdiction from advertising outside the pharmacy quasi-pharmaceutical goods which they are authorised to sell.

23. That rule, which applies without distinction as to the origin of the products in question to all pharmacists regulated by the Professional Association, does not affect the marketing of goods from other Member States differently from that of domestic products.

24. Accordingly, the reply to be given to the Verwaltungsgerichtshof Baden-Wuerttemberg is that Article 30 of the EEC Treaty is to be interpreted as not applying to a rule of professional conduct, laid down by the pharmacists' professional body in a Member State, which prohibits pharmacists from advertising quasi-pharmaceutical products outside the pharmacy.

B. Commentary

1. European Law

Hünermund, heard in parallel to *Keck* and decided shortly thereafter (ECJ [1993] ECR I–6097: Case no 7 in this Casebook), contains a number of clarifications of the new case law relating to the free movement of goods in the wake of *Keck*. At the same time it gives the first example of a national provision which is a 'selling arrangement' outside Article 28 (ex Article 30) EC Treaty. Advocate-General Tesauro encapsulated the crux of the problem by asking:

Is Article 30 of the Treaty a provision intended to liberalize intra-Community trade or is it intended more generally to encourage the unhindered pursuit of commerce in individual Member States?

In other words, must all restrictions of business activity be justified on the basis of 'mandatory requirements' pursuant to the decision in *Cassis de Dijon* (Case no 3 in this Casebook) or is it the case that this requirement only relates to such measures which hinder imports from other Member States? The ECJ's answer in *Keck* and *Hünermund* is clearly worded: the free movement of goods governed by Article 28 (ex Article 30) EC Treaty only protects cross-border trade. The ECJ adopted the wording of the formula from the judgment in *Keck* relating to 'certain selling arrangements' and applied them to the German prohibition on advertising by pharmacists for goods commonly sold in pharmacies. Admittedly a prohibition on advertising such as this may be capable of restricting the volume of sales and thereby the volume of sales from other Member States because the ban deprives pharmacists of a way of promoting the sale of such products (paragraph 20). On the facts, a restriction on trade was therefore given according to the old *Dassonville* formula. According to this formula, Article 28 (ex Article 30) EC Treaty embraces all trading rules which are capable of hindering directly or indirectly, actually or potentially intra-Community trade (ECJ *Dassonville* [1974] ECR 837 paragraph 5). According to *Keck*, however, this does not apply to rules governing certain selling practices 'so long as those provisions apply to all relevant traders operating within the national territory and so long as they affect in the same manner, in law and in fact, the marketing of domestic products and of those from other Member States'. Precisely this requirement was present in the *Hünermund* case. That is to say the prohibition on advertising did not affect the marketing of goods from other Member States differently from that of domestic products (paragraph 23).

The *Hünermund* case serves as an example of the extent to which the *Keck* decision expands the freedom of Member States in using domestic law as a means to regulate their national market. The German prohibition on goods commonly sold in pharmacies would have been unlikely to pass the strict 'rule of reason' test laid down in the *Cassis de Dijon* formula. The aims of the prohibition may also have been to protect the health of the public (ensuring expert advice by pharmacists). However it would have been quite disproportionate since less drastic means were available to deal with this (the Advocate-General also shared this view, paragraphs 30 and 31 and the Commission, report of the proceedings in the *Hünermund* case). The ECJ's new case law on Article 28 (ex Article 30) EC Treaty therefore allows Member States to impose restrictions on commercial activities which would have been prohibited by earlier case law. Community law does not interfere with disproportionate measures relating to consumer protection and other methods of market intervention provided that Article 28 (ex Article 30) EC Treaty does not apply (post-*Keck*). Whether this development is seen to be beneficial for consumer protection depends on the observer's view of economics.

ECJ CASE LAW REFERENCES

see references given in the European Law Commentary to K*eck*: Case no 7 in this Casebook.

LITERATURE REFERENCES

W Möschel (1994) *Neue Juristische Wochenschrift* 782 (Casenote on *Hünermund*); M Petschke 'Die Warenverkehrsfreiheit in der neuesten Rechtsprechung des EuGH' (1994) *Europäische Zeitschrift für Wirtschaftsrecht* 107; W Roth (1994) *Common Market Law Review* 845 (Casenotes on *Keck* and *Hünermund*).

HS-N/JJ

2. England & Wales

The rules of conduct of the English pharmacists' professional body, the Royal Pharmaceutical Society of Great Britain, were reviewed by the European Court of Justice in 1989. In the seminal case of *R v the Royal Pharmaceutical Society of Great Britain, ex parte API*, the Court extended the notion of 'measures enacted by Member States' within the meaning of Article 28 (ex Article 30) EC Treaty to rules of professional conduct laid down by a professional body, provided that that body is able to impose disciplinary sanctions on its members. Accordingly, the *Hünermund* judgment builds upon this ruling and classifies rules of conduct of the equivalent German association as 'state measures'.

The *Hünermund* decision, which provides one of the very first applications of the *Keck* ruling, did not raise any particular interest in the UK, even though the clarification given in *Keck* was subject to discussion in the academic environment. As yet, no cases concerning advertising have arisen in the English courts in the post-*Keck* era. English courts, however, seem more than ready and willing to exclude the application of Article 28 (ex Article 30) EC Treaty under the criteria laid down in *Keck*. Two examples of this attitude can be found in *R v Luton Borough Council, ex parte Mirza* and in *Stedman v Hogg Robinson Travel Agents*. In the first case, the Queen's Bench Division held that technical specifications for manufacturing taxis did not offend Article 28 (ex Article 30) as they applied to all traders in the UK and affected the marketing of domestic products in the same way as those from other states. This argument was supported by a reference to the *Keck* ruling, as (mis)understood by the English court.

In the other case, an argument based on the incompatibility of UK Sunday Trading legislation with Article 28 (ex Article 30) EC Treaty was readily rejected (without further enquiry) by Hoffmann LJ in the Court of Appeal on grounds that 'the European Court has told us that Article 30 (new Article 28) EC Treaty does not apply and there is no other basis that I can see upon which Sunday trading could come within the scope of European law at all'.

CASE LAW REFERENCES

R v the Royal Pharmaceutical Society of Great Britain, ex parte API [1989] ECR 1295; *R v Luton Borough Council, ex parte Mirza* (judgments of 4 November 1994, 5 February 1995, Lexis); *Stedman v Hogg Robinson Travel Agents* (judgment of 27 October 1994, Lexis).

LITERATURE REFERENCE

D Chalmers 'Repackaging the Internal Market—The Ramifications of the *Keck* Judgment', (1994) *European Law Review* 385; FS Hakura 'The Weakening Impact of Article 30 on Advertising' (1988) *Entertainment Law Review* 170; S Weatherill 'After Keck: some thoughts on how to clarify the clarification' (1996) *Common Market Law Review* 885; M Jarvis *The Application of EC Law by National Courts* (1998) 118–132. On *Royal Pharmaceutical Society's rules of conduct: Medicines, Ethics and Practice: a guide for Pharmacists Issue*, n 21, January 1999, The Pharmaceutical Press.

PN

3. *Germany*

The judgment in *Hünermund* was published in most of the well-known German journals but hardly played an independent role in academic articles. Rather, it stood in the shadow of *Keck* and mainly served to assist in the interpretation of the change in case law introduced by *Keck*. Many court decisions deal with both *Keck* and *Hünermund* together. Judgments of the German courts referring to *Hünermund* alone are difficult to find (eg *Oberlandesgericht* Nürnberg (Higher Regional Court) judgment of 18 August 1994 on the compatibility of the *Rabattgesetzes* (Discount Law) with Article 28 (ex Article 30) EC Treaty). The *Verwaltungsgerichtshof* Baden-Württemberg (Higher Administrative Court) which had referred the *Hünermund* case to the ECJ decided against the pharmacists after it had received the answer to its question (ruling of 18 April 1994). The *Hünermund* judgment therefore did not cause any changes in German law but on the contrary left the strict competition law regarding pharmacies untouched. This demonstrates the limited effect of the principle of the free movement of goods on the laws of the Member States. It allows the Member States great freedom in the development of their legal systems by means of laws which have little influence on cross-border trade.

CASE LAW REFERENCES

Verwaltungsgerichtshof Baden-Württemberg ruling of 18 April 1994 (1994) *Die öffentliche Verwaltung* 831; Oberlandesgericht Nürnberg judgment of 18 August 1994 (1995) *Europäisches Wirtschafts-und Steuerrecht* 53.

LITERATURE REFERENCES

T Ackermann 'Warenverkehrsfreiheit und "Verkaufsmodalitäten"' (1994) *Recht der Internationalen Wirtschaft* 189; W Möschel (1994) *Neue Juristische Wochenschrift* 782 (Casenote on *Hünermund*); M Petschke 'Die Warenverkehrsfreiheit in der neuesten Rechtsprechung des EuGH' (1994) *Europäische Zeitschrift für Wirtschaftsrecht* 107.

HS-N

4. France

French writers have only paid marginal attention to the judgment in *Hünermund*; it is normally only mentioned in connection with *Keck*. There are very few references made to *Hünermund* in the published decisions of French courts. This can be due to the fact that the decisions of French courts are not normally published (for example, the *Hünermund* judgment is mentioned in the unpublished Opinion to the judgment of the *Conseil d'État* of 7 July 1995). *Hünermund* demonstrates that the reception of the ECJ's decisions in individual Member States can also depend on the degree to which the Member States are dependent on the outcome of the case. As a rule the European cases which attract the most interest are those which are either of great importance to the development of Community law or which threaten to change the domestic legal system. The latter case arises when the submission originates from the interested state itself, or, for example, in proceedings where the breach of the EC Treaty is alleged against the state which is a party to the action. As far as France is concerned, the judgment in *Hünermund* fulfilled none of these criteria.

CASE LAW REFERENCES

Conseil d'État judgment of 7 July 1995 (1995) *Recueil des dÉcisions du Conseil d'État* 287 (see M Jarvis 'The Application of EC Law by National Courts' *The Free Movement of Goods* (1998) 124).

LITERATURE REFERENCES

F Picod 'La nouvelle approche de la Cour de justice en matière d'entraves aux échanges' (1998) *Revue trimestrielle de droit européen* 169.

BD

5. *Italy*

For comments on misleading advertising and case law see *Nissan*: Case no 5 in this Casebook.

6. *Austria*

After the *Oberster Gerichtshof* (Supreme Court) had used the principles of *Keck* in the case *Computerkurse I* to justify the strict standards in Austrian consumer protection (see the Austrian Commentary to *Keck*: Case no 7 in this Casebook), it utilised *Hünermund* to clarify the concept of 'selling arrangements'.

Pursuant to § 59 of the Austrian Pharmaceuticals Law (*AMG*), pharmaceuticals may generally only be sold to the end consumer from pharmacies. After an Austrian chain of chemist shops had sold garlic capsules produced in Germany outside its shops, an Austrian Pharmaceuticals Organisation sued them. The *Oberster Gerichtshof* (judgment of 19 September 1995) questioned whether § 59 *AMG* was compatible with Article 28 (ex Article 30) EC Treaty. It confirmed that it was and in the process referred to *Hünermund* and *Commission v Greece* (ECJ [1995] ECR I–1621). It stated that this rule constituted a 'selling arrangement' within the meaning of *Keck* which did not infringe Article 28 (ex Article 30) EC Treaty. The Court held this to be so obvious that it rendered the request for a preliminary ruling from the ECJ redundant (*Knoblauch-Kapseln*).

The *Oberster Gerichtshof* also regarded the provisions of the Austrian Opening Times Law (*Bundesgesetzblatt* 1992 no 50) as a selling arrangement within the meaning of *Keck* (judgment of 12 November 1996). The court did refer to the ECJ's decisions in *Punto Casa* (ECJ [1994] ECR I–2355), *Tankstation* (ECJ [1994] ECR I–2199) and *Semerano Casa* (ECJ [1996] ECR I–2975) (*Öffnungszeiten*). The *Oberster Gerichtshof* doubted whether the Austrian Opticians Provisions (§ 94(64)) and § 96 of the Austrian Trade Law (*Gewerbeordnung, Bundesgesetzblatt* 1994, no 194) constituted 'selling arrangements' (ruling of 7 October 1997). These provisions state that the sale of prescription glasses is only permitted by opticians who have the necessary license to trade. According to the facts in the preliminary proceedings, a warehouse chain sold ready made-reading spectacles imported from Germany by way of self-service. This infringed the Opticians Provisions. The *Oberster Gerichtshof* considered that opticians may be more interested in selling spectacles which had been produced by themselves (and therefore also more expensive) than cheap ready-made reading glasses. The Opticians Provisions therefore affected domestic and foreign products certainly in a legal sense, but possibly not in a factual sense in the same way; the glasses produced by the opticians themselves were manufactured within the domestic market, whilst the ready-made glasses originated at least in part from outside Austria. The *Oberster Gerichtshof* therefore decided to make a reference to the ECJ. The proceedings were however subsequently struck from the register. Obviously, the parties reached an out-of-court settlement.

A further application for a preliminary ruling was made by the *Oberster Gerichtshof* concerning § 53a of the Trade Law (ruling of 30 June 1998). According to this provision, grocers are only able to offer their goods for sale 'when moving around from place to place or from house to house' if they own a fixed business premises in the relevant administrative area (or immediately neighbouring it) which also offers these goods. The issue therefore concerned the control of certain kinds of marketing arrangements which, from a purely legal point of view, affected domestic and foreign grocers to the same degree. Even so, the *Oberster Gerichtshof* suspected that 'hidden restriction' on trade and thereby an infringement of Article 28 (ex Article 30) EC Treaty could be detected, because the provision in real terms was clearly more likely to present an obstacle to businesspersons from other Member States, who generally would only rarely own a branch in the relevant Austrian administrative district (*Tiefkühl-Heimservice I*). The ECJ found the latter to be true and ruled that the provision does not fall within the definition of 'selling arrangement' laid down by *Keck*. It therefore infringes Article 28 (ex Article 30) EC Treaty (ECJ judgment of 13 January 2000 Case C–254/98).

Interestingly the facts of this case concern a purely domestic matter. The *Oberster Gerichtshof* nevertheless took the view in its reasoning that the question of whether § 53a of the Trade Law conforms to Community law is of crucial importance. Domestic discrimination, ie a worsening of the position of Austrian business persons towards their competitors from other Member States would infringe the right to equality contained in Austria's constitutional law. In other words, if § 53a of the Trade Law could no longer be applied against businesspersons from foreign EU States due to its incompatibility with Community law then it could no longer be cited against Austrian business persons—otherwise it would infringe the principle of equality in the Austrian Constitution. Consequently the *Oberster Gerichtshof* has submitted an application for nullification of § 54a *Gewerbeordnung* to the *Verfassungsgerichtshof* (Constitutional Court). The case is still pending. It can be expected, however, that § 54a will be made void.

CASE LAW REFERENCES

Oberster Gerichtshof *Knoblauch-Kapseln* judgment of 19 September 1995 (1996) *Österreichische Blätter für gewerblichen Rechtsschutz und Urheberrecht* 88; Oberster Gerichtshof *Öffnungszeiten* judgment of 12 November 1996 *Sammlung der Entscheidungen des Obersten Gerichtshofes in Zivilsachen* 69/250; Oberster Gerichtshof *Augenoptiker* judgment of 7 October 1997 (1997) *Wirtschaftsrechtliche Blätter* 527; Oberster Gerichtshof *Tiefkühl-Heimservice I* judgment of 30 June 1998 (1998) *Wirtschaftsrechtliche Blätter* 461; Oberster Gerichtsho *Tiefkühl-Heimservice II* judgment of 1 February 2000 (2000) *Österreichische Blätter für gewerblichen Rechtsschutz und Urheberrecht* 191.

LITERATURE REFERENCES

F Leidenmühler 'Warenverkehrsfreiheit im Wandel der Judikatur' (2000) *Wirtschaftsrechtliche Blätter* 245; P Lewisch/K Hornbanger 'Neues von der Warenverkehrsfreiheit'

(2000) *Recht der Wirtschaft* 334; M Tüchler 'Apothekenmonopol für Säuglingsmilch und freier Warenverkehr' (1995) *Wirtschaftsrechtliche Blätter* 526.

AE

CASE NO. 9 — *Mars C–470/93*

Verein gegen Unwesen in Handel und Gewerbe Köln eV v Mars GmbH
[1995] ECR I–1923

A. Judgment of the ECJ of 6 July 1995

1. Held

Article 30 of the EC Treaty is to be interpreted as precluding a national measure from prohibiting the importation and marketing of a product lawfully marketed in another Member State, the quantity of which was increased during a short publicity campaign and the wrapping of which bears the marking '+ 10%',

a) on the ground that that presentation may induce the consumer into thinking that the price of the goods offered is the same as that at which the goods had previously been sold in their old presentation,

b) on the ground that the new presentation gives the impression to the consumer that the volume and the weight of the product have been considerably increased.

2. Facts of the Case

The *Landgericht* Köln (Regional Court, Cologne) requested a preliminary ruling from the Court under Article 177 (new Article 234) EC Treaty a question relating to the interpretation of Article 30 (new Article 28) EC Treaty. The question was raised in proceedings between an association for combating unfair competition, the Verein gegen Unwesen in Handel und Gewerbe Köln e.V., and Mars GmbH (hereafter 'Mars') concerning the use of a certain presentation for the marketing of ice-cream bars of the Mars, Snickers, Bounty and Milky Way brands. Mars imported those goods from France where they are lawfully produced and packaged by an undertaking belonging to the American group, Mars Inc.,

McLean, in a uniform presentation for distribution throughout Europe. At the material time, the ice-cream bars were presented in wrappers marked '+ 10%'. That presentation had been chosen as part of a short publicity campaign covering the whole of Europe during which the quantity of each product was increased by 10 per cent.

Under § 1 of the Law against Unfair Competition (*Gesetz gegen den unlauteren Wettbewerb*, hereafter 'the *UWG*' (*UWG, Reichsgesetzblatt* 1909, 499, amended inter alia, *Bundesgesetzblatt* I 1969, 633)) proceedings may be brought in order to restrain improper competitive practices while under § 3 of that law proceedings may be brought in order to restrain the use of misleading information (§ 3 *UWG* reproduced above in the German commentary to *Nissan*: Case no 5 in this Casebook). Furthermore, under § 15 of the Law against Restraints of Competition (*Gesetz gegen Wettbewerbsbeschränkungen*, hereafter 'the *GWB*' (*GWB Bundesgesetzblatt* I 1957 1081)), agreements between undertakings restricting the freedom of one of the parties to fix prices in contracts concluded with third parties for the supply of goods are void.

The Verein gegen Unwesen in Handel und Gewerbe Köln e.V. brought proceedings under those provisions before the *Landgericht* Köln in order to prevent the '+ 10%' marking from being used in Germany. It contended first of all that the consumer was bound to assume that the advantage indicated by the '+ 10%' marking was granted without any price increase, since a product whose composition was only slightly changed and which was sold at a higher price offered no advantage. So, in order not to mislead the consumer, the retailer should have maintained the final price previously charged. Since the marking in question had been binding on the retail trade as regarded the fixing of the price for sale to the ultimate consumer, it constituted a breach of § 15 *GWB* which had to be brought to an end in accordance with § 1 *UWG*.

Secondly, the plaintiff in the main proceedings contended that the way in which the '+ 10%' marking was incorporated in the presentation gave the consumer the impression that the product had been increased by a quantity corresponding to the coloured part of the new wrapping. The coloured part occupied considerably more than ten percent of the total surface area of the wrapping and this, in the plaintiff's view, was misleading and therefore contrary to § 3 *UWG*.

In interlocutory proceedings the *Landgericht* Köln had, by order of 10 December 1992, granted an interim restraining order against the defendant. The *Landgericht* took the view that the presentations in question, conveying the idea that more of the product, negligible in quantitative terms, was being offered without any increase in price, restricted freedom of retail trade in the matter of the fixing of prices. When it came to rule on the substance of the case, the *Landgericht* Köln decided to refer the following question to the Court:

Is it compatible with the principles of the free movement of goods to prohibit the marketing in a Member State of ice-cream snacks in a particular presentation which are produced in another Member State and lawfully marketed there in that same presentation, which is described in the application,

1. on the ground that the (new) presentation is liable to give consumers the impression that the goods are offered for the same price as under the old presentation,

2. on the ground that the visual presentation of the new feature '+ 10% ice-cream' gives consumers the impression that either the volume or the weight of the product has been considerably increased?

3. *Extract from the Grounds of the ECJ's Judgment*

Applicability of Article 30 of the Treaty

11. The first question to be examined is whether a prohibition of the marketing of goods bearing on their packaging a publicity marking such as that in question in the main proceedings constitutes a measure having an effect equivalent to a quantitative restriction within the meaning of Article 30 of the Treaty.

12. According to the case law of the Court, Article 30 is designed to prohibit any trading rules of Member States which are capable of hindering, directly or indirectly, actually or potentially, intra-Community trade (see the judgment in Case 8/74 *Procureur du Roi v Dassonville* [1974] ECR 837, paragraph 5). The Court has held that, in the absence of harmonization of legislation, obstacles to the free movement of goods that are the consequence of applying, to goods coming from other Member States where they are lawfully manufactured and marketed, rules that lay down requirements to be met by such goods, such as those relating, for example, to their presentation, labelling and packaging, are prohibited by Article 30, even if those rules apply without distinction to national products and to imported products (judgment in Joined Cases C–267/91 and C–268/91 *Keck and Mithouard* [1993] ECR I–6097, paragraph 15).

13. Although it applies to all products without distinction, a prohibition such as that in question in the main proceedings, which relates to the marketing in a Member State of products bearing the same publicity markings as those lawfully used in other Member States, is by nature such to hinder intra-Community trade. It may compel the importer to adjust the presentation of his products according to the place where they are to be marketed and consequently to incur additional packaging and advertising costs.

14. Such a prohibition therefore falls within the scope of Article 30 of the Treaty.

The grounds of justification relied on

15. It is settled law that obstacles to intra-Community trade resulting from disparities between provisions of national law must be accepted in so far as such provisions may be justified as being necessary in order to satisfy overriding requirements relating, *inter alia,* to consumer protection and fair trading. However, in order to be permissible, such provisions must be proportionate to the objective pursued and that objective must be incapable of being achieved by measures which are less restrictive of intra-Community trade (see the judgments in Case 120/78 *Rewe-Zentral* [1979] ECR 649; Case C–238/89 *Pall* [1990] ECR I–4827 paragraph 12; and Case C–126/91 *Yves Rocher* [1993] ECR I–2361 paragraph 12).

16. It is contended in the main proceedings that the prohibition is justified on two legal grounds, which are indicated in the first and second parts of the preliminary question.

The consumer' s expectation that the price previously charged is being maintained

17. It is argued that the '+ 10%' marking may lead the consumer to think that the 'new' product is being offered at a price identical to that at which the 'old' product was sold.

18. As the Advocate-General points out in paragraphs 39 to 42 of his Opinion, on the assumption that the consumer expects the price to remain the same, the referring court considers that the consumer could be the victim of deception within the meaning of paragraph 3 of the UWG and that if the price did not increase the offer would meet the consumer's expectation but then a question would arise concerning the application of paragraph 15 of the GWB, which prohibits manufacturers from imposing prices on retailers.

19. As regards the first possibility, it must be observed first of all that Mars has not actually profited from the promotional campaign in order to increase its sale prices and that there is no evidence that retailers have themselves increased their prices. In any case, the mere possibility that importers and retailers might increase the price of the goods and that consequently consumers may be deceived is not sufficient to justify a general prohibition which may hinder intra-Community trade. That fact does not prevent the Member States from taking action, by appropriate measures, against duly proved actions which have the effect of misleading consumers.

20. As regards the second possibility, the principle of freedom of retail trade in the matter of the fixing of prices, provided for by a system of national law, and intended in particular to guarantee the consumer genuine price competition, may not justify an obstacle to intra-Community trade such as that in question in the main proceedings. The constraint imposed on the retailer not to increase his prices is in fact favourable to the consumer. It does not arise from any contractual stipulation and has the effect of protecting the consumer from being misled in any way. It does not prevent retailers from continuing to charge different prices and applies only during the short duration of the publicity campaign in question.

The visual presentation of the '+ 10%' marking and its alleged misleading effect.

21. It is accepted by all the parties that the '+ 10%' marking is accurate in itself.

22. However, it is contended that the measure in question is justified because a not insignificant number of consumers will be induced into believing, by the band bearing the '+ 10%' marking, which occupies more than 10% of the total surface area of the wrapping, that the increase is larger than that represented.

23. Such a justification cannot be accepted.

24. Reasonably circumspect consumers may be deemed to know that there is not necessarily a link between the size of publicity markings relating to an increase in a product's quantity and the size of that increase.

25. The reply to the preliminary question must therefore be that Article 30 of the Treaty is to be interpreted as precluding a national measure from prohibiting the importation and marketing of a product lawfully marketed in another Member State, the quantity of which was increased during a short publicity campaign and the wrapping of which bears the marking '+ 10%',

(a) on the ground that that presentation may induce the consumer into thinking that the price of the goods offered is the same as that at which the goods had previously been sold in their old presentation,

(b) on the ground that the new presentation gives the impression to the consumer that the volume and weight of the product have been considerably increased.

B. Commentary

1. European Law

The judgment in *Mars* clearly demonstrates (more so than previous decisions) that the ECJ is guided by the concept of the reasonably circumspect consumer (*verständiger Verbraucher, consommateur raisonablement avisé* paragraph 24). According to the *Landgericht* Köln (which referred the questions to the Court), the marking '+10%', which took up about one quarter of the wrapping was misleading, inter alia, because it could give the impression to a significant number of consumers that the enlargement of the ice-cream bar was greater than 10 per cent. The ECJ dismissed this consideration almost brusquely:

Reasonably circumspect consumers may be deemed to know that there is not necessarily a link between the size of publicity markings relating to an increase in a product's quantity and the size of that increase (*Mars* paragraph 24).

This image of the consumer limits the possibilities for Member States to use more extensive measures in order to protect the 'not reasonably circumspect' consumers, if such measures contain obstacles to the free movement of goods governed by Article 28 (ex Article 30) EC Treaty. The judgment in *Mars* clearly demonstrates that rules relating to the packaging of products even after the new case law introduced by the judgment in *Keck* (ECJ [1993] ECR I–6097: Case no 7 in this Casebook) fall within the ambit of Article 28 (ex Article 30) EC Treaty. Such measures therefore require, pursuant to the *Cassis de Dijon* decision (ECJ [1979] ECR 649: Case no 3 in this Casebook), justification on the basis of mandatory requirements. Consumer protection may, as the ECJ stressed once again in *Mars*, be considered as justifying restrictions on the free movement of goods only if they are 'proportionate to the objective pursued' (paragraph 15). With the judgment in *Mars*, the ECJ has made clear that it will tolerate Member States' measures relating to consumer protection which present obstacles to trade only if they serve to protect the 'reasonably circumspect' consumer. In other words, the Member States may not take measures to protect 'not reasonably circumspect' or merely inattentive consumers.

This served to strengthen the ECJ's tendency to impose an obligation on the consumer to take responsibility for protecting his own interests. The consumer, who has a right to information (ECJ *GB-INNO* [1990] ECR I–667; *Yves Rocher* [1993] ECR I–2361: Case no 6 in this Casebook), must also take note of this information and consider it. The ECJ has in the past used inconsistent wording in its case law to describe these requirements. For example, the 'average consumer' (ECJ *Schott-Zwiesel* [1994] ECR I–3879, paragraph 18), the 'especially well-informed purchaser' (usually in the auctions) (ECJ *Boscher* [1991] ECR I–2023 paragraph 20). The ECJ seems to have settled on one description: the 'average consumer who is reasonably well informed and reasonably observant and circumspect' (*Gut Springenheide* [1998] ECR I–4657 paragraph 31: Case no 17 in this Casebook; *Sektkellerei Kessler* [1999] ECR I–513, paragraph 36; *Lancaster* [2000] ECR I–117 paragraph 27; *Darbo* [2000] ECR I–2297 paragraph 20; *Cidrerie Ruwet* [2000] ECR I–8749).

This image of the consumer also leaves room to acknowledge consumer groups in special need of protection (see also *Aragonesa de Publicidad Exterior*: Case no. 4 in this Casebook and ECJ, *Konsumentombudsmannen* [2001] ECR I–1795). In *Buet* the ECJ left intact a French prohibition on doorstep selling of teaching material because this method of marketing was aimed at 'a category of people who, for one reason or another, are behind in their education' and who are therefore 'particularly vulnerable' (ECJ *Buet* [1989] ECR 1235 paragraph 13). The question could also have been raised in *Mars* whether similar considerations would not have been appropriate in respect of children and teenagers, who probably make up a large number of such customers. On the other hand, it could be argued that the actual economic interest of consumers were only marginally affected by the low-priced ice cream bars.

ECJ CASE LAW REFERENCES

Cassis de Dijon [1979] ECR 649: Case no 3 in this Casebook; *Buet* [1989] ECR 1235; *GB-INNO* [1990] ECR I–667; *Boscher* [1991] ECR I–2023; *Yves Rocher* [1993] ECR I–2361: Case no 6 in this Casebook; *Keck* [1993] ECR I–6097: Case no 7 in this Casebook; *Schott-Zwiesel* [1994] ECR I–3879; *Gut Springenheide* [1998] ECR I–4657: Case no 17 in this Casebook; *Sektkellerei Kessler* [1999] ECR I–513; *Lancaster* [2000] ECR I–117; *Darbo* [2000] ECR I–2297; *Cidrerie Ruwet* [2000] ECR I–8749; *Konsummentombudsmannen* [2001] ECR I–1795.

LITERATURE REFERENCES

C Berr (1996) *Journal du droit international* 503 (Casenote on *Mars*); M Mok (1995) *TVVS ondernemingsrecht en rechtspersonen* 340 (Casenote on *Mars*); R Streinz/S Leible '10 per cent mehr Eiskrem für alle!' (1995) *Zeitschrift für Wirtschaftsrecht* 1236.

HS-N/JJ

2. England & Wales

In the English courts, the issue of the allegedly misleading chocolate wrapper would be assessed in light of the law relating to trade description and price.

In the first place, the word '+10%' affixed on the wrapper could be considered as an indication of the quantity or size of the good and therefore fall within the definition of trade description of the Trade Description Act 1968 (see sections 2, 3 and 4); if false or misleading, such a trade description would constitute an offence under section 1 of the Act, unless the defendant could bring himself within one of the specified defences provided by the Act.

Whether the indication '+10%' would be considered by an English judge as 'misleading' on the two grounds put forward by the plaintiff in the case referred to the ECJ cannot be easily determined; nor has any case arisen in the English courts concerning the compatibility of Article 28 (ex Article 30) EC Treaty and national rules on presentation of goods, such as the Trade Description Act 1968.

Promotional indications on chocolate bar wrappers, however, were the subject of proceedings in the Queen's Bench Division a few years ago. In *Cadbury Ltd. v Halliday* the appellants' chocolate wrappers had the words 'extra value' printed on them in order to indicate that more chocolate was supplied for the same price. After a few months the wrappers were discontinued and cheaper bars were introduced. For a period, the bars were available in both old and new wrappers, but the bars in the old wrappers no longer represented additional value. It was alleged that this constituted an offence under section 1 of the Trade Description Act. The Queen's Bench Division held that the word 'extra value' could not be a trade description as the meaning of it did not necessarily denote extra weight: while it was clear that extra weight was the explanation why the wrappers were originally introduced, it was doubtful whether that could be the only and obvious meaning of the two words: accordingly, no offence had been committed.

In the second place, the allegation that consumers would think that the price of the goods offered for sale is the same at which the goods had previously been sold could be considered as a pricing offence under section 20 of the Consumer Protection Act 1987. According to section 2.1(e) of the Act, a misleading price indication is, *inter alia*, one where the facts or circumstances by reference to which consumers might reasonably be expected to judge the validity of any relevant comparison made or implied by the indication are not what in fact they are: that is to say, the consumer reading a certain indication gains an incorrect impression of what is being offered or of the comparison being suggested by the indication.

CASE LAW REFERENCES

Cadbury v Halliday [1975] 2 *All England Reports* 226.

LITERATURE REFERENCES

CJ Miller/B Harvey/D Parry *Consumer and Trading Law* (1998) 601–71; D Oughton/ J Lowry *Textbook on Consumer Law* (1997) 441–64 and 486–506.

PN

3. Germany

The *Mars* case once again highlights the stark differences in the concepts of the consumer employed by German competition law and Community law. According to the *Landgericht* Köln (ruling of 11 November 1993) the marketing of ice-cream bars with the marking '+10%' infringed the German law on competition in several ways. One of these infringements lay in the fact that the highlighted area on the wrapper upon which the information '+10%' was printed was considerably greater than one tenth of the wrapper. This led the *Landgericht* to take the view that a significant number of consumers would assume that the area marked in colour designated the additional amount of the product in terms of weight and volume. The *Landgericht's* opinion of the consumer was expressed in the comment that the consumer would be accustomed to the graphic explanation of verbal statements and would have—literally—'no cause to consider the information critically'. The *Landgericht* regarded this contrast between the visual presentation and verbal statements as misleading according to § 3 of the Law against Unfair Competition (*UWG*, text from § 3 is reproduced above in the German commentary *Nissan*: Case no 5 in this Casebook).

In analysing German law, the ECJ stated that Article 28 (ex Article 30) EC Treaty did not allow restrictions to be imposed on the free movement of goods for the purposes of consumer protection which went too far. The German practice of assuming a deception contrary to § 3 *UWG* in the case of a 'not inconsiderable number' (approximately 10–15 per cent) of misled consumers came into question. The small number of misled consumers needed in order for the assumption to arise was not tenable in the long run (see *Baumbach/Hefermehl*). The judgment in *Mars* clearly shows the effects of the ECJ's case law on German competition law. In reality this meant that the consumer, lacking in sound judgment, whether due to immaturity, senility, level of education or intellectual ability, could lose some of the protection specifically afforded to him under German competition law. In view of the advantages which the Internal Market and the cross-border trade offer to the consumer, however, these disadvantages can be tolerated.

German courts have attempted to defend the deception presumption against the views expressed by the ECJ (eg *Kammergericht* Berlin judgment of 10 January 1994). The *Mars* case has directly influenced the decision of the *Oberlandesgericht* Karlsruhe of 27 November 1996. The defendant advertised 'Slim-Line Earrings' in a women's magazine. In the publicity material sent on request to those interested, she claimed among other things:

> Die wissenschaftliche Grundlage der Ohrakkupressur (Aurikulartherapie) beruht auf dem Stimulieren der Reflexzonen und den Reflexpunkten am und im Ohr. Ausschlaggebend für diese Theorie ist die Erkenntnis, daß das menschliche Ohr ein Körperreflexzentrum aller Organe darstellt. Durch Stimulation kann die Funktion der einzelnen Organe beeinflußt werden. Der Slim-Line Ohrring beruht auf dieser wissenschaftlichen Erkenntnis. Die Wirkung wird hervorgerufen bzw. ausgelöst durch zwei unterschiedliche Metalle an den Ohrringenden: Gold, nickelfreier Stahl.

Citing § 3 *UWG*, the *Oberlandesgericht* ruled that these claims were misleading. In looking at this case however it remains unclear whether the court used the concept 'casual consumer' or 'reasonably circumspect interested individual'. The *Oberlandesgericht* expressly cited the judgment in *Mars*, stating that a not inconsiderable number of 'reasonably circumspect' (or diligent) consumers would not dismiss the advertising in question as mere 'humbug' straight away; they might therefore believe the advertising complained of or at least have arrived at the assumption that there might possibly 'be something in it'. This case clearly demonstrates how the *Oberlandesgericht* at the very least attempted to comply with the requirements of the ECJ concerning the 'reasonably circumspect' consumer. In several other decisions German courts have relied on the *Mars* case in order to clarify the scope of Article 28 (ex Article 30) EC Treaty (eg *Oberlandesgericht* Stuttgart and judgment of 8 May 1998; *Oberlandesgericht* Dresden, judgment of 6 July 1999).

CASE LAW REFERENCES

Landgericht Köln judgment of 11 November 1993 (1994) *Wettbewerb in Recht und Praxis* 907; Kammergericht (Berlin) judgment of 10 January 1994 (1994) *Europäische Zeitschrift für Wirtschaftsrecht* 541; Oberlandesgericht Karlsruhe judgment of 27

November 1996 (1997) *Neue Juristische Wochenschrift Entscheidungsdienst Wettbewerbsrecht* 174; Oberlandesgericht Stuttgart judgment of 8 May 1998 *Juris*; Oberlandesgericht Dresden judgment of 6 July 1999 (2000) *Gewerblicher Rechtsschutz und Urheberrecht* 88.

LITERATURE REFERENCES

A Baumbach/W Hefermehl *Wettbewerbsrecht* (22nd edn, 2001) Einleitung UWG, no 650–659; R Streinz/ S Leible '10% mehr Eiskrem für alle!' (1995) *Zeitschrift für Wirtschaftsrecht* 1236.

HS-N

4. France

French writers expressed incomprehension at the German law on competition, which classifies an acceptable competitive practice in France as '*contre les bonnes mœurs*' (*Berr*, see the wording of § 1 *UWG*: '*gegen die guten Sitten*'). Misleading advertising is prohibited in France pursuant to the Article L. 121–1 *Code de la Consommation* (text reproduced in the French commentary to the ECJ, *Nissan*: Case no 5 in this Casebook). According to the case law, even statements on the wrapper are capable of amounting to misleading advertising (*Cour d'Appel* Paris judgment of 24 March 1987). The law does not prohibit exaggerated advertisement in the form of a parody or emphasis if it is clear that the exaggeration, assessed according to the ability to differentiate and to reach a judgement of the *consommateur moyen*, is not capable of misleading anyone (*Cour de Cassation* judgment of 21 May 1984). Here the comparison is not the ideal of the '*bon père de famille*' (as in the *Code civil*) who constantly displays a very diligent standard of conduct, but rather the *consommateur moyen*. This concept is dependent on the target group of the advertising message. The concept of the reasonably circumspect/diligent consumer ('*consommateur raisonnablement avisé*') established by the ECJ is seen as identical to the French law concept of the *consommateur moyen* (*Pizzio*).

CASE LAW REFERENCES

Cour de Cassation chambre criminelle judgment of 21 May 1984 (1985) *Recueil Dalloz Sirey* Jurisprudence 105; Cour d'Appel Paris judgment of 24 March 1987 (1987) *Recueil Dalloz Sirey* Informations rapides 103.

LITERATURE REFERENCES

C Berr (1996) *Journal du droit international* 503 (Casenote on *Mars*); J Pizzio (1995) *Recueil Dalloz Sirey* Sommaire 316 (Casenote on *Mars*); A Rigaux/D Simon (1995) *Europe* Commentaires 297 14 (Casenote on *Mars*).

BD

5. Italy

Italian writers have paid little attention to the ECJ's judgment in *Mars*. Some have pointed out that the Court used *Mars* in order to implement its new case law relating to the free movement of goods in the area of advertising. The Court recognised the consequences which would ensue if it had merely transferred its decision in *Keck* to advertising law (*Mengozzi*). An example of a comparable decision of an Italian court is provided by the criminal law decision of the *Pretura* Forlì of 6 July 1988. The company '*Tre Effe di Fondi Claudio & C sad.*' imported a drink under the name of 'McTwo' into Italy. The label stated '*Limonade-Bier-Mix-McTwo*' in German and a picture of a lemon. The *Pretura* considered this to be an infringement of (the since repealed) Article 13 of *Legge* no 283 of 30 April 1962 on *Disciplina igienica della produzione e della vendetta dell sostanze alimentari e dell bevande.* This prohibited misleading advertising for foodstuffs and drinks (for the current state of the law see the Italian commentary to the ECJ, *Gut Springenheide:* Case no 17 in this Casebook). He held that the label was likely to mislead the consumer. In German, the word '*Limonade*' merely meant a fizzy drink and not necessarily a lemonade drink as did '*limonata*' in Italian. The '*figura astratte dell' aquirente di normale intelligenza e prudenza*' (ie the fictional consumer of normal intelligence and diligence) could not be expected to know the exact meaning of the German word '*limonade*'. The *Pretura* took the view that this interpretation of Article 13 of *Legge* no 283 of 1962 did not infringe Article 28 (ex Article 30) EC Treaty, since it protected the consumer from misleading information.

CASE LAW REFERENCES

Pretura di Forlì judgment of 6 July 1988 (1989) *Il Foro italiano* II 562.

LITERATURE REFERENCES

F Capelli 'I malintesi provocati dalla sentenza Cassis de Dijon, vent'anni dopo' (1996) *Diritto Comunitario e degli Scambi Internazionali* 673; L Klesta Dosi (1996) *Nuova Giurisprudenza Civile Commentata* II 166 (Casenote on *Mars*); P Mengozzi 'L'informazione commerciale nel diritto comunitario' (1996) *Contratto e Impresa Europa* 576.

AM

III

Consumer Contract Law

INTRODUCTION

The European Union has passed a number of pieces of legislation relating to consumer contract protection. The most important Directives include those regulating Doorstep Selling (Directive 85/577 OJ 1985 L372/31), Consumer Credit (Directive 87/102 OJ 1987 L42/48 with later amendments), Package Travel (Directive 90/314 OJ 1990 L158/59), Unfair Terms in Consumer Contracts (Directive 93/13 OJ 1993 L95/29), Timeshare (Directive 94/47 OJ 1994 L280/83) and Distance Selling (Directive 97/7 OJ 1997 L144/19), Sale of Consumer Goods (Directive 1999/44 OJ 1999 L171/12) Electronic Commerce (Directive 2000/31 OJ 2000 L178/1). A number of further Directives and Regulations on insurance and banking law, law relating to negotiable instruments and other securities, data protection and telecommunication law contain at least a few consumer contract protection provisions. European consumer contract law is being created which is influencing and complementing the contract law of Member States in various ways.

Despite the many pieces of Community legislation there have been relatively few decisions of the ECJ in this area. The small number of references submitted by the courts is due in part to the fact that a number of these legislative provisions have only been passed very recently. Practitioners are only gradually becoming aware of the extent to which European law is permeating contract law.

The five decisions of the ECJ relating to consumer contract law which are presented here should therefore be regarded as only the tip of an approaching iceberg, particularly since the references are now beginning to mount up. It is indeed no coincidence that three of the decisions chosen deal with one of the oldest Directives in this field, namely the so-called Doorstep Sales Directive 85/577. Of these three judgments one deals with the consequences of failing to implement a Directive (*Dori*: Case no 11 in this Casebook) and two with the ECJ's interpretation of a Directive in cases in which the Directive had been implemented by the Member States concerned (*Di Pinto* and *Dietzinger*: Cases no 10 and no 14 in this Casebook). The other two decisions concern Directives 97/102 (Consumer Credit) and 90/314 (Package Tours). Their facts are once more indicative of the slow progress in harmonising consumer contract law and the significant role of the ECJ in this process. The case *El Corte Inglés* (Case no 12 in this Casebook) concerned the 'horizontal' direct effect of the provision of Directive 87/102 which had not been implemented in Spain. The *Dillenkofer* judgment (Case no 13 in this Casebook) dealt with the question of whether Germany was liable on account of failing to implement Directive 90/314. Some further recent decisions of the ECJ concerning the Consumer Directives are examined in the commentaries.

LITERATURE REFERENCES

S Grundmann *Europäisches Schuldvertragsrecht* (1998); 'G Howells/T Wilhelmsson *EC Consumer Law* (1997) 85–120, 165–258; S Weatherill *EC Consumer Law and Policy* (1997) 76–91; N Reich *Europäisches Verbraucherrecht* (3rd edn 1996) 334–392.

CASE NO. 10 — *Di Pinto* C–361/89

Criminal Proceedings v Patrice di Pinto
[1991] ECR I–1189

A. Judgment of the ECJ of 14 March 1991

1. Held

1. *A trader canvassed with a view to the conclusion of an advertising contract concerning the sale of his business is not to be regarded as a consumer protected by Council Directive 85/577 of 20 December 1985 to protect the consumer in respect of contracts negotiated away from business premises.*

2. *Directive 85/577 does not preclude national legislation on canvassing from extending the protection which it affords to cover traders acting with a view to the sale of their business.*

Article 8 of that Directive, which leaves Member States free to adopt or maintain more favourable provisions to protect consumers in the field covered by the Directive, cannot be interpreted as precluding those States from adopting measures in an area with which it is not concerned, such as that of the protection of traders.

2. Facts of the Case

The *Cour d'Appel* Paris had referred two questions to the court for a preliminary ruling on the interpretation of Directive 85/577 concerning consumer protection in respect of contracts concluded away from business premises (OJ 1985 L372 p 31; hereinafter: 'the Directive'). These questions arose in criminal proceedings against Patrice di Pinto due to his alleged infringement of the French Law no 72–1137 of 22 December 1972 (amended) protecting consumers regarding canvassing and door-to-door selling (hereinafter referred to as 'the Law on Canvassing'). As in the case of Directive 85/577, that Law provides that a consumer who is canvassed may renounce the effects of his undertaking within a period of seven days and that this option must be specified in the contract. The defendant was the manager of the private limited liability company *Groupement de l'Immobilier et du Fonds de Commerce*, which published a periodical entitled '*GI Commerce. Le Partenaire du Commerçant et de la Franchise*' in which businesses are advertised for sale. For the purpose of collecting such advertisements, Mr di Pinto employed representatives to canvass, either at their homes or at their places of business, those traders who had expressed an intention to sell their business during an initial contact by telephone.

On 28 March 1989 the *Tribunal de Grande Instance* Paris, imposed a one year suspended prison sentence on him and a fine of FF 15,000 for having, in July 1985 and during 1986 and 1987, contravened the Law on Canvassing. Although Article 4 of that Law prohibits canvassers from requesting payment in cash before expiry of the seven-day cooling-off period, the contracts concluded by the representatives of the accused in the course of their canvassing were accompanied by immediate payment of the price for the service which varied between FF 3,000 and FF 30,000 depending on the format of the advertisement. In addition, the contracts did not refer to the consumer's right of cancellation during the period of reflection. The accused and the Public Prosecutor both appealed on 4 April 1989 against this judgment to the *Cour d'Appel* Paris. That Court confirmed, by default, the judgment at first instance on the criminal liability of Mr di Pinto and sentenced him to one year's imprisonment and a fine of FF 15,000. On 11 July 1989, Mr di Pinto appealed against the enforcement of that judgment.

According to Article 1, the French Law on Canvassing applies in principle to:

quiconque pratique ou fait pratiquer le démarchage au domicile d'une personne physique, à sa résidence ou à son lieu de travail pour proposer la vente, la location ou la location-vente de marchandises ou d'objets quelconques ou pour offrir des prestations de services.

Article 8(I)(e), however, excludes from the scope of the Law:

les ventes, locations ou locations-ventes de marchandises ou d'objets ou les prestations de services lorsqu' elles sont proposées pour les besoins d'une exploitation agricole, industrielle ou commerciale ou d'une activité professionnelle.

Article 1 of Directive 85/577 provides that it shall apply to:

contracts under which a trader supplies goods or services to a consumer and which are concluded: (. . .)

—during a visit by a trader

i) to the consumer's home or that of another consumer

ii) to the consumer's place of work.

Article 2 provides that:

—'Consumer' a natural person who, in transactions covered by this Directive, is acting for purposes which can be regarded as outside his trade or profession;

—'Trader' a natural or legal person who, for the transaction in question acts in his commercial or professional capacity, and anyone acting in the name or on behalf of a trader.

Being uncertain as to the proper interpretation to be given to the Directive, the *Cour d'Appel* Paris referred the following two questions to the Court of Justice for a preliminary ruling:

1. Is a trader canvassed at home in connection with the sale of his business entitled to the protection accorded to consumers by Directive 85/577?

2. Is Article 8(I)(e) of the Law of 22 December 1972 compatible with the aforementioned Directive and the other provisions of Community Law protecting consumers in case of doorstep canvassing?

3. *Extract from the Grounds of the ECJ's Judgment*

The first question

14. In its first question, the Cour d'Appel de Paris seeks in substance to ascertain whether a trader who is canvassed for the purpose of concluding an advertising contract concerning the sale of his business must be regarded as a consumer entitled to protection under the Directive.

15. It is necessary on this point to refer to Article 2 of the Directive. It follows from that provision that the criterion for the application of protection lies in the connection between the transactions which are the subject of the canvassing and the professional activity of the trader: the latter may claim that the Directive is applicable only if the transaction in respect of which he is canvassed lies outside his trade or profession. Article 2, which is drafted in general terms, does not make it possible, with regard to acts performed in the context of such a trade or profession, to draw a distinction between normal acts and those which are exceptional in nature.

16. Acts which are preparatory to the sale of a business, such as the conclusion of a contract for the publication of an advertisement in a periodical, are connected with the professional activity of the trader although such acts may bring the running of the business to an end, they are managerial acts performed for the purpose of satisfying requirements other than the family or personal requirements of the trader.

17. The Commission, which favours the application of the Directive in such a case, objects that a trader, when canvassed in connection with the sale of his business, finds himself in an unprepared state similar to that of an ordinary consumer. For that reason, it argues, traders ought also to be entitled to the protection which the Directive confers.

18. That argument cannot be accepted. There is every reason to believe that a normally well-informed trader is aware of the value of his business and that of every measure required by its sale, with the result that, if he enters into an undertaking, it cannot be through lack of forethought and solely under the influence of surprise.

19. The answer to the first question must therefore be that a trader canvassed with a view to the conclusion of an advertising contract concerning the sale of his business is not to be regarded as a consumer protected by Directive 85/577.

The second question

20. In its second question, the Cour d'Appel de Paris seeks in substance to ascertain whether the Directive precludes national legislation on canvassing from extending the protection which it affords to cover traders acting with a view to the sale of their business.

21. It should be recalled in this regard that Article 8 of the Directive provides that it 'shall not prevent Member States from adopting or maintaining more favourable provisions to protect consumers in the field which it covers'.

22. The object of that provision is to determine the freedom left to Member States in the area covered by the Directive, namely that of consumer protection. It cannot therefore be interpreted as precluding States from adopting measures in an area with which it is not concerned, such as that of the protection of traders.

23. The answer to the second question must therefore be that the Directive does not preclude national legislation on canvassing from extending the protection which it affords to cover traders acting with a view to the sale of their business.

B. Commentary

1. European Law

The *Di Pinto* decision specifies the concept of the 'consumer' which is defined in Article 2 of Directive 85/577 to protect the consumer in cases of contracts concluded away from business premises (OJ 1985 L372/31). Since most of the consumer Directives relating to contract law contain quite similar terminology, the decision is of fundamental importance for European consumer contract law. In general this is only applicable in transactions between a trader on the one hand and a consumer on the other. Examples of these are Article 1, paragraph 2a of Directive 87/102 (Consumer Credit OJ 1987 L42/48), Article 2b of Directive 93/13 (Unfair Terms in Consumer Contracts OJ 1993 L95/29), Article 2 of Directive 94/47 (Timeshare OJ 1994 L280/83), Article 2(2) of Directive 97/7 (Distance Selling OJ 1997 L158/59), Article 2a of Directive 99/44 (Consumer Sales OJ 1999 L171/12) and Article 2e of Directive 00/31 (E-Commerce OJ 2000 L178/1). In contrast, however, see Article 2(4) of Directive 90/314 (Package Holidays OJ 1990 L158/59), according to which a commercial trade also falls under this Directive. A 'consumer' is, according to the generally accepted definition of the Directive in issue, a natural person who is acting outside his or her trade, business or profession. Patrice di Pinto had sold advertisements to traders in which they offered to sell their businesses. What was doubtful was whether providing such an advertisement could be attributed to the trader's professional or commercial activity (Article 2 Directive 85/577).

The definition of a consumer in Directive 85/577 is in a sense conclusive: one and the same person can be a consumer in one transaction but not in another (as the Advocate-General pointed out in paragraph 19 of his Opinion). The distinction is therefore made not by reference to persons, but by transactions. The transactions entered into by a trader are divided into two kinds: consumer transactions, on the one hand, and transactions where European law offers no consumer protection, on the other. The demarcation between the two areas proved controversial in the *Di Pinto* case.

The European Commission, France and following them the Advocate-General were in favour of more expansive protection. They submitted that even those business transactions of a trader for which he does not possess the special experience and knowledge which would differentiate him from a private individual should be covered by this Directive (see the Opinion of the Advocate-General paragraph 22). This would have resulted in far more comprehensive protection in all commercial transactions which formed part of the business practice but which lay outside the trader's usual sphere of activity. In the case of such an unusual transaction as the sale of the entire business, the trader would then generally be viewed as a 'consumer' and afforded the protection of the Directive.

The Court of Justice however set narrower boundaries. It followed the submission of the British Government. Preparing for the sale of a business forms part of the commercial practice and the trader is not a consumer. The Court of Justice did present its model for transactions which are covered by consumer contract law. A trader only deals as a consumer when he enters into transactions in order to satisfy his ordinary or personal requirements (paragraph 16). The Commission's argument that a trader could be just as unprepared for a transaction with which he is generally unaccustomed as an ordinary consumer (eg the sale of his entire business) was not accepted. The ECJ relied on the 'normally well-informed trader' who does not enter into a transaction without reflection (paragraph 18).

One of the points to consider in this case is that the European Commission and some Member States aimed to extend the protection of the EC Consumer Directive concerning consumer contracts to include certain traders, and above all, smaller self-employed traders. The Advocate-General, who supported this aim, gave as examples butchers, bakers and hotel proprietors (paragraph 21 of the Opinion). The ECJ rejected this argument. The *Di Pinto* decision clearly states that traders only enjoy consumer protection if they trade as private individuals, in particular in order to satisfy their ordinary and personal requirements. This narrow interpretation of 'consumer' has recently been confirmed by the ECJ (*Dietzinger* [1998] ECR I–1199: Case no 14 in this Casebook). In the cases *Bertrand* (ECJ, [1978] ECR 1431: Case no 1 in this Casebook) and *Benincasa* (ECJ [1997] ECR I–3767: Case no 2 in this Casebook) the ECJ has also taken a similarly restrictive interpretation of the term 'consumer' under Article 13 of the Brussels Convention on Jurisdictions and Enforcement relating to judicial decisions in civil and trade matters (European Convention on Jurisdictions and Enforcement OJ 1978 L304/1).

The ECJ makes clear in its answer to the second question, that Community Law does not prevent Member States from extending consumer protection in national law to certain transactions entered into by traders. Article 8 of Directive 85/577 provides a minimum protection and therefore does not only allow Member States the freedom to legislate for higher protection for the 'consumer' (narrowly interpreted according to the *Di Pinto* judgment) than Directive 85/577, but to also include other groups, who are not 'consumers' (according to the Directive).

ECJ CASE LAW REFERENCES

Bertrand [1978] ECR 1431: Case no 1 in this Casebook; *Cassis de Dijon* [1979] ECR 649: Case no 3 in this Casebook; *Benincasa* [1997] ECR I–3767: Case no 2 in this Casebook; *Bayerische Hypotheken- und Wechselbank* [1998] ECR I–119: Case no 14 in this Casebook.

LITERATURE REFERENCES

W Faber 'Elemente verschiedener Verbraucherbegriffe in EG-Richtlinien, zwischen-staatlichen Übereinkommen und nationalem Zivil- und Kollisionsrecht' (1998) *Zeitschrift für Europäisches Privatrecht* 854; K Mortelmans Colportage en minimum-harmonisatie, Kan het Europees consumentenrecht ook handelaren bescherming bieden?' (1991) *Tijdschrift voor Consumentenrecht* 185.

HS-N/JJ

2. *England & Wales*

The United Kingdom participated in the *Di Pinto* proceedings by submitting observations to the European Court of Justice. They expressed the view that a trader canvassed at home in connection with the sale of his business is not entitled to the protection accorded to consumers by Directive 85/577. According to the United Kingdom's argument, a 'consumer' within the meaning of the Directive is a person acting for purposes which can be regarded as outside his trade or profession; the sale of a business, even though it is not a usual or necessary 'day-to-day' activity of a particular trade or profession, can still be regarded as an activity undertaken for the purposes of, rather than outside, that trade or profession. The sale of a business, it added, may be an activity common to all businesses rather than to a particular one, but it is certainly not an activity common to all consumers.

The lack of interest in this case expressed by practitioners and academics in the UK, together with the varied approach of English courts in differing areas of the law to the question of what is done or not 'in the course of a business', makes it difficult to assess the impact of *Di Pinto* on the English legal system. The interpretation of what is done 'in the course of a business' which has most commonly been used by English judges are whether a transaction is integral to the course of a business or, if only incidental to the carrying on of the relevant business, whether there is a degree of regularity in entering into such a transaction. In this respect, the approach taken by the UK in its observations seems to extend the application of such a formula to activities which do not fully respond to concepts such as regularity, incidental sales and integral part of a business.

Directive 85/557 was implemented in the UK by the Consumer Protection (Cancellation of Contracts Concluded Away from Business Premises) Regulations 1987. It defines the consumer as:

> a person, other than a body corporate, who in making a contract to which these Regulations apply, is acting for purposes which can be regarded as outside his business.

Like the Directive, the Regulations do not apply in favour of corporations or partnerships; however, by omitting the requirement that the person is 'natural', the Regulations may go a little further than the Directive as legal persons other than a body corporate (eg associations) may well be entitled to protection.

The Department of Trade and Industry recently noticed that traders had been seeking to avoid the protection given to consumers by the Regulations by getting them to sign a paper on the doorstep selling signifying their willingness to be visited. This is done before they open the negotiation leading to a contract, so that the subsequent visit would appear solicited rather than unsolicited. The Consumer Protection (Cancellation of Contracts Concluded Away from Business Premises) (amendment) Regulations 1998 have accordingly been adopted to close this loophole. The Regulations also amended the principal Regulations, making it an offence for a trader to fail to give the consumer written notice of his right to cancel the contract together with a cancellation form. In this case, however, the amending Regulations also provide for a 'due diligence' defence and for liability of persons other than the principal offender in a number of specified circumstances.

CASE LAW REFERENCES

Stevenson & Anor v Rogers [1999] 2 *Weekly Law Reports* 1064; *Symmons v Cook, New Law Journal* 1981, 758; *Davies v Sumner* [1984] 1 *Weekly Law Reports* 1301; *R & B Customs Brokers v United Dominions Trust Ltd.* [1988] 1 *Weekly Law Reports* 321.

LITERATURE REFERENCES

J De Lacy 'Selling in the course of business under the Sale of Goods Act 1979' (1999) *Modern Law Review* 776; G Howells/S Weatherill *Consumer Protection Law* (1995) 291–295.

PN

3. Germany

The judgment in *Di Pinto* has aroused little interest among German writers. Indeed, it has been published in a few journals only. Despite this, the questions of law raised by this judgment are quite significant for German law. Directive 85/577 has been implemented by the Law on Doorstep Sales (*Gestez über den Widerruf von Haustürgeschäften und ähnlichen Geschäften, Bundesgesetzblatt* I 1986, 122, as amended in *Bundesgesetzblatt* I 2000, 955). A number of courts had recognised relatively early on that this statute must be interpreted in conjunction with the Directive (eg *Oberlandesgericht* Stuttgart (Higher Regional Court) judgment of 8 January 1988; *Landgericht* Frankfurt on Main (Regional Court) judgment of 10 January 1989; *Bundesgerichtshof* (Federal Court of Justice) judgment of 12 June 1991; *Oberlandesgericht* Koblenz, ruling of 9 February 1994). The Law on Doorstep Sales grants consumers the right to revoke transactions which have been concluded 'on the doorstep' and under similar circumstances. The question whether business persons also enjoy such protection in the case of doorstep sales is now governed in the amended § 1 Law on Doorstep Sales (*Bundesgesetzblatt* I 2000, 955).

> Einem Verbraucher steht ein Widerrufsrecht nach § 361a des Bürgerlichen Gesetzbuchs bei Verträgen mit einem Unternehmer zu, . . .

The term '*Verbraucher*' (consumer) is defined in § 13 Civil Code (*BGB*; printed above in the German Commentary to *Benincasa*: Case no 2 in this Casebook). According to this new law a business person is only protected under the Law on Doorstep Sales if he or she is a '*Verbraucher*'.

As the legislator only wanted to change the terminology but not the substance of the law, the court decisions before the amendment in 2000 are still valid. The former version of § 6 no 1 of the Law on Doorstep Sales stated:

> Anwendungsbereich. Die Vorschriften dieses Gesetzes finden keine Anwendung,
>
> 1. wenn der Kunde den Vertrag in Ausübung einer selbständigen Erwerbstätigkeit abschließt (. . .).

Therefore, whoever acts in 'the course of a business' does not have a right of cancellation pursuant to the Law on Doorstep Sales. The interpretation of this requirement for protection was clarified by the judgment of the *Bundesgerichtshof* (Federal Court of Justice) of 4 May 1994. A married couple, who ran a small bakery concluded a leasing agreement with a visiting representative in their shop. They leased a coffee machine and table for the purpose of giving customers visiting their shop free coffee. The next day they revoked the contract on the basis of the Law on Doorstep Sales. The *Landgericht* and *Oberlandesgericht* held that the Law on Doorstep Sales was applicable and accordingly, that the cancellation was valid. The *Oberlandesgericht* submitted, inter alia, that (the former) § 6 no 1 of the Law on Doorstep Sales referred to transactions which were directly connected with the business currently being carried on. This was not the case where a coffee machine was hired in order to start a new, additional business activity. The condition of 'direct connection' is strongly reminiscent of the '*rapport direct*' in French law (see the French Commentary to this case below).

On appeal to the *Bundesgerichtshof* (4 May 1994) the court decided against the bakers. Paragraph 6 no 1 the Law on Doorstep Sales was not applicable if a customer who was a self-employed business person concluded the contract with a view to commencing a new and different kind of business. Due to the fact that this provision was designed for typical cases it did not come down to the question of whether the self-employed business consumer appeared in need of protection due to his inexperience or clearly being caught unawares. This is a judgment along the lines of decision of the ECJ in *Di Pinto* without actually mentioning the connection. German law in principle therefore grants no protection to business persons in the case of doorstep sales. In this respect German law follows Directive 85/577, but not French law. In contrast however, transactions which are concluded by employees with the intention of starting a self-employed activity were in some cases decided under the Law on Doorstep Sales (eg *Oberlandesgericht* Karlsruhe judgment of 11 May 1993; but different *Oberlandesgericht* Nürnberg judgment of 17 January 1995). After the 2000 amendment of the Law on Doorstep Sales this jurisprudence which was backed by the wording of the former § 6 no 1, is no longer good law.

CASE LAW REFERENCES

Oberlandesgericht Stuttgart judgment of 8 January 1988 (1988) *NJW–Rechtsprechungsreport Zivilrecht* 558; Landgericht Frankfurt on Main judgment of 10 January 1989, (1989) *NJW–Rechtsprechungsreport Zivilrecht* 824; Bundesgerichtshof judgment of 12 June 1991 (1991) *Der Betrieb* 2237; Oberlandesgericht Karlsruhe judgment of 11 May 1993 (1993) *NJW–Rechtsprechungsreport Zivilrecht* 1274; Oberlandesgericht Koblenz ruling of 9 February 1994 (1994) *Neue Juristische Wochenschrift* 1418; Bundesgerichtshof judgment of 4 May 1994 (1994) *Neue Juristische Wochenschrift* 2759; Oberlandesgericht Nürnberg judgment of 17 January 1995 (1995) *Wertpapiermitteilungen* 481.

LITERATURE REFERENCES

W Faber 'Elemente verschiedener Verbraucherbegriffe in EG-Richtlinien, zwischen-staatlichen Übereinkommen und nationalem Zivil-und Kollisionsrecht' (1998) *Zeitschrift für Europäisches Privatrecht* 854; P Mankowski (1998) *Juristenzeitung* 898 (Casenote on *Benincasa*).

HS-N

4. France

The French government submitted before the ECJ that Directive 85/577 also protects business persons who advertise the sale of their business premises. This argument therefore attempted to interpret the term 'consumer' in such a way that the result correlated with the legal situation in France. The ECJ chose not to follow this line of argument. Instead it held that the French law was compatible with the Directive on the basis of Article 8 (paragraph 21). This did not alter the plight of the accused, di Pinto, who was prosecuted (*Cour de Cassation* judgment of 26 May 1993).

The protection of the consumer when concluding transactions away from business premises was governed by French law no 72–1137 of 22 December 1972 *relative à la protection des consommateurs en matière de démarchage et de vente à domicile.* The law formed the basis of the decision in *Di Pinto.* According to Article 8(1)(e) transactions which were concluded in the course of an agricultural or commercial business or a professional activity were excluded from the ambit of the law (the wording of the law is reproduced above in the facts of the case). Taking the literal meaning of this text it appeared that even di Pinto's advertisements were displayed in the course of his business. The *Cour de Cassation* had extended the protection of the Law no 72–1137 to include business persons who acted outside their area of professional experience (eg judgment of 15 April 1982; for further examples see the French commentary to the ECJ, *Benincasa:* Case no 2 in this Casebook). The French courts in the *Di Pinto* case which referred the matter to the ECJ also decided along the same lines. The provisions on doorstep sales and similar contracts have in the meantime been adapted to the case law of the ECJ. They are now contained in Articles L 121–21 to L 121–33 *Code de la Consommation.* The area of application has now been drawn considerably wider. According to L 121–22(2) no 4 *Code de la Consommation* the rules for doorstep sales are not to be applied if they are directly connected to a commercial activity:

Ne sont pas soumis aux dispositions des articles L 121–23 à L 121–28:

(. . .)

4° Les ventes, locations ou locations-ventes de biens ou les prestations de services lorsqu'elles ont un rapport direct avec les activités exercées dans le cadre d'une exploitation agricole, industrielle, commerciale ou artisanale ou de toute autre profession.

The ECJ's narrow interpretation of the term 'consumer' in Directive 85/577, therefore, to a certain extent at least, contradicts the rather wide definition of the term in the French *Code de la Consommation*. Since the ECJ has expressly confirmed the right of Member States to grant more extensive protection, the judgment in *Di Pinto* has not hindered the statutory broadening of the application of Articles L 121–21 to L 121–28 *Code de la Consommation*. Nevertheless in France, there appears to be a tendency towards a narrower view of protecting the consumer (see *Calais-Auloy/Steinmetz* 8, 9; see also the French commentary to ECJ *Benincasa*: Case no 2 in this Casebook). This development may be strengthened by the ECJ's position in this issue. Due to the Directive's minimum harmonisation measure it cannot be claimed that *Di Pinto* has had an influence on French law on this point.

CASE LAW REFERENCES

Cour de Cassation 1ère chambre civile judgment of 15 April 1982 *Bulletin des arrêts de la Cour de Cassation* chambres civiles 1982 I no 133: (1984) *Recueil Dalloz Sirey* Jurisprudence 439; Cour de Cassation chambre criminelle judgment of 26 May 1993 *Bulletin des arrêts de la Cour de Cassation* chambre criminelle 1993 no 193.

LITERATURE REFERENCES

J Calais-Auloy/F Steinmetz *Droit de la consommation* (4th edn 1996) 8, 93.

BD

5. Italy

The *Di Pinto* judgment did not arouse much interest among Italian legal writers. The major importance of this decision lies in the fact that the ECJ opposed calls to expand the concept of the 'consumer' which had been made by legal writers and in the judgments of national courts (*Succi*, similarly *Luongo*).

Directive 85/577 was implemented in Italy by *Decreto Legge* no 50 of 15 January 1992. The Directive is relatively short in length, containing only 10 grounds and seven articles. The *Decreto Legge*, on the other hand, is no mere transcription but a longer and more complex document. The *Decreto* was enacted about four years too late: the implementation period had expired as early as December 1987. The delay led to the Italian courts attempting to fulfil the aims of the Directive by interpreting existing law (*Tribunale* Rome *Ordinanza* of 17 December 1994; *Pretura* Livorno judgment of 10 December 1993; *Pretura* Rho judgment of 14 November 1991; *Conciliatore* Rome judgment of 24 June 1991; *Conciliatore* Rome judgment of 22 August 1991). In comparison with the state, the courts therefore acknowledged that even Directives which had not yet been implemented were capable of having 'vertical' direct effect. Additionally, the Italian judges attempted to compensate for the inaction of the legislator by applying the right of cancellation from the former Article 18 ter(3)(1) of *Legge* no 216 of 7 June 1974 on the Broking of Investment in Securities for Doorstep Sales. Sometimes it was assumed that the dealer had acted fraudulently during the course of negotiations if he had persuaded the consumer that his signing the contract constituted a mere preparatory and non-binding step to the conclusion of a contract.

The courts also based their decisions on various voluntary codes of practice laid down by professional bodies—for example, the self-regulatory code for the mail order trade laid down in 1974 by ANVEC (*Associazione nazionale di vendita per corrispondenza*), or the code of practice adopted by AVEDISCO (*Associazione nazionale vendite dirette servizio consumatori*). A self-regulatory instrument of special importance was a protocol signed by consumer organisations and the trading bodies on 11 October 1989 in Rome, which provided the consumer with a period of reflection in the case of mail order contracts. However, the limited adoption of such self-regulations by traders was not sufficient to provide the consumer with comprehensive protection. Codes of practice and protocols only bind the members of the participating bodies. Moreover, an infringement of such regulatory instruments did not affect the efficacy of contracts which had already been concluded. Only when *Decreto Legge* no 50 was passed in 1992 were the gaps in protection which had arisen in Italian law due to the delayed implementation of Directive 85/577 finally filled. This *Decreto Legge* controls the area of application for all transactions covered in Article 2 which defines the consumer as 'a natural person who trades for a purpose which lies outside his normal business activity'. The wording of Article 2 of *Decreto Legge* no 50 from 1992 sticks closely to the Italian version of the Directive:

Definizioni.—1. Ai fini del presente decreto si intende per:

a) consumatore: la persona fisica che, in relazione ai contratti o alle proposte contrattuali disciplinati dal presente decreto, agisce per scopi che possono considerarsi estranei alla propria attività professionale;

b) operatore commerciale: la persona fisica o giuridica che, in relazione ai contratti o alle proposte contrattuali disciplinati dal presente decreto, agisce nell'ambito della propria attività commerciale o professionale, nonchè la persona che agisce in nome o per conto di un operatore commerciale.

By way of example, the *Pretura* Bologna (judgment of 28 February 1995) and the *Pretura* Milan (judgments of 12 June 1996 and 30 January 1997) had to resolve issues similar to those dealt with by the ECJ in the *Di Pinto* case. These three judgments serve to develop the concept of the 'consumer' in Italian law, although they largely apply similar criteria to those of the ECJ in *Di Pinto*. Following the decision of the *Pretura* Bolgna, a director or organ of a company may cancel the contract according to Article 4 of *Decreto Legge* no 50 of 1992 provided that the goods had been acquired away from business premises and were not connected with the business carried on by the company. This also applies if the name of the company is stamped on the contractual document. The basis of the decision was a case whereby a Mr Ciprinai, director of the Cipritex company, had acquired various publications concerning economic issues. It was questioned whether Ciprinai constituted a 'consumer' for the purpose of Article 2 (a) of the *Decreto Legge* no 50. The *Pretura* Bologna held that the concept of a 'consumer' had to be determined according to objective criteria. In the event it came down to the purpose for which the goods or services are acquired as laid down in the contract. The *Pretura* had to rule on two objections:

1. On the contract document which had been signed by Cipriani four stamps with extensive information on the company, including its tax number, had been provided; and

2. Cipritex had additionally stated that the publications were to be used for commercial purposes.

Both objections failed. The *Pretura* held that the statement concerning the purpose of the acquisition was to be disregarded because it had been submitted for tax purposes. In addition, it held that there existed no connection between the type of the publications acquired (publications) and the business carried on by Cipritex (DIY advertising). In this way the *Pretura* made clear that a connection between the purpose of the doorstep sale and the nature of the business carried on by the customer is necessary in order to exclude the protection conferred by the *Decreto Legge* no 50 of 1992.

A similar approach was also taken by the *Pretura* Milan in its judgment of 12 June 1996. This case concerned the order of air purifying equipment which a Mr Gabriele Manzoni had concluded in his apartment with a sales representative of the firm IWM SAS. Manzoni revoked the contract within seven days. IWM SAS claimed that *Decreto Legge* no 50 did not apply because the customer had stated in writing that the air purifier was to be used for professional purposes. The *Pretura* rejected the argument that Manzoni was not a consumer for the purposes of Article 2(a) of *Decreto Legge* no 50 1992. It held that the written statement provided by Manzoni was to be disregarded. The court stated that the fact that the purchase of the air purifier was unconnected with the professional occupation was decisive. This would not have been the case, however, if Manzoni had, for example, worked as a reporter on environmental issues. In this case the decision was based on the absence of a connection between the goods purchased and the professional activity of the purchaser, whereby a mere statement of the purchaser in the contract is to be disregarded. The judgment by the *Pretura* Milan of 30 January 1997 rested on similar facts. In this case, an individual had also purchased an air purifier away from business premises and had given a statement in the contract that the equipment was to be used for professional purposes in order to take advantage of a price reduction. The *Pretura* did not invoke the exclusions provided for in the *Decreto* because the concept of the 'consumer' had to be determined according to objective criteria, regardless of the parties' statements to the contrary.

According to Article 8 of Directive 85/577, on which the ECJ based its arguments relating to the second question of the preliminary proceedings, Member States were free to accept or retain provisions which guarantee more extensive consumer protection in this field. The Italian legislator used this option and made further provision in Article 12 of the *Decreto Legge* 1992, designating the living quarters of the consumer to be the exclusive venue of jurisdiction. This provision is regarded as being a positive exception to the usual practice in Italy of adopting the Directive in its entirety without creating instruments which go beyond the minimum standard in order to realise the aims the Directive seeks to achieve (*Luongo*).

CASE LAW REFERENCES

Conciliatore di Roma judgment of 24 June 1991 (1991) *Il Foro Italiano*, Repertorio, see 'Vendita', no 70; Conciliatore di Roma judgment of 22 August 1991 (1993) *Responsabilità Civile* 187; Pretura di Rho judgment of 14 November 1991 (1992) *Il Foro Italiano* I 1599; Pretura di Livorno judgment of 10 December 1993 *I Contratti* no 5, 1994 525; Tribunale di Roma, Ordinanza of 17 December 1994 *I Contratti* no 1 1996, 13; Pretura di Bologna judgment of 28 February 1995 (1995) *Il Foro Italiano* II 2304; Pretura di Milano judgment of 12 June 1996 *I Contratti* no 6 1997 603; Pretura di Milano judgment of 30 January 1997 (1997) *Foro Padano* I 168; Corte di Cassazione judgment of 1 September 1997 n 8302 (1997) *Massimario Guistizia Civile*; Pretura di Milano judgment of 30 January 1997 (1997) *Foro Padano* I 168.

LITERATURE REFERENCES

P Luongo 'Alcune riflessioni circa la nozione di consumatore', (1997) *Il Foro Padano* I 168; A Succi *I Contratti* I (1996) 13; Merola nota a Corte di Giustizia Comunità Europee 16 March 1989 n 382/87 (1990) *Il Foro Italiano* IV 262; GB Ferro 'La vendita "porta a porta" ' (1998) *Nuova Giurisprudenzena Civile* II 137.

AM

6. Austria

Like France, Austria had legal provisions protecting the consumer in the case of doorstep selling in force long before Directive 85/577 had been enacted; indeed even long before Austria had joined the European Union. The Law governing part payment (*Ratengesetz*) of 1961 (*Bundesgesetzblatt* 1961 no 279 repealed by the Law on Consumer Protection), which however, only applied in the case of instalment transactions, already had a provision in § 4 for a right of revocation for the purchaser if the contract had been concluded away from the business premises.

The Law governing part payment was replaced in 1979 by the Law on Consumer Protection (*Konsumentenschutzgesetz* hereafter '*KSchG*' *Bundesgesetzblatt* 1979 no 140) which now governs the right of cancellation in the case of doorstep sales (§ 3). In addition, the Law which had been conceived as a comprehensive code of consumer rights was amended so as to implement (at least in part) Directives 87/102 (Consumer Credit), 90/314 (Package Tours) and 93/13 (Unfair Terms). Paragraph 1 of the *KSchG* is central in these types of transactions. Reference is also made to this law in the special statutes concerning consumer contract law (eg the Time-Share Law (*Teilzeitnutzungsgesetz* (*TNG Bundesgesetzblatt* 1997 no 32 the implementing law of the Time-Share Directive (94/47))). It defines 'consumer' and the 'businessman' (interpreted as 'entrepreneur' by the *KSchG*) as follows:

(1) Dieses Hauptstück gilt für Rechtsgeschäfte, an denen

    1. einerseits jemand, für den das Geschäft zum Betrieb seines Unternehmens gehört (im folgenden kurz Unternehmer genannt) und

    2. andererseits jemand, für den dies nicht zurifft (im folgenden kurz Verbraucher genannt) beteiligt sind.

(2) Unternehmen im Sinn des Abs. 1 Z. 1 ist jede auf Dauer angelegte Organisation selbständiger wirtschaftlicher Tätigkeit, mag sie auch nicht auf Gewinn gerichtet sein. Juristische Personen des öffentlichen Rechts gelten immer als Unternehmer.

(. . .)

The background materials to the Law (Explanatory notes to the Government *KSchG* bill, no 744 of the appendices of the minutes of the National Council in its fourteenth legislative session 16) expressly leave it to the courts to interpret the rules of the *KSchG* teleologically where applicable.

An assessment of the facts in the *Di Pinto* case decided under Austrian law could justify the application of § 3 *KSchG* and thereby the existence of a right of revocation. If, on the other hand, a lawyer in his capacity as a private individual and as a consumer were to conclude a doorstep sale, he would have no right of cancellation because he would not be deserving of protection. The *Oberster Gerichtshof* (Supreme Court) has attempted to standardise its approach to this issue, only being guided by the formal characteristics of the 'consumer' or 'business', without it ever coming to the point that an imbalance of power is actually present (judgments of 21 April 1982, 21 October 1982 and 24 October 1993). Due to the fact that the court takes the same approach as the ECJ and in the *Di Pinto* case, joining the Community has not resulted in the need to adapt Austrian law.

A small difference of minor practical importance to the EC Directives and most other domestic legal systems lies in the fact that the concept of the 'consumer' contained in § 1 *KSchG* is not limited to natural persons, so that for example, a non-profit organisation is also included, serving to widen the protection. This is in line with *Di Pinto*.

CASE LAW REFERENCES

Oberster Gerichtshof judgment of 21 April 1982 *Sammlung der Entscheidungen des Obersten Gerichtshofes in Zivilsachen* 55/51; Oberster Gerichtshof judgment of 21 October 1982 *Sammlung der Entscheidungen des Obersten Gerichtshofes in Zivilsachen* 55/157; Oberster Gerichtshof judgment of 24 November 1993 *Wohnrechtliche Blätter* 1994/68.

LITERATURE REFERENCES

F Bydlinski *System und Prinzipien des Privatrechts* (1996) 708; W Faber 'Elemente verschiedener Verbraucherbegriffe in EG-Richtlinien, zwischenstaatlichen Übereinkommen und nationalem Zivil-und Kollisionsrecht' (1998) *Zeitschrift für Europäisches Privatrecht* 854; W Schuhmacher *Verbraucher und Recht aus historischer Sicht* 981; A Tangl 'Konsumentenschutz bei Haustürgeschäften: Unterschiede im Anwendungsbereich der einschlägigen Regelungen in Frankreich und Österreich' (1997) *Zeitschrift für Rechtsvergleichung* 99.

AE

CASE NO. 11 — *Dori* C–91/92

Paola Faccini Dori v Recreb SRL
[1994] ECR I–3325

A. Judgment of the ECJ of 14 July 1994

1. Held

1) *Article 1(1), Article 2 and Article 5 of Council Directive 85/577/EEC of 20 December 1985, concerning protection of the consumer in respect of contracts negotiated away from business premises, are unconditional and sufficiently precise as regards determination of the persons for whose benefit they were adopted and the minimum period within which notice of cancellation must be given.*

2) *In the absence of measures transposing Directive 85/577 within the prescribed time limit, consumers cannot derive from the Directive itself a right of cancellation as against traders with whom they have concluded a contract or enforce such a right in a national court. However, when applying provisions of national law, whether adopted before or after* *the Directive, the national court must interpret them as far as possible in the light of the wording and purpose of the Directive.*

2. Facts of the Case

The *Giudice Conciliatore* Firenze (Judge-Conciliator, Florence), Italy, referred to the Court for a preliminary ruling under Article 177 (new Article 234) EC Treaty a question on the interpretation of Council Directive 85/577/EEC, concerning protection of the consumer in respect of contracts negotiated away from business premises (OJ 1985 L372 p 31), and on the possibility of relying on that Directive in proceedings between a trader and a consumer.

The question was raised in proceedings between Paola Faccini Dori of Monza, Italy, and Recreb Srl. A contract for an English language correspondence course was concluded between Ms Faccini Dori and an enterprise called Recreb Inter-diffusion Srl. in front of (or, as the Advocate-General pointed out, 'at') the Milan main Railway Station. The contract was therefore concluded away from Interdiffusion Srl.'s business premises. On 23 January 1989, Ms Faccini Dori informed that company via registered letter that she was cancelling her order. The company replied on 3 June 1989 that it had assigned its claim to Recreb Srl. On 24 June 1989, Ms Faccini Dori wrote to Recreb confirming that she had cancelled her subscription to the course, indicating *inter alia* that she relied on the right of cancellation provided for by Directive 85/577. On 30 June 1989, Recreb Srl. asked the *Giudice Conciliatore* Firenze to order Ms Faccini Dori to pay it the agreed sum with interest and costs.

By order of 20 November 1989, the judge ordered Ms Faccini Dori to pay the sums in question. She lodged an objection to that order with the same judge. She again stated that she had withdrawn from the contract under the conditions laid down by Directive 85/577.

However, it was common ground that at the material time Italy had not taken any steps to transpose the Directive into national law, although the period set for transposition had expired on 23 December 1987. It was not until the adoption of *Decreto Legislativo* no 50 of 15 January 1992, which entered into force on 3 March 1992, that Italy finally transposed the Directive. The national court was uncertain whether, even though the Directive had not been transposed at the material time, it could apply its provisions. It therefore referred the following question to the Court for a preliminary ruling:

Is Community Directive 85/577/EEC of 20 December 1985 to be regarded as sufficiently precise and detailed and, if so, was it capable, in the period between the expiry of the 24-month time-limit given to the Member States to comply with the Directive and the date on which the Italian State did comply with it, of taking effect as between individuals and the Italian State and as between individuals themselves?

3. *Extract from the Grounds of the ECJ's Judgment*

11. The Directive requires the Member States to adopt certain rules intended to govern legal relations between traders and consumers. In view of the nature of the dispute, which is between a consumer and a trader, the question submitted by the national court raises two issues, which should be considered separately. The first is whether the provisions of the Directive concerning the right of cancellation are unconditional and sufficiently precise. The second is whether a Directive which requires the Member States to adopt certain rules specifically intended to govern relations between private individuals may be relied on in proceedings between such persons in the absence of measures to transpose the Directive into national law.

Whether the provisions of the Directive concerning the right of cancellation are unconditional and sufficiently precise

12. Article 1(1) of the Directive provides that the Directive is to apply to contracts concluded between a trader supplying goods and services and a consumer, either during an excursion organised by the trader away from his business premises or during a visit by him to the consumer's home or place of work, where the visit does not take place at the express request of the consumer.

13. Article 2 states that 'consumer' means a natural person who, in transactions covered by the Directive, is acting for purposes which can be regarded as outside his trade or profession and that 'trader' means a natural or legal person who, for the transaction in question, acts in his commercial or professional capacity.

14. Those provisions are sufficiently precise to enable the national court to determine upon whom, and for whose benefit, the obligations are imposed. No specific implementing measure is needed in that regard. The national court may confine itself to verifying whether the contract was concluded in the circumstances described by the Directive and whether it was concluded between a trader and a consumer as defined by the Directive.

15. In order to protect consumers who have concluded contracts in such circumstances, Article 4 of the Directive provides that traders are to be required to give consumers written notice of their right of cancellation, together with the name and address of a person against whom that right may be exercised. It adds that, in the case of Article 1(1), that information must be given to the consumer at the time of conclusion of the contract. Finally, it provides that Member States are to ensure that their national legislation lays down appropriate consumer protection measures for cases where the information in question is not supplied.

16. Furthermore, pursuant to Article 5(1) of the Directive, the consumer is to have the right to renounce the effects of his undertaking by sending notice within a period of not less than seven days from the time at which the trader informed him of his rights in accordance with the terms and conditions laid down by national law. Article 5(2) provides that the giving of such notice is to have the effect of releasing the consumer from any obligations under the contract.

17. Admittedly, Articles 4 and 5 allow the Member States some latitude regarding consumer protection when information is not provided by the trader and in determining the time limit and conditions for cancellation. That does not, however, affect the precise and unconditional nature of the provisions of the Directive at issue in this case. The latitude allowed does not make it impossible to determine minimum rights. Article 5 provides that the cancellation must be notified within a period of not less than seven days after the time at which the consumer received the prescribed information from the trader. It is therefore possible to determine the minimum protection which must on any view be provided.

18. As regards the first issue therefore, the answer to be given to the national court must be that Article 1(1), Article 2 and Article 5 of the Directive are unconditional and sufficiently precise as regards determination of the persons for whose benefit they were adopted and the minimum period within which notice of cancellation must be given.

Whether the provisions of the Directive concerning the right of cancellation may be invoked in proceedings between a consumer and a trader

19. The second issue raised by the national court relates more particularly to the question whether, in the absence of measures transposing the Directive within the prescribed time limit, consumers may derive from the Directive itself a right of cancellation against traders with whom they have concluded contracts and enforce that right before a national court.

20. As the Court has consistently held since its judgment in Case 152/84 *Marshall v Southampton and South-West Hampshire Health Authority* [1986] ECR 723 paragraph 48, a Directive cannot of itself impose obligations on an individual and cannot therefore be relied upon as such against an individual.

21. The national court observes that if the effects of unconditional and sufficiently precise but untransposed Directives were to be limited to relations between State entities and individuals, this would mean that a legislative measure would operate as such only as between certain legal subjects, whereas, under Italian law as under the laws of all modern States founded on the rule of law, the State is subject to the law like any other person. If the Directive could be relied on only as against the State, that would be tantamount to a penalty for failure to adopt legislative measures of transposition as if the relationship were a purely private one.

22. It need merely be noted here that, as is clear from the judgment in *Marshall*, cited above (paragraphs 48 and 49), the case law on the possibility of relying on Directives against State entities is based on the fact that under Article 189 a Directive is binding only in relation to 'each Member State to which it is addressed'. That case law seeks to prevent 'the State from taking advantage of its own failure to comply with Community law'.

23. It would be unacceptable if a State, when required by the Community legislature to adopt certain rules intended to govern the State's relations—or those of State entities—with individuals and to confer certain rights on individuals, were able to rely on its own failure to discharge its obligations so as to deprive individuals of the benefits of those rights. Thus the Court has recognised that certain provisions of Directives on conclusion of public works contracts and of Directives on harmonization of turnover taxes may be relied on against the State (or State entities) (see the judgment in Case 103/88 *Fratelli Costanzo v Comune di Milano* [1989] ECR 1839 and the judgment in Case 8/81 *Becker v Finanzamt Muenster-Innenstadt* [1982] ECR 53).

24. The effect of extending that case-law to the sphere of relations between individuals would be to recognise a power in the Community to enact obligations for individuals with immediate effect, whereas it has competence to do so only where it is empowered to adopt Regulations.

25. It follows that, in the absence of measures transposing the Directive within the prescribed time-limit, consumers cannot derive from the Directive itself a right of cancellation as against traders with whom they have concluded a contract or enforce such a right in a national court.

26. It must also be borne in mind that, as the Court has consistently held since its judgment in Case 14/83 *Von Colson and Kamann v Land Nordrhein-Westfalen* [1984] ECR 1891 paragraph 26, the Member States' obligation arising from a Directive to achieve the result envisaged by the Directive and their duty under Article 5 of the Treaty to take all appropriate measures, whether general or particular, is binding on all the authorities of Member States, including, for matters within their jurisdiction, the courts. The judgments of the Court in Case C–106/89 *Marleasing v La Comercial Internacional de Alimentacion* [1990] ECR I–4135 paragraph 8, and Case C–334/92 *Wagner Miret v Fondo de Garantia Salarial* [1993] ECR I–6911 paragraph 20, make it clear that, when applying national law, whether adopted before or after the Directive, the national court that has to interpret that law must do so, as far as possible, in the light of the wording and the purpose of the Directive so as to achieve the result it has in view and thereby comply with the third paragraph of Article 189 of the Treaty.

27. If the result prescribed by the Directive cannot be achieved by way of interpretation, it should also be borne in mind that, in terms of the judgment in Joined Cases

C–6/90 and C–9/90 *Francovich and Others v Italy* [1991] ECR I–5357 paragraph 39, Community law requires the Member States to make good damage caused to individuals through failure to transpose a Directive, provided that three conditions are fulfilled. First, the purpose of the Directive must be to grant rights to individuals. Second, it must be possible to identify the content of those rights on the basis of the provisions of the Directive. Finally, there must be a causal link between the breach of the State's obligation and the damage suffered.

28. The Directive on contracts negotiated away from business premises is undeniably intended to confer rights on individuals and it is equally certain that the minimum content of those rights can be identified by reference to the provisions of the Directive alone (see paragraph 17 above).

29. Where damage has been suffered and that damage is due to a breach by the State of its obligation, it is for the national court to uphold the right of aggrieved consumers to obtain reparation in accordance with national law on liability.

30. So, as regards the second issue raised by the national court, the answer must be that in the absence of measures transposing the Directive within the prescribed time-limit consumers cannot derive from the Directive itself a right of cancellation as against traders with whom they have concluded a contract or enforce such a right in a national court. However, when applying provisions of national law, whether adopted before or after the Directive, the national court must interpret them as far as possible in the light of the wording and purpose of the Directive.

B. Commentary

1. European Law

The importance to the Community legal system which the ECJ attributed to *Dori* can be seen even by the way the court arranged the proceedings. All Member States were requested to make observations: the judgment was not decided in chamber, but in the full Court. Concerning the key question, the ECJ, contrary to the Opinion of the Advocate-General, confirmed its previous case law first enunciated in *Marshall* ([1986] ECR 723). The Directives of the Community are not capable of having 'horizontal' direct effect. The citizens of the Community are not able to enforce rights deriving from Directives in their dealings with other Community citizens. The ECJ put it as follows: a Directive cannot of itself impose obligations on an individual and cannot therefore be relied upon as such against an individual (paragraph 20). In this the ECJ strengthened the fundamental difference between primary law and Regulations on the one hand and Directives on the other. The decisive provision of the EC Treaty is Article 249 (ex Article 189):

In order to carry out their task and in accordance with the provisions of this Treaty, the European Parliament acting jointly with the Council, the Council and the Commission shall make Regulations and issue Directives, take Decisions and make Recommendations or deliver Opinions.

A Regulation shall have general application. It shall be binding in its entirety and directly applicable in all Member States.

A Directive shall be binding as to the result to be achieved, upon each Member State to which it is addressed, but shall leave to the national authorities the choice of form and methods.

(. . .)

Among the different types of Community legislation only Regulations are capable of directly creating obligations on individuals. On the other hand Directives only directly bind Member States and always require the co-operation of the legal systems of Member States in order to bind individuals. The ECJ briefly summarised the indirect effects which Directives are capable of having in relation to individuals (paragraphs 26–29). Basically, it is possible to divide a Directive's effect into four parts:

A Directive contains an order to Member States to transpose the Directive by adapting domestic law so as to achieve the legal situation it intends to create within domestic law (duty to transpose).

In relation to the State, an individual is also capable of deriving rights from a Directive which has not been transposed ('vertical' direct effect, ECJ *Marshall* [1986] ECR 723).

The courts are under a duty in the case of an inadequately or non-transposed Directive to interpret domestic law as far as possible according to the wording and purpose of the Directive in order to achieve the aim intended by the Directive (duty to interpret domestic law to comply with Community law, *Von Colson and Kamann* [1984] ECR 1891; *Marleasing* [1990] ECR, I–4135).

Community law grants individuals a claim in damages against Member States which have not fulfilled their Community obligations (State liability for failing to transpose Directives, ECJ *Francovich* [1991] ECR I–5357; *Dillenkofer* [1996] ECR I–4845: Case no 13 in this Casebook).

At first sight the judgment in *Dori* appears to downgrade consumer protection in Community law. A consumer is incapable of directly relying on consumer protection Directives. The remaining possibility of pursuing a claim for damages under *Francovich* demands that the consumer has more time and energy and is willing to take a bigger risk. Having said this, it is still plausible that the decision in *Dori* will lead to a considerable strengthening of the protection of the consumer in Community law. Above all, the threat of state liability for failing to transpose (consumer) Directives puts Member States under considerable pressure to fulfil their obligations to transpose. The experience of a claim of state liability in Germany (see the German commentary to the ECJ, *Dillenkofer:* Case no 13 in this Casebook) has shown that a large number of consumers are clearly prepared to take on the risk of such a case. The decision in *Dori* therefore indirectly contributes towards improving the legal position of consumers by reducing the number of untransposed Directives.

From the viewpoint of Member States' legal systems, the ECJ answered the controversial question of the 'horizontal' direct effect of Directives in a laissez-faire way. The way in which the changes demanded by the Directive are to be introduced into domestic private law remains the preserve of the Member States. The Community's Directives do not impose duties on the individual directly; rather, they demand the co-operation of Member States in attaining the aims of the Directives for the purposes of Article 10 (ex Article 5) EC Treaty. This co-operation is—as shown by the reference to the duty to interpret domestic law in conformity with Directives and state liability (paragraphs 26–29)—not only expected from the legislator, but also of all emanations of the State. The application of domestic law must ensure that the aims of Community law are realised.

Concerning the interpretation of Directive 85/577 the decision in *Dori* raises more questions than it answers. The ECJ did admittedly establish that the provisions in the Directive relating to the beneficiaries and the right of cancellation were unconditional and sufficiently precise, with the result that consumers were able to derive rights from this Directive (if only indirectly and only against Member States). The point however lay in the circumstances of the case. Ms Dori had concluded the contract for the English course in front of Milan's main railway station (arguably also in the main station itself). Article 1(1) of Directive 85/577 states:

> This Directive shall apply to contracts under which a trader supplies goods or services to a consumer and which are concluded:
>
> 1. during an excursion organized by the trader away from his business premises, or
>
> 2. during a visit by a trader
>
>   a. to the consumer's home or to that of another consumer;
>   b. to the consumer's place of work;
>
> 3. where the visit does not take place at the express request of the consumer.

Article 1 of Directive 85/577 therefore only provides an express right of cancellation where the contract was concluded in the consumer's home or at his place of work during either an excursion organised by the business person or on the occasion of an unsolicited visit by the business person to the consumer. Since Ms Dori was not part of such an excursion, nor lived or worked at Milan main railway station, the contract made, at least as far as the wording is concerned, did not fall under the Directive. However, the 4th and 5th recitals of Directive 85/577 state:

Whereas the special feature of contracts concluded away from business premises of the trader is that as a rule it is the trader who initiates the contract negotiations, for which the consumer is unprepared or which he does not expect; whereas the consumer is often unable to compare the quality and price of the offer with other offers; whereas this surprise element generally exists not only in contracts made at the doorstep but also in other forms of contract concluded by the trader away from his business premises;

Whereas the consumer should be given a right of cancellation over a period of at least seven days in order to enable him to assess the obligations arising under the contract.

The question whether the ECJ intends to interpret the provisions of Directive 85/577 widely, having regard to the recitals and its title ('concerning the protection of the consumer in the case of contracts concluded away from business premises'), is left unanswered in the judgment. The Advocate-General hinted in his Opinion that contracts which are concluded in public streets do not come under the protection of Directive 85/577.

ECJ CASE LAW REFERENCES

Von Colson and Kamann [1984] ECR 1891; *Marshall* [1986] ECR 723; *Marleasing* [1990] ECR I–4135; *Francovich* [1991] ECR I–5357; *El Corte Inglés* [1996] ECR I–1281: Case no 12 in this Casebook; *Dillenkofer* [1996] ECR I–4845: Case no 13 in this Casebook.

LITERATURE REFERENCES

W Hakenberg 'Keine horizontale Richtlinienwirkung' (1994) *Zeitschrift für Wirtschaftsrecht* 1510; S Prechal *Sociaal-economische wetgeving* (1995) 436; W Robinson (1995) *Common Market Law Review* 629 (Casenote on *Dori*); D Simon *La Directive européenne* (1997) 70–75.

HS-N/JJ

2. England & Wales

In spite of having been directly involved in cases concerning direct effect of Directives more than once (see eg C–41/74 *Van Duyn v Home Office*; C–152/84 *Marshall v Southampton Area Health Authority* C–188/89 *Foster v British Gas*), the UK only participated in the *Faccini Dori* case during the oral procedure, after the Court asked for Member States' views. Like the great majority of the other intervening States, the UK urged the Court not to depart from its previous case law and to hold that Directive 85/577 did not have 'horizontal' direct effect.

The decision, however, did not pass unnoticed in the British academic world and was heavily criticised in legal literature: according to *Craig*, the reasons for a distinction between vertical and horizontal direct effect of Directives were considered to be rather weak. The opposition by the Member States to the latter is surprising if considered in the light of the *Francovich* principle, which makes States subject to the possibility of monetary liability for their failures (which could obviously be avoided if such direct effect was allowed). In addition, *Coppel* stressed that the right to sue the relevant State in damages is limited to the most serious cases of default only. State liability does not aid consumers much, who in most cases, due to the small amounts involved, would wish to rely simply on rights under a Directive against the trader, rather than to sue the State.

Directive 85/577 was duly implemented in the UK within the prescribed time limit by the Consumer Protection (Cancellation of Contracts Concluded away from Business Premises) Regulations 1987, as amended in 1988 and 1998. As yet, the Regulations, which follow the Directive quite closely and do not impose stricter rules, have not given rise to any problems of interpretation.

Before the Directive, UK law already provided for cooling-off periods and cancellations in the fields of consumer credit, life insurance and investment agreements. It also banned unsolicited doorstep selling of money loans. However, it lacked a more general discipline of such a sales method. In this respect, a significant role was played by the Code of Practice of the Direct Selling Association which requires its members to allow consumers a cooling-off period of fourteen days.

LITERATURE REFERENCES

J Coppel 'Rights, Duties and the End of Marshall' (1994) *Modern Law Review* 859; J Coppel 'Horizontal effect of Directives' (1997) *Industrial Law Journal* 69; P Craig 'Directives, Direct Effect, Indirect Effect and the Construction of National Legislation' (1997) *European Law Review* 519.

PN

3. Germany

The German government, like almost all other European governments, vehemently opposed Directives having horizontal direct effect in its submission to the *Dori* case. This question was debated both in legal journals (see *Herber* for overview) and in a number of courts, some of which even accepted horizontal direct effect of Directives which had not been transposed (for example, the *Oberlandesgericht* Hamm (Higher Regional Court), judgment 1 December 1988; *Oberlandesgericht* Celle judgment of 28 April 1990; *Landgericht* Wiesbaden judgment of 14 August 1990; *Landgericht* Hildesheim (Regional Court) judgment of 11 December 1991). The judgment in *Dori* therefore led to a much called for clarification of the application of law. The courts (for example the *Bundesarbeitsgericht* (Federal Labour Court) judgment of 2 April 1996; *Oberverwaltungsgericht* (Higher Administrative Court) for the Land Nordrhein-Westfalen judgment of 29 March 1995) as well as most legal writers agree with the decision of the ECJ (for example, *Hakenberg, Herber, Ukrow*; for a different opinion see *Bleckmann*).

The effects of the decision on consumer protection in Germany was not far reaching because Germany had transposed Directive 85/577 (the Doorstep Sales Law) long before the transposition deadline. The central provision—section 1(1)—states:

(1) Einem Verbraucher steht ein Widerrufsrecht nach sections 361a des Bürgerlichen Gesetzbuchs bei Verträgen mit einem Unternehmer zu, die eine entgeltliche Leistung zum Gegenstand haben und zu denen er

1. durch mündliche Verhandlungen an seinem Arbeitsplatz oder im Bereich seiner Privatwohnung

2. anläßlich einer von der anderen Vertragspartei oder von einem Dritten zumindest auch in ihrem Interesse durchgeführten Freizeitveranstaltung oder

3. im Anschluß an ein überraschendes Ansprechen in Verkehrsmitteln oder im Bereich öffentlich zugänglicher Verkehrslächen

bestimmt worden ist. (. . .)

The German Law in section 3(3) exceeds the demands required by Directive 85/577. According to German law Ms Dori, who had concluded the contract in front of Milan main station, would also have had a right of cancellation.

CASE LAW REFERENCES

Oberlandesgericht Hamm judgment of 1 December 1988 (1989) *NJW–Rechtsprechungsreport Zivilrecht* 496; Landgericht Wiesbaden judgment of 14 August 1990 (1991) *Monatsschrift für Deutsches Recht* 156; Oberlandesgericht Celle judgment of 28 August 1990 (1990) *Europäische Zeitschrift für Wirtschaftsrecht* 550; Landgericht Hildesheim judgment of 11 December 1991 (1993) *Praxis des internationalen Privat- und Verfahrensrechts* 173; Oberverwaltungsgericht für das Land Nordrhein-Westfalen judgment of 29 March 1995 (1996) *Nordrhein-Westfälische Verwaltungsblätter* 356; Bundesarbeitsgericht judgment of 2 April 1996 (1996) *Der Betrieb* 1725: *Betriebs-Berater* 1997 1259.

LITERATURE REFERENCES

A Bleckmann *Europarecht* (6th edn 1997) 169; W Hakenberg 'Keine horizontale Richtlinienwirkung' (1994) *Zeitschrift für Wirtschaftsrecht* 1510; R Herber (1996) *Zeitschrift für Europäisches Privatrecht* 121 (Casenote on *Dori*); J Ukrow 'Unmittelbare Wirkung von Richtlinien und gemeinschaftsrechtliche Staatshaftung nach Maastricht' (1994) *Neue Juristische Wochenschrift* 2469.

HS-N

4. France

French writers have also discussed the controversial question of whether Directives are capable of having horizontal direct effect (see eg *Level, Simon* for an overview). The French government gave a written submission in the proceedings to *Dori* in which it opposed Directives having horizontal direct effect. The ECJ's judgment in *Dori* is considered to be a clear confirmation of the decision in *Marshall* and thereby as a clarification of the ECJ's position. It has been welcomed by academics (*Gautier, Level*). Despite this, there are some commentators who still demand that the horizontal direct effect of non-transposed Directives be acknowledged (*Emmert/Pereira de Azevedo*). The *Conseil d'État* retained its hitherto negative attitude towards the horizontal direct effect of Directives and cited the ECJ's decision in *Dori* as authority (see *SA LILLY France* for an overview of the relevant case law of the *Conseil d'État* and the accompanying literature, for example in the Opinion of the Advocate-General to the judgment of the *Conseil d'État* of 23 June 1995).

The problem relating to the law of consumer protection which proved fundamental to the *Dori* case did not arise in French law because a right of revocation relating to contracts concluded away from business premises has been in force in France for a long time. Even as Directive 85/577 was transposed, Law no 72–1137 of 22 December 1992 *relative à la protection des consommateurs en matière de démarchage et de vente à domicile* was in force in France, which to a large extent, fulfilled the requirements of the Directive. The provisions of this Law are now contained with a number of amendments in the *Code de la Consommation*, Articles L 121–21 to L 121–41. The central provisions state:

Article L 121–21

Est soumis aux dispositions de la présente section quiconque pratique ou fait pratiquer le démarchage, au domicile d'une personne physique, à sa résidence ou à son lieu de travail, même à sa demande, afin de lui proposer l'achat, la vente, la location, la location-vente ou la location avec option d'achat de biens ou la fourniture de services.

Est également soumis aux dispositions de la présente section le démarchage dans les lieux non destinés à la commercialisation du bien ou du service proposé et notamment l'organisation par un commerçant ou à son profit de réunions ou d'excursions afin de réaliser les opérations définies à l'alinéa précédent.

Article L 121–25

Dans les sept jours, jours fériés compris, à compter de la commande ou de l'engagement d'achat, le client a la faculté d'y renoncer par lettre recommandée avec accusé de réception. Si ce délai expire normalement un samedi, un dimanche ou un jour férié ou chômé, il est prorogé jusqu'au premier jour ouvrable suivant.

Toute clause du contrat par laquelle le client abandonne son droit de renoncer à sa commande ou à son engagement d'achat est nulle et non avenue.

CASE LAW REFERENCES

Conseil d'État judgment of 23 June 1995 *SA LILLY France* (1995) *Recueil des décisions du Conseil d'État* 257.

LITERATURE REFERENCES

F Emmert/M Pereira de Azevedo 'Les jeux sont faits: rien ne va plus ou une nouvelle occasion perdue par la CJCE' (1995) *Revue trimestrielle de droit européen* 11; Y Gautier (1995) *Journal du droit international* 425 (Casenote on *Dori*); P Level *Jurisclasseur périodique—La semaine juridique* édition générale 1995 II 22358 (Casenote on *Dori*); C Maugüé 'L'Etat ne peut se prévaloir d'une Directive qu'il n'a pas transposée' (1995) *Revue française de droit administrative* 1037; G Raymond 'Droit Communautaire.—Une Directive européene, s'applique-t-elle directement au consommateur?' *Contrats—Concurrence—Consommation* (1994) no 255, 16; D Simon *La Directive européenne* (1997) 70–75.

BD

5. Italy

Directive 85/577 had not been transposed into Italian law at the time Ms Dori lodged an objection against the order to pay the sum for an English course. Only shortly after she had concluded the contract did Italy transpose Directive 85/577 by *Decreto Legge* no 50 of 15 January 1992: a delay of some years. Italian law was nevertheless familiar with the right of cancellation before the transposition. The earlier Article 18(3)(1) of *Legge* no 216 of 7 June 1974 on the placement of investment securities in conjunction with Article 12 of *Legge* no 77 of 23 March 1983 later amended by *Legge* no 15 Article 281 of 4 June 1985 (repealed in 1986) provided that the contract could be rescinded within five days of signing. An agreement between the most important mail order business associations was signed in Rome on 11 October 1989. It provided that a seven day cooling-off period be adopted in the General Terms and Conditions of Sale. The case law on the legal position of the consumer has however been inconsistent (see the Italian commentary to the ECJ *Di Pinto*: Case no 10 in this Casebook).

Different opinions exist pertaining to the interpretation of Article 4 of *Decreto Legge* no 50 of 1992, which transposed the cooling-off period proscribed by Directive 85/577 into Italian law. This Article states that:

Diritto di recesso.—1. Per i contratti e per le proposte contrattuali soggetti alledisposizioni del presente decreto è attribuito al consumatore undiritto di recesso nei termini ed alle condizioni indicati negli articoli seguenti.

It is uncertain whether the power to rescind a contract affects either the conclusion or the validity of a contract, ie whether, for example, the contract has been repudiated or the consumer's statement has been revoked.

Only after a period of time did the ECJ's judgment in *Dori* begin to have an effect on Italian law. At Ms Dori's trial the *Corte di Cassazione* (judgment of 21 February 1995) declined to indirectly apply the non-transposed Directive 85/577 by means of an interpretation in compliance with the Directive. Nor did the *Corte di Cassazione* follow the direction of the ECJ's judgment. Rather, the Court reaffirmed its view that a binding contractual offer can only be held ineffective pursuant to an express legal provision, and not by adopting a certain interpretation of existing Italian law alone.

The judgment of the *Corte di Cassazione* of 20 March 1996 dealing with an appeal against a judgment of the *Conciliatore* Rome of 5 June 1992 heralded a change of direction. The *Conciliatore* granted a right of cancellation in the case of a doorstep sale which had been concluded before Directive 85/577 had been transposed into Italian law. The court based this power on '*equità*', pursuant to Article 113 *Codice di procedure*. This provision facilitated a summary equitable decision in response to an appeal on the basis of '*equità*'. In 1995 this procedure was abolished. The appeal asserted that the legal principles in force at the time had been infringed. The *Corte di Cassazione* held that in the proceedings before the *Conciliatore* Directive 85/577 which had not been transposed at the time could be relied upon due to the fact that it contained a provision relating to the interpretation of the contract according to the principles of equity ('*interpretazione equitativa*'). The appeal was therefore rejected. The *Corte di Cassazione* added *obiter dictum*:

> la direttiva in questione, indipendentemente dal suo successivo recepimento, si colloca ormay tra le fonti del diritto rilevanti nell'ordinamento interno e di essa non può non tenersi conto nella configurazione dei principi regolatori degli istituti disciplinati da tale ordinamento.

A number of academics have interpreted this sentence as providing the possibility for citizens to pursue 'horizontal' enforcement of Directives which have not been transposed by the deadline in the ordinary courts, provided the Directives are sufficiently clear and precise.

The case of *Dori* gave an opportunity to criticise Italy's frequent delay in complying with Community law. This also suggests a certain indifference towards European consumer protection legislation. A possible consequence of this attitude is an increase in *Francovich*-type cases.

CASE LAW REFERENCES

Corte di Cassazione judgment of 21 February 1995 no 2275, *Giurisprudenza Italiana* I 1 99; Corte di Cassazione judgment of 20 March 1996 no 2369 (1996) *Giustizia Civile* I 2970; Tribunale Roma judgment of 21 January 2000; Corte di Cassazione judgment of 14 January 2000; Preura di Bologna 6 August 1998; Tribunale di Palermo judgment of 2 June 1998; Giudice di Pace di Palermo judgment of 15 December 1999.

LITERATURE REFERENCES

G Alpa 'L'Italia riscopre il diritto di recesso, ma resta "al palo" sulla tutela del consumatore' *Guida al diritto* no 2 of 30 October 1994 113; F Astone 'I contratti negoziati fuori dei locali commerciali in diritto privato europeo ed integrazione dei diritti soggettivi', Norme sostanziali, organi istituzionali, tutela giurisdizionale in N Lipari (ed) *Diritto Privato Europeo* (1997) 31; N Scannicchio 'Dal diritto comunitario al diritto privato europeo nella giurisprudenza della Corte di Giustizia' in N Lipari (ed) *Diritto Privato Europeo* (1997) 58.

AM

CASE NO. 12 — *El Corte Inglés* C–192/94

El Corte Inglés SA v Cristina Blázquez Rivero
[1996] ECR I–1281

A. Judgment of the ECJ of 7 March 1996

1. Held

In the absence of measures implementing Council Directive 87/102/EEC of 22 December 1986 for the approximation of the laws, regulations and administrative provisions of the Member States concerning consumer credit within the prescribed period, a consumer may not, even in view of Article 129a of the EC Treaty, base a right of action on the Directive itself against a lender who is a private person, on account of inadequacies in the supply of goods or provision of services by the supplier or provider with whom the lender concluded an exclusive agreement with regard to the grant of credit and assert that right before a national court.

2. Facts of the Case

The *Juzgado de Primera Instancia* no 10 (Court of First Instance no 10), Seville, made a reference to the ECJ questioning the interpretation of Article 129a (new Article 153) EC Treaty and Article 11 of Council Directive 87/102 for the approximation of the laws, regulations and administrative provisions of the Member States concerning consumer credit (OJ 1987 L42 p 48). The question was raised in proceedings brought by a finance company, El Corte Inglés (hereinafter 'the finance company'), against Ms Blázquez Rivero.

Ms Blazquez Rivero entered into a contract for holiday travel with the travel agency Viajes El Corte Inglés SA (hereinafter 'the travel agency') which she financed in part by a loan obtained from the finance company. The finance company had the exclusive right to grant loans to the travel agency's customers under an agreement between the two companies. Ms Blázquez Rivero accused the travel agency of shortcomings in performing its obligations and made several complaints against it. When those complaints proved unsuccessful, she ceased to pay instalments on the loan, whereupon the finance company brought proceedings in the *Juzgado de Primera Instancia* Seville for payment of the outstanding balance. Before the national court, Ms Blázquez Rivero entered the defence against the finance company that the travel contract had not been performed, without drawing any distinction between the finance company and the travel agent in view of the close bond between them.

The national court took the view that Article 11(2) of the Directive enabled the consumer to bring an action against the finance company. Article 11(2) provides as follows:

Where:

a) in order to buy goods or obtain services the consumer enters into a credit agreement with a person other than the supplier of them;

and

b) the grantor of the credit and the supplier of the goods or services have a preexisting agreement whereunder credit is made available exclusively by that grantor of credit to customers of that supplier for the acquisition of goods or services from that supplier;

and

c) the consumer referred to in subparagraph (a) obtains his credit pursuant to that preexisting agreement;

and

d) the goods or services covered by the credit agreement are not supplied, or are supplied only in part, or are not in conformity with the contract for supply of them; and

e) the consumer has pursued his remedies against the supplier but has failed to obtain the satisfaction to which he is entitled, the consumer shall have the right to pursue remedies against the grantor of credit. Member States shall determine to what extent and under what conditions these remedies shall be exercisable.

The national court found, however, that Article 11(2) of the Directive had not been transposed into Spanish law even though the period prescribed for implementation had run out at the material time and that the result intended by that provision could not be attained by interpreting national law in conformity with the Directive. Indeed, Article 1257 of the Spanish Civil Code, under which 'contracts shall have effects only between the parties which concluded them and their heirs', prevents the consumer from pleading the shortcomings of the travel agency as against the finance company.

Although the national court considered that Article 11(2) was sufficiently clear, precise and unconditional to be relied on before it, it suspended the proceedings and asked the ECJ to give a preliminary ruling on the following question:

Is Article 11 of Council Directive 87/102/EEC of 22 December 1986 for the approximation of the laws, regulations and administrative provisions of the Member States concerning consumer credit, which has not been implemented in national law by the Spanish State, directly applicable in a case where a consumer seeks to rely, against a claim by the grantor of credit, on the defects in the service supplied by the supplier with whom the said grantor of credit has concluded an exclusive agreement for granting credit to his customers?

3. Extract from the Grounds of the ECJ's Judgment

10. Shortly after this question was referred, the Court gave judgment in Case C–91/92 *Faccini Dori* [1994] ECR I–3325, in which it reaffirmed its case-law according to which Directives do not have any horizontal direct effect. The Court forwarded a copy of that judgment to the national court and asked it whether, in the light of that judgment, it wished to maintain its question.

11. The national court considered that the judgment in *Faccini Dori* provided a clear answer to the question of the horizontal direct effect of unimplemented Directives, but observed that, unlike in the case of the dispute before it, *Faccini Dori* was concerned with facts antedating the entry into force of the Treaty on European Union. That Treaty introduced a new consumer protection provision, Article 129a.

12. Article 129a provides as follows:

'1. The Community shall contribute to the attainment of a high level of consumer protection through:

(a) measures adopted pursuant to Article 100a in the context of the completion of the internal market;

(b) specific action which supports and supplements the policy pursued by the Member States to protect the health, safety and economic interests of consumers and to provide adequate information to consumers.

2. The Council, acting in accordance with the procedure referred to in Article 189b and after consulting the Economic and Social Committee, shall adopt the specific action referred to in paragraph 1(b).

3. Action adopted pursuant to paragraph 2 shall not prevent any Member State from maintaining or introducing more stringent protective measures. Such measures must be compatible with this Treaty. The Commission shall be notified of them.'

13. The national court maintained its question on the ground that it wondered whether that rule establishing the principle of a high degree of consumer protection might have any bearing on the direct effect as between individuals of Article 11 of the Directive.

14. By its question, the national court essentially seeks to establish whether, in the absence of measures implementing the Directive within the prescribed period, a consumer may, in view of Article 129a of the Treaty, base a right of action on the Directive itself against a lender who is a private person, on account of inadequacies in the supply of goods or provision of services by the supplier or provider with whom the lender concluded an exclusive agreement with regard to the grant of credit and assert that right before a national court.

Whether the provisions of the Directive relating to the consumer's right of action may be relied on in proceedings between the consumer and a lender.

15. As the Court has consistently held (see, in particular, Case 152/84 *Marshall I* [1986] ECR 723 paragraph 48), a Directive may not of itself impose obligations on an individual and may therefore not be relied upon as such against such a person.

16. As for the case-law on when Directives may be relied upon against State entities, it is based on the binding nature of Directives, which applies only with regard to the Member States to which they are addressed, and seeks to prevent a State from taking advantage of its own failure to comply with Community law (see *Marshall I*, paragraphs 48 and 49).

17. The effect of extending that case-law to the sphere of relations between individuals would be to recognise a power in the Community to enact obligations for individuals with immediate effect, whereas it has competence to do so only where it is empowered to adopt regulations or decisions (see *Faccini Dori* paragraph 24).

18. Article 129a of the Treaty cannot alter that case-law, even if only in relation to Directives on consumer protection.

19. Suffice it to say in this connection that the scope of Article 129a is limited. On the one hand, it provides that the Community is under a duty to contribute to the attainment of a high level of consumer protection. On the other, it creates Community competence with a view to specific action relating to consumer protection policy apart from measures taken in connection with the internal market.

20. In so far as it merely assigns an objective to the Community and confers powers on it to that end without also laying down any obligation on Member States or individuals, Article 129a cannot justify the possibility of clear, precise and unconditional provisions of Directives on consumer protection which have not been transposed into Community law within the prescribed period being directly relied on as between individuals.

21. Consequently, a consumer cannot base on the Directive itself a right of action against a lender who is a private person following shortcomings in the supply of goods or the provision of services and assert that right before a national court.

22. Moreover, if the result prescribed by the Directive cannot be achieved by way of interpretation, it should also be borne in mind that, in terms of the judgment in Joined Cases C–6/90 and C–9/90 *Francovich and Others v Italy* [1991] ECR I–5357 paragraph 39, Community law requires the Member States to make good damage caused to individuals through failure to transpose a Directive, provided that three conditions are fulfilled. First, the purpose of the Directive must be to grant rights to individuals. Second, it must be possible to identify the content of those rights on the basis of the provisions of the Directive. Finally, there must be a causal link between the breach of the State's obligation and the damage suffered (*Faccini Dori* paragraph 27).

23. In the light of the foregoing, it should be stated in reply to the national court's question that, in the absence of measures implementing the Directive within the prescribed period, a consumer may not, even in view of Article 129a of the Treaty, base a right of action on the Directive itself against a lender who is a private person, on account of inadequacies in the supply of goods or provision of services by the supplier or provider with whom the lender concluded an exclusive agreement with regard to the grant of credit and assert that right before a national court.

B. Commentary

1. European Law

The case *El Corte Inglés*—like that of *Dori*—illustrates the consequences that a delayed transposition of a Directive can have on the legal position of a consumer. Ms Blázquez Rivero sought to assert a right that was available to her under Article 11(2) of Directive 87/102 (text reproduced above under A2). This Article provided for the possibility that the consumer in the case of a consumer contract financed by credit being able, under certain circumstances, to have the right to pursue remedies against the lender if the goods or services delivered under the principal contract were defective. Directive 87/102 had not been transposed into Spanish law despite the deadline having passed. Spanish law did not have a legal provision protecting the consumer equivalent to Article 11(2) of the Directive. Additionally on this point the Spanish court did not consider it possible to adopt an interpretation of national law which conformed to Community law.

The ECJ also rejected the contention that a Directive was capable of being directly effective as between the two parties. For victims such as Ms Blázquez Rivero there remained, as the ECJ has repeatedly stated, only the possibility of suing the Spanish State for damages on the grounds that it failed to transpose Directive 87/102 in time in accordance with the principles laid down in *Francovich* (ECJ *Francovich* [1991] ECR I–5357). The result of this therefore was that the ECJ affirmed its long-standing case law (*Marshall* (ECJ [1986] ECR 723), *Dori* (ECJ [1994] ECR I–3325: Case no 11 in this Casebook)) without qualification.

The novelty of the decision in *El Corte Inglés* lay in the clarification that not even the Treaty on the European Union (the so-called Maastricht Treaty OJ 1992 C191/1) could cause the ECJ to change its case law. The Maastricht Treaty has charged the Community—much more clearly than before—with making a contribution to the attainment of a high level of consumer protection (ex Article 129a(1): text reproduced above in the judgment under A3 paragraph 12; new Article 153) EC Treaty. This provision had raised hopes of a more comprehensive consumer protection policy. The referring Spanish court had held it possible that the Maastricht Treaty did have a bearing on the horizontal direct effect of Directives relating to consumer protection. The ECJ clearly opposed such moves. Article 129a of the Maastricht Treaty only had a 'limited scope' (paragraph 19). It limited itself to assigning an objective to the Community and conferring powers on it to that end. The Treaty could not justify the possibility that provisions from Directives referring to consumer protection could be directly enforced between individuals (paragraphs 17, 20). The aim of anchoring the policy of consumer protection in the primary law of the Union which the Maastricht Treaty sought to achieve has therefore only led to the establishment of aims and the granting of jurisdiction to the Union. The effects of the legislation passed by the Union, especially Directives, do not change by virtue of the Union's greater jurisdiction. From this principle it may be concluded that the repeated strengthening of consumer protection by the Treaty of Amsterdam (OJ 1997 C340/1) will probably not influence the effect of non-transposed Directives (dissenting opinion: *Reich*).

The new provisions of the EC Treaty contained in the Treaty of Amsterdam state:

Article 153

In order to promote the interests of consumers and to ensure a high level of consumer protection, the Community shall contribute to protecting the health, safety and economic interests of consumers, as well as to promoting their right to information, education and to organise themselves in order to safeguard their interests.

Consumer protection shall be taken into account in defining and implementing other Community policies and activities.

The Community shall contribute to the attainment of the objectives referred to in paragraph 1 through:

measures adopted pursuant to Article 95 in the context of the completion of the internal market;

measures which support, supplement and monitor the policy by the Member States.

The Council, acting in accordance with the procedure referred to in Article 251 and after consulting the Economic and Social Committee, shall adopt the measures referred to in paragraph 3(b).

Measures adopted pursuant to paragraph 4 shall not prevent any Member State from maintaining or introducing more stringent protective measures. Such measures must be compatible with this Treaty. The Commission shall be notified of them.

The ECJ's position on the ranking of consumer protection within Community law becomes clear in its judgment in the case *Germany v Parliament and Council* ([1997] ECR I–2405 paragraph 48), which dealt with Directive 94/19 (OJ 1994 L135/5) on deposit-guarantee schemes:

In that regard it suffices to point out that, although consumer protection is one of the objectives of the Community, it is clearly not the sole objective. As has already been stated, the Directive aims to promote the right of establishment and the freedom to provide services in the banking sector. Admittedly, however, there must be a high level of consumer protection concomitantly with those freedoms; however, no provision of the Treaty obliges the Community legislature to adopt the highest level of protection which can be found in a particular Member State.

ECJ CASE LAW REFERENCES

ECJ, *Marshall* [1986] ECR 723; *Francovich* [1991] ECR I–5357; *Dori* [1994] ECR I–3325; *Dillenkofer* [1996] ECR I–4845; *Verein für Konsumenteninformation* [1998] ECR I–2949.

LITERATURE REFERENCES

Y Gautier (1997) *Journal du droit international* 484 (Casenote on *El Corte Inglés*); S Grund-mann (1998) *Europäisches Schuldvertragsrecht* 655–680; J Stuyck (1996) *Common Market Law Review* 1261 (Casenote on *El Corte Inglés*).

HS-N/JJ

2. England & Wales

The case is known in English legal journals for re-affirming that Directives cannot be applied directly to legal relations between private persons. It is accordingly subject to the criticism that the denial of horizontal direct effect deprives a Directive of some of its strength in creating consumer rights within a national legal system.

On the other hand, from a substantive point of view the case did not trigger any discussions or comments in the academic world, nor did it entail any proposals for changes in the English legal system: the legislation in force in the UK, namely the Consumer Credit Act 1974 (CCA), offers to UK consumers a standard of protection which in many aspects goes further than Directive 87/102. This explains why, in order to implement the Directive, only minor amendments to subordinate legislation were made, and the Consumer Credit Act 1974 is still fully in force.

Liability of the grantor of credit for breaches of the supplier is covered by section 75 CCA. It establishes joint and several liability between the creditor and the supplier in respect of a misrepresentation or a breach of contract by the supplier:

75. Liability of creditor for breaches of the supplier.

If the debtor under a debtor-creditor-supplier agreement falling within section 12(b) or (c) has, in relation to a transaction financed by the agreement, any claim against the supplier in respect of a misrepresentation or breach of contract, he shall have a like claim against the creditor, who, with the supplier, shall accordingly be jointly and severally liable to the debtor (. . .)

The wording of section 75 was actually proposed as a blue print for Article 11 of the Directive. The formula finally adopted in the European legislation however only provides for subsidiary liability, so that the consumer can claim against the creditor only after having unsuccessfully claimed against the supplier. The UK legislation is more advanced in another respect: whilst in most of the Member States the use of credit cards does not fall within the scope of subsidiary liability, section 75 also applies where the consumer purchases goods using a credit card.

The UK government has recently been looking to deregulate the consumer credit business, and as part of this process the Office of Fair Trading (OFT) has made a number of recommendations for change. With regard to section 75, the OFT has made recommendations to the effect that this provision should be changed so as to lessen liability imposed on credit card issuers and to replace the existing joint and several liability by 'second-in-line' liability. The Department of Trade and Industry, however, has subsequently issued a consultation document where it was argued that they were not at present convinced of any need for change as the mentioned provision gives useful and desirable protection to consumers who buy goods or services on credit and they do not impose an unwarranted burden on businesses.

LITERATURE REFERENCES

M Leder/P Shears *Consumer Law* (1997) 146–150; *Connected Lender Liability—a Second Report by the Director General of Fair Trading on s 75 of the CCA 1974* Office of Fair Trading, Report no 132 of May 1995; A Davis 'European Union—consumer credit' (1996) *Consumer Law Journal* CS31 (Casenote on *El Corte*).

PN

3. Germany

The judgment in the case *El Corte Inglés* has been published in many German legal journals and is primarily regarded as affirming the ECJ's case law up to that point relating to the horizontal direct effect of Directives. The decision was not able to make much of a contribution to German consumer credit law since § 9 of the Law on Consumer Credit (*Verbraucherkreditgesetz*, as amended in *Bundesgesetzblatt* I 2000, 940) contains a provision regulating connected trading and credit transactions which exceeds the requirements of Article 11 of Directive 87/102. Paragraph 9 of the Law on Consumer Credit states:

§ 9 Verbundene Geschäfte.

(1) Ein Kaufvertrag bildet ein mit dem Kreditvertrag verbundenes Geschäft, wenn der Kredit der Finanzierung des Kaufpreises dient und beide Verträge als wirtschaftliche Einheit anzusehen sind. Eine wirtschaftliche Einheit ist insbesondere anzunehmen, wenn der Kreditgeber sich bei der Vorbereitung oder dem Abschluß des Kreditvertrages der Mitwirkung des Verkäufers bedient.

(2) (. . .)

(3) Der Verbraucher kann die Rückzahlung des Kredits verweigern, soweit Einwendungen aus dem verbundenen Kaufvertrag ihn gegenüber dem Verkäufer zur Verweigerung seiner Leistung berechtigen würden. Dies gilt nicht, wenn der finanzierte

Kaufpreis 200 Euro nicht überschreitet sowie bei Einwendungen, die auf einer zwischen dem Verkäufer und dem Verbraucher nach Abschluß des Kreditvertrages vereinbarten Vertragsänderung beruhen. Beruht die Einwendung des Verbrauchers auf einem Mangel der gelieferten Sache und verlangt der Verbraucher auf Grund vertraglicher oder gesetzlicher Bestimmungen Nachbesserung oder Ersatzlieferung, so kann er die Rückzahlung des Kredits erst verweigern, wenn die Nachbesserung oder Ersatzlieferung fehlgeschlagen ist.

(4) Die Absätze 1 bis 3 gelten entsprechend für Kredite, die zur Finanzierung des Entgelts für eine andere Leistung als die Lieferung einer Sache gewährt werden.

LITERATURE REFERENCES

P Bülow (1996) *Entscheidungen zum Wirtschaftsrecht* 599 (Casenote on *El Corte Inglés*); K Finke 'Die Haftung der Mitgliedstaaten für die Verletzung von Gemeinschaftsrecht' (1996) *Deutsche Zeitschrift für Wirtschaftsrecht* 361; B Lurger *Entscheidungssammlung zum Wirtschafts- und Bankrecht* I E 2 Art 11 RL 87/102 196 (Casenote on *El Corte Inglés*).

HS-N

4. *France*

The decision in *El Corte Inglés* has mainly evoked positive reactions with very few exceptions (*Boutard-Labarde, Gautier*). It is principally acknowledged as having clearly rejected the horizontal direct effect of Directives.

France had already enacted provisions concerning connected trading and credit transactions with the Law no 78–22 of 10 January 1978 *relative à l'information et à la protection des consommateurs dans le domaine de certaines opérations de crédit*. It did not prove necessary to amend these provisions in order to transpose Article 11 of Directive 87/102, with the result that France did not experience problems comparable to that in the case of *El Corte Inglés*. The provisions have been incorporated in the *Code de la Consommation*. Articles L 311–20 and L 311–21 state:

Article L 311–20.

Lorsque l'offre préalable mentionne le bien ou la prestation de services financé, les obligations de l'emprunteur ne prennent effet qu'à compter de la livraison du bien ou de la fourniture de la prestation; en cas de contrat de vente ou de prestation de services à exécution successive, elles prennent effet à compter du début de la livraison ou de la fourniture et cessent en cas d'interruption de celle-ci. Le vendeur ou le prestataire de services doit conserver une copie de l'offre préalable remise à l'emprunteur et la présenter sur leur demande aux agents chargés du contrôle.

Article L 311–21.

En cas de contestation sur l'exécution du contrat principal, le tribunal pourra, jusqu'à la solution du litige, suspendre l'exécution du contrat de crédit. Celui-ci est résolu ou annulé de plein droit lorsque le contrat en vue duquel il a été conclu est lui-même judiciairement résolu ou annulé.

Les dispositions de l'alinéa précédent ne seront applicables que si le prêteur est intervenu à l'instance ou s'il a été mis en cause par le vendeur ou l'emprunteur.

It is believed that a gap exists in the protection of the consumer. According to the wording of Article L 311–20, the Article is only applicable if the product or provision of services which forms the subject matter of the finance is mentioned in the offer of credit (*Calais-Auloy/Steinmetz*). This requirement can hardly be reconciled with Article 11(2)(b) of Directive 87/102 (text reproduced under part 2), since the latter does not demand such a requirement. According to the case law of the *Cour de Cassation*, an express reference of this nature is however essential if the two transactions have been presented to the consumer as connected in some way (judgment of 19 January 1993).

CASE LAW REFERENCES

Cour de Cassation, chambre commerciale judgment of 19 January 1993 (1993) *Revue trimestrielle de droit commercial* 707.

LITERATURE REFERENCES

M Boutard-Labarde *Juris-classeur périodique—La semaine juridique*, édition générale 1996 I 3940 (Casenote on *El Corte Inglés*); J Calais-Auloy/F Steinmetz *Droit de la Consommation* (4th edn 1996) 338–340; Y Gautier (1997) *Journal du droit international* 484 (Casenote on *El Corte Inglés*); D Simon *La Directive européenne* (1997) 70–75.

BD

5. Italy

The decision in *El Corte Inglés* was criticised by Italian writers because the ECJ had repeatedly rejected the horizontal direct effect of non-transposed Directives (*Faini, Regaldo*). At the same time, the judgment is considered as confirming the decision in *Francovich* (*Faini*). As a result, every person is basically entitled to claim damages if a Member State has not transposed a Directive and the courts are unable to achieve the aims set out by the Directive by interpreting the applicable provisions of domestic law in conformity with the Directive. In this case the Italian courts were bound to allow a claim of damages under domestic provisions via state liability.

CASE LAW REFERENCES

Corte di Cassazione judgment of 11 October 2000 n 10617 Corte di Cassazione judgment of 3 February 1995 n 1271, (1995) *Massimario Giustizia Civile* (1995) *Nuova*

Giurisprudenza Civile Commentata I, 837 n Calò; Corte di Cassatione, judgment of 20 November 1997 n 11571 (1997) *Massimario Giustizia Civile*; Tribunale di Pavia judgment of 22 March 1997 (1997) *Giurisprudenza commerciale* II 426 n Lucchini Guastalla; Consiglio di Stato sez IV judgment of 18 January 1996 n 54 (1997) *Rivista Italiema di Diritto Pubblico Comunitario* 177; Corte di Cassatione judgment of 3 February 1995 n 1271 (1996) *Rivista Italiema di Diritto Pubblico Comunitario*, 1021 n Scambiato.

LITERATURE REFERENCES

A Barone (1996) *Il Foro Italiano* IV 358; D Faini 'Se manca il recepimento statale non è invocabile la tutela dei consumatori prevista dal Trattato' *Guida al Diritto* n 27 1996 71; F Regaldo 'Recenti sviluppi in tema di responsabilità dello Stato per la mancata attuazione delle direttive comunitarie' (1998) *Giurisprudenza Italiana* IV 1; C Nizzo 'Mancata attuazione di direttive comunitarie e responsabilità patrimoniale dello Stato memnbro inadempiente' (1997) *Resp. Comunicazione Imprese* 45; G Roscioni 'Mancata attuazione delle direttive comunitarie: la Cassazione nega l'illecito dello Stato' (1996) *Danno e responsabilità* 80; L Daniele 'Brevi note in tema di attuazione delle direttive comunitarie da parte degli stati membri' (1992) *Rivisto Italiemo Diritto Pubblico Comunitario* 803; S Tassone 'Sulla responsabilità dello stato membro per omessa attuazione di direttive comunitarie nell'ordinamento interno' (1992) *Responsibilita civile e Previdenza* 847; E Cannizzaro 'Delegazione legislativa e delegificazione nella attuazione di direttive comunitarie' (1990) *Rivisto di Diritto Internazionale* 912.

AM

CASE NO. 13 — *Dillenkofer* Joined Cases C–178/94, C–179/94, C–188/94, C–189/94, C–190/94

Erich Dillenkofer, Christian Erdmann, Hans-Jürgen Schulte, Anke Heuer, Werner, Ursula and Torsten Knor v Germany
[1996] ECR I–4845

A. Judgment of the ECJ of 8 October 1996

1. Held

1. *Failure to take any measure to transpose a Directive in order to achieve the result it prescribes within the period laid down for that purpose constitutes* per se *a serious breach of*

Community law and consequently gives rise to a right of reparation for individuals suffering injury if the result prescribed by the Directive entails the grant to individuals of rights whose content is identifiable and a causal link exists between the breach of the State's obligation and the loss and damage suffered.

2. *The result prescribed by Article 7 of Council Directive 90/314 on package travel, package holidays and package tours entails the grant to package travellers of rights guaranteeing a refund of money paid over and their repatriation in the event of the organizer's insolvency; the content of those rights is sufficiently identifiable.*

3. *In order to comply with Article 9 of Directive 90/314 on package travel, package holidays and package tours, which provides that the Member States are to bring into force the measures necessary to comply with the Directive before 31 December 1992, the Member States should have adopted, within the period prescribed, all the measures necessary to ensure that, as from 1 January 1993, individuals would have effective protection against the risk of the insolvency of the organizer.*

4. *If a Member State allows the package travel organizer and/or retailer party to a contract to require payment of a deposit of up to 10% towards the travel price, but subject to a certain maximum amount, the protective purpose pursued by Article 7 of Directive 90/314 is not satisfied unless a refund of that deposit is also guaranteed in the event of the insolvency of the package travel organiser and/or retailer party to the contract.*

5. *Article 7 of Directive 90/314 is, furthermore, to be interpreted as meaning, first, that the 'security' of which organisers must offer sufficient evidence is lacking even if, on payment of the travel price, travellers are in possession of documents of value which, although guaranteeing a direct right against the actual provider of services, do not necessarily require that party, who is himself likewise exposed to the risks consequent on insolvency, to honour them and, secondly, that a Member State may not omit to transpose a Directive on the basis of a judgment of a domestic supreme court, according to which package travel purchasers are no longer required to pay more than 10% of the travel price before they obtain such documents of value.*

6. *Neither the objective of Directive 90/314 nor its specific provisions require the Member States to adopt particular provisions in relation to Article 7 to protect package travellers from their own negligence. Where a Directive has not been transposed within the prescribed period, a national court may, in order to determine the damage which must be made good, always inquire whether the injured person showed reasonable care so as to avoid the loss or damage or to mitigate it. However, a package traveller who has paid the whole travel price cannot be regarded as acting negligently simply because he did not take advantage of the possibility, which a judgment of the kind referred to above afforded him, of paying no more than 10% of the total travel price before obtaining documents of value.*

2. Facts of the Case

The *Landgericht* Bonn (Regional Court) referred to the Court for a preliminary ruling under Article 177 (new Article 234) EC Treaty twelve questions on the interpretation of Council Directive 90/314 on package travel, package holidays and package tours (OJ 1990 L158/59). These questions were raised in the course of actions for compensation brought against the Federal Republic of Germany by Erich Dillenkofer and others (hereinafter 'the plaintiffs') for damage they had suffered because the Directive was not transposed within the prescribed period.

   The plaintiffs claimed compensation for damage caused by the late transposition of the Directive. The plaintiffs who purchased travel packages, following the insolvency of the operators from whom they had bought their packages in 1993, either never left for their destination or had to return from their holiday location at their own expense. They did not succeed in obtaining reimbursement of the sums they had paid to the operators or of the expenses they had incurred in returning home.

   The plaintiffs brought actions for compensation against the Federal Republic of Germany relying on the principles laid down by the ECJ in *Francovich* ([1991] ECR I–5357) on the ground that Directive 90/314 on package travel had not been transposed within the prescribed period. Article 7 of this Directive provides:

> The organizer and/or retailer party to the contract shall provide sufficient evidence of security for the refund of money paid over and for the repatriation of the consumer in the event of insolvency.

According to Article 9, Member States were required to bring into force the measures necessary to comply with the Directive before 31 December 1992. Not until mid-1994 did Germany pass a law implementing the Directive; up until then no action had been taken in this matter. The *Landgericht* Bonn held that German law did not afford any basis for upholding the claims for compensation but having doubts regarding the consequences of the *Francovich* judgment it decided to stay the proceedings and refer the following questions to the Court for a preliminary ruling:

1. Is the EC Council Directive of 13 June 1990 on package travel, package holidays and package tours (90/314/EEC) intended to grant individual package travellers, via national transposing provisions, the individual right to security for money paid and repatriation costs in the event of the insolvency of the travel organiser (see paragraph 40 of the judgment in *Francovich*)?

2. Is the content of that right sufficiently identified on the basis of that Directive?

3. What are the minimum requirements for the 'necessary measures' to be taken by the Member States within the meaning of Article 9 of the Directive?

4. In particular, did it satisfy Article 9 of the Directive if the national legislature by 31 December 1992 provided the legislative framework for imposing a legal obligation on the travel organiser and/or retailer to take measures for security within the meaning of Article 7 of the Directive? Or did the necessary change in the law, taking into account the lead times involved in consultation of the travel, insurance and credit sectors, have to come into effect sufficiently in advance of 31 December 1992 for that security actually to function in the package travel market from 1 January 1993?

5. Is the protective purpose, if any, of the Directive satisfied if the Member State allows the travel organiser only to require a deposit towards the travel price of up to 10% of the travel price with a maximum of DM 500 before documents of value are handed over?

6. To what extent are the Member States obliged under the Directive to act (by legislating) in order to protect package travellers against their own negligence?

7. (a) Could the Federal Republic of Germany, in view of the 'advance payment' judgment (*Vorkasse*-Judgment) of the *Bundesgerichtshof* (Federal Court of Justice) of 12 March 1987 (*NJW* 87 1931), have omitted altogether to transpose Article 7 of the Directive by means of legislation?

7. (b) Is there no 'security' within the meaning of Article 7 of the Directive even where, on payment of the travel price, travellers were in possession of documents of value confirming a right to performance against those responsible for providing particular services (airline companies, hotel operators)?

8. (a) Does the mere fact that the time-limit specified in Article 9 of the Directive has been exceeded suffice to confer a right to compensation involving State liability as defined in the *Francovich* judgment of the Court of Justice, or can the Member State put forward the objection that the period for transposition proved to be inadequate?

8. (b) If that objection fails, does the response to the previous question apply even where the Member State concerned cannot achieve the protective purpose of the Directive simply by a change in the law (as for instance with payments in lieu of wages to employees in the event of insolvency), the cooperation of private third parties (travel organizers, the insurance and credit sector) being essential?

9. Does liability on the part of a Member State for an infringement of Community law presuppose a serious, that is to say a manifest and grave, breach of obligations?

10. Is it a precondition of State liability that a judgment in infringement proceedings establishing a breach of Treaty obligations has been delivered before the event giving rise to damage?

11. Does it follow from the *Francovich* judgment of the Court of Justice that the right to compensation on grounds of breach of Community law is not dependent on a finding of fault in general, or at any rate of wrongful non-adoption of legislative measures, on the part of the Member State?

12. If that conclusion is not correct, could the 'advance payment' judgment of the *Bundesgerichtshof* have been an acceptable reason justifying or excusing the Federal Republic of Germany for transposing the Directive, as defined in the answers of the Court of Justice to Questions 4 and 7, only after expiry of the time-limit specified in Article 9?

3. Extract from the Grounds of the ECJ's Judgment

16. The crux of these questions is whether a failure to transpose a Directive within the prescribed period is sufficient per se to afford individuals who have suffered injury a right to reparation or whether other conditions must also be taken into consideration.

17. More specifically, the national court raises the question of the importance to be attached to the German Government's contention that the period prescribed for transposition of the Directive proved inadequate (Question 8). It asks, further, whether State liability requires a serious, that is to say, a manifest and grave, breach of Community obligations (Question 9), whether the breach must have been established in infringement proceedings before the loss or damage occurred (Question 10), whether liability presupposes the existence of fault, of either commission or omission, in the adoption of legislative measures by the Member State (Question 11) and, lastly, in the event that Question 11 is answered in the affirmative, whether liability can be excluded by reason of a judgment such as the 'advance payment' judgment of the Bundesgerichtshof referred to in Question 7 (Question 12).

18. The German, Netherlands and United Kingdom Governments have submitted in particular that a State can incur liability for late transposition of a Directive only if there has been a serious, that is to say, a manifest and grave, breach of Community law for which it can be held responsible. According to those Governments, this depends on the circumstances which caused the period for transposition to be exceeded.

(. . .)

21. In *Brasserie du Pecheur* ([1996] ECR I–1029) and *Factortame* ([1990] ECR I–2433) at paragraphs 50 and 51, *British Telecommunications* ([1996] ECR I–1631), at paragraphs 39 and 40, and *Hedley Lomas* ([1996] ECR I–2553) at paragraphs 25 and 26, the Court, having regard to the circumstances of the case, held that individuals who have suffered damage have a right to reparation where three conditions are met: the rule of law infringed must have been intended to confer rights on individuals; the breach must be sufficiently serious; and there must be a direct causal link between the breach of the obligation resting on the State and the damage sustained by the injured parties.

22. Moreover, it is clear from the *Francovich* case which, like these cases, concerned non-transposition of a Directive within the prescribed period, that the full effectiveness of the third paragraph of Article 189 of the Treaty requires that there should be a right to reparation where the result prescribed by the Directive entails the grant of rights to individuals, the content of those rights is identifiable on the basis of the provisions of the Directive and a causal link exists between the breach of the State's obligation and the loss and damage suffered by the injured parties.

(...)

Grant to individuals of rights whose content is sufficiently identifiable (Questions 1 and 2)

30. By its first two questions, the national court asks whether the result prescribed by Article 7 of the Directive entails the grant to package travellers of rights guaranteeing the refund of money paid over and repatriation in the event of the insolvency of the travel organizer and/or the retailer party to the contract (hereinafter 'the organiser'), and whether the content of those rights can be sufficiently identified.

31. According to the plaintiffs and the Commission, these two questions must be answered in the affirmative. Article 7, they say, clearly and unequivocally recognizes the right of the package traveller, *qua* consumer, to obtain a refund of money paid over and of the costs of repatriation in the event of the organizer's insolvency.

32. The German, Netherlands and United Kingdom Governments disagree with that point of view.

33. The question whether the result prescribed by Article 7 of the Directive entails the grant of rights to individuals must be examined first.

34. According to the actual wording of Article 7, this provision prescribes, as the result of its implementation, an obligation for the organiser to have sufficient security for the refund of money paid over and for the repatriation of the consumer in the event of insolvency.

35. Since the purpose of such security is to protect consumers against the financial risks arising from the insolvency of package travel organisers, the Community legislature has placed operators under an obligation to offer sufficient evidence of such security in order to protect consumers against those risks.

36. The purpose of Article 7 is accordingly to protect consumers, who thus have the right to be reimbursed or repatriated in the event of the insolvency of the organizer from whom they purchased the package travel. Any other interpretation would be illogical, since the purpose of the security which organizers must offer under Article 7 of the Directive is to enable consumers to obtain a refund of money paid over or to be repatriated.

37. That result is, moreover, confirmed by the penultimate recital in the preamble to the Directive, according to which both the consumer and the package travel industry would benefit if organisers were placed under an obligation to provide sufficient evidence of security in the event of insolvency.

38. In that connection, the German and United Kingdom Governments' argument that the Directive, which is based on Article 100a of the Treaty, is aimed essentially at ensuring freedom to provide services and, more generally, freedom of competition cannot be valid.

39. First, the recitals in the preamble to the Directive repeatedly refer to the purpose of protecting consumers. Secondly, the fact that the Directive is intended to assure other objectives cannot preclude its provisions from also having the aim of protecting consumers. Indeed, according to Article 100a(3) of the Treaty, the Commission, in its proposals submitted pursuant to that article, concerning inter alia consumer protection, must take as a base a high level of protection.

40. Similarly, the German and United Kingdom Governments' argument that the actual wording of Article 7 shows that this provision simply requires package travel organizers to provide sufficient evidence of security and that its lack of reference to any right of consumers to such security indicates that such a right is only an indirect and derived right must be rejected.

41. In this regard, it suffices to point out that the obligation to offer sufficient evidence of security necessarily implies that those having that obligation must actually take out such security. Indeed, the obligation laid down in Article 7 would be pointless in the absence of security actually enabling money paid over to be refunded or the consumer to be repatriated, should occasion arise.

42. Consequently, it must be concluded that the result prescribed by Article 7 of the Directive entails the grant to package travellers of rights guaranteeing the refund of money that they have paid over and their repatriation in the event of the organizer's insolvency.

43. The next point to be examined is whether the content of the rights in question are identifiable on the basis of the provisions of the Directive alone.

44. The persons having rights under Article 7 are sufficiently identified as consumers, as defined by Article 2 of the Directive. The same holds true of the content of those rights. As explained above, those rights consist in a guarantee that money paid over by purchasers of package travel will be refunded and a guarantee that they will be repatriated in the event of the insolvency of the organiser. In those circumstances, the purpose of Article 7 of the Directive must be to grant to individuals rights whose content is determinable with sufficient precision.

45. That conclusion is not affected by the fact that, as the German Government points out, the Directive leaves the Member States considerable latitude as regards the choice of means for achieving the result it seeks. The fact that States may choose between a wide variety of means for achieving the result prescribed by a Directive is of no importance if the purpose of the Directive is to grant to individuals rights whose content is determinable with sufficient precision.

46. The reply to the first two questions must therefore be that the result prescribed by Article 7 of the Directive entails the grant to package travellers of rights guaranteeing a refund of money paid over and their repatriation in the event of the organizer's insolvency; the content of those rights is sufficiently identifiable.

B. Commentary

1. European Law

With this decision the ECJ for the first time extended its case law on state liability arising from a Member State's infringement of Community law to the field of consumer protection. The claim of state liability which had been developed in the cases of *Francovich* (ECJ [1991] ECR I–5357), *Brasserie du pêcheur* (ECJ [1996] ECR I–1029), *British Telecommunications* (ECJ [1996] ECR I–1631) and *Hedley Lomas* (ECJ [1996] ECR I–2553) primarily served to enforce Community law against the Member States by introducing an effective sanction. At the same time this case law leads to the indirect effect of non-transposed Community law. This benefits consumers. The decision in *Dillenkofer* clearly strengthened the legal position of the consumer in Community law. This strengthening compensates for the lack of a 'horizontal direct effect' of non-transposed (consumer protection) Directives which the consumer may only assert against the State and not against other individuals (ECJ *Dori* [1994] ECR I–3325: Case no 11 in this Casebook).

The ECJ reaffirmed in *Dillenkofer* that a claim of state liability depends on the following conditions being fulfilled:

1. The rule of Community law which has been infringed must have been intended to confer rights on individuals and the content of those rights must be identifiable on the basis of the provisions of the infringed rule;

2. The infringement is sufficiently serious;

3. There must be a direct causal link between the breach of the State's obligation and the loss and the damage suffered by the injured parties.

For the purposes of consumer protection the implementation of the first condition is important. In *Dillenkofer* it was whether Article 7 of Directive 90/314 (text reproduced above in A2) intended to grant a right to the travellers the content of which was sufficiently identifiable. In light of its wording (and that of the recitals), the ECJ held that the conditions were fulfilled (paragraphs 33–40). In so doing it regarded the protection of the consumer to be an independent objective of the Directive, not only ancillary to the completion of the Internal Market (paragraph 39). The ECJ was thereby clearly opposed to the contrary opinion which had been put forward by the German and British governments amongst others. They had relied in particular on (the pre-Maastricht) Article 100a EC Treaty upon which the enactment of the Directive was based.

Article 100a

1. By way of derogation from Article 100 and save where otherwise provided in this Treaty, the following provisions shall apply for the achievement of the objectives set out in Article 8a. The Council shall, acting by a qualified majority on a proposal from the Commission in co-operation with the European Parliament and after consulting the Economic and Social Committee, adopt the measures for the approximation of the provisions laid down by law, regulation or administrative action in Member States which have as their object the establishment and functioning of the internal market.

(. . .)

3. The Commission, in its proposals envisaged in paragraph 1 concerning health, safety, environmental protection and consumer protection, will take as a base a high level of protection.

The wording of the old Article 100a resulted in the Community having jurisdiction only to create measures for the purpose of completing the Internal Market, whereas the protection of the consumer was mentioned only as a type of subsidiary objective in paragraph 3. The first Treaty amendment giving the Community jurisdiction on consumer protection matters came in Article 129a of the Maastricht Treaty (amended by the Treaty of Amsterdam (OJ 1997 C340/1) and now Article 153 EC Treaty, text reproduced above in the European law Commentary to the ECJ *El Corte Inglés*: Case no 12 in this Casebook). The decision of the Court makes clear that even in the case of legislative acts which have been passed on the basis of Article 100a EC Treaty, the protection of the consumer may have an independent objective from which it may be possible for the consumer to lay a claim in state liability. In the meantime, the ECJ has confirmed through its decision in *Verein für Konsumenteninformation* (ECJ [1998] ECR I–2949, for more details to this case see under 6) that Article 7 of Directive 90/314 has as its objective the granting of rights to the consumer and has defined these rights further.

Concerning the issue of general state liability arising from an infringement of Community law, the decision in *Dillenkofer* clarified that a 'sufficiently serious' breach is made out per se if a Member State remains wholly inactive during the period of implementation (paragraph 29). The ECJ did not have to answer the question pertaining to whether the passing of a law is necessary in order to implement a Directive or whether the Member State may forego a statutory rule by relying on precedent (paragraph 67).

ECJ CASE LAW REFERENCES

Francovich [1991] ECR I–5357; *Dori* [1994] ECR I–3325: Case no 11 in this Casebook; *Brasserie du pêcheur* [1996] ECR I–1029; *British Telecommunications* [1996] ECR I–1631; *Hedley Lomas* [1996] ECR I–2553; *Verein für Konsumenteninformation* [1998] ECR I–2949.

LITERATURE REFERENCES

F Berrod 'Responsabilité des États membres en cas de violation du droit communautaire' (1996) *Revue du marché unique européen* no 4 197; P Oliver (1997) *Common Market Law Review* 675 (Casenote on *Dillenkofer*); N Reich 'Der Schutz subjektiver Gemeinschaftsrechte durch Staatshaftung', (1996) *Europäische Zeitschrift für Wirtschaftsrecht* 709; D Simon (1997) *Journal du droit international* 493 (Casenote on *Dillenkofer*); R Streinz/S Leible 'Staatshaftung wegen verspäteter Umsetzung der EG-Pauschalreiserichtlinie' (1996) *Zeitschrift für Wirtschaftsrecht* 1931.

HS-N/JJ

2. *England & Wales*

The UK took part in the *Dillenkofer* proceedings by supporting the German Government's argument that the actual wording of Article 7 of Directive 90/314 simply required package travel organisers to provide sufficient evidence of security and that its lack of reference to any right of consumers to such security indicated that such a right was only an indirect and derived right.

The UK, though, complied punctually with their obligations under EC law and implemented the Directive by the Package Travel, Package Holidays and Package Tours Regulations 1992, which came into force one week before the deadline for implementation had expired. The 1992 Regulations were recently amended by the

Package Travel (Amendment) Regulations 1998 and have constituted the ground for some litigation concerning mainly inaccurate brochures and improper performance of holiday contracts.

The question of consumer security is addressed by Regulations 16 to 27. According to regulation 16:

> the other party to the contract shall at all times be able to provide sufficient evidence of security for the refund of money paid over and for the repatriation of the consumer in the event of insolvency.

This evidential requirement is reinforced by criminal law sanctions (Regulation 23 and Schedule 3), but no civil liability arises from non-compliance (Regulation 27). The Regulations do not set up any government-run system, but offer the organisers a menu of options to provide security, either by way of a bond, an insurance policy or a trust (regulations 17–21). Those new provisions, however, have not entailed any major changes in the holiday industry within the United Kingdom.

Since the 1970s, the Civil Aviation Authority has required tour operators who use air travel as a means of transport to obtain an ATOL (Air Travel Organisers' Licence). One of the conditions of the grant of the licence is that applicants show that their financial resources are adequate to discharge their obligations in respect of the activities in which they are engaged. Other tour operators' associations such as the Association of British Travel Agents (ABTA) and the Association of Independent Tour Operators (AITO) provide financial bonds against the financial collapse of their members with the aim of refunding deposits and repatriating holidaymakers. Given this pre-existing bonding structure, the main effect of the Regulations has been to considerably extend the number of travel activities in respect of which security must be provided. Given the width of the definition of 'organiser', even more organisations are now going to be obliged to provide evidence of security.

Reference to the *Dillenkofer* case can be found in two UK cases concerning State liability for failure to comply with obligations under EC law. One of these cases, *R v Secretary of State, ex parte Sutton*, was referred to the ECJ for a preliminary ruling concerning incorrect transposition of Directive 79/7 on equal treatment for men and women in matters of social security; in the second case, *R v Attorney General for Northern Ireland, ex parte Burns*, the Queen's Bench Division applied *Dillenkofer* to declare that UK's failure to comply with Directive 93/104 on working time was a sufficiently serious breach to automatically give rise to liability for losses suffered by any person.

CASE LAW REFERENCES

R v Secretary of State, ex parte Sutton [1997] 3 *All England Reports* 497; *R v Attorney General for Northern Ireland, ex parte Burns* [1999] *Northern Ireland Law Reports* 175.

LITERATURE REFERENCES

D Grant/S Mason *Holiday Law* (1998); V King 'The fault issue in state liability: from *Francovich* to *Dillenkofer*' *European Competition Law* (1997) 110; J Dalby 'Advance deposits and the Package Travel Directive' (1996) *Travel Law Journal* 11; A Davis 'European Union: late implementation of Directive by a Member State-compensation to consumers' (Casenote) (1997) *Consumer Law Journal* CS1.

PN

3. Germany

In the summer of 1993 several travel agents went bankrupt (including a company with the name MP–Travel-Line). Thousands of German tourists were either left stranded at their holiday resorts or lost the money they had already paid. The question of possible state liability for the Federal Republic caused great interest even in the daily press. The *Bundesministerium der Justiz* (Federal Ministry of Justice) received approximately 9,000 applications for compensation claims totalling over 20 million German Marks, 11 million German Marks of which has been paid. The *Dillenkofer* case was seen as the tip of the iceberg. The spectre of state liability led to a law implementing Directive 90/314 being rushed through Parliament (*Bundesgesetzblatt* I 1994 1322).

Before the Directive was implemented, German law did not have legislation protecting consumers in the case of a travel organiser's insolvency. On the contrary, protection of this kind was only provided in a few contractual situations, most notably in labour law. As the draft Directive 90/314 was being discussed, Germany vehemently opposed any protection against insolvency. In the so-called '*Vorkasse* Judgment' ('Advance Payment' judgment of 12 March 1987), the *Bundesgerichtshof* was developing the foundations for tourist protection in case of the travel organiser's insolvency (*BGHZ* 100 157 *NJW* 1993 293). According to this judgment, the traveller could only be required to give an advance payment which exceeded a relatively low deposit in return for essential travel documents. However, according to the ECJ, this state of law did not comply sufficiently with the requirements of Article 7 of the Directive (paragraphs 62–65).

The law implementing Directive 90/314 (*Bundesgesetzblatt* I 1994 1322 as amended by *Bundesgesetzblatt* I 2000 897 and 2001 1658) inserted a new paragraph into the Civil Code (*Bürgerliches Gesetzbuch*). Paragraphs 1 and 3 state:

(1) Der Reiseveranstalter hat sicherzustellen, daß dem Reisenden erstattet werden:

1. der gezahlte Reisepreis, soweit Reiseleistungen infolge Zahlungsunfähigkeit oder Eröffnung des Insolvenzverfahrens über das Vermögen des Reiseveranstalters ausfallen, und

2. notwendige Aufwendungen, die dem Reisenden infolge Zahlungsunfähigkeit oder Eröffnung des Insolvenzverfahrens über das Vermögen des Reiseveranstalters für die Rückreise entstehen.

Die Verpflichtungen nach Satz 1 kann der Reiseveranstalter nur erfüllen

1. durch eine Versicherung bei einem im Geltungsbereich dieses Gesetzes zum Geschäftsbetrieb befugten Versicherungsunternehmen oder

2. durch ein Zahlungsversprechen eines im Geltungsbereich dieses Gesetzes zum Geschäftsbetrieb befugten Kreditinstituts.

(. . .)

(3) Zur Erfüllung seiner Verpflichtung nach Absatz 1 hat der Reiseveranstalter dem Reisenden einen unmittelbaren Anspruch gegen den Versicherer oder das Kreditinstitut zu verschaffen und durch Übergabe einer von diesem Unternehmen ausgestellten Bestätigung (Sicherungsschein) nachzuweisen.

(. . .)

The old § 651k(4) of the Civil Code (*Bundesgesetzblatt* I 1994 1322) was clearly in line with the '*Vorkasse*' case, but not with European law.

(4) Der Reiseveranstalter darf Zahlungen des Reisenden auf den Reisepreis, außer einer Anzahlung bis zur Höhe von zehn vom Hundert des Reisepreises, höchstens jedoch fünfhundert Deutsche Mark vor der Beendigung der Reise nur fordern oder annehmen, wenn er dem Reisenden einen Sicherungsschein übergeben hat.

In *Dillenkofer* the ECJ unequivocally stated that according to Article 7 of Directive 90/314 even the refund of the deposit must be protected (paragraphs 56–60). This time Germany reacted quickly to the danger of state liability and amended § 651k paragraph 4 of the Civil Code so that even with a payment of a deposit a security document must be handed over. The decision of the *Landgericht* Bonn and the decision of the ECJ in the *Dillenkofer* case have effectively removed a lacuna in transposing of EC consumer protection law. Due to the enormous attention it has received in the legal press, this case has also made the general public aware of the influence of European private law on German civil law. In legal journals a clear reversal of opinion can be ascertained. Whilst the content of Directive 90/314 and in particular the duty to offer protection from insolvency encountered considerable criticism at first, the *Dillenkofer* decision has been generally well received; Germany's breach of Community Law could not be disputed (eg *Streinz/Leible*).

In the meantime Germany has paid damages in many cases where the facts were undisputed. It has remained doubtful, however, whether a claim of state liability also exists in relation to loss suffered under a package holiday contract, which had been concluded before the expiration of the transposition period of Directive 90/314 (31 December 1992). The *Oberlandesgericht* Köln (Higher Regional Court), without making a reference to the ECJ, gave a clear answer to this question in its judgment of 15 July 1997: it is neither within the meaning nor in accordance with the purpose of Directive 90/314 to force Member States to interfere in valid contracts in a way which is constitutionally questionable and thereby impose a burden on travel organisers. Accordingly, Germany was not liable in respect of the *Dillenkofer* case for losses incurred by package travellers who had concluded the contract for the package holiday with an insolvent travel organiser before 1 January 1993, notwithstanding the fact that they had paid a deposit before or after the relevant date of 1 January 1993.

CASE LAW REFERENCES

Bundesgerichtshof judgment of 12 March 1987 (1987) *Neue Juristische Wochenschrift* 1931; Oberlandesgericht Köln judgment of 15 July 1997 (1998) *Europäische Zeitschrift für Wirtschaftsrecht* 95.

LITERATURE REFERENCES

M Huff 'Eine erste Bewertung des EuGH-Urteils *Dillenkofer*' (1996) *Neue Juristische Wochenschrift* 3190; N Reich 'Der Schutz subjektiver Gemeinschaftsrechte durch Staatshaftung' (1996) *Europäische Zeitschrift für Wirtschaftsrecht* 709; K Stöhr 'Schadensersatzansprüche wegen verspäteter Umsetzung der EG-Pauschalreiserichtlinie' (1999) *Neue Juristische Wochenschrift* 1063; R Streinz/S Leible 'Staatshaftung wegen verspäteter Umsetzung der EG-Pauschalreiserichtlinie' (1996) *Zeitschrift für Wirtschaftsrecht* 1931.

HS-N

4. France

French writers, when discussing the decision in *Dillenkofer* mainly concentrate on the importance of the decision for the development of state liability in Community law (*Berrod, Simon*). There had been little incentive to mention the legal situation in France, for the standards set by Directive 90/314 had already been fulfilled. Moreover, this Directive had in many respects been inspired by French law. The main provisions of travel law have not been incorporated into the *Code de la Consommation*. They are in fact contained in Law no 92–645 of 13 June 1992 as well as in *Decret* no 94–490 of 15 June 1994. Cases which refer to Directive 90/314 are hard to find (an example is the judgment of the *Cour de Cassation* of 12 June 1995). Article 4 of Law no 92–645 secures the claims of the traveller in the case of the bankruptcy or insolvency of the tour organiser or travel agent which is required by Article 7 of Directive 90/314. This security is achieved by means of an administrative admissions procedure. Accordingly, the tour organisers and the travel agency must have a license, the issue of which is subject to strict conditions. Among them is the need to prove a *garantie financière* (a type of financial guarantee) which secures the costs of a possible return journey.

CASE LAW REFERENCES

Cour de Cassation chambre criminelle judgment of 12 June 1995 *Bulletin des arrêts de la Cour de Cassation* chambre criminelle 1995 no 212.

LITERATURE REFERENCES

A Batteur 'La protection illusoire du consommateur par le droit spécial de la consommation: réflexions sur la législation nouvelle régissant le contrat de vente de voyages' (1996) *Recueil Dalloz Sirey* Chronique, 82; F Berrod 'Responsabilité des États membres en cas de violation du droit communautaire' (1996) *Revue du marché unique européen* no 4 197; D Simon (1997) *Journal du droit international* 493 (Casenote on *Dillenkofer*).

BD

5. *Italy*

Directive 90/314 on package travel was transposed into Italian law by the *Decreto Legge* no 111 of 17 March 1995 which had been passed on the basis of *Legge* no 146 of 22 February 1994. The period of transposition had expired on 31 December 1992.

It is claimed that the *Dillenkofer* decision contributed to the extension of Community law relating to state liability in two respects. On the one hand, it provided Italian law with more precise criteria for the purpose of deciding an issue of state liability. On the other hand, it has become clearer that Italian courts must regard entire national provisions as invalid to the extent to which they stand in the way of a claim for state liability (*Scardocchia*). The *Dillenkofer* judgment is regarded as being of fundamental importance because it laid down common principles for the application of Community law designed to aid national courts to develop a uniform Community law, rather than developing the law nationally (*Furlan*).

Before the decision in *Dillenkofer* Italian law made it very difficult to pursue a claim for state liability. Italian law made a distinction between two legal positions of the citizen vis-à-vis the State. Where the State acted in the field of private law, the citizen had *diritti soggettivi* (full rights) against the State. There was a private law claim for full compensation of damage suffered which could be pursued in the civil courts (Article 2043 *Codice civile*). On the other hand, concerning acts of the State in public law, the citizen only had *interessi legitimi* (legitimate interests). However, in this case the amount of compensation was far less than that which he could claim according to private law principles; it also had to be pursued in the administrative tribunal. The restriction of the citizen's legal position to *interessi legitimi* proved difficult to square with the judgment in *Francovich*. The decision of the Court in *Dillenkofer* contributed to the 'softening' of the distinction between *diritti soggettivi* and *interessi legitimi*. An example of this development

can be found in the decisions of the *Corte di Cassazione* relating to industrial relations law. Whilst one judgment rejected the liability of public authorities for
failure to transpose a Directive by relying on the traditional distinction, a judgment of 23 April 1996 allowed a compensation claim in a similar case on the basis
of private law principles. More recently, the *Corte di Cassazione* established the
possibility of compensation based not only on *diritto soggettivi*, but also *diritto
legittimi*, as well as re-affirming the liability of public authorities.

CASE LAW REFERENCES

Corte di Cassazione judgment of 11 October 1995 no 10617 (1996) *Il Foro Italiano* I 503;
Corte di Cassazione judgment of 23 August 1996 no 7770, (1996) *Il Foro Italiano* Massi-
mario 705;Corte di Cassazione sez un 22 July 1999 no 500 (1999) *Giustia Civile* I 2261 n
Morelli.

LITERATURE REFERENCES:

S Furlan 'Il Risarcimento dei danni causati dalla mancata attuazione di una direttiva:
la sentenza *Dillenkofer*' (1997) *Rivista Italiana di Diritto Pubblico Comunitario* 463; S
Scardocchia 'Un Passo avanti della Corte di Giustizia nella tutela dei singoli contro gli
inadempimenti' *Guida al Diritto*, no 43 of 2 November 1996 76 (Casenote on *Dillenkofer*).

AM

6. Austria

After joining the European Economic Area in 1993 the Austrian legislator found
itself for the first time in the situation of having to transpose private law provisions relating to the consumer. Directive 90/314 on Package Travel became part
of the Law on Consumer Credit (*Konsumentenschutzgesetz*, hereafter *KSchG*,
Bundesgesetzblatt 1979 no 140, *Bundesgesetzblatt* 1993 no 247, §§ 31b–31f),
and partially implemented in trade law regulations (Informationspflichten
Bundesgesetzblatt 1994 no 599; Travel Agency Security Regulation, *Reisebüro-
Sicherungsverordnung*; hereafter *R-SV, Bundesgesetzblatt* 1994 no 881).

In connection with this matter the question arose as to how Directive 90/314,
which protected not only the consumer but also business travellers (Article 2(4)
of the Directive), could be transposed into the Austrian *KSchG*. It only applied to
contracts concluded by consumers. Paragraph 1 of the *KSchG* (text reproduced in
the Austrian Commentary to the ECJ's decision in *Di Pinto*: Case no 10 in this
Casebook) was only applicable to Part 1 of the statute. The provisions relating to
package tours were inserted in Part 3 of the *KSchG* entitled 'Supplementary Provisions'. The transposition into the *KSchG* is therefore most probably correct but
can nevertheless be criticised because it leaves gaps. The statute has, however, been
extended to cover the travel contracts of business persons.

In order to implement Article 7 of Directive 90/314 dealing with insolvency insurance, the Austrian legislator passed the *Reisebüro-Sicherungsverordnung* (Travel Agency Security Regulation (*R-SV, Bundesgesetzblatt* 1994 no 881, repealed by the new *Reisebürosicherungsverordnung, Bundesgesetzblatt* 1998–II no 10)). According to this law, the tour organiser had to guarantee the reimbursement of instalments already paid and the necessary costs of providing a return journey by arranging an insurance policy or by providing a bank or a public authority willing to act as guarantor. However, in practice it cannot be expected that an insurance company or bank would be willing to undertake unlimited liability; therefore the necessary amount of insurance or the required extent of the bank guarantee in § 3(2) R-SV was restricted to 5 per cent of the turnover from the tour organiser's business activity in the first quarter of the previous year (in the case of a deposit of over 10 per cent of the package tour price the corresponding amount is 10 per cent of the turnover; by amendment, *Bundesgesetzblatt* 1996 no 170, the percentage values were raised to 10 per cent and 15 per cent respectively).

In 1995 the Austrian tour organiser Karthago-Reisen declared itself bankrupt. The Greek hotelier with whom several holidaymakers had booked their stay (through Karthargo-Reisen) found out about this. He therefore demanded from the travellers that they pay the hotel bill themselves. In so doing he prevented them from leaving the hotel, using physical force, until they had paid the bill. The Austrian Consumers' Information Association took the Österreichische Kreditversicherungs AG to court, claiming the hotel costs on behalf of the travellers. The *Handelsgericht* Vienna (Commercial Court) doubted whether the facts of the case came within the term 'necessary expenditure for the return journey' for the purposes of the *R-SV*. It was of the opinion that this Law was dependent on the interpretation of Article 7 of Directive 90/314 due to the obligation to interpret domestic law in conformity with the Directive. It therefore submitted an application for preliminary judgment to the ECJ (ruling of 21 October 1996). The ECJ held that Article 7 in aiming to cover the risk to the consumer in case of the organiser's insolvency also applied to the facts of this case (ECJ, *Verein für Konsumenteninformation* [1998] ECR I–2949). The parties to the initial proceedings accordingly reached an out-of-court settlement in which the insurance company agreed to reimburse the hotel costs.

The insolvency of the Austrian tour organiser Arena was a case where the liability of the insurance company, limited according to § 3(2) *R-SV*, was not sufficient to satisfy the claims of all the applicants. A claim of state liability against Austria was commenced. In contrast to the facts in *Dillenkofer*, Austria had not implemented Article 7 of Directive 90/314 too late but rather incorrectly. The fault lay in the fact that the insolvency insurance had only to be paid up to a corresponding percentage of the previous year's profits. Losses which exceed this amount are not covered. However, an incorrect transposition may also provide sufficient grounds to make a claim of state liability (ECJ *British Telecommunications* [1996] ECR I–1631). This raised the question whether there had been a sufficiently serious breach of Community law. The ECJ had stated in *Dillenkofer* that there was no leeway in the transposition of Article 7 of Directive 90/314 inasmuch as the provision demanded a complete guarantee to reimburse without restricting the amounts already paid and the price of the return journey. It comes as no surprise, therefore, that Austria was found in breach of Community law by the ECJ in *Rechberger* ([1999] ECR I–3499).

Clearly, the Austrian legislator had recognised the inadequacy of the (ex) *R-SV* and had once more passed a new *Reisebürosicherungsverordnung* (Travel Agency Insurance Regulation) (*RSV, Bundesgesetzblatt* 1998 no 10 in the *Bundesgesetzblatt* 1998 no 118, now replaced by *Reisebürosicherungsverordnung, Bundesgesetzblatt* 1999–II no 316). Paragraph 8 of the new *RSV* makes provision for the tour organiser to participate in an insurance association. In the event that the insurance (still provided for) or guarantee proves inadequate, the insurance association must satisfy the claims of the package tourists to an amount of fifty million schillings (approximately 3.5 million Euro). It is however not obligatory to be a member of such an insurance association. Where the tour organiser chooses not to participate in such an association, the percentage of the sales from the previous year, which must be covered by an insurance policy or bank guarantee, is simply raised. In addition an advisory committee was set up in the Federal Ministry for Economic Affairs (*Bundesministerium für wirtschaftliche Angelegenheiten*) which is responsible for making sure that the calculation of the companies' turnover accords with the provisions. Even the new *RSV* therefore does not completely guarantee the package tourists' claims of restitution. A claim of state liability against Austria due to the incorrect implementation of Directive 90/314 is therefore still possible in the future.

CASE LAW REFERENCES

Handelsgericht Wien judgment of 21 October 1996 (1997) *Wirtschaftsrechtliche Blätter* 33.

LITERATURE REFERENCES

H Dossi 'Die Geltendmachung der EU-Staatshaftung in Österreich: die Praxis in einem System unvollständiger Rechtsgrundlagen' *ecolex,* 2000 337; S Hödl 'System der gemeinschaftsrechtlichen Staatshaftung nach dem Urteil *Dillenkofer*' (1996) *Wirtschaftsrechtliche Blätter* 472; S Schermayer *Der gemeinschaftsrechtliche Staatshaftungsanspruch, Entwicklung, Perspektiven und Auswirkungen auf das österreichische Haftungsrecht* (1998); C Srix-Hackl 'Pauschalreisen und 'Staatshaftung'—eine unendliche Geschichte' (1999) *Österreichisches Anwaltsblatt* 470.

AE

IV

The Description of Goods

INTRODUCTION

The provisions regulating the labelling and description of goods illustrate the complex relationship between consumer protection and the realisation of the Internal Market. An effective protection of the consumer demands, on the one hand, comprehensive information pertaining to the ingredients and properties of products in a language which is easy to understand, preferably in the consumer's native language. On the other hand, different national provisions on labelling which derogate from the norm restrict cross-border trade, for in certain cases they proscribe different labels for different countries and thereby cause costs to rise. The ECJ has in addition assigned a key function to the labelling of goods by means of its 'labelling doctrine' which it developed in its well-known judgment in the *Cassis de Dijon* case ([1979] ECR 649: Case no 3 in this Casebook). The prohibition on the import of goods on the basis of public interest, for example public health and the protection of the consumer, is disproportionate and contravenes Article 28 (ex Article 30) EC Treaty if the protection intended may be achieved by a warning on the packaging of the product (see the European Law Commentary to ECJ, *Cassis de Dijon*: Case no 3 in this Casebook). The Community therefore enacted relatively early on a number of legal measures primarily in the field of foodstuffs concerning labelling. Of special importance is Directive 79/112 on the approximation of the laws of the Member States relating to labelling, presentation advertising of foodstuffs for sale to the ultimate consumer (OJ 1979 L33/1) which has now been replaced by Directive 2000/13 on the approximation of the laws of the Member States relating to the labelling, presentation and advertising of foodstuffs (OJ 2000 L109/29). The wording of many of the relevant provisions of Directive 79/112 has not been changed by this replacement.

The three ECJ decisions presented here elucidate some provisions central to this Directive from different perspectives, such as the obligation to use a language on the label which can be easily understood by the buyer (*Piageme I*: Case no 16 in this Casebook), and the fundamental prohibition imposed on Member States not to adopt provisions which exceed the requirements of the Directive (*SARPP*: Case no 15 in this Casebook). In the case *Gut Springenheide* (Case no 17 in this Casebook) the issue concerned the labelling provisions for eggs on the basis of which the ECJ interpreted the general prohibition of misleading the consumer which is to be found in Directive 79/112 and other Community legislation. The three decisions presented here also illustrate how the ECJ seeks to realise the aims of consumer protection. These aims sometimes conflict with the policy of the Internal Market and powerful economic interests.

LITERATURE REFERENCES

G Howells/T Wilhelmsson *EC Consumer Law* (1997) 126–133; N Reich *Europäisches Verbraucherrecht* (3rd edn 1996) 301–317; S Weatherill *EC Consumer Law and Policy* (1997) 48–52.

CASE NO. 14 — *Bayerische Hypotheken- und Wechselbank C–45/96*

Bayerische Hypotheken-und Wechselbank AG v Edgar Dietzinger **[1998] ECR I–1199**

A. Judgment of the ECJ of 17 March 1998

1. Held

On a proper construction of the first indent of Article 2 of Directive 85/577/EEC of 20 December 1985 to protect the consumer in respect of contracts negotiated away from business premises, a contract of guarantee concluded by a natural person who is not acting in the course of his trade or profession does not come within the scope of the Directive where it guarantees repayment of a debt contracted by another person who, for his part, is acting within the course of his trade or profession.

2. Facts of the Case

The *Bundesgerichtshof* (Federal Court of Justice) made a reference to the Court concerning the interpretation of Council Directive 85/577/EEC of 20 December 1985 to protect the consumer in respect of contracts negotiated away from business premises (OJ 1985 L372/31). That question was raised in proceedings between Bayerische Hypotheken- und Wechselbank AG ('the Bank') and Edgar Dietzinger concerning the performance of a contract of guarantee concluded by Mr Dietzinger with the Bank. Article 1(1) of Directive 85/577 provides:

This Directive shall apply to contracts under which a trader supplies goods or services to a consumer and which are concluded:

—during an excursion organised by the trader away from his business premises, or

—during a visit by a trader

  i) to the consumer's home or to that of another consumer;
 ii) to the consumer's place of work,

where the visit does not take place at the express request of the consumer.

Article 2 provides:

For the purposes of this Directive:

—'consumer' means a natural person who, in transactions covered by this Directive, is acting for purposes which can be regarded as outside his trade or profession

—'trader' means a natural or legal person who, for the transaction in question, acts in his commercial or professional capacity, and anyone acting in the name or on behalf of a trader.

Under Article 4 of Directive 85/577, traders are required to give consumers written notice of their right to cancel the contract within a specified period. Article 5 provides that that period is to be not less than seven days from receipt by the consumer of the notice of his right to renounce the effects of the contract.

Mr Dietzinger's father ran a building firm in respect of which the Bank, inter alia, granted a current account overdraft facility. On 11 September 1992, Mr Dietzinger gave a direct recourse written guarantee, for a sum not to exceed DM 100,000, covering his parents' obligations to the Bank. The contract of guarantee was concluded at the house of Mr Dietzinger's parents during a visit by an employee of the Bank. Mr Dietzinger's mother had agreed to the contract over the telephone. Mr Dietzinger was not informed of his right of cancellation. In May 1993, the Bank called in, with immediate effect, all the loans which it had granted to Mr Dietzinger's parents, which at that time totalled more than DM 1.6 million. The bank also sued Mr Dietzinger for payment of DM 50,000 under the guarantee. Mr Dietzinger sought to renounce the guarantee, maintaining that he had not been informed of his right of cancellation, contrary to the *Gesetz über den Widerruf von Haustürgeschäften und ähnlichen Geschäften* ('Law on the Cancellation of Doorstep Transactions and Analogous Transactions', *Bundesgesetzblatt* I 122) of 16 January 1986, which transposed Directive 85/577 into German law.

The *Landgericht* (Regional Court) found in favour of the Bank. Mr Dietzinger then appealed to the *Oberlandesgericht* (Higher Regional Court), which quashed the decision given at first instance. The Bank then appealed on a point of law to the *Bundesgerichtshof*, which held that an interpretation of Directive 85/577 was necessary in order to determine the dispute. It therefore referred the following question to the ECJ for a preliminary ruling:

Where a contract of guarantee or suretyship is concluded under German law between a financial institution and a natural person who is not acting in that connection in the course of his trade or profession, in order to secure a claim by the financial institution against a third party in respect of a loan, is it covered by the words 'contracts under which a trader supplies goods or services to a consumer' (Article 1(1) of Council Directive 85/577/EEC of 20 December 1985 to protect the consumer in respect of contracts negotiated away from business premises, OJ 1985 L372/31)?

3. Extract from the Grounds of the ECJ's Judgment

11. By its question, the Bundesgerichtshof is asking in effect whether a contract of guarantee concluded by a natural person who is not acting in the course of a trade or profession is covered by Directive 85/577.

12. Mr Dietzinger and the Commission consider that Directive 85/577 applies to a contract of guarantee by virtue of the Directive's aim, which is to protect those consumers who conclude a contract where, because it involved doorstep selling, they were unable to prepare themselves for its negotiation. Like a purchaser, a guarantor undertakes to perform obligations and is even more in need of protection since he receives no consideration in exchange for his commitment.

13. In the Commission's view, Article 1 of Directive 85/577 is applicable to any contract concluded between a natural person and a trader who, in the course of his business activities, supplies goods or services to consumers in general, even if the contract in question does not involve such consideration. In referring to contracts under which a 'trader supplies goods or services to a consumer', the Directive is simply making clear that its scope is not restricted to sellers of goods.

14. The German, Belgian, French and Finnish Governments, on the other hand, consider that guarantees are not covered by Directive 85/577, essentially because a guarantee is not a 'contract under which a trader supplies goods or services to a consumer' within the meaning of Article 1.

15. According to those Governments, the wording of the provision implies that goods or services are supplied by a trader to a consumer who relies on the protection afforded by Directive 85/577, so that it is not enough for the trader to be a supplier of goods or services in general. They point out that such an interpretation is strongly suggested by the English version of the Directive ('contracts under which a trader supplies goods or services to a consumer'). In circumstances such as those of the instant case, the guarantor's commitment gives rise to no consideration, in the sense that the guarantor receives no goods or services from the trader to whom the commitment was given.

16. Those Governments argue further that Directive 85/577 does not cover guarantees; if it did, the Directive would have contained specific rules providing, in particular, for the fate of the contract whose performance is guaranteed by the guarantor in the event of his exercising the right of cancellation. Consequently, protection of guarantors is a matter for national law alone. In particular, the French Government argues that, since Directive 85/577 does not govern the effects, on the principal contract, of possible invalidity of a contract of guarantee, such guarantees must, in view of their ancillary nature, be excluded from the scope of the Directive.

17. The Court observes that, according to Article 1, Directive 85/577 applies to contracts under which 'a trader supplies goods or services to a consumer' which are concluded away from the trader's business premises, unless the trader was expressly requested by the consumer to visit him with a view to the negotiation of the contract.

18. In determining whether a contract of guarantee securing performance of a credit agreement by the principal debtor can fall within the scope of Directive 85/577, it should be noted that, apart from the exceptions listed in Article 3(2), the scope of the Directive is not limited according to the nature of the goods or services to be supplied under a contract; the only requirement is that the goods or services must be intended for private consumption. The grant of a credit facility is indeed the provision of a service, the contract of guarantee being merely ancillary to the principal contract, of which in practice it is usually a precondition.

19. Furthermore, nothing in the wording of the Directive requires that the person concluding the contract under which goods or services are to be supplied be the person to whom they are supplied. Directive 85/577 is designed to protect consumers by enabling them to withdraw from a contract concluded on the initiative of the trader rather than of the customer, where the customer may have been unable to see all the implications of his act. Consequently, a contract benefiting a third party cannot be excluded from the scope of the Directive on the sole ground that the goods or services purchased were intended for the use of the third party standing outside the contractual relationship in question.

20. In view of the close link between a credit agreement and a guarantee securing its performance and the fact that the person guaranteeing repayment of a debt may either assume joint and several liability for payment of the debt or be the guarantor of its repayment, it cannot be excluded that the furnishing of a guarantee falls within the scope of the Directive.

21. Moreover, the possible termination of a contract of guarantee concluded in the context of 'doorstep selling' within the meaning of Directive 85/577 is merely one particular situation where the question may arise as to the effect of the possible invalidity of an ancillary contract upon the principal contract. In those circumstances, the mere fact that the Directive contains no provision governing the fate of the principal contract where the guarantor exercises the right of renunciation conferred by Article 5 cannot be taken to mean that the Directive does not apply to guarantees.

22. However, it is apparent from the wording of Article 1 of Directive 85/577 and from the ancillary nature of guarantees that the Directive covers only a guarantee ancillary to a contract whereby, in the context of 'doorstep selling', a consumer assumes obligations towards the trader with a view to obtaining goods or services from him. Furthermore, since the Directive is designed to protect only consumers, a guarantee comes within the scope of the Directive only where, in accordance with the first indent of Article 2, the guarantor has entered into a commitment for a purpose which can be regarded as unconnected with his trade or profession.

23. The answer to the question referred to the Court must therefore be that, on a proper construction of the first indent of Article 2 of Directive 85/577, a contract of guarantee concluded by a natural person who is not acting in the course of his trade or profession does not come within the scope of the Directive where it guarantees repayment of a debt contracted by another person who, for his part, is acting within the course of his trade or profession.

B. Commentary

1. European Law

For the first time the ECJ, in *Dietzinger*, had the opportunity to interpret one of the key European consumer contract law Directives. This offered the ECJ a chance to strengthen its involvement in private law, an important ingredient of a well-functioning Community legal order. In sharp contrast, the previous cases relating to consumer protection in contract law had merely focussed on the consequences of incorrectly transposed Directives (eg ECJ *Dillenkofer* [1996] ECR I–4845: Case no 13 in this Casebook) or the so-called direct effect of Directives not yet implemented (eg *Dori* [1994] ECR I–3325: Case no 11 in this Casebook; *El Corte Ingles* [1996] ECR I–1281: Case no 12 in this Casebook). *Dietzinger* is the first in a series of decisions by the ECJ which deal with the effect of substantive parts of transposed Directives in ordinary private law litigation, eg *AFS Intercultural Programs* [1999] I–825; *Travel VAC* [1999] ECR I–2195 *Berliner Kindl* [2000] ECR I–1741; *Océano* [2000] ECR I–4941 and Case C–167/00 *Henbel* see also Case C–168/00 *Leitner*).

The central question in *Dietizinger* was whether a guarantee as defined under German law fell to be considered under Directive 85/577. Article 1(2) of the Directive states:

> This Directive shall apply to contracts under which a trader supplies goods or services to a consumer (. . .)

The German version (and similarly most other language versions) state:

Diese Richtlinie gilt für Verträge, die zwischen einem Gewerbetreibenden, der Waren liefert oder Dienstleistungen erbringt, und einem Verbraucher geschlossen werden (...)

When interpreting this provision the question arises whether the Directive only applies to a contract for the provision of goods or services to a consumer, not a trader. A guarantee establishes a one-sided obligation on the guarantor to pay. A service is not provided to the consumer, nor a supply of goods. The wording of Article 1(1) is capable of several meanings. The German language version of the Directive can be interpreted to the effect that the trader has only to provide goods or services to anyone, not necessarily to a consumer. This means that the Directive could also apply to guarantees. The English language version states that 'contracts under which a trader supplies goods and services to a consumer'. According to this version, it is difficult to argue that the Directive also applies to guarantees.

The ECJ settled the question with the surprising announcement that a loan constituted the provision of a service and that a contract of guarantee is ancillary in nature (paragraph 18). It was not conclusive that the person concluding the contract was the receiver of the service being provided. The Directive also covered those contracts the performance of which was provided to third parties (paragraph 19). A guarantee is therefore capable of falling within the scope of Directive 85/577 (paragraph 20).

Similarly surprising is the Court's answer to the concluding question as to whether the guarantor is to be considered a consumer and whether the guarantee in the case at hand falls within the Directive. Article 2 states:

For the purposes of this Directive:

—'consumer' means a natural person who, in transactions covered by this Directive, is acting for purposes which can be regarded as outside his trade or profession (...);

In this instance the Court did not focus on the guarantee, but on the principal obligation, the loan. The loan was granted to the principal debtor, the father of the defendant, for his building firm. It was therefore connected with a business activity. Even the guarantee for this loan was not to be considered as coming within the Directive due to its ancillary nature (paragraph 22). A guarantee therefore only falls to be considered under the Directive if it is given for a non-business private consumer loan. Whoever acts as guarantor for business loans is not protected by European consumer law.

Additionally the protection of guarantors is restricted by a further condition. According to paragraph 22 of the judgment it should follow from Article 1 of the Directive that 'the Directive covers only a guarantee ancillary to a contract whereby, in the context of "doorstep selling", a consumer assumes obligations towards the trader with a view to obtaining goods or services from him.' This sentence, which is no clearer in other language versions, can be understood as meaning that the debtor must have concluded the contract in a doorstep transaction. The ECJ however did not expressly demand that the guarantor must be caught unawares. This interpretation therefore leads to a parallel protection of the principal debtor and the guarantor. According to the Directive, only if the main debtor has a right of cancellation does the private guarantor have a right of cancellation (if so, then he always has that right). A guarantee does not come within the Directive per se but only if the principal obligation comes within it. Concerning the revocation of a guarantee it does not depend on the guarantor being caught unawares but on the main debtor being surprised.

On first impressions this result appears illogical and has been subjected to a great deal of criticism, especially in connection with the Court's inadequate reasoning (*Pfeiffer, Reinicke/ Tiedke, Temmink*). A private individual who acts as guarantor for a business loan appears, when caught unawares in one of the situations provided for by Directive 85/577, to be much more deserving of protection than the guarantor who is fully aware of a consumer loan. As a rule, it is easier to understand. Yet one can also find good reasons for the ECJ's decision. This judgment is consistent with the Court's case law which states that the scope of European consumer law is limited to non-business activities (concerning the Brussels Convention see the seminal decision in *Bertrand* [1978] ECR 1431: Case no 1 in this Casebook; concerning consumer contract law *Di Pinto* [1991] ECR I–1189: Case no 10 in this Casebook). Accordingly, a private individual who concludes contracts with the view to founding a business is not a consumer and not to be regarded as a consumer in the case of such transactions for the purposes of the Brussels Convention (ECJ *Benincasa* [1997] ECR I–3767: Case no 2 in this Casebook). Whoever acts as guarantor for a business loan will be treated as a trader. This only means that the guarantor is not protected by European consumer contract law. Any protection afforded the guarantor is therefore left to national law.

Dietzinger is a case illustrative of the only very limited claims available under European private law. European consumer law does not aim to provide overall systematic regulation. It merely contains minimum standards for the protection of defined individuals ('consumers') in relation to defined transactions and to limited sectors. In contrast, it is the task of domestic civil legal systems to integrate these minimum standards into their own legal systems and possibly to iron out contradictions. To this end, Directives on consumer protection in contract law create a freedom of implementation: such an example is Article 7 of Directive 85/577:

> If the consumer exercises his right of renunciation, the legal effect of such renunciation shall be governed by national laws, particularly regarding the reimbursement of payments for goods, services provided and the return of goods received.

Further examples of domestic law's dominance in this area results from the so-called minimum harmonisation clauses which are normally provided in Directives on consumer protection contract law. Accordingly, Article 8 of Directive 85/577 states:

> This Directive shall not prevent Member States from adopting or maintaining more favourable provisions to protect consumers in the field which it covers.

In *Di Pinto* (ECJ [1991] ECR I–1189: Case no 10 in this Casebook), the ECJ expressly confirmed the possibility that domestic law could extend the protection to consumers (under Community law) in order to include traders as well.

The decision in *Dietzinger* offers a series of important clarifications of Directive 85/577, some of which can be summarised as follows:

> the term 'contract' which is to be interpreted independently also includes contracts which bind only one party, such as a guarantee. The argument that a 'contract' in the sense of the Directive basically includes only synallagmatic contracts has thus been rejected (see, eg the submissions of several governments in the *Dietzinger* case). Transactions laying down obligations which bind only one party and which are capable of being created in the absence of a contract (in the sense of a *stipulatio* of Roman law) may well be included as well.

> In assessing whether an obligation in a legal transaction is covered by the Directive, the laws of some Member States alone are not to be taken as decisive for certain contracts. Rather, several contracts between different persons are to be regarded as an economically unified or a single transaction and thereby to be assessed together (paragraphs 18, 22).

> The person concluding the contract ('the consumer') who is protected does not himself have to be the recipient of the supply of goods or provision of services. Even a contract providing performance to a third party falls within the Directive (paragraph 19).

As a rule, these principles are capable of being utilised to interpret other consumer contract law Directives because of the similarity in wording of these articles (among them are, for example, Directive 87/102 Consumer Credit OJ 1987 L42/48; Directive 90/314 Package Tours, OJ 1990 L158/59; Directive 93/13 Unfair Clauses, OJ 1993 L95/29; Directive 94/47 Time-Share OJ 1994 L280/83; Directive 97/7 Distance Selling OJ 1997 L144/19; Directive 99/44 Consumer Sales OJ 1999 L171/12; Directive 2000/31 E-Commerce OJ 2000 L178/1).

ECJ CASE LAW REFERENCES

Bertrand [1978] ECR 1431: Case no 1 in this Casebook; *Di Pinto* [1991] ECR I–1189: Case no 10 in this Casebook; *Shearson Lehmann Hutton* [1993] ECR I–139; *Dori* [1994] ECR I–3325: Case no 11 in this Casebook; *El Corte Inglés* [1996] ECR I–1281: Case no 12 in this Casebook; *Dillenkofer* [1996] ECR I–4845: Case no 13 in this Casebook; *Benincasa* [1997] ECR I–3767: Case no 2 in this Casebook; *AFS Intercultural Programs* [1999] I–825; *Travel VAC* [1999] ECR I–2195; *Berliner Kindl* [2000] ECR I–1741; *Océano* [2000] ECR I–4941.

LITERATURE REFERENCES

N Bamforth (1999) *European Law Review* 410; S Grundmann *Europäisches Schuldvertragsrecht* (1998) 204–220; H Micklitz (1998) *Europäische Zeitschrift für Wirtschaftsrecht* 253 (Casenote on *Dietzinger*); T Pfeiffer 'Die Bürgschaft unter dem Einfluss des deutschen und europäischen Verbraucherrechts' (1998) *Zeitschrift für Wirtschaftsrecht* 1129; G Straetmans *Droit de la Consommation* (1998) 256 (Casenote on *Dietzinger*); H Temmink *Tijdschrift voor Consumentenrecht* (1998) 224 (Casenote on *Dietzinger*).

HS-N/JJ

2. England & Wales

The *Dietzinger* case is of some interest to English lawyers not just because it seeks to clarify the phrase 'in the course of business', but because the actual events which gave rise to it are familiar to English judges. Cases where a person in a relationship of trust and confidence in another has entered into an obligation to stand as guarantor for the business debts of the other are frequently found in English case law. In most of these cases, just like in the *Dietzinger* case, the guarantee is given by the guarantor on the occasion of the creditor (usually a bank employee) visiting at his place. Once the seriousness of the consequences of his or her obligation are realised, the guarantor seeks to set aside the contract by pleading that he or she had not entered into the transaction freely and in the knowledge of the true facts; in other words, the principal debtor has misrepresented the effects of the guarantee or has exercised undue pressure in order to obtain the guarantee. These cases are often founded on the doctrines of misrepresentation and undue influence. In setting aside this type of transaction, judges have also considered whether the creditor himself has taken reasonable steps to make sure that the transaction was freely made and that the guarantor has received independent legal advice as to the amount of his or her potential liability, as well as the risks involved.

Judging by the large number of cases, however, it appears that the law is still far from clear (see, eg the contrasting approaches of the Court of Appeal to the creditors' duties in the case *Credit Lyonnais Bank Netherland NV v Burch* and *Banco Exterior Internacional SA v Thomas*, both decided in 1997). Accordingly, if the *Dietzinger* case had been decided differently, it would have contributed to consolidating the protection afforded in the UK to guarantors of others' business liabilities by allowing them a cooling-off period during which they could fully realise the extent of their liabilities, and possibly cancel the contract.

During the proceedings, the German government argued, inter alia, that, as the guarantor's commitment gives rise to no consideration, in the sense that the guarantor receives no goods or services from the trader to whom the commitment was given, the protection afforded by Directive 85/577 did not apply. Such an argument was mainly grounded on the wording of the English version of the Directive which refers to 'contracts under which a trader supplies goods or services to a consumer'. The European Court of Justice, however, refused to uphold the German government's argument and declared that the grant of a credit facility amounts to the provision of a service. Accordingly, Regulation 3 of the Consumer Protection (Cancellation of Contracts Concluded away from Business Premises) Regulations 1987 (as amended in 1988 and 1998), which sticks to the formula used by the Directive and refers to 'the supply by a trader of goods or services to a consumer . . . ', will also have to be read in the light of the Court's clarification.

CASE LAW REFERENCES

Barclays Bank Plc v Coleman [2000] 3 *Weekly Law Reports* 405; *Royal Bank of Scotland Plc. v Etridge (No.2)* [1998] 4 *All England Reports* 705; *Barclays Bank Plc. v O'Brien* [1993] 4 *All England Reports* 417.

LITERATURE REFERENCES

J Horan 'Wives *v Banks*: Is there still an *O'Brien* defence?' (1999) *Solicitors Journal* 1198; D Geary 'Notes on family guarantees in English and Scottish law—a comment' (2000) *ERPL* 25; P Giliker '*Barclays Bank v O'Brien* revisited: what a difference five years can make' (1999) *Modern Law Review* 609; E Stone 'Infants, Lunatics and Married Women: Equitable Protection in *Garcia v National Australia Bank*' (1999) *Modern Law Review* 604.

PN

3. Germany

The traditionally strict German law relating to guarantees is in a state of flux. Following a ground-breaking decision of the *Bundesverfassungsgericht* (Federal Constitutional Court, ruling of 19 October 1993), the *Bundesgerichtshof* has granted an improved protection to close family members in extreme cases of ruinous guarantee arrangements (eg *Bundesgerichtshof* judgment of 24 February 1994). An interesting side effect of this development has been the German Law on Doorstep Sales (*Gesetz über den Widerruf von Haustürgeschäften und ähnlichen Geschäften*, as amended in *Bundesgesetzblatt* I 2000 955), since guarantees are often signed during a visit of a bank representative at the home of the debtor or guarantor. Directive 85/577 was transposed by the Law on Doorstep Sales, § 1(1) of which states:

> Einem Verbraucher steht ein Widerrufsrecht nach § 361a des Bürgerlichen Gesetzbuchs bei Verträgen mit einem Unternehmer zu, die eine entgeltliche Leistung zum Gegenstand haben und zu denen er

1. durch mündliche Verhandlungen an seinem Arbeitsplatz oder im Bereich einer Privatwohnung

(. . .)

bestimmt worden ist.

Within the two chambers (called 'senates') of the *Bundesgerichtshof* there is a difference of opinion on the question as to whether a guarantee can be understood as an *'entgeltliche Leistung'* ('a service for payment') within the meaning of this provision. The *IX Senat* has rejected this and has held the Law on Doorstep Sales inapplicable. In contrast, the *XI Senat* basically gave the guarantor who has been called on at his private residence a right of renunciation (evidence of this can be found in the judgment of the *Bundesgerichtshof* of 14 May 1998). Legal writers are also divided on this question (see *Lorenz, Reinicke/Tiedke*).

In the light of these background arguments the reference in the *Dietzinger* case (ruling from 11 January 1996 made by the *IX Senat*) and the judgment of the ECJ aroused a great deal of interest among German writers. Dissenting opinions to the ECJ's ruling currently appear to predominate (*Reinicke/Tiedke, Pfeiffer,* rather conciliatory *Micklitz*). Only a few weeks after the ECJ's judgment the *II Senat* of the *Bundesgerichtshof* passed a judgment in a different case in which it made express reference to *Dietzinger* (judgment of 21 April 1998). This case concerned the question as to whether a guarantee comes within the German Law on Consumer Credit Arrangements (*Verbraucherkreditgesetz,* as amended in *Bundesgestzblatt* I 2000 940) which was enacted to implement Directive 87/102 (Consumer Credit Directive, OJ 1987 L42/48). The *Bundesgerichtshof* concluded from the ECJ's judgment that in any event a guarantee for a business loan did not come within Directive 87/102 and that therefore there was no obligation to interpret the German Consumer Credit Law in line with the Directive.

Since then the *IX Senat* has also passed judgment in *Dietzinger* (judgment of 14 May 1998). Consistent with its current case law it refused the guarantor a right of revocation according to the Law on Doorstep Sales since a guarantee arrangement was not a 'contract for remuneration'. The *Bundesgerichtshof* has referred the case back to the *Oberlandesgericht München* and instructed it to consider whether it is possible to protect the guarantor on the grounds that the guarantee arrangement was unconscionable (pursuant to § 138 *Bürgerliches Gesetzbuch*).

From the viewpoint of German law this result is unsatisfactory principally because of the uncertainty surrounding the applicability of the Law on Doorstep Sales to guarantee arrangements for business loans. The ECJ's judgment leads to doubt in appraising whether the Law on Doorstep Sales applies to guarantors. Should the guarantor lose the case against the Bayerische Hypotheken-und Wechselbank then it remains open for him to appeal to the *Bundesverfassungsgericht* on the grounds that he has not been treated equally with guarantors who are protected by the Law on Doorstep Sales. The *IX Senate* must however be credited with the fact that in cases falling outside the scope of European Directives on consumer protection it will prefer where possible a solution which takes into account the facts of the individual case on the basis of the general limits of contractual freedom as being more equitable than the application of consumer contract law which tends to standardise such transactions. It also remains to be seen how the ECJ continues to interpret Directives relating to consumer contract law. A reference made by the *Landgericht* Berlin (ECJ *VR-Leasing GmbH* Case C–30/98) will not be heard, whilst in the case of *Berliner Kindl* [2000] ECR I–1741, the ECJ decided that a guarantee does not fall under Directive 87/102 (Consumer Credit). Both of these references also show the sensitisation of the German civil justice system to European private law. The *Dietzinger* case appears to have significantly enhanced this development.

CASE LAW REFERENCES

Bundesverfassungsgericht ruling of 19 October 1993 (1994) *Neue Juristische Wochenschrift* 36; Bundesgerichtshof judgment of 24 February 1994 (1994) *Neue Juristische Wochenschrift* 1278; Bundesgerichtshof ruling of 11 January 1996 (1996) *Neue Juristische Wochenschrift* 930; Bundesgerichtshof judgment of 21 April 1998 (1998) *Neue Juristische Wochenschrift* 1939; Bundesgerichtshof judgment of 14 May 1998 (1998) *Neue Juristische Wochenschrift* 2356.

LITERATURE REFERENCES

P Bydlinski/J Klauninger (1998) *Zeitschrift für Europäisches Privatrecht* 996 (Casenote on *Dietzinger*); S Lorenz 'Richtlinienkonforme Auslegung, Mindestharmonisierung und "Krieg der Senate"' (1998) *Neue Juristische Wochenschrift* 2937; H Micklitz (1998) *Europäische Zeitschrift für Wirtschaftsrecht* 253 (Casenote on *Dietzinger*); T Pfeiffer 'Die Bürgschaft unter dem Einflu des deutschen und europäischen Verbraucherrechts' (1998) *Zeitschrift für Wirtschaftsrecht* 1129; D Reinicke/K Tiedtke 'Schutz des Bürgen durch das Haustürwiderrufsgesetz' (1998) *Zeitschrift für Wirtschaftsrecht* 893; K Tiedke 'Rechtsprechung des BGH auf dem Gebiet des Bürgerschaftsrechts seit 1997' (2001) *Neue Juristische Wochenschrift* 1015.

HS-N

4. France

The relationship between the main debt (*contrat principal*) and the contract of surety (*contrat de cautionnement*) is also described by the concept of *théorie de l'accessoire*, ie the dependence of collateral on principle debt. According to the *Code civil* the guarantee is ancillary in nature because the guarantor can point out all circumstances to the creditor which reduce the debt of the principal debtor (for an example of the legal situation of a guarantee for a balance on a current account see the *Cour de Cassation*, judgment of 20 December 1983). The central provisions of the *Code civil* state:

Article 2013 1. Le cautionnement ne peut excéder ce qui est dû par le débiteur, ni être contracté sous des conditions plus onéreuses.

Article 2036. La caution peut opposer aux créanciers toutes les exceptions qui appartiennent au débiteur principal, et qui sont inhérentes à la dette;

Mais elle ne peut opposer les exceptions qui sont purement personnelles au débiteur.

According to French law the provisions of the *Code de la Consommation* on Consumer Credit Arrangements and Real Estate Credit protect the guarantors in the same way as the principal debtor. Article L 311–2(1) of the *Code de la Consommation* states:

Les dispositions du présent chapitre s'appliquent à toute opération de crédit, ainsi qu'à son cautionnement éventuel, consentie à titre habituel par des personnes physiques ou morales, que ce soit à titre onéreux ou gratuit.

In contrast to this the provisions on doorstep selling (*démarcharge*) in Articles L 121–21 to L 121–33 of the *Code de la Consommation* do not expressly mention the contract of guarantee. The decision in *Bayerische Hypotheken-und Wechselbank* could attain considerable importance in French law. The question as to whether Directive 86/577 is applicable to guarantees has not yet arisen in connection with French law. A consumer who enters into a guarantee for a doorstep transaction may likewise be protected by the provisions on *démarchage* which *per se* only operate to the benefit of the principal debtor.

CASE LAW REFERENCES

Cour de Cassation, 1ère chambre civile, judgment of 20 December 1983, *Bulletin des arrêts de la Cour de Cassation*, chambres civiles 1983 I no 306; Cour d'Appel de Douai, judgment of 15 September 1994, *Gazette du Palais*, 19–20 April 1996 2.

LITERATURE REFERENCES

V Avena-Robardet (1998) *Dalloz Affaires* 708 (Casenote on *Bayerische Hypotheken-und Wechselbank*).

BD

5. Italy

Bayerische Hypotheken- und Wechselbank was a case which influenced Italian law mainly because it served to rejuvenate the discussion about the concept of the consumer. Italian writers consider the ECJ's interpretation of the concept of the 'consumer' to be authoritative.

In comparison with German law, the Italian *Decreto Legge* no 50 of 1992 (see also the Italian commentary to the ECJ, *Di Pinto*: Case no 10 in this Casebook) grants a somewhat lower level of consumer protection, since the period in the case where no instruction has been provided is much shorter. If the consumer has not been informed of his power of revocation then it will expire in 60 days (Article 6(2) of this *Decreto*). Where the information is correct the period of revocation is seven days (running either from the day the order was made, ie the day the information was communicated or the day the goods were received, Article 6(1)). In the case of Mr Dietzinger, the period would therefore have already expired.

LITERATURE REFERENCES

P Moreschini 'La fidejussione è regolata dalle norme nazionali se assiste un credito di natura "non privata"' (1998) *Guida al Diritto* 77.

AM

6. Austria

Austrian law regards a guarantee agreement as a contract (as expressly stated by § 1346 of the *Allgemeines Bürgerliches Gesetzbuch, ABGB*). The *ABGB* distinguishes between contracts with and without payment but does not assign the contract of guarantee to either category. Therefore it must be decided in each case whether the provisions relating to contracts for payments or for contracts without payment apply.

The Law on the Protection of the Consumer (*Konsumentenschutzgesetz*, hereafter '*KSchG*', *Bundesgesetzblatt* 1979 no 140), however, applies to all kinds of contracts and even offers as well as other one-sided declarations, eg notices of termination and the like. Only the mere granting of a gift does not fall within the law's scope of application (*Oberster Gerichtshof* (Supreme Court), judgment of 27 January 1999). Paragraph 3 of the law which regulates the consumer's revocation of a doorstep sale merely makes mention of the consumer's 'declaration of intent to conclude a contract' (*Vertragserklärung*). In contrast to § 1 of the German Law on Doorstep Sales (*Haustürwiderrufsgesetz*), § 3 does not require the transaction which the consumer intended to conclude to be for renumeration. Accordingly, Austrian law grants the consumer the right to revoke a contract of guarantee provided the remaining conditions for a doorstep sale are fulfilled. This applies regardless of the nature of the transaction which the guarantee arrangement is deigned to secure. Therefore, had the facts of the case in *Bayerische Hypotheken- und Wechselbank* arisen in Austria, Mr Dietzinger would have been able to revoke the contract of guarantee in accordance with Austrian law.

CASE LAW REFERENCES

Oberster Gerichtshof, judgment of 16 December 1992 (1993) *Österreichisches Bankarchiv* 479 with commentary by P Bydlinski; Oberster Gerichtshof, judgment of 27 January 1999 (1999) *Recht der Wirtschaft* 458.

LITERATURE REFERENCES

P Bydlinski *Kreditbürgschaft anhand aktueller Rechtsprechung* (1993); T Rabl *Die Bürgerschaft* (2000).

AE

CASE NO. 15 — *SARPP* C–241/89

Société d'application et de recherches en pharmacologie et phytothérapie [SARPP] v Chambre syndicale des raffineurs et conditionneurs de sucre de France
[1990] ECR I–4695

A. Judgment of the ECJ of 12 December 1990

1. Held

1) *The provisions of Council Directive 79/112/EEC of 18 December 1978 on the approximation of the laws of the Member States relating to the labelling, presentation and advertising of foodstuffs for sale to the ultimate consumer, and in particular Articles 2 and 15, must be interpreted as meaning that they preclude the application to national and imported products of national provisions which prohibit any statement in the labelling of artificial sweeteners alluding to the word 'sugar' or to the physical, chemical or nutritional properties of sugar that artificial sweeteners also possess.*

2) *Articles 30 and 36 of the EEC Treaty must be interpreted as meaning that they preclude the application to imported products of national provisions which prohibit any statement in the advertising of artificial sweeteners alluding to the word 'sugar' or to the physical, chemical or nutritional properties of sugar that artificial sweeteners also possess.*

2. Facts of the Case

The *Tribunal de grande instance* Paris made a reference to the Court for a preliminary ruling under Article 177 (new Article 234) EC Treaty concerning the interpretation of Article 30 (new Article 28) EC Treaty with a view to determining whether the French rules on labelling, presentation and advertising of artificial sweeteners were compatible with the Treaty. The rules in question appear in Article 10(1) of Law no 88–14 of 5 January 1988 on legal actions brought by approved consumer associations and on the provision of information to consumers. Article 10(1) prohibits all statements alluding to the physical, chemical or nutritional properties of sugar or to the word 'sugar' in the labelling of sweeteners that are sweeter than sugar but do not have the same nutritional qualities, in the labelling of foodstuffs containing such substances, as well as in the sale and presentation of such substances and foodstuffs and in the information supplied to consumers on them. However, the names and trademarks of sweeteners marketed before 1 December 1987 by the medical and pharmaceutical sector may be retained. Those provisions were supplemented by the Order of 11 March 1988 amending the Order of 20 July 1987 on dietary products.

The question referred by the *Tribunal de grande instance* Paris was raised in proceedings brought by SARPP (Société d'application et de recherches en pharmacologie et phytotherapie, hereinafter 'SARPP') against the Chambre syndicale des raffineurs et conditionneurs de sucre de France ('the Association') and a number of companies that import or market artificial sweeteners in France. On an application from the Association, the President of the *Tribunal de grande instance* Nantes (Regional Court, Nantes, 5 January 1989) ordered the withdrawal from sale of products marketed by SARPP under the trademark '*Sucrandel*', the packaging of which did not comply with Article 10(1) of Law no 88–14. Following that decision, SARPP brought an action against the Association before the *Tribunal de grande instance* Paris for a declaration that that law and the Order of 11 March 1988 were contrary to Article 30 (new Article 28) EC Treaty.

The *Tribunal de grande instance* Paris considered that the French legislation, and in particular the prohibition on any statement alluding to the word 'sugar' or to the physical, chemical or nutritional properties of sugar in the labelling of artificial sweeteners could constitute a measure having equivalent effect to a quantitative restriction on imports prohibited by Article 30 (new Article 28) EC Treaty, and the question therefore arose whether that legislation could be justified by reasons relating to consumer protection or public health. Accordingly, the *Tribunal de grande instance* Paris decided to stay the proceedings and refer the following question to the Court of Justice for a preliminary ruling:

> Are Article 10(1) of Law no. 88–14 of 5 January 1988 and the Order of 11 March 1988 compatible with Article 30 of the Treaty of Rome, inasmuch as they prohibit any statement alluding to the physical, chemical or nutritional properties of sugar or to the word 'sugar' in the labelling or advertising of artificial sweeteners?

3. Extract from the Grounds of the ECJ's Judgment

8. By way of a preliminary observation, it should be pointed out that although the Court may not, within the framework of Article 177 of the Treaty, rule on the compatibility of a provision of national law with the Treaty, it may provide the national court with all those elements by way of interpretation of Community law which may enable it to assess that compatibility for the purposes of the case before it. Moreover, in doing so it may deem it necessary to consider provisions of Community law to which the national court has not referred in its question.

9. The documents before the Court show that by its question, the national court seeks to determine whether Community law precludes the application, to national and imported products, of national rules prohibiting any statement alluding to the word 'sugar' or to the physical, chemical or nutritional properties of sugar in the labelling and advertising of artificial sweeteners intended to be supplied to consumers.

The applicable Community provisions

10. On 18 December 1978 the Council adopted Directive 79/112/EEC on the approximation of the laws of the Member States relating to the labelling, presentation and advertising of foodstuffs for sale to the ultimate consumer (OJ 1979 L33 p. 1).

11. As is evident from its preamble, the objective of the Directive is to promote the free movement of foodstuffs by the approximation of the laws of the Member States on labelling. To that end, it lays down a number of common general rules applicable horizontally to all foodstuffs put on the market.

12. Article 2 of the Directive lays down the principle upon which any provisions on labelling and advertising must be based. Article 2(1)(a) provides that the labelling of foodstuffs intended for sale to the ultimate consumer must not be such as could mislead the purchaser, particularly 'as to the characteristics of the foodstuff' or 'by attributing to the foodstuff effects or properties which it does not possess', or 'by suggesting that the foodstuff possesses special characteristics when in fact all similar foodstuffs possess such characteristics'. In addition, Article 2(1)(b) provides that labelling may not attribute medicinal properties to foodstuffs. Article 2(3) extends those prohibitions to the presentation and advertising of foodstuffs.

13. In order to ensure that consumers are informed and protected, Article 3 of the Directive lists the only particulars which are compulsory on the labelling of foodstuffs. The conditions under which those particulars must appear on labelling are given in Articles 4 to 14, which also lay down a certain number of derogations from Article 3.

14. Article 15(1) of the Directive provides that Member States may not forbid trade in foodstuffs which comply with the rules laid down in the Directive by the application of non-harmonized national provisions governing the labelling and presentation of certain foodstuffs or of foodstuffs in general. However, under Article 15(2) that prohibition does not apply to non-harmonized national provisions justified on one of the grounds exhaustively listed in that provision. Those grounds include, in particular, the protection of public health and the prevention of unfair competition.

15. It should be pointed out that the provisions of the Directive relating to labelling differ in one essential way from those relating to advertising. As is evident from the ninth recital, because the Directive is general and applicable horizontally, it allows the Member States to maintain or adopt rules in addition to those laid down by the Directive. With regard to labelling, the limits of the power retained by the Member States are set by the Directive itself in so far as it lists exhaustively, in Article 15(2), the grounds on which the application of non-harmonized national provisions prohibiting trade in foodstuffs may be justified. However, that provision is not applicable to advertising. Consequently, the question whether in this field Community law precludes the application of national rules in addition to those laid down by the Directive must be considered in the light, in particular, of the provisions of the Treaty on the free movement of goods and especially Articles 30 and 36.

16. That difference gives rise to an important consequence. As the Court pointed out in its judgment in Case 98/86 *Ministère public v Mathot* [1987] ECR 809, paragraph 11, Directive 79/112 created obligations concerning the labelling of foodstuffs marketed throughout the Community without permitting any distinction to be drawn according to the origin of those foodstuffs, subject only to the condition contained in Article 3(2). Consequently, if the provisions of the Directive preclude the application of certain national rules on the labelling of foodstuffs, such rules may not be applied either to imported foodstuffs or to national foodstuffs. However, when national rules on advertising are contrary to Articles 30 and 36 of the Treaty, the application of those rules is prohibited only in respect of imported products and not national products.

17. Having regard to that difference, separate consideration must be given to the aspects of the national rules at issue relating to labelling on the one hand and to advertising on the other.

The aspects of the rules at issue relating to labelling

18. With regard to the aspects of the national rules relating to labelling, it should be pointed out, first of all, that the prohibition of any statement alluding to the word 'sugar' or to the physical, chemical or nutritional properties of sugar in the labelling of artificial sweeteners exceeds the requirements laid down by Article 2(1) of Directive 79/112 in order to prevent the consumer from being misled as to the characteristics, effects or properties of that foodstuff. In order to achieve that objective, it is sufficient to prohibit any particulars which indicate, suggest or lead one to believe that artificial sweeteners possess properties similar to those of sugar when in fact they do not. However, concern to ensure that consumers are not misled cannot justify a general prohibition of any statement alluding to the word 'sugar' or to the properties of sugar that artificial sweeteners also possess, such as their sweetening effect.

19. The national prohibition at issue must be regarded as a 'non-harmonized' rule within the meaning of Article 15 of the Directive. It forbids trade in artificial sweeteners whose labelling complies with the rules laid down in the Directive, since that foodstuff may not be marketed if its labelling includes inter alia any statement alluding to the word 'sugar' or to the properties of sugar. Consequently, the prohibition of any statement in the labelling of artificial sweeteners alluding to the word 'sugar' or to the physical, chemical or nutritional properties of sugar that artificial sweeteners also possess can be applied to that foodstuff, whether imported or domestic, only if it is justified on one of the grounds mentioned in Article 15(2) of the Directive.

20. In this regard, the Association claimed that the purpose of the prohibition was to prevent unfair competition between sugar and artificial sweeteners. It maintained that as a result of repeated campaigns disparaging sugar mounted by the producers of artificial sweeteners, any allusion to the word 'sugar' or to the properties of that product in the labelling of artificial sweeteners constitutes unfair competition.

21. That argument cannot be upheld. Not every statement in the labelling of artificial sweeteners alluding to the word 'sugar' or to its properties necessarily has the effect of denigrating sugar. That applies particularly to the brand names of artificial sweeteners that include the radical 'suc'. Consequently, although the objective of the prohibition at issue is to prevent unfair competition, it is manifestly disproportionate to that objective, which can be achieved either by having recourse to the general rules against unfair competition or by prohibiting in the labelling of artificial sweeteners only statements whose object or effect is to disparage sugar.

22. It should be pointed out, moreover, that the French legislature allowed for an exception to the prohibition at issue in so far as it provided that the names and trade marks of artificial sweeteners marketed before 1 December 1987 by the medical and pharmaceutical sector might be retained, regardless of their form. It follows that the French legislature itself does not consider that the prohibition of any allusion to the word 'sugar' in the labelling of artificial sweeteners is necessary to prevent all unfair competition between those products, since some artificial sweeteners may be marketed under a trade mark alluding to the word 'sugar', while the fact that those sweeteners were previously marketed by the medical and pharmaceutical sector is no guarantee against unfair trading.

23. Moreover, a derogation on grounds of protection of public health cannot apply to a national provision such as the one at issue.

24. The prohibition at issue is not intended to warn purchasers of any risks to human health involved in consuming artificial sweeteners.

25. Consequently, the reply to the national court must be that the provisions of Directive 79/112, and in particular Articles 2 and 15, must be interpreted as meaning that they preclude the application to national and imported products of national rules which prohibit any statement in the labelling of artificial sweeteners alluding to the word 'sugar' or to the physical, chemical or nutritional properties which artificial sweeteners also possess.

The aspects of the rules at issue relating to advertising.

26. With regard to the aspects of the national rules relating to advertising, it should be pointed out, first, that those rules are identical to the rules relating to labelling and that, secondly, the provisions of Article 2(1) of Directive 79/112 applicable to advertising are also identical to those governing labelling. Consequently, having regard to what has been said above (paragraphs 18 and 19), the prohibition of any statement in the advertising of artificial sweeteners alluding to sugar or to the physical, chemical or nutritional properties of sugar that artificial sweeteners also possess must be considered to be a rule which has not been harmonized by the aforementioned Directive.

27. It must therefore be considered whether, and to what extent, Article 30 of the Treaty precludes the application of that prohibition.

28. The Court has consistently held (for the first time in Case 8/74 *Procureur du Roi v Dassonville* [1974] ECR 837) that the prohibition of measures having an effect equivalent to quantitative restrictions on imports laid down in Article 30 of the Treaty applies to all trading rules enacted by Member States which are capable of hindering, directly or indirectly, actually or potentially, intra-Community trade.

29. Legislation such as that at issue here which restricts or prohibits certain forms of advertising may, although it does not directly affect imports, be such as to restrict their volume because it affects marketing opportunities for the imported products (see the judgment in Case 286/81 *Oosthoek's Uitgeversmaatschappij* [1982] ECR 4575, paragraph 15). The possibility cannot be ruled out that to compel a producer either to modify the form or the content of an advertising campaign depending on the Member States concerned or to discontinue an advertising scheme which he considers to be particularly effective may constitute an obstacle to imports even if the legislation in question applies to domestic products and imported products without distinction.

30. Moreover, that obstacle to intra—Community trade is the result of a disparity between the national legislative schemes. The documents before the Court show that although French law prohibits any statements alluding to the word 'sugar' or to the physical, chemical or nutritional properties of sugar in the advertising of artificial sweeteners, such statements are allowed in other Member States.

31. In this regard, the Court has consistently held (see, in particular, the judgments in Case 120/78 *REWE v Bundesmonopolverwaltung für Branntwein* [1979] ECR 649, Case 261/81 *Rau v De Smedt* [1982] ECR 3961 and Case 178/84 *Commission v Germany* [1987] ECR 1227) that in the absence of common rules relating to the marketing of the products concerned, obstacles to free movement within the Community resulting from disparities between the national laws must be accepted provided that such rules are applicable without distinction to domestic and to imported products and can be justified as being necessary on one of the grounds of public interest set out in Article 36 of the Treaty, such as the protection of human health, or to satisfy imperative requirements relating inter alia to consumer protection. Nevertheless, the rules must be proportionate to the aim to be achieved. If a Member State has a choice between various measures to attain the same objective, it should choose the means which least restricts free trade.

32. The grounds relied on to justify the aspects of the national rules at issue relating to advertising are identical in scope to the grounds relied on to justify the aspects of those rules relating to labelling, namely the prevention of unfair trading and the protection of human health. For the reasons already given (in paragraphs 20 to 24, above), the arguments relied on in this regard cannot be accepted.

33. Consequently, the reply to the national court must be that Articles 30 and 36 of the EEC Treaty must be interpreted as meaning that they preclude the application to imported products of national provisions which prohibit any statement in the advertising of artificial sweeteners alluding to the word 'sugar' or to the physical, chemical or nutritional properties of sugar that artificial sweeteners also possess.

B. Commentary

1. European Law

The prohibition at issue in the case of *SARPP* which banned the usage of the word '*sucre*' on labels and in advertisements for artificial sweeteners was part of a French statute which had as its express aim the specifications for consumer information on labels (Law no 88–14 of 5 January 1988 *relative aux actions en justice des associations agréées de consommateurs et à l'information des consommateurs*). The nature of the prohibition and the vehement reactions of the parties in the case gave rise to the suspicion that, under the guise of consumer protection, an attempt to protect the interests of the sugar producers at the expense of the manufacturers was being made (especially at the expense of the importers of artificial sweeteners). Examples of SARPP's advertisement statements on the packaging of its products included 'replaces the taste of sugar' or 'helps to avoid obesity caused by sugar' (on '*Sucrandel*'). The *Chambre syndicale* held that these statements were an 'advertisement campaign' with the 'effect of denigrating sugar' carried out by the 'unfair competition' of the manufacturers of artificial sweeteners (quotations from the report of the hearing [1990] ECR I–4698, 4705).

The ECJ examined the prohibition at issue on the labelling of artificial sweetener packaging and the advertising employed to promote these products. With respect to the labelling, the Court held that Directive 79/112 on the labelling and presentation of foodstuffs designated for the ultimate consumer was applicable. In the meantime this Directive has been replaced by Directive 2000/13 on the approximation of the laws of the Member States relating to the labelling, presentation and advertising of foodstuffs (OJ 2000 L109/29). The wording of the relevant provisions in Article 15 of Directive 79/112 (now Article 18 of Directive 2000/13) has not been changed.

Article 18(1) of Directive 2000/13 prohibits the Member States from adopting labelling provisions which exceed the standards laid down by the Directive. Article 18(2) nevertheless contains an exception from this prohibition in the case that stricter labelling provisions have as their aim the protection of public health or the prevention of unfair competition.

Article 18

1. Member States may not forbid trade in foodstuffs which comply with the rules laid down in this Directive by the application of non-harmonised national provisions governing the labelling and presentation of certain foodstuffs or of foodstuffs in general.

2. Paragraph 1 shall not apply to non-harmonised national provisions justified on grounds of:

—protection of public health,

—prevention of fraud, unless such provisions are liable to impede the application of the definitions and rules laid down by this Directive,

—protection of industrial and commercial property rights, indications of provenance, registered designations of origin and prevention of unfair competition.

The French government and the *Chambre syndicale* sought to rely on paragraph 2 of this provision. The Court regarded this as a pretence. This becomes clear in the Opinion of the Advocate-General:

Far from ensuring that the information supplied to consumers is accurate, a prohibition which is so comprehensive and indiscriminate is likely to achieve the opposite effect, forming an obstacle to the satisfactory and full provision of information (paragraph 6 of the Opinion).

Elsewhere this is expressed yet more clearly:

> Let me add that that argument appears to be motivated by a rather low opinion of the ability of consumers to understand and to form judgements (paragraph 7 of the Opinion).

This reflects the ECJ's concept of the aware, critical consumer whose 'accurate, 'satisfactory' and 'full information' is to be ensured by Community law (on the ECJ's model 'consumer' see the European law commentary to the ECJ, *Gut Springenheide*: Case no 17 in this Casebook).

The ECJ did not examine the admissibility of restricting the advertising of sweeteners in accordance with Directive 79/112 which it did not believe to be applicable in this instance. Instead it relied on Articles 28 and 30 (ex Articles 30 and 36) EC Treaty. In this respect it is doubtful whether the judgment in *SARPP* has been superseded by the change in the ECJ's case law since its judgment in *Keck* (ECJ, [1993] ECR I–6787: Case no 7 in this Casebook) since provisions which solely restrict the advertising for sweeteners are possibly (as mere 'selling arrangements') no longer perceived as a restriction on the free movement of goods according to Article 28 (ex Article 30) EC Treaty (ECJ, *Hünermund* [1993] ECR I–6787: Case no 8 in this Casebook; *Leclerc-Siplec* [1995] ECR I–179; *De Agostini* [1997] ECR I–3843). The application of the decision in *Keck* to the facts of the case in *SARPP* would however lead to a strange result. The labels on which the word '*sucre*' legitimately appeared would not be allowed to show in the advertising. Accordingly there is much to be said for continuing to measure domestic rules on advertising against Article 28 (ex Article 30) EC Treaty to the extent that they prohibit measures which are permissible according to the European provisions on labelling.

The judgment in *SARPP* also highlights an important difference in the effect of primary (eg EC Treaty) and secondary (eg Regulations and Directives) legislation. If domestic provisions conflict with directly effective secondary law, then these former provisions may not be applied to goods of both foreign and domestic origin. Where the fundamental freedoms of the Treaty are contravened, primary law prohibits the application of domestic laws only in relation to those products which have been imported from other Member States and not in relation to domestic products.

ECJ CASE LAW REFERENCES

Keck [1993] ECR I–6097: Case no 7 in this Casebook; *Hünermund* [1993] ECR I–6787: Case no 8 in this Casebook; *Leclerc-Siplec* [1995] ECR I–179; *Sauce hollandaise* [1995] ECR I–3599; *De Agostini* [1997] ECR I–3843; *Gut Springenheide* [1998] ECR I–4657: Case no 17 in this Casebook.

LITERATURE REFERENCES

C Berr (1992) *Journal du droit international* 438 (Casenote on *SARPP*); G Raymond *Con-trats—Concurrence—Consommation*, 1991 no 3 and 12 (Casenote on *SARPP*); A Teubner (1991) *Sociaal-economische wetgeving* 800 (Casenote on *SARPP*).

HS-N/JJ

2. *England & Wales*

The *SARPP* case did not raise much interest in the UK, despite the fact that food laws constitute a rather controversial topic in the country. Food regulation has a long history in the UK. A Food Standards Committee was set up in 1947 in order to advise the appropriate ministers before regulations concerning the composition of food were issued. This Committee, together with the Food Additives and Contaminants Committee, has issued a number of valuable reports which led to important legislative changes. In 1983, these two committees were merged and became the Food Advisory Committee. More recently, the Food Standards Act 1999 has created a Foods Standards Agency endowed with the specific tasks of (1) providing advice and information to the public and to the Government on food safety, (2) protecting consumers through effective enforcement and monitoring, and (3) supporting consumer choice through promoting accurate and meaningful labelling.

At legislative level, matters concerning food safety are then regulated by statutory instrument under the power conferred by sections 16 and 17 of the Food Safety Act 1990 (as amended by the Food Standards Act 1999) to the Secretary of State (before the amendment such power was conferred to various Ministers).

Misleading labelling of foods finds its general legal framework in the Food Safety Act 1990 itself, which makes it an offence to falsely or misleadingly describe or advertise food. In particular, it is forbidden to affix labels which falsely describe the food or are likely to mislead as to the nature or substance or quality of the food (section15). In addition, the Food Labelling Regulations 1996 (amending the previous Food Labelling Regulations 1980 and 1984; see UK commentary to *Piageme*: Case no 16 in this Casebook) make detailed provisions specifying requirements as to the manner of marking and labelling of the food and prohibit, inter alia, the misleading presentation of food, including its shape, appearance or packing and the way it is arranged or displayed for sale. The Regulations include a few provisions on the use and labelling of sweeteners, but a more detailed legal framework is provided by the Sweeteners in Food Regulations 1995 (statutory instrument 1995/3123, twice amended by the Sweeteners in Food (Amendment) Regulations 1996, statutory instrument 1996/1477 and Sweeteners in Food (Amendment) Regulations 1997, statutory instrument 1997/814). A ban on statements alluding to the physical chemical or nutritional properties of sugar in the labelling, sale or presentation of sweeteners is not included in the UK legislation.

LITERATURE REFERENCES

A Painter (ed), *Butterworth's Law of Food and Drugs* (1990); Joint Food Safety and Standards Group Food Law MAFF, 1998.

PN

3. Germany

Germany did not have a provision which was comparable to the French prohibition on using the word 'sugar' when labelling and advertising artificial sweeteners. German writers showed little interest in the *SARPP* judgment. It has been published in only a few legal journals (mainly dealing with the law relating to foodstuffs). The German government did not make a submission to the ECJ during the proceedings, even though German exporters of sweeteners were affected by the prohibition.

Shortly before the judgment in *SARPP* the *Oberverwaltungsgericht* Münster (Higher Administrative Court) in the *Halbfettbutter* case (judgment of 24 October 1989) did not realise that Article 15 of Directive 79/112 (now Article 18 of Directive 2000/13) also applied to purely domestic facts in a case. In this decision the *Oberverwaltungsgericht* considered whether a trading prohibition on fat-reduced butter under the description '*Halbfettbutter*' (half-fat butter) infringed Community law. The *Oberverwaltungsgericht* rejected this on the ground that the case concerned a purely domestic product. In the light of the ECJ's judgment in *SARPP* this reasoning can no longer be maintained. The influence of the *SARPP* judgment can be recognised in a decision of the *Bundesverwaltungsgericht* (Federal Administrative Court, judgment of 23 January 1992, *becel-Diät-Wurst*). The *Bundesverwaltungsgericht* cited *SARPP* as supporting the statement that as far as the description of foodstuffs is concerned, Community law applies not only to imported but also to domestic foodstuffs. Like the ECJ in *SARPP* (see paragraph 23), the *Bundesverwaltungsgericht* proceeded on the assumption that the same aspects can be considered in the interpretation of Directive 79/112 (now Directive 2000/13) as those developed by the ECJ under Article 28 (ex Article 30) EC Treaty in justifying 'measures having equivalent effect to a quantitative restriction'. In its judgment of 23 January 1992 the *Bundesverwaltungsgericht* departed from its previous case law on misleading advertisement. As justification for this change in direction the court expressly cited the judgments in *SARPP* and *Smanor* (ECJ, [1988] ECR 4489, see the French commentary to *Cassis de Dijon*: Case no. 3 in this Casebook). These two judgments provided precedent for the interpretation of the labelling Directive 79/112 in the issues relevant to the decision. When interpreting the relevant provisions in the German Law on Foodstuffs and Consumer Goods (§ 17(1) no 5 S 1 and S 2 lit. b *Lebensmittel- und Bedarfsgegenständegesetz, Bundesgesetzblatt* I 1997, 2296) with Community law it was no longer possible to proceed on the assumption that there had been a misrepresentation in the marketing of the products. Accordingly, in contrast with the previous state of affairs, a meat product where animal fat had been replaced by vegetable fat may now be described as '*Wurst*' provided that the label clearly indicates the presence of vegetable fat. German law relating to the labelling of foodstuffs has been relaxed by this change to the case law. The judgment of the *Bundesverwaltungsgericht* illustrates how German law adapted to the requirements of European law in a purely domestic case, without a reference being made to the ECJ.

With this amendment the consumer protection has taken a new direction with a double effect: on the one hand, the new case law makes it easier to market animal-vegetable mixed products and enlarges the range of (from a nutritional-physiological point of view) foodstuffs on offer; on the other hand, in the case of a product which is marketed under the description '*Wurst*' the consumer is only able to find out that the product contains mostly vegetable ingredients by carefully reading the label. Where the consumer only glances at the label or has only a limited knowledge of the German language, there remains the danger that he will make a wrong assumption about the contents of the product. In contrast, the attentive consumer will find a new product on offer and can decide for himself whether or not to purchase it. Especially clear from this example is the fact that the emphasis traditionally made by German law in relation to consumer protection differs from that under European law.

A newer judgment of the *Oberlandesgericht Zweibrücken* (21 August 1997) proves that this is not a one-off judgment. This case concerned the question whether the consumer in respect of the rather nostalgic description of a product as '*Hausmacher Bratwurst*' (home-made bratwurst) could legitimately expect that no modern additives were employed in its manufacture. The *Oberlandesgericht* cited the case law of the ECJ on Directive 79/112 (judgments *SARPP* and *Sauce hollandaise* [1995] ECR I–3599). According to this case law the appropriate information about the constitution of the product will normally amount to the least restrictive means of protecting the consumer from deception and will take precedence over prohibitions on trade in accordance with the principle of proportionality. In accordance with the provisions of the German Regulation on the labelling of foodstuffs (*Lebensmittelkennzeichnungsverordnung, Bundesgesetzblatt* I 1984, 1222, new version in 1999, 2464), if the labelling includes a list of ingredients, it will be sufficient to exclude the possibility of deception.

CASE LAW REFERENCES

Oberverwaltungsgericht Münster, *Halbfettbutter*, judgment of 24 October 1989 (1990) *Europäische Zeitschrift für Wirtschaftsrecht* 198; Bundesverwaltungsgericht, *becel-Diät-Wurst*, judgment of 23 January 1992 (1992) *Europarecht* 298, (1993) *Wettbewerb in Recht und Praxis* 16; Oberlandesgericht Zweibrücken, ruling of 21 August 1997 (1998) *Recht der Internationalen Wirtschaft* 241.

LITERATURE REFERENCES

G Hohmann 'Einwirkungen des Gemeinschaftsrechts auf die Auslegung von § 3 UWG unter besonderer Berücksichtigung des "becel"-Urteils des BVerwG' (1993) *Wettbewerb in Recht und Praxis* 225; M Horst (1992) *Europarecht* 305 (Casenote on *becel-Diät-Wurst*).

HS-N

4. France

France has a long tradition of restricting the marketing of artificial sweeteners by statutory measures. As the report of the hearing to the *SARPP* case demonstrates, the use of artificial sweeteners which were sweeter in effect than sugar without indicating its nutritional value had been banned since 1902. There was an exception for therapeutically and pharmaceutical purposes as well as sugar not produced for use in edible products. This general prohibition of sweeteners came into conflict with the provisions of Community law. The *Cour d´Appel* Paris, in its judgment of 16 December 1987, decided that the prohibition infringed Article 28 (ex Article 30) EC Treaty (information thereon may be found in the report of the hearing to the *SARPP* case, [1990] ECR I–4696). In reaction to the judgment of the *Cour d'Appel* the old prohibition was repealed by Law no 88–14 of 5 January 1988 at issue in the *SARPP* case. The new law liberalised the sale of artificial sweeteners, at the same time introduced restrictions on labelling and advertising. Article 10 of Law no 88–14 stated:

> I. Aucune indication évoquant les caractéristiques physiques, chimiques ou nutritionnelles du sucre ou évoquant le mot sucre ne doit être utilisée:
>
> a) Dans l'étiquetage de substances édulcorantes possédant un pouvoir sucrant supérieur à celui du sucre sans en avoir les qualités nutritives;
>
> b) Dans l'étiquetage des denrées alimentaires contenant de telles substances;
>
> c) Dans les procédés de vente, les modes de présentation ou les modes d'information des consommateurs relatifs à ces substances ou denrées.
>
> (. . .)
>
> Pourront être conservées les denominations et marques de fabriques de substances édulcorantes commercialisées antérieurement au 1er décembre 1987 par le secteur médical et pharmaceutique.

Above all, the exception contained in the last sub-paragraph applying to sweeteners which had been marketed before 1 December 1987 rendered the provision untenable and showed that protectionist motives may also have been at work in its enactment. One of those involved in the proceedings stated, without being challenged, that this exception would operate mainly to the benefit of French producers who, due to the narrow domestic market, would practically have been the only ones who had marketed their products in France before 1 December 1987.

Seen from the French point of view the *SARPP* decision scarcely came as a surprise (*Berr*). Even the French government had indicated in its submission to the ECJ that a modification to the provision would not be excluded if the usage of the word 'sugar' on labels for sweeteners were held 'no longer likely to deceive the consumer' (report of the hearing [1990] ECR I–4706). Following the ECJ's judgment in *SARPP*, the restrictions on advertising for sweeteners contained in Law no 88–14 have been repealed (by Law no 92–60). French law put up considerable resistance to the pressure exerted by the European Community to harmonise laws. This was mainly for economic reasons. The enforcement of Community law has led to an improvement in consumer protection. For example, it removes the danger of too high a price being charged to the benefit of the sugar producers and the domestic producers of sweetener and at the expense of the consumer. Moreover, French law now permits useful information to be given to the consumer with regard to the properties of artificial sweeteners.

LITERATURE REFERENCES

C Berr (1992) *Journal du droit international* 438 (Casenote on *SARPP*).

BD

5. Italy

Italian writers have hardly discussed the judgment of the ECJ in *SARPP*. It is not possible to establish whether this case has had any influence on Italian law. Unlike France, Italy has no comparable provision prohibiting the word 'sugar' in advertising and labelling of artificial sweeteners. Directive 79/112 has been transposed into Italian law by the *Decreto Presidente della Repubblica* no 322 of 18 May 1982, which was replaced by *Decreto Legge* no 109 of 27 January 1992 for the purpose of transposing Directives 89/395 and 89/396 (OJ 1989 L186/17, L186/21).

LITERATURE REFERENCES

P Mengozzi 'L'uniformazione commerciale nel diritto comunitario' (1996) *Contratto e Impresa Europa* 576.

AM

CASE NO. 16 — *Piageme I* C–369/89

ASBL Piageme and others v BVBA Peeters
[1991] ECR I–2971

A. Judgment of the ECJ of 18 June 1991

1. Held

Article 30 of the EC Treaty and Article 14 of Council Directive 79/112 of 18 December 1978 on the approximation of laws of the Member States relating to the labelling, presentation and advertising of foodstuffs for sale to the ultimate consumer preclude a national law from requiring the exclusive use of a specific language for the labelling of foodstuffs, without allowing for the possibility of using another language easily understood by purchasers or of ensuring that the purchaser is informed by other measures.

2. Facts of the Case

The *Rechtbank van Koophandel* Leuwen (Belgium) referred to the court for a preliminary ruling under Article 177 (new Article 234) EC Treaty a question on the interpretation of Article 30 (new Article 28) EC Treaty and Article 14 of Council Directive 79/112 on the approximation of the laws of the Member States relating to the labelling, presentation and advertising of foodstuffs for sale to the ultimate consumer (OJ 1979 L33/1). This question arose in the context of proceedings between on the one hand the Association of manufacturers, importers and general agents of foreign mineral water (Piageme), the Société générale des grandes sources et eaux minérales françaises (SGGSEMF) and the Évian, Apollinaris and Vittel companies (hereafter 'plaintiffs'), who import and distribute various mineral waters in Belgium and on the other hand Peeters, a company established in the Flemish-speaking region of that country where it sells those mineral waters in bottles labelled only in French or in German.

Considering themselves to have suffered damage, the plaintiffs started proceedings against Peeters in the *Rechtbank van Koophandel* Leuwen. They alleged that Article 10 of the Royal Decree of 2 October 1980, replaced by Article 11 of the Royal Decree of 13 November 1986 (*Moniteur Belge* of 2 December 1986, 16317), which was intended to transpose Directive 79/112 into Belgian law, provided that the particulars required on labels must at least appear in the language or languages of the linguistic region where the foodstuffs are offered for sale. Peeters pleaded the incompatibility of the Belgian legislation with Article 30 (new Article 28) EC Treaty and Article 14 of the Directive. It provided that the relevant particulars are to appear in 'a language easily understood by purchasers, unless other measures have been taken to ensure that the purchaser is informed'. Consequently, the *Rechtbank* stayed the proceedings and referred the following question to the court:

> Is Article 10 of the Royal Decree of 2 October 1980, now Article 11 of the Royal Decree of 13 November 1986, contrary to Article 30 of the EC Treaty and Article 14 of Directive 79/112 of 18 December 1978?

3. Extract from the Grounds of the ECJ's Judgment

Jurisdiction

6. The plaintiffs in the main action contest the Court's jurisdiction on two grounds. First of all, they maintain that the Court has no jurisdiction to assess the conformity of the national provisions with Community law nor consequently to reply to the question referred by the national court. Secondly, they contend that the preliminary question which has been asked is unnecessary.

7. On the first point it should be noted that the Court has consistently held that, whereas it is not for the Court, in the context of Article 177 of the Treaty, to rule on the compatibility of a national law with Community law, it does have jurisdiction to provide the national court with all the elements of interpretation under Community law to enable it to assess that compatibility for the purpose of deciding the case before it (see for example the judgment in Case C–373/89 *Caisse d'assurances sociales pour travailleurs independants 'Integrity' v Rouvroy* [1990] ECR I–4243, paragraph 9).

8. By the preliminary question, the national court seeks to establish, in substance, whether Article 30 of the EEC Treaty and Article 14 of Directive 79/112 preclude a Member State from requiring by legislation the use of the language of the linguistic region in which the foodstuffs are marketed and preventing the possible use of another language easily understood by purchasers, or any derogation in cases where the purchaser is informed by other means.

9. By their second submission, the plaintiffs in the main action maintain that the issue in the proceedings before the national court is not whether Belgian legislation should provide, by way of derogation, for the possibility of informing the purchaser by means other than a label worded in the language of the region, but whether, in so far as that derogation were permitted, other means would enable the purchaser to be informed effectively. The proceedings relate therefore to a question of evidence falling exclusively within the jurisdiction of the national court and not within that of the Court, to which a preliminary question having no relevance to the outcome of the main proceedings has been referred.

10. It is worth remembering that it has been consistently held that it is only for national courts before which actions have been brought, and which must assume responsibility for the subsequent judgment, to assess, in the light of the circumstances of each case, both the necessity for a preliminary ruling in order to be able to give their judgment and the relevance of the questions they refer to the Court. Consequently where questions referred by national courts relate to the interpretation of a Community-law provision, the Court is, in principle, obliged to make a ruling (judgment in Case C–231/89 *Gmurzynska- Bscher v Oberfinanzdirektion Koeln* [1990] ECR I–4003 paragraph 20).

The preliminary question

11. The plaintiffs in the main action consider that the requirement to label in the language of the linguistic region where the products are offered for sale is reasonable in the light of the aim of the Directive, which is to supply the consumer with details of the products sold and in that respect to ensure the necessary legal certainty in view of the different languages spoken in a region they stress that Article 14 of the Directive imposes on Member States the obligation to prohibit the marketing of products whose labelling is not in accordance with the rules and does not limit itself to a requirement of tolerance allowing labelling which is easily understood by the purchaser.

12. It should be noted that the requirement imposed on Member States by Article 14 of the Directive consists in 'ensuring that the sale of foodstuffs within their own territories is prohibited' if the required particulars 'do not appear in a language easily understood by purchasers, unless other measures have been taken to ensure that the purchaser is informed'.

13. The only obligation is therefore to prohibit the sale of products whose labelling is not easily understood by the purchaser rather than to require the use of a particular language.

14. It is true that, according to a literal interpretation, Article 14 does not preclude a national law which allows, for the information of the consumer, only the use of the language or languages of the region where the products are sold, in so far as such a law would allow purchasers to understand easily the particulars appearing on the products. The language of the linguistic region is the language which seems to be the most 'easily understood'.

15. Such an interpretation of Article 14 fails, however, to take account of the aims of the Directive. It follows from the first three recitals in the preamble that Directive

79/112 seeks in particular to eliminate the differences which exist between national provisions and which hinder the free movement of goods. It is because of that aim that Article 14 is limited to the requirement of a language easily understood by the purchaser and provides that the entry of foodstuffs into the territory of a Member State may be authorized where the relevant particulars do not appear in a language easily understood 'if other measures have been taken to ensure that the purchaser is informed'.

16. It follows from the foregoing that, on the one hand, imposing a stricter obligation than the use of a language easily understood, that is to say for example the exclusive use of the language of a linguistic region and, on the other hand, failing to acknowledge the possibility of ensuring that the purchaser is informed by other measures, goes beyond the requirements of the Directive. The obligation exclusively to use the language of the linguistic region constitutes a measure having equivalent effect to a quantitative restriction on imports, prohibited by Article 30 of the Treaty.

17. Consequently, the reply to the question referred by the national court should be that Article 30 of the EEC Treaty and Article 14 of Directive 79/112 preclude a national law from requiring the exclusive use of a specific language for the labelling of foodstuffs, without allowing for the possibility of using another language easily understood by purchasers or of ensuring that the purchaser is informed by other measures.

B. Commentary

1. *European Law*

The judgment in *Piageme I* illustrates the often complicated relationship which exists between consumer protection and the free movement of goods with regard to the labelling of foodstuffs. The best way of ensuring that the consumer is effectively informed is by using his native language. However, provisions which lay down which language is to be used on labels restrict the free movement of goods and in particular, parallel imports which are so important to the operation of the Internal Market.

The European Community had regulated the language problems of labels in Directive 79/112 on the approximation of the laws of the Member States relating to the labelling, presentation and advertising of foodstuffs for sale to the ultimate consumer. Article 14 of the Directive states:

> The Member States shall, however, ensure that the sale of foodstuffs within their own territories is prohibited if the particulars in Article 3 and Article 4(2) do not appear in a language easily understood by purchasers, unless other measures have been taken to

ensure that the purchaser is informed. This provision shall not prevent such particulars from being indicated in various languages. (now amended, see below)

Community law therefore declined to proscribe the use of a specific language, eg such as that employed in the market area. It was sufficient to use an 'easily understood' language or 'other measures' for information purposes. According to the provision of Belgian law which was at issue in *Piageme I* the information on the label had to appear at least in the language or the languages of the linguistic region in which the foodstuffs were for sale. Since the mineral water in issue was marketed in the Flemish speaking area, Belgian law proscribed the compulsory use of the Flemish language.

The ECJ held this to be an infringement of Article 14(2) of Directive 79/112; the Directive was implemented in order to remove the differences between the domestic laws of Member States which restricted the free movement of goods. For this reason Article 14(2) was limited to the requirement of a language easily understood by the purchaser (paragraph 15). Since Directive 79/112 established general, horizontal Community rules for all foodstuffs (see the Advocate-General in his Opinion, paragraph 6), a national law which proscribes the use of a certain language was contrary to Community law.

This decision has been criticised from a consumer law point of view (*Reich*): it places a too high demand on the consumer who is expected and assumed to be able to understand even those labels which are presented in a language different to that used in the product's area of sale, provided it is 'easily understood'. It is assumed that many consumers in the Flemish speaking part of Belgium are able to read labels in French and perhaps also in German (for a different opinion in this matter see *Hof van Beroep* (Court of Appeal) Brussels, judgment of 27 June 1996; also see *van Bunnen*). However, using a foreign language makes it more difficult for consumers to access information specifically targeted for them. If Community law (as was the case in *Piageme I*) prohibited national law from proscribing the language to be used on labels, then the level of consumer protection would decrease. That in turn would not benefit the free movement of goods. This becomes especially clear from the case in which large importers of mineral waters cited the provision relating to labelling in order to restrict unwanted competition through parallel importers. Such consumer protection measures may also have negative consequences for the consumer. The restriction of competition reduces the range of products on offer and may therefore lead to higher prices being passed on to the consumer.

In response to the decision in *Piageme I* the Commission issued a Communication (COM [93] 456) demanding that Member States have the freedom to proscribe the use of their own language. In a Resolution on consumer law even the European Parliament expressed the view that 'consumers will enjoy proper protection only if all information is available in their own language' (OJ 1992 C94/217 219). The ECJ, however, considering the *Piageme* case a second time in relation to a similar issue, reinforced the view that a requirement to use a certain language in the labelling of foodstuffs infringed Article 14(2) of Directive 79/112 (*Piageme II* [1995] ECR I–2955).

A change in political will has led to a strengthening of consumer protection. In *Schott-Zwiesel* ([1994] ECR I–3879) the ECJ had to consider whether a German provision relating to the description of crystal glass infringed Article 28 (ex Article 30) EC Treaty. It did not object to the requirement that the German language be used in the description. Since then Article 14(2) of Directive 79/112 has been repealed. The new Article 13a which has been inserted in Directive 79/112 by Directive 97/4 (OJ 1997 L43/21), permits Member States to proscribe that labels be presented in at least one of the official languages of the EU. Influenced by this change in the law relating to the description of foodstuffs the ECJ has since let it be known that it places more emphasis on consumer interests by having the information presented in his own language (*Goerres* [1998] ECR I–4431). The decision on whether the language used is easily understood by the consumer is an issue which the domestic courts alone have to decide. Despite this development the ECJ has recently ruled that Article 28 (ex Article 30) EC Treaty and Article 14 of Directive 79/112 (old version) preclude a national provision from requiring the use of a specific language easily understood by purchasers to be used or for the purchaser to be informed by other means (*Geffroy* [2000] ECR I–6579). But this case is based on facts which took place before the insertion of Article 13a. The ECJ will have to adapt its position where the new Article 13a is applicable.

Meanwhile, Directive 79/112 has been replaced by Directive 2000/13 on the approximation of the laws of the Member States relating to the labelling, presentation and advertising of foodstuffs (OJ 2000 L109/29). The content of the relevant provisions in Article 13a of Directive 79/112 (now Article 6 of Directive 2000/13) has not been changed. Article 16 of Directive 2000/13 states:

> Member States shall ensure that the sale is prohibited within its own territories of foodstuffs for which the particulars provided for in Article 3 and Article 4(2) do not appear in a language easily understood by the consumer, unless the consumer is in fact informed by means of other measures determined in accordance with the procedure laid down in Article 20(2) as regards one or more labelling particulars.

> Within its own territory, the Member State in which the product is marketed may, in accordance with the rules of the Treaty, stipulate that those labelling particulars shall be given in one or more languages which it shall determine from among the official languages of the Community.

> Paragraphs 1 and 2 shall not preclude the labelling particulars from being indicated in several languages.

The language which is used on labels is an example which demonstrates the shift in importance away from market (economic) law biased of the suppliers of goods to a legal system orientated around the needs of citizens and consumers. Directive 79/112 clearly had as its primary aim the approximation of labelling laws in order to protect the consumer only to a moderate level; the main aim was the free movement of goods. It has become clear from the position adopted by the ECJ in the *Piageme I* and *II* and *Geffroy* cases that the old idea of Directive 79/112 no longer belongs to today's Community consumer policy, especially after the enactment of the Single European Act (OJ 1987 L169/1) and the Maastricht Treaty (OJ 1992 C191/1). The main reason for this change came from the Commission, the European Parliament and the Member States themselves. The longest to hold on to the old notion of consumer protection was the European Court. The demands made by Community law on the consumer have therefore been somewhat relaxed. The information provided on labels aims at consumers with lower language skills. This is not to imply a departure from the concept of the 'informed consumer' but rather a departure from the overburdened consumer. Above all, the ECJ's decisions on the use of language on labelling show how under-developed Community law still is in this area, despite numerous advances made. More effective consumer protection in an open market would require that labels be in all or at least in most of the official languages of the EU. The fact that this is possible can be seen from the packaging of numerous food products.

ECJ CASE LAW REFERENCES

Schott-Zwiesel [1994] ECR I–3879; *Piageme II* [1995] ECR I–2955; *Goerres* [1998] ECR I–4431; *Geffroy* [2000] ECR I–6579.

LITERATURE REFERENCES

L van Bunnen 'Du bon usage des langues dans l'étiquetage' (1996) *Journal des tribunaux* 679; M Goyens (1996) *Droit de la Consommation* 109 (Casenote on *Piageme II*); G Howells/Wilhelsson *EC Consumer Law* (1997) 128; N Reich *Europäisches Verbraucherrecht* (3rd edn 1996) 306–307; P Wytinck (1992) *Revue de droit commercial belge* 415 (Casenote on *Piageme I*).

HS-N/JJ

2. England & Wales

In England and Wales, the Food Labelling Directive 79/112 was implemented by the Food Labelling Regulations 1980, followed by the Food Labelling Regulations 1984 and by the Food Labelling Regulations 1996 (statutory instrument 1996/1499). The combination of these regulations have finally unified the law in the United Kingdom. Up until that time Scotland had separate legislation. Lastly, the Food Labelling (Amendment) Regulations 1998 (statutory instrument 1998/1399; the Food Labelling (Amendment) Regulations 1999 statutory instrument 1999/747; Food Labelling (Amendment) no 2 Regulations 1999 statutory instrument 1999/1483) have implemented the more recent Directive 97/4 with effect from 1 July 1999.

The language requirement which has been maintained almost unchanged in its present form throughout the different enactments, is set out in Regulation 38 of the 1996 Regulations on 'Intelligibility' (Regulation 30 in the 1980 Regulations):

Intelligibility

(1) The particulars with which a food is required to be marked or labelled by these Regulations, or by Regulation 1139/98 or which appear on a menu, notice, ticket or label pursuant to these Regulations, shall be easy to understand, clearly legible and indelible and, when a food is sold to the ultimate consumer, the said particulars shall be marked in a conspicuous place in such a way as to be easily visible.

(2) Such particulars shall not in any way be hidden, obscured or interrupted by any other written or pictorial matter.

(3) Paragraph (1) of this regulation shall not be taken to preclude the giving of such particulars at a catering establishment, in respect of foods the variety and type of which are changed regularly, by means of temporary media (including the use of chalk on a blackboard).

No reference is therefore made to a specific language; the formula used here, however, appears popular in UK legislation when requirements of comprehensibility are imposed.

The relationship between language requirements and consumer information does not usually raise much interest in the United Kingdom. This was confirmed in 1993 by the Commission, which stated that 'in certain Member States, the use of languages in relation to consumers is little discussed, either by trade and industry or by consumers representatives. This applies to Germany, Ireland, Luxembourg and the UK' (paragraph 29 COM(93) 456).

The matter, however, has been addressed in the last few years by the Office of Fair Trading (OFT). In a speech addressed to the Consumer Education Liaison Group on Consumer Education, the Director General of the OFT has declared that, in order to determine its future strategies, the Office of Fair Trading was focusing particular attention to specially vulnerable groups, and that research into consumer experience suggested that people from ethnic minorities might have particular difficulties in exercising their rights. However, it seemed that producing written information in minority languages, with the exception of Welsh, was not an effective way to reach those most in need of information as many of those who could not read English could not read any other language. Accordingly, the Director invited suggestions on how to reach this important group of consumers.

LITERATURE REFERENCES

R Burden 'Vulnerable Consumer Groups: Quantification and Analysis' *OFT Reasearch Paper* 15 April 1998; Consumer Education towards 2000: Speech to the Consumer Education Liaison Group by JS Bridgeman 9 Jan 1997; M Cornwell/G McFarlane 'Eau what a muddle' (1995) *New Law Journal*, 1661; European Court of Justice News section (1991) *European Competition Law*, R157.

PN

3. Germany

In Germany, the judgments in *Piageme I* and *II* have only been published in journals on European law and law relating to foodstuffs. They have aroused little interest in general legal literature and have only been briefly cited in judgments (eg *Kammergericht* Berlin (Higher Regional Court) judgment of 31 October 1994). The German legislator, on the other hand, probably felt obliged to amend the law on the description of foodstuffs (*Verordnung über die Kennzeichnung von Lebensmitteln* (*Bundesgesetzblatt* I 1984 1222)). Paragraph 3(3) of this statutory instrument stipulates that the information is to be provided on the packaging itself or on a label attached to it be in German, in a clearly visible place, easily understandable, clearly readable and permanent. As a result of the decision in *Piageme I*, a second sentence was added in 1992. According to this sentence the information can be given in another easily understandable language provided that the information given to the consumer is not affected by it (*Bundesgesetzblatt* I 1992 2423). Writers consider this amendment to be of little practical importance (*Schilling*) since as a rule only German will be considered to be an 'easily understood' language. In a decision of the *Oberlandesgericht Dresden* (Higher Regional Court judgment of 6 July 1999) which expressly quoted the *Piageme* cases, labels on mineral water bottles in Italian were held not to be easily understandable. The *Oberlandesgericht* held that labels in a language other than German were only easily understandable if nearly all consumers who can read were able to understand them.

CASE LAW REFERENCES

Kammergericht Berlin judgment of 31 October 1994 *Gewerblicher Rechtsschutz und Urheberrecht* 1995 684; Oberlandesgericht Dresden judgment of 6 July 1999 *Gewerblicher Rechtsschutz und Urheberrecht*, 2000, 88.

LITERATURE REFERENCES

B Ackermann 'Das Sprachenproblem im europäischen Primär-und Sekundärrecht und der Turmbau zu Babel' (2000) *Wettbewerb in Recht und Praxis* 807; T Schilling (1996) *Europäische Zeitschrift für Wirtschaftsrecht* 14 (Casenote on *Piageme II*).

HS-N

4. France

In France products basically have to be labelled in French. Relevant provisions include Article 4 of the *Décret* no 84–1147 of 7 December 1984 *concernant l'étiquetage des denrées alimentaires* and Law no 75–1349 of 31 December 1975, which was replaced by the *Loi Toubon*, Law no 94–665 of 4 August 1994 *relative à l'emploi de la langue française*. However, because some Articles of the *Loi Toubon* were unconstitutional, Articles 1 and 2 of the 1975 Law have remained in force. The *Loi Toubon* states:

Article 1. Langue de la République en vertu de la Constitution, la langue française est un élément fondamental de la personnalité et du patrimoine de la France.

Elle est la langue de l'enseignement, du travail, des échanges et des services publics.

Elle est le lien privilégié des Etats constituants la communauté de la francophonie.

Article 2. Dans la désignation, l'offre, la présentation, le mode d'emploi ou d'utilisation, la description de l'étendue et des conditions de garantie d'un bien, d'un produit ou d'un service, ainsi que dans les factures et quittances, l'emploi de la langue française est obligatoire.

Les mêmes dispositions s'appliquent à toute publicité écrite, parlée ou audiovisuelle.

Les dispositions du présent article ne sont pas applicables à la dénomination des produits typiques et spécialités d'appellation étrangère connus du large public.

The provisions' main aim is to protect the French language. However, they also lead to a better protection of the French speaking consumer by prohibiting instructions for use from being printed exclusively in English or even in Japanese. The actual presentation of consumer information lies within the control of the French courts. Therefore the copying of a cigarette carton advertisement in English, for example, will contravene the requirement to use the French language if a French translation is not supplied (*Cour de Cassation* judgment of 12 March 1984). Non-compliance with these provisions may lead to prosecution for a criminal offence by the *Direction Générale de la Concurrence, de la Consommation et de la Répression des Fraudes* (Article 16 of Law no 94–665 of 4 August 1994). Cases which have been prosecuted include menus (*Cour d'Appel* Paris 28 February 1995), labels on bottles of oil (*Cour d'Appel Aix-en-Provence* 24 September 1997) and instructions for the use of electrical appliances (*Cour d'Appel* Paris 13 April 1999).

Until Directive 79/112 was amended by Directive 97/4 French law was somewhat stricter than Community law because it only permitted the use of French and not the use of another language which was capable of being easily understood by the consumer. The present legal situation probably does not infringe Directive 79/112, as amended by Directive 97/4. Doubts as to whether the laws protecting the French language infringe Community law have been considerably allayed by this amendment.

CASE LAW REFERENCES

Cour de Cassation chambre criminelle judgment of 12 March 1984 (1984) *Recueil Dalloz Sirey* Informations rapides 349; Cour de Cassation chambre criminelle judgment of 22 October 1985 *Bulletin d'information et de documentation de la Direction générale de la concurrence, de la consommation et de la répression des fraudes* 1986 no 5 59; Tribunal de Grande Instance Nancy judgment of 4 June 1996 *Bulletin d'Iformation et de Documenation* 1997 no 1 29; Cour d'Appel de Paris judgment of 28 February 1995 *Contrat Concurrence Consommation* December 2000 jurisprudence no 167; Cour d'Appel d'Aix-en-Provence judgment of 24 September 1997 *Contrat Concurrence Consommation* December 2000 jurisprudence no 168; Cour d'Appel de Paris judgment of 13 April 1999 *Contrat Concurrence Consummation* December 2000 jurisprudence no 169.

LITERATURE REFERENCES

A Cherel 'L'emploi de la langue française' *Revue de la concurrence et de la consommation* 1997 no 96 10; S Feuillerat 'Emploi de la langue française: Information des consommateurs et loyauté des transactions' *Revue de la concurrence et de la consommation* 1997 no 100, 41.

BD

5. Italy

The decisions in *Piageme I* and *II* have not as yet been discussed by Italian writers. Article 3 of the *Decreto Presidente della Repubblica* no 322 of 18 May 1982, which had been passed in order to transpose Directive 79/112 (see the Italian commentary to ECJ *SARPP:* Case no 15 in this Casebook), prohibited trade in products which failed to supply the necessary information on a label in Italian. This provision clearly infringed the earlier Article 14 of Directive 79/122 as interpreted by the ECJ in *Piageme*. The currently applicable *Decreto Legge* no 109 of 27 January 1992 (replacing the 1982 law) no longer contains provisions which expressly require labels to be printed in Italian.

Comparing the provisions of European law with Italian law, some commentators believe that the Italian duties of helping and informing the consumer still apply. Articles 1337 and 1439 *Codice civile* regulate the principle of good faith (*buona fede*) in pre-contractual relations as well as malice (*dolo*). They state:

Article 1337. Le parti, nello svolgimento delle trattative e nella formazione del contratto, devono comportarsi secondo buona fede.

Article 1439 (1). Il dolo è causa di annullamento del contratto quando i raggiri usati da uno dei contraenti sono stati tali che, senza di essi, l'altra parte non avrebbe contrattato.

The rules of Community law primarily protect the party to the contract who has been put at a disadvantage due to a lack of information. It is argued that Italian law can achieve a better protection of the consumer by combining the above rules of the *Codice civile* and the provisions of Community law (*Sacco/de Nova, Musy*).

LITERATURE REFERENCES

P Mengozzi 'L'uniformazione commerciale nel diritto comunitario' (1996) *Contratto e Impresa Europa* 576; A Musy 'Responsabilità precontrattuale (culpa in contrahendo)' *Digesto IV* sezione Civile Band XVII 1997; R Sacco/G De Nova (1993) *Il contratto* 1 436–440.

AM

CASE NO. 17 — *Gut Springenheide* C–210/96

Gut Springenheide GmbH, Rudolf Tusky v Oberkreisdirektor des Kreises Steinfurt, Amt für Lebensmittelüberwachung [1998] ECR I–4657

A. Judgment of the ECJ of 16 July 1998

1. Held

In order to determine whether a statement intended to promote the sale of eggs is liable to mislead the purchaser, in breach of Article 10(2)(e) of Regulation (EEC) No 1907/90 on certain marketing standards for eggs, the national court must take into account the presumed expectations it evokes in an average consumer who is reasonably well-informed and reasonably observant and circumspect. However, Community law does not preclude the possibility that, where the national court has particular difficulty in assessing the misleading nature of the statement or description in question, it may have recourse, under the conditions laid down by its own national law, to a consumer research poll or an expert's report as guidance for its judgment.

2. Facts of the Case

The *Bundesverwaltungsgericht* (Federal Administrative Court) referred three questions to the Court for a preliminary ruling under Article 177 (new Article 234) EC

Treaty on the interpretation of Council Regulation (EEC) no 1907/90 of 26 June 1990 on certain marketing standards for eggs (OJ 1990 L173/5). The questions were raised in proceedings brought by Gut Springenheide GmbH (hereinafter 'Gut Springenheide') and its director, Rudolf Tusky, against *Oberkreisdirektor des Kreises Steinfurt—Amt für Lebensmittelüberwachung* (Chief Administrative Officer of the Rural District of Steinfurt—Office for Supervision of Foodstuffs, hereinafter 'the Office for Supervision of Foodstuffs') concerning a description appearing on packs of eggs marketed by Gut Springenheide and an insert enclosed in the packs. The plaintiff marketed eggs ready-packed under the description '*6—Korn—10 frische Eier*' ('6 grain—10 fresh eggs'). According to the plaintiff the six varieties of cereals in question accounted for 60 per cent of the feed mix used to feed the hens. A slip of paper enclosed in each pack of eggs extolled the beneficial effect of this feed on the quality of the eggs. The Office for the Supervision of Foodstuffs repeatedly advised Gut Springenheide of its reservations with regard to the description '6 grain—10 fresh eggs and the pack insert. On 24 July 1989 the Office then gave the company written notice that it must remove them. In addition, a fine was imposed on its director, the plaintiff, on 5 September 1990. The *Verwaltungsgericht* Münster (Administrative Court) dismissed the declaratory action brought by the plaintiffs in its judgment of 11 November 1992 on the ground that the description and the information contained on the pack insert infringed paragraph 17(1) of the Lebensmittel-und Bedarfsgegenständegesetzes (Law on Foodstuffs and Consumer Goods). The plaintiffs appealed unsuccessfully against that judgment. The appeal court held that the description and the pack insert infringed Article 10(1)(a) and (2)(e) of Regulation 1907/90. The description '6 grain—10 fresh eggs', which is also a trade mark, and the pack insert were likely to mislead a significant proportion of consumers in that they implied falsely that the feed given to the hens was made up exclusively of the six cereals indicated and that the eggs for sale had particular characteristics.

The plaintiffs then appealed to the *Bundesverwaltungsgericht*. They argued that the description and the pack insert at issue provided the consumer with vital information. The appeal court had not produced any expert opinion to prove that they misled consumers. The *Bundesverwaltungsgericht* took the view that the outcome of the proceedings turned on Article 10 of Regulation 1907/90. However, it held that Article 10(2)(e), which allows packs to bear statements designed to promote sales provided that they are not likely to mislead the consumer, could be interpreted in two ways. It could be argued that the misleading nature of the statements is to be assessed in the light of the actual expectations of the consumers they address. In this case the expectations ought to be ascertained by means of a representative sample of consumers or on the basis of an expert's report. However, the provision could also be based on an objective notion of a purchaser which is only open to legal interpretation, irrespective of the actual expectations of consumers. Accordingly, the *Bundesverwaltungsgericht* ordered that proceedings be stayed and the following questions be referred to the Court of Justice for a preliminary ruling:

1. In order to assess whether, for the purposes of Article 10(2)(e) of Regulation (EEC) no 1907/90, statements designed to promote sales are likely to mislead the purchaser, must the actual expectations of the consumers to whom they are addressed be determined, or is the aforesaid provision based on a criterion of an objectified concept of a purchaser, open only to legal interpretation?

2. If it is consumers' actual expectations which matter, the following questions arise:
a) Which is the proper test: the view of the informed average consumer or that of the casual consumer?
b) Can the proportion of consumers needed to prove a crucial consumer expectation be determined in percentage terms?

3. If an objectified concept of a purchaser open only to legal interpretation is the right test, how is that concept to be defined?

3. Extract from the Grounds of the ECJ's Judgment

27. By its three questions, which it is appropriate to answer together, the referring court is essentially asking the Court of Justice to define the concept of consumer to be used as a standard for determining whether a statement designed to promote sales of eggs is likely to mislead the purchaser, in breach of Article 10(2)(e) of Regulation 1907/90.

28. In answering those questions, it should first be noted that provisions similar to Article 10(2)(e), intended to prevent consumers from being misled, also appear in a number of pieces of secondary legislation, applying generally or in particular fields, such as Council Directive 79/112/EEC of 18 December 1978 on the approximation of the laws of the Member States relating to the labelling, presentation and advertising of foodstuffs for sale to the ultimate consumer (OJ 1979 L33 p 1), or Council Regulation (EEC) 2392/89 of 24 July 1989 laying down general rules for the description and presentation of wines and grape musts (OJ 1989 L232 p 13).

29. The protection of consumers, competitors and the general public against misleading advertising is also regulated by Council Directive 84/450/EEC of 10 September 1984 relating to the approximation of the laws, regulations and administrative provisions of the Member States concerning misleading advertising (OJ 1984 L250 p 17). Under Article 2(2) of that Directive, misleading advertising means any advertising which in any way, including its presentation, deceives or is likely to deceive the persons to whom it is addressed or whom it reaches and which, by reason of its deceptive nature, is likely to affect their economic behaviour or which, for those reasons, injures or is likely to injure a competitor.

30. There have been several cases in which the Court of Justice has had to consider whether a description, trademark or promotional text is misleading under the provisions of the Treaty or of secondary legislation. Whenever the evidence and information before it seemed sufficient and the solution clear, it has settled the issue itself rather than leaving the final decision for the national court (see, in particular, *Pall* [1990] ECR I–4827; *Yves Rocher* [1993] ECR I–2361: Case no 6 in this Casebook; *Clinique* [1994] ECR I–317; *Langguth* [1995] ECR I–1737; and *Mars* [1995] ECR I–1923: Case no 9 in this Casebook).

31. In those cases, in order to determine whether the description, trade mark or promotional description or statement in question was liable to mislead the purchaser, the Court took into account the presumed expectations of an average consumer who is reasonably well-informed and reasonably observant and circumspect, without ordering an expert's report or commissioning a consumer research poll.

32. So, national courts ought, in general, to be able to assess, on the same conditions, any misleading effect of a description or statement designed to promote sales.

33. It should be noted, further that, in other cases in which it did not have the necessary information at its disposal or where the solution was not clear from the information before it, the Court has left it for the national court to decide whether the description, trade mark or promotional description or statement in question was misleading or not (see, in particular, *Gutshof-Ei* [1992] ECR I–1003; *De Kikvorsch* [1983] ECR 947; and *Graffione* [1996] ECR I–6039).

34. In *Nissan* ([1992] ECR I–131 paragraphs 15 and 16: Case no 5 in this Casebook) in which Directive 84/450 was on point, the Court held, *inter alia*, that it was for the national court to ascertain in the circumstances of the particular case and bearing in mind the consumers to which the advertising was addressed, whether advertising describing cars as new despite the fact that they had been registered for the purposes of importation, without ever having been driven on a road, could be misleading in so far as, on the one hand, it sought to conceal the fact that the cars advertised as new were registered before importation and, on the other hand, that fact would have deterred a significant number of consumers from making a purchase. The Court also held that advertising regarding the lower prices of the cars could be held to be misleading only if it were established that the decision to buy on the part of a significant number of consumers to whom the advertising in question was addressed was made in ignorance of the fact that the lower price of the vehicles was matched by a smaller number of accessories on the cars sold by the parallel importer.

35. The Court has not therefore ruled out the possibility that, in certain circumstances at least, a national court might decide, in accordance with its own national law, to order an expert's opinion or commission a consumer research poll for the purpose of clarifying whether a promotional description or statement is misleading or not.

36. In the absence of any Community provision on this point, it is for the national court, which may find it necessary to order such a survey, to determine, in accordance with its own national law, the percentage of consumers misled by a promotional description or statement that, in its view, would be sufficiently significant in order to justify, where appropriate, banning its use.

37. The answer to be given to the questions referred must therefore be that, in order to determine whether a statement or description designed to promote sales of eggs is liable to mislead the purchaser, in breach of Article 10(2)(e) of Regulation No 1907/90, the national court must take into account the presumed expectations which it evokes in an average consumer who is reasonably well-informed and reasonably observant and circumspect. However, Community law does not preclude the possibility that, where the national court has particular difficulty in assessing the misleading nature of the statement or description in question, it may have recourse, under the conditions laid down by its own national law, to a consumer research poll or an expert's report as guidance for its judgment.

B. Commentary

1. European Law

With *Gut Springenheide* the ECJ for the first time gave a clear answer on which basis the Community concept of a consumer was founded with regard to the prohibition on misleading descriptions. The Court did not limit its premise to Regulation 1907/90 on certain marketing standards for eggs which was decisive in the case, but enumerated further provisions of Community law which deal with the protection of the consumer against misleading information (paragraphs 28–34). The ECJ was therefore clearly concerned with establishing a uniform concept of the consumer for these provisions. Of particular importance to the catalogue of statutory definitions for misleading information are:

Article 2(1) of Directive 79/112 (now Article 2(1) of Directive 2000/13) on Labelling and Packaging of Goods Sold to the End Consumer and its Advertising (OJ 1979 L33/1, now replaced by Directive 2000/13 on the approximation of the laws of the Member States relating to the labelling, presentation and advertising of foodstuffs, OJ 2000 L109/29);

Article 2(2) of Directive 84/450 on misleading advertising and comparative advertising (OJ 1984 L250/17, title amended by Directive 97/55 OJ 1997, L290/18);

Article 28 (ex Article 30) EC Treaty which limits the freedom of Member States to protect the consumer from misleading descriptions, trade marks or advertising statements (see the European law Commentaries to, *Nissan, Yves, Rocher, Mars* and *SARPP*: Cases no 5, 6, 9 and 15 in this Casebook).

The question to be answered is which definition of the consumer is decisive in the assessment of whether a particular description, trade mark or promotional statement is likely to mislead those it addresses. For consumer protection law the answer determines the standards which Community law places on individual consumers and suppliers. The lower the standard expected of the consumer, the stricter Community competition law will be and the greater the likelihood of the State or the Community adopting interventionist market regulation. It is evident that a badly informed, 'casual' consumer is more likely to be misled than a circumspect one. The ECJ, adding to its current case law (see *Mars*, among others: Case no 9 in this Casebook), tackled this issue by stating that it depends on the presumed expectations of an 'average consumer who is reasonably well-informed, reasonably observant and circumspect' (approved, inter alia, by ECJ *Kessler Hochgewächs* [1999] ECR I–513 paragraph 36). Thereby the Court came down in favour of extensive freedom in competition law at the expense of a relatively low level of consumer protection. A marketing strategy can therefore only be said to be misleading for the purposes of Community law if the 'reasonably well-informed, observant and circumspect average consumer' is also misled. According to Community law, provided only the average grossly uninformed, unobservant or non-circumspect consumer is misled, then there can be no objection to the trading practice of the supplier. Community law fails in part to protect the consumer who could be easily misled.

The ECJ's current case law does differentiate between the various advertising and labelling target groups. Accordingly, the concept of the average consumer is a relative term to be determined by reference to the target group. For example, if an advertising provision were directed at potential purchasers who may belong to 'a category of people who, for one reason or another, are behind in their education and are seeking to catch up' (ECJ *Buet* [1989] ECR 1235 paragraph 13), then Member States would be able to pass laws protecting those consumers. This reasoning was employed by the ECJ in *Buet* to justify a French law restricting competition by prohibiting the doorstep advertising of teaching materials. The danger of making a badly judged purchase is particularly marked in such cases. The desire to make up for below average education made potential customers particularly vulnerable towards the vendors of teaching materials who attempted to persuade them that purchase thereof would improve their career prospects.

In *Gut Springenheide* the ECJ also addressed the question of how national courts ought to ascertain whether a given piece of information is misleading. Both conceivable alternatives are clearly visible in the questions put by the *Bundesverwaltungsgericht* in the preliminary proceeding. According to the first, the answer rests on the actual expectations of those consumers to whom the information is addressed. In this case, the court will frequently only be able to determine whether a consumer was misled or not by means of market research. The other alternative is an objective concept of the consumer which is only open to legal interpretation. In this case, the court may reach a decision without the aid of market research on how observant a consumer is expected to be. The ECJ made clear that the concept of the consumer should be determined objectively. In doing so it referred to a series of decisions concerning the definition of 'misleading' in which it had neither ordered an expert's report nor commissioned a consumer research poll (paragraph 31). According to the ECJ's view, national courts ought to be able to determine whether a promotional statement is misleading in the same way. However, the ECJ granted national courts a certain freedom in the handling of cases concerned with competition law. If a court has 'particular difficulty' in assessing whether a statement is misleading, Community law will not prevent it from having recourse, under the conditions laid down by its own national law, to a consumer research poll or an expert's report for guidance in its judgment (paragraph 37). This jurisprudence has been approved in the cases *Lifting-Crème* [2000] ECR I–117 and *Kessler Hochgewächs* [1999] ECR I–513. In these cases the ECJ confirmed that it is for the national court to decide, having regard to the presumed expectations of the average consumer, whether a trade mark or advertisement statement is misleading. According to these judgments, should it experience difficulties in deciding whether or not a name is misleading, Community law does not preclude the national court commissioning an opinion poll or an expert opinion. The ECJ has not, however, stated the percentage of 'deceived' consumers required. The Court in *Gut Springenheide* also pointed out that it will only decide for itself whether a description or a brand name is misleading in exceptional circumstances. For example where the information at the Court's disposal is sufficient and a solution is clearly possible (paragraph 30; confirmed in *Geffroy* [2000] ECR I–6579 paragraph 19). A recent example of a decision of the ECJ in this area is *Darbo* ([2000] ECR I–2297) concerning the labelling of strawberry jam with the adjective '*naturrein*' (naturally pure). The ECJ held that the use of the description '*naturrein*' for strawberry jam which contains the gelling agent pectin and small traces of lead, cadmium and pesticides is not misleading.

ECJ CASE LAW REFERENCES

Buet [1989] ECR 1235; *SARPP* [1990] ECR I–4695: Case no 15 in this Casebook; *Nissan* [1992] ECR I–131: Case no 5 in this Casebook; *Yves Rocher* [1993] ECR I–2361: Case no 6 in this Casebook; *Mars* [1995] ECR I–1923: Case no 9 in this Casebook; *Kessler Hochgewächs* [1999] ECR I–513; *Lifting-Crème* [2000] ECR I–117; *Darbo* [2000] ECR I–2297; *Geffroy* [2000] ECR I–6579.

LITERATURE REFERENCES

S Leible (1998) *Europäische Zeitschrift für Wirtschaftsrecht* 528 (Casenote on *Gut Springenheide*); U Reese 'Das "6-Korn-Eier"-Urteil des EuGH—Leitentscheidung für ein Leitbild?'

(1998) *Wettbewerb in Recht und Praxis* 1035; G Schmid (1998) *European Law Reporter* 464 (Casenote on *Gut Springenheide*).

HS-N/JJ

2. England & Wales

In the United Kingdom protection from falsely describing food benefits from multi-layered protection. Section 15 of the Food Safety Act 1990 re-enacts the offence of falsely or misleadingly describing and advertising food rooted in section 6 of the Food Act 1984:

> Section 15: Falsely describing or presenting food.
>
> (1) Any person who gives with any food sold by him, or displays with any food offered or exposed by him for sale or in his possession for the purpose of sale, a label, whether or not attached to or printed on the wrapper or container, which-
> (a) falsely describes the food; or
> (b) is likely to mislead as to the nature or substance or quality of the food, shall be guilty of an offence.
>
> (2) Any person who publishes, or is a party to the publication of, an advertisement (not being such a label given or displayed by him as mentioned in subsection (1) above) which-
> (a) falsely describes any food; or
> (b) is likely to mislead as to the nature or substance or quality of any food, shall be guilty of an offence.
>
> (3) Any person who sells, or offers or exposes for sale, or has in his possession for the purpose of sale, any food the presentation of which is likely to mislead as to the nature or substance or quality of the food shall be guilty of an offence.
>
> (. . .)

Since *Concentrated Foods Ltd. v Champ* in 1944 the question whether a label is 'misleading' has been a matter to be decided not by an expert, but by the court; it decides whether or not the ordinary man is misled by the statement made.

More detailed prohibitions are contained in the Labelling of Food Regulations 1996 (as amended), issued in pursuance of sections 16–17 of the Food Safety Act 1990. In addition, the Trade Description Act 1968 in prohibiting false trade descriptions at the same time necessarily prohibits false and misleading advertisements. Section 1(1) makes it an offence to apply a false trade description to any goods, or to supply or offer to supply any goods to which a false trade description is applied. A 'trade description' includes the indication, direct or indirect, by whatever means given, of composition, and any other physical characteristics of the good (section 2). 'Applying a trade description' includes affixing or annexing it, or in any manner marking or incorporating it with the good, or with anything with which the good is supplied (section 4). Section 3 includes in the definition of 'false description' a description that, without being materially false, is likely to mislead the 'reasonable consumer' (*London Borough of Southwark v Time Computer Systems Ltd*), or which, though not trade description as defined, is likely to be taken for an indication of the matters set out in section 2.

In deciding cases of 'misleading' information, English courts do not seem to feel the need for experts' reports and statistical information on consumers; rather, they prefer to refer to the abstract notion of the 'ordinary man' and the 'reasonable customer'. However, things are different at the level of governmental policy. The Office of Fair Trading, which is responsible for publishing information designed to help consumers avoid these kinds of problems and to advise them what to do when things go wrong, is focusing its publications on providing information for the young, the elderly, people with disabilities and those with limited education.

CASE LAW REFERENCES

Concentrated Foods Ltd. v Champ [1944] KB 342; *London Borough of Southwark v Time Computer Systems Ltd., The Independent Law Reports* 14 July 1997.

LITERATURE REFERENCES

B Harvey/D Parry *The Law of Consumer Protection and Fair Trading* (1996) 400–10.

PN

3. Germany

The ECJ's decision in *Gut Springenheide* was eagerly awaited in Germany. For a number of years the *Bundesgerichtshof* had developed the concept of the 'casual' or 'passing' average observer in its case law (eg the judgments of 23 October 1956 and 22 October 1992). According to this settled case law, a promotional practice is to be considered isleading under § 3 of the Law on Unfair Competition Act (*Gesetz gegen den unlauteren Wettbewerb*, the text is reproduced in the German commentary to *Nissan*: Case no 5 in this Casebook) if at least 10 to 15 per cent of the purchasers addressed are misled. Legal writers have voiced their opinion that this concept of the consumer is incompatible with the ECJ's concept (see *Sack* for an overview of the current opinion). Hitherto the case law had shown a tendency to remain the same. The *Kammergericht* Berlin expressed a particularly sharp opinion in its judgment of 10 January 1994, stating:

> Es kann derzeit noch nicht festgestellt werden, daß sich der EuGH zur Beurteilung wettbewerbsrechtlicher Irreführungen auf das Leitbild eines kritischen, vernünftigen und verständigen Verbrauchers festgelegt hat.

Right up until the judgment in *Gut Springenheide* legal writers had propagated the opinion that the European concept of a well-informed consumer was not necessarily incompatible with the German concept of a casual or passing average consumer (*Sack*). Following the decision in *Gut Springenheide* it could be presumed that the more or less 'open rebellion' against the ECJ concerning competition law in which the German courts had found themselves (*Reese*) would come to an end. Firstly, several higher regional courts accepted the definition of the consumer developed by the ECJ in *Gut Springenheide* and other cases and applied this definition under the Law on Unfair Competition in purely domestic cases (eg *Oberlandesgericht* Frankfurt judgment of 17 June 1998; *Oberlandesgericht* Hamburg judgment of 28 January 1999; *Oberlandesgericht* Bremen judgment of 24 June 1999; *Schleswig-Holsteinisches Oberlandesgericht* judgment of 13 July 1999). In addition, the *Bundesgerichtshof* has introduced the 'observant' consumer instead of the 'casual' consumer as the relevant addressee of consumer protection of the German law of advertising (judgment of 19 August 1999). The next milestone was the judgment of the *Bundesgerichtshof* of 20 October 1999 in which the court developed its own concept of an 'average informed and circumspect consumer'. This new consumer model is a relative one: the attention required of the consumer depends on the nature of the transaction the consumer is faced with. If the consumer is buying expensive products he is deemed to be much more attentive than with other, ordinary purchases. It is unclear whether these new elements in the German law of advertising and unfair competition have already led to a definition of the consumer similar to the jurisprudence of the ECJ (*Kemper/ Rosenow*). However, the German competition law has clearly moved in the direction of the European concept. This can already be seen in purely domestic cases.

It will presumably be impossible to stick to the low quota (10–15 per cent) relating to the proportion of cases where consumers have to be misled. It is uncertain, however, how high a threshold will be set before the State will intervene. This is not a question which can be answered generally. Rather, it can only be answered by considering the individual circumstances of a case whereby it will depend on the protection required by that group of consumers which the statement seeks to address. Only time will tell whether a consumer 'deception' quota of 20–25 per cent or even 50 per cent will be the norm (*Leible*). In Germany the *Gut Springenheide* case goes on. After receiving the opinion of the ECJ, the *Bundesverwaltungsgericht* (judgment of 23 March 1999) referred the case back to the *Oberverwaltungsgericht* Münster (Higher Administrative Court) which has not yet given its final ruling.

CASE LAW REFERENCES

Bundesgerichtshof *Steinhäger* judgment of 23 October 1956 (1957) *Gewerblicher Rechtsschutz und Urheberrecht* 128; Bundesgerichtshof *Teilzahlungspreis II* judgment of 22 October 1992 (1993) *Gewerblicher Rechtsschutz und Urheberrecht* 127; Kammergericht Berlin judgment of 10 January 1994 (1994) *Europäische Zeitschrift für Wirtschaftsrecht* 541; Oberlandesgericht Frankfurt judgment of 17 June 1998 (1999) *NJW-Rechtsprechungsreport* 1347; Oberlandesgericht Hamburg judgment of 28 January 1999 (1999) *Gewerblicher Rechtsschutz und Urheberrecht-Internationaler Teil* 780; Bundesverwaltungsgericht *Gut Springenheide* judgment of 23 March 1999 Case 1 C 1/99 *Juris*; Oberlandesgericht Bremen judgment of 24 June 1999 (1999) *Wettbewerb in Recht und Praxis* 945; Schleswig-Holsteinisches Oberlandesgericht judgment of 13 July 1999 (2000) *Oberlandesgerichtsreport Schleswig* 35.

LITERATURE REFERENCES

R Kemper/J Rosenow 'Der Irreführungsbegriff auf dem Weg nach Europa' (2001) *Wettbewerb in Recht und Praxis* 370; S Leible (1998) *Europäische Zeitschrift für Wirtschaftsrecht* 528 (Casenote on *Gut Springenheide*); U Reese 'Das "6–Korn–Eier—Urteil des EuGH—Leitentscheidung für ein Leitbild?' (1998) *Wettbewerb in Recht und Praxis* 1035; R Sack 'Das Verbraucherleitbild und das Unternehmerleitbild im europäischen und deutschen Wettbewerbsrecht' (1998) *Wettbewerb in Recht und Praxis* 264.

HS-N

4. France

In assessing whether a statement is misleading, French civil law has traditionally been guided by the '*bon père de famille*'. The '*bon père de famille*' is normally observant enough to avoid the dangers which may result from statements on packaging. French consumer case law is guided by the average member of the consumer group at which the product is aimed at. The courts impose higher or lower standards when assessing whether a statement is misleading. This is dependent on the group of potential customers. One commentator (*Laurent*) criticises the '*capitis deminutio*' of the national judges. It is the ECJ who must decide whether or not the requirements for the 'average consumer' are present.

LITERATURE REFERENCES

F Berrod 'Le consommateur de référence' (1998) *Europe Commentaires* 14 319 (Casenote on *Gut Springenheide*); P Laurent 'La capitis demunitio du juge national dans la procédure préjudicielle' *Contrats, Concurrence, Consommation*, 1999 doctrine no 2 (Casenote on *Gut Springenheide*).

BD

5. Italy

Italian commentators have as yet not discussed the *Gut Springenheide* case. In Italy the trade in eggs is governed by Community law and by *Legge* no 419 of 3 May

1971. The latter statute gives the Minister for Agriculture supervisory powers. The supervision of the trade in eggs is laid down in *Legge* no 137 of 10 April 1991. Article 1, §§ 4 to 6 have been amended by *Decreto Ministeriale* no 434 of 14 December 1991. However, these provisions do not contain specific provisions governing statements on egg packaging.

A situation like the one in the *Gut Springenheide* case has never arisen in Italy. The ruling of the ECJ on the concept of misrepresentation in promotional statements for eggs are, however, comparable with Italian case law relating to the earlier *Decreto Presidente della Repubblica* no 322 of 18 May 1982 and to the *Decreto Legislativo* no 74 of 25 January 1992. These two decrees were issued in order to transpose Directives 79/112 and 84/450 into Italian law. *Decreto Legislativo* no 74 of 1992 on misleading advertising states:

> Article 1(2) La pubblicità deve essere palese, veritiera e corretta.
>
> Article 2(1) Ai fini del presente decreto si intende: (. . .)
>
> b) per 'pubblicità ingannevole', qualsiasi pubblicità che in qualunque modo, compresa la sua presentazione, induca in errore o possa indurre in errore le persone fisiche o giuridiche alle quali è rivolta o che essa raggiunge e che, a causa del suo carattere ingannevole, possa pregiudicare il loro comportamento economico ovvero che, per questo motivo, leda o possa ledere un concorrente.

In *Gut Springeheide*, the ECJ held that the prohibition on misleading statements contained in Directives 79/122 and 84/450 was synonymous with the prohibition on misleading statements contained in Article 10(2)(e) of Regulation 1907/90. Before Directives 79/112 and 84/450 had been transposed into Italian law, the case law occasionally had recourse to Article 2598 *Codice civile*. It governed unfair competition in order to protect the consumer against misleading statements. In assessing the misleading effect of statements judges had applied the rule of the '*consumatore medio*' (average consumer). The *Corte d'Appello* Milan held on 19 December 1975 that the likelihood of deceptive promotional statements misleading the consumer could only be assessed from the statement's content as a whole and not from one part only; the guiding concept adopted would be a '*consumatore di media diligenza ed avvedutezza*' (averagely circumspect and observant consumer) from the relevant consumer group. The application of this standard has been criticised by a number of commentators as preventing the adoption of a uniform standard in the field of advertising (*Alpa*). The majority of writers regard the control of promotional statements by means of provisions on unfair competition as largely ineffective. These provisions aim above all at protecting businesses. They therefore do not address the right of the consumer to better information (see *Alpa*).

In addition to Article 2598 *Codice Civile*, there have been rare cases where civil case law has also relied on *dolo* (Article 1439 *Codice civile*) and relevant mistake (Article 1337, 1338 *Codice civile*). Some Italian courts have also applied provisions of the criminal law, including commercial misrepresentation (Article 515 *Codice penale*), sale or trade with industrial products under a description, trade mark or labelling which could mislead the consumer concerning the origin or properties (Article 517 *Codice penale*), fraud (Article 640 *Codice penale*) and exploitation of gullibility (Article 661 *Codice penale*). Such statutory criminal definitions are rarely effective because all of the elements of the offence must be present. In any case they often only lead to a fine.

In addition, Article 12 of *Legge* no 283 of 30 April 1962 prohibits the employment of inaccurate labelling in promotional statements which give misleading information on the ingredients in foodstuffs (see also the Italian commentary to the ECJ, *Mars*: Case no 19 in this Casebook). One example of the application of this article can be found in a judgment of the *Corte di Cassazione* of 19 September 1989. This case illustrates the elements which must be fulfilled before Italian law will regard a promotional statement as likely to mislead the consumer. The case concerned the sale of two products which contained 1.5 per cent dry frozen *propolis* (a honey product) and 3.5 per cent extract of *propolis*. The packaging labelled this product as '*propolis*'. The *Corte di Cassazione* held that this statement was misleading. In so holding it assumed that:

> La tutela del consumatore nei confronti della pubblicità ingannevole non si riferisce agli acquirenti dotati di specifica competenza, avvedutezza o di particolari cognizioni merceologiche, ma agli acquirenti di media accortezza o meglio alla generalità dei consumatori, i quali hanno minore attitudine a rendersi conto delle eventuali manovre ingannevoli del venditore. (The protection of the consumer against misleading advertising does not aim to protect purchasers with special abilities, of special observation or with special market knowledge but those purchasers of average circumspection measured against consumers as a whole who only rarely bargain with the seller supplying misleading information)

Article 13 of *Legge* no 283 of 30 April 1962 was repealed by *Decreto Legge* no 109 of 27 January 1992 which transposed Directives 89/395 and 89/396 (OJ 1989 L186/17, L186/21) into Italian law. Directive 79/112 had been transposed into Italian law by *Decreto Presidente della Repubblica* no 322 of 18 May 1982. This *Decreto* was repealed by *Decreto Legislativo* no 74 of 25 January 1992 on Misleading Advertising and *Decreto Legge* no 109 of 27 February 1992.

Even when applying these provisions, Italian courts assess whether an advertisement is likely to mislead on the basis of what an average consumer (*consumatore medio*) expects. This standard becomes particularly clear in a judgment of the *Corte di Cassazione* of 25 February 1993. The court applied the criteria of the average consumer's expectations in order to establish the misleading nature of the statement 'Your Daily Bread'. This statement was printed on the packaging of a loaf of bread which had been produced fifteen days earlier. It was possible to store the bread for several months. In this case the consumer would expect the bread to be fresh and not capable of being stored for so long. Italian case law had therefore developed the same criterion as that which had gradually been developed by the ECJ. As far as is possible to ascertain, Italian judges do not normally employ opinion polls in order to establish consumers' expectations.

CASE LAW REFERENCES

Corte d'Appello di Milano judgment of 19 December 1975 (1976) *Il Foro Padano* I 29; Corte di Cassazione *Alimenti* judgment of 19 September 1989 (1989) *Massimario Giustizia Civile* 7463; Corte di Cassazione judgment of 25 February 1993 (1995) *Il Foro Italiano* I 657.

LITERATURE REFERENCES

G Alpa *Il diritto dei consumatori* (1995) 64; L Sordelli 'Pubblicità commerciale ed altre informazioni pubblicitarie' *Novissimo Digesto* Appendice Volume VI 1986 179; Casenote on the judgment of the *Corte di Cassatione* of 25 February 1993 (1995) *Il Foro Italiano* I 657.

AM

V

Product Safety and Product Liability

INTRODUCTION

European Consumer law attempts, on the one hand, to protect the consumer from dangerous products by means of preventative measures (product safety law), on the other hand, Community law grants the consumer a right to claim damages against the manufacturer or the importer of defective goods (product liability law). The Community has taken measures to improve product safety. These can be seen in numerous rules individually tailored to the most varied product types. The visible evidence of this policy is the CE symbol (which stands for *Communauté Européenne*) which is to be found on many products and guarantees that the product conforms to European safety standards. Since 1992 a 'horizontal' product safety measure has taken its place alongside the 'vertical' individual measures for specified types of products. This is Directive 92/59 concerning general product safety (OJ 1992 L228/24).

The decisions of the ECJ presented here serve as an introduction to both individual measures (using the spectacular wine scandal in the *Francesconi* case: Case no 18 in this Casebook) as well as to the general product safety law on the basis of a Member State's action against the Council (*Federal Republic of Germany v Council*: Case no 19 in this Casebook). The product liability law of the European Community is based on Directive 85/374 on the approximation of laws, regulations and administrative provisions of Member States in concerning liability for defective products (OJ 1985 L210/29). The ECJ was concerned with this Directive in connection with infringement proceedings in which the Commission accused a Member State of inadequately transposing a Directive (*Commission v The United Kingdom*: Case no 20 in this Casebook). The three cases mentioned highlight the different types of proceedings before the ECJ. The case of *Francesconi* arose from a claim for compensation made against the Community by citizens in accordance with Articles 235 and 288(2) (ex Articles 178 and 215) EC Treaty. In *Federal Republic of Germany v the Council of the European Community*, a Member State brought an action against a Directive under Article 230(1) (ex Article 173(1)) EC Treaty. In *Commission v United Kingdom* the Commission commenced proceedings against a Member State for breach of the EC Treaty pursuant to Article 226 (ex Article 169) EC Treaty. All other cases dealt with in this Casebook are so-called references for preliminary ruling pursuant to Article 234 (ex Article 177) EC Treaty, in which domestic courts have submitted questions to the ECJ concerning the interpretation of Community law.

LITERATURE REFERENCES

T Askham/A Stoneham *EC Consumer Safety* (1994); N Brown/T Kennedy *The Court of Justice of the European Communities* (1994); G Howells *Consumer Product Safety* (1998); P Kelly/R Attree (eds) *European Product Liabilities* (1997); H Micklitz/T Roethe/S Weatherill (eds) *Federalism and Responsibility: a Study on Product Safety Law and Practice in the European Community* (1994); H Micklitz *Internationales Produktsicherheitsrecht* (1995); N Reich, *Europäisches Verbraucherrecht* (3rd edn 1996) 445–499; D Simon *Le système juridique communautaire* (1997); J Stapleton *Product Liability* (1994).

CASE NO. 18 — *Francesconi* Joined Cases C–326/86 and 66/88

Benito Francesconi and others v The Commission of the European Communities
[1989] ECR 2087

A. Judgment of the ECJ of 4 July 1989

1. Held

THE COURT *(Second Chamber)*

hereby:

1) *Dismisses the application.*

2) *(. . .)*

2. Facts of the Case

Twenty dealers, restaurateurs and producers of Italian wine and the personal representatives of persons who died after drinking Italian wine containing methanol brought two actions under Article 178 and Article 215(2) (new Articles 235 and 288(2)) EC Treaty against the Commission of the European Communities for compensation for damage suffered as a result of the presence of adulterated wine on the wine market. The applicants claimed they had suffered damage consisting for some of them in the reduction in exports of Italian wine and the resulting reduction in turnover and for others in the loss of a member of their family.

In April 1985 Austrian wine adulterated with diethylene glycol was discovered on the market in Germany. At a press conference on 27 August 1985 the Commission stated that very slight traces of diethylene glycol had also been discovered in certain Italian wines. On 19 March 1986 the Italian authorities informed the Commission that certain Italian wines were adulterated with methanol. The next day the Commission conveyed that information to the other Member States. The first deaths as a result of the consumption of Italian wine adulterated with methanol were reported on 2 March 1986.

The applicants considered that the Commission was guilty of a wrongful act or omission. They complained first of all of bad management and failure to supervise the wine market inasmuch as the Commission did not ensure the proper implementation of the general measures governing the wine market in the Member States. The applicants also alleged that those general measures were inappropriate. They submitted that the measures adopted in the wine sector were such as to encourage the manufacture of adulterated wines, inter alia, for consumption. Finally, the applicants claimed that the Commission ought to have noticed the considerable increase in the quantity of wine in 1984. As early as August 1985 it ought to have adopted appropriate measures to limit the damage suffered by the traders concerned as a result of the scandal caused by the presence of adulterated wines on the market.

The Commission denied any wrongful act or omission, or that it was possible to establish a causal link between the alleged wrongful act or omission and the damage which the applicants had suffered.

3. Extract from the Grounds of the ECJ's Judgment

8. With a view to considering whether the action is well founded it is appropriate to recall the conditions under which the Community may be held to be liable under the second paragraph of Article 215 of the EEC Treaty. The Court has consistently held (see in particular the judgment of 15 January 1987 in the case *GAEC de la Segaude v Council and Commission* [1987] ECR 123) that Community liability depends on the coincidence of a set of conditions as regards the unlawfulness of the acts alleged against the institution, the fact of damage and the existence of a causal link between the wrongful act or conduct and the damage complained of.

9. It must first be determined whether the applicants have established unlawful conduct on the part of the Commission, and if so whether the two other conditions of Community liability are satisfied.

10. As a preliminary point it should be observed that it is for the Member States to ensure that the Community provisions in the wine sector are observed.

11. Pursuant to Article 64 of Council Regulation 337/79 of 5 February 1979 on the common organization of the market in wine (OJ 1979 L54 p 1) Member States must designate one or more authorities to be responsible for verifying compliance with these provisions. Moreover, under Article 3 of Council Regulation 359/79 of 5 February 1979 on direct cooperation between the bodies designated by Member States to verify compliance with Community and national provisions in the wine sector (OJ 1979 L54 p 136) the competent bodies of the Member States must study in detail any grounds for suspecting that the product does not conform to the wine provisions. It is also the Member States who, pursuant to Council Decision 84/133/EEC of 2 March 1984 introducing a Community system for the rapid exchange of information on dangers arising from the use of consumer products (OJ 1984 L70 p 16), may decide to take urgent steps to prevent the marketing of a product because of the serious and immediate risk which that product presents for the health or safety of consumers.

12. It follows from the terms of that legislation that the Community institutions are required to intervene only if there is evidence that the national bodies are not fulfilling their task of supervision satisfactorily.

13. Before considering the submissions put forward by the applicants it should be observed that the Commission has adopted a certain number of measures in relation to the management structures for the wine market. In particular it adopted Regulation no 2102/84 of 13 July 1984 on harvest production and stock declarations relating to wine-sector products (OJ 1984 L194 p 1) and Regulation 2396/84 of 20 August 1984 laying down detailed rules for drawing up the forward estimate in the wine-sector (OJ 1984 L224 p 14). In addition the Commission procured certain changes to the distillation system by the adoption of Council Regulation 2687/84 of 18 September 1984 (OJ 1984 L255 p 1) amending Council Regulation 2179/83 of 25 July 1983 laying down general rules for distillation operations involving wine and the by-products of wine-making (OJ 1983 L212 p 1).

14. The applicants claim that the measures thus adopted in the wine sector are inappropriate in so far as they are likely to encourage the manufacture of artificial wines, especially in view of the lack of detailed chemical analysis of products delivered for distillation.

15. As the Commission observed, no link has been established between the system of distillation and the manufacture of adulterated wines. The toxic substances were discovered in wine intended for human consumption and not in wine delivered for distillation.

16. Moreover, the applicants observed at the hearing that only unadulterated wine was delivered for distillation and that adulterated wine came on to the market for human consumption. The applicants' argument that the distillation system absorbed all the natural wine and the manufacture of adulterated wine was necessary in order to satisfy consumption must be rejected, since there is a surplus of natural wine.

17. The same is true of the argument alleging insufficient analysis. Even assuming that adulterated wines were delivered for distillation it is sufficient to observe that pursuant to Article 27 of Council Regulation 2179/83 it is for the Member States to take the necessary measures to check that the distillation system is properly applied. This checking of the characteristics of products delivered for distillation, which, pursuant to Article 22, relates in particular to quantity, colour and alcoholic strength, is sufficient to allow the competent authorities to oversee the Community system for distillation of wine and detect adulterated wines delivered for distillation.

18. The applicants also consider that the Commission ought to have been aware of the considerable increase in the quantity of wines delivered for distillation in 1984 and the stocks of Italian wines at the end of that year.

19. It did not necessarily follow from the increase in those quantities of wine that adulterated wine had come on to the market. As the Commission has pointed out, the large size of the harvest in 1983, mistaken estimates of consumption and inaccuracies in declarations of stocks played a significant part.

20. Finally, the applicants submit that the Commission ought the day after the press conference on 27 August 1985 to have taken steps to withdraw wines adulterated with diethylene glycol from the market, inform consumers of the scandal of adulterated wines and increase checking by the competent national authorities in their supervision of the Community system of distillation.

21. It must first of all be observed that the Commission has no power to withdraw adulterated wine from the market, that being a matter for the national authorities.

22. The Commission is under no obligation to publish the identity of traders who may be involved in scandals. The information system established to detect fraud and irregularities in the wine sector and to avert dangers which might arise from the use of consumable products leaves it to the national authorities to take steps to inform the consumer.

23. Furthermore, on 16 August 1985 the competent United Kingdom authorities gave the authorities of the other Member States information on Italian wine adulterated with diethylene glycol. When the Commission gave its press conference it was aware only of very slight traces of diethylene glycol in some Italian wines. It could therefore legitimately take the view that a reserved approach was preferable to the disclosure of the identity of the companies involved in trade in those wines, which would have led to adverse publicity even more damaging to sales of Italian wine. It must also be borne in mind that when on 26 March 1986 the applicants requested the Commission to disclose the names of the companies concerned Italian wine adulterated with methanol had already been the cause of several deaths. The Commission immediately passed on the information in relation to Italian wine adulterated with methanol which it received in March 1986 from the Italian authorities to the other Member States.

24. Finally, it must be held that even after the appearance in 1985 of Italian wine containing traces of diethylene glycol, the Commission had insufficient facts at its disposal to require a review of the Italian monitoring measures in relation to the distillation system. It should be added that inspection pursuant to Article 9 of Regulation 729/70 of the Council of 21 April 1970 on the financing of the common agricultural policy (OJ English Special Edition 1970(I) p 218) would have related to the financing of distillation by the European Agricultural Guidance and Guarantee Fund and not, as the applicants argue, to the sale of wine on the market.

25. It follows from all the above considerations that the applicants have not succeeded in establishing unlawful conduct on the part of the Commission after the discovery of the scandal of Italian wines containing methanol. In consequence there is no need to determine whether the other conditions necessary in order to establish liability on the part of the Community are satisfied.

26. Accordingly the application must be dismissed as unfounded.

B. Commentary

1. European Law

The *Francesconi* case makes clear that the Commission owes a duty of care towards consumers and in the event of its breach a claim against the Community can arise. The background to the case is a particularly crass instance of dangerous products caused by adulterating wine with methanol which led to a number of fatalities. Apart from traders, claims for compensation were also made against the Commission by survivors of the deceased. The claims rested on a breach of statutory duty in the regulation of the wine market, in particular due to failures in supervising the enforcement of Community law in the Member States (paragraph 5). The ECJ rejected the claim, holding that it had not been proved that the Commission had acted illegally. However, the grounds of the decision set out the conditions under which the Commission is obliged to act in order to ensure the safety of the consumer. In the case concerned, the Commission did not have jurisdiction over the enforcement of the provisions of Community law relating to the general organisation of the wine market. Responsibility for ensuring the provisions were followed lay exclusively with Member States' authorities (paragraph 11). According to the ECJ the Community institutions are obliged to intervene in such a case only where the facts suggest that the authorities of a Member State have not satisfactorily carried out their supervisory duties. The ECJ thereby clearly stated that where the Commission breaches its duty to intervene, a direct claim of compensation arises against the Community under Article 288(2) (ex Article 215(2)) EC Treaty. This had not, however, been made out in *Francesconi*.

In addition, the judgment could also lead one to conclude that where the Community deals within its own competence, the consumer must have his own legal remedies against the Community (*Reich*). One example of Commission competence with which the consumer could have reservations is its power under Article 9 of Directive 92/59 to demand the appropriate measures in so-called product safety emergencies (see European commentary, *German Federal Republic v Council*: Case no 19 in this Casebook). It has been claimed that the *Francesconi* decision fundamentally acknowledges a 'duty to protect consumers imposed by Community Law on the Commission' (*Weatherill*). Some writers go further and draw from the references to consumer protection in Articles 95 and 153 (ex Articles 100a and 129a) EC Treaty a 'right of protection' with regard to product safety which is enjoyed by all EC citizens (*Micklitz*). It is doubtful, however, that such a right of protection exists as subjective law and is actionable at the present stage of Community law's development. To the extent that Community law offers definite obligations to protect the consumer then these are enforceable as tortious claims. This conclusion can be drawn from the *Francovich* case in relation to breaches of obligations by organs of the Member States (see *Francovich* [1991] ECR I–5357; and the European law commentary to ECJ *Dillenkofer*: Case no 13 in this Casebook). The *Francesconi* decision demonstrates that consumer rights may be enforced against the Community by means of claims in tort arising from Article 288 (ex Article 215(2)) EC Treaty.

ECJ CASE LAW REFERENCES

Francovich [1991] ECR I–5357; *Dillenkofer* [1996] ECR I–4845: Case no 13 in this Casebook.

LITERATURE REFERENCES

A Borrás Rodríguez/B Vilá Costa (1990) *Revista Jurídica de Catalunya* 531 (Casenote on *Francesconi*); H Micklitz (1995) *Internationales Produktsicherheitsrecht* 169–241; N Reich *Europäisches Verbraucherrecht* (3rd edn 1996) 533, 534; S Weatherill 'Shaping Responsibilities in the Legal Order of the European Community' in H Micklitz/T Roethe/

S Weatherill (eds) *Federalism and Responsibility: A Study on Product Safety Law and Practice in the European Community* (1994) 153, 204, 205.

HS-N/JJ

2. England & Wales

The *Francesconi* case raised the delicate issue of state liability in the field of product safety. In the UK, the question has been addressed with regard to wrongful prosecutions rather than to omissions.

According to section 27 of the Consumer Protection Act 1987 (CPA), responsibility for consumer safety law enforcement mainly lies with local government trading standard officers. Communication between the different local trading standards officers is ensured by means of connecting computer databases (TS LINK and HAZPROD) and a Bulletin for less urgent matters. The most powerful tools in the hands of the enforcement officers are the powers to serve suspension notices and seizure and forfeiture orders.

Initially, officers can prohibit a trader from supplying or offering to supply certain goods which are suspected of contravening safety provisions (section 14 CPA). Contravention of a suspension notice is an offence, but a suspension notice can be challenged in the magistrates' court, with right to appeal to the Crown Court. If the enforcement officers feel that the trader cannot be trusted, they have the power, under section 29(6) CPA, to seize and detain the relevant goods (again, appeal is guaranteed to the magistrates' court and to the Crown Court). Finally, enforcement authorities can apply to the magistrates' courts for an order for the forfeiture of the goods on the grounds that there has been a contravention of a safety provision (section 16 CPA; this will usually occur during the time when an offence is being prosecuted or a trader is challenging a suspension notice or a seizure order).

In all of these cases, enforcement authorities risk paying compensation if their action turns out not to have been justified. Compensation will be paid to any person having an interest in the goods (sections 14 and 34 CPA). This leaves officers in a difficult situation: even though they are not likely to be held personally liable for the unlawful action, the desire to avoid the problems connected with a compensation claim may affect their behaviour. On the other hand, the Act does not make similar provisions for cases of failure to act, so that no sanctions other than simple blame will be imposed on the enforcement authorities if, being too cautious, they permit dangerous products to be marketed. Similar compensation provisions do not exist for actions taken by the Secretary of State: no comparable penalties will therefore be applied should he exercise his powers unfairly (see UK commentary to *Germany v Council*: Case no 19 in this Casebook).

LITERATURE REFERENCES

K Cardwell/P Kay 'The Consumer Protection Act 1987: Liability of the Enforcement Authorities' (1988) *Trading Law* 212; K Cardwell 'Consumer Protection Act 1987' (1987) *Modern Law Review* 625; G Howells *Consumer Product Safety* (1998); Miller, *Product Liability and Safety Encyclopedia* 1999 IV 162–168.

PN

3. Germany

The *Francesconi* decision has remained relatively unknown in Germany, although it has been published in some of the more important general journals. Influences on German law have not been attributed to the decision. One may find some references to its importance for Community law in relation to state liability law only. Under German law a failure to follow measures or effectively supervise the carrying out of safety regulations can give rise to state liability according to general rules (§ 839 Civil Code, in conjunction with Article 34 of the German Constitution). The prerequisite for liability is that someone acting as an official breached the official duty of care he owed to a third party.

LITERATURE REFERENCES

E Grabitz/M Hilf *Kommentar zur Europäischen Union* Article 215 EC Treaty no 78, 79, 152 (A von Bogdandy) (1998); N Reich *Europäisches Verbraucherrecht* (3rd edn 1996) 533.

HS-N

4. France

The *Francesconi* decision has not been discussed in France. The scandal surrounding the blood banks which had been infected with AIDS, on the other hand, has lead to an interesting development in state liability law. The *Conseil d'État* (in its judgment of 9 April 1993) held that on the basis of its regulations concerning blood transfusions, one of the ministers of the French government was liable for the damage caused by numerous mistakes in the exercise of its powers. In connection with the scandal, the *Cour de Justice de la République* held that the former State Secretary was responsible for every breach of the duty of care during his period in office (judgment of 9 March 1999). He was held negligent because he had failed in his duty to protect the health of the citizens accorded him under the Public Health Code (*Code de la Santé publique*).

CASE LAW REFERENCES

Conseil d'État judgment of 9 April 1993 (1993) *Recueil des décisions du Conseil d'État* 110; Cour de Justice de la République judgment of 9 March 1999 *Gazette du Palais* April 1999 no 112, 27.

LITERATURE REFERENCES

E Aubin 'Lépilogue inattendu de l'affaire du sang contaminé devant la Cour de Justice de République (Casenote) *Revue de la Recherche Juridique—Droit Prospectif*, October 1999 no 4 1325.

BD

5. Italy

In the spring of 1986 Italian officials discovered during the course of their investigations of several deaths as a consequence of excessive alcohol consumption that a number of wine manufacturers were using the highly toxic substance methanol. This discovery came less than a year after traces of diethylenglycol had been found in Italian wines. The manufacture and distribution of grape juices and wines had hitherto been regulated by the *Decreto Presidente della Repubblica* no 162 of 12 February 1965 and by several provisions of Community law. The wine scandal highlighted the inadequacy of the Italian authorities' measures relating to such widely distributed products. The *Regio Decreto Legge* no 2033 of 15 October 1923 regulating agricultural products and the substances used in their production granted responsibility for control over the manufacture and trade of wine to the Ministries of Agriculture, Health and Finance. This control was assigned to special institutions. Complaints had often been made about the inefficiency of the supervision (for example, at a conference about wine control in October 1983). The appropriate measures were not, however, taken in response. The lack of regulation allowed the Italian producers to add methanol to the wine in order to raise the alcohol content. Economically, the reason for this practice was a result of the *Legge* no 408 of 28 July 1984. This provision served to increase the tax on methanol as a result of which its price sank to a tenth of the price of ethanol (normal alcohol; ethyl alcohol). Ethanol had been illegally used on occasion as a substitute for sugar in order to raise the alcohol content of wine.

These failures in supervision were first reported to the European Commission on 25 May 1986: much too late therefore to prevent the incidences of 1985 and 1986 and for an action under Article 226 (ex Article 169) EC Treaty to be taken. Italy introduced a series of measures, such as the governmental ordinances (*Regulamenti Ministeriale*) of 2 April, and 4 and 23 May 1986 containing urgent measures to protect the health of the public from the dangers presented by wine containing methanol. The *Decreto Legge* no 104, which had been issued on 11 April 1986, was replaced by *Legge* no 462 of 7 August 1986 (known as the post–methanol *Legge*). This law legislated for an improved preventative control rather than simply increasing criminal sanctions. More particularly, it created new competence for supervision and sanctions, improved existing control methods and provided a procedure for the event that products which presented a danger to the health of the consumer were discovered. Of especial significance is Article 8 which has enabled both producer and consumer groups to initiate criminal proceedings in the event of a breach of the conditions concerning the production and sale of wine. After the methanol scandal, *Legge* no 460 of 4 November 1987 was also issued. With this provision, Italy introduced a criminal statutory definition for breaches of EC Regulations in the agricultural sector.

It is this wine scandal which forms the background to the *Francesconi* judgment. Its importance may be seen in the fact that the ECJ, even if the problem had not actually presented itself, for all intents and purposes held that liability may be incurred for neglecting to supervise the implementation of Community law (*Carunta*). It is noteworthy that the ECJ, which has denied the Commission's ability to commit tortious acts and rejected numerous claims of compensation against the Community itself, has with this judgment emphasised the responsibility of the Italian authorities. In contrast to the judges of the ECJ, the Italian courts have consistently rejected the liability of the Italian state for neglect of supervision (*Corte d'Appello* Milan judgment of 30 March 1990; *Corte d'Appello* Genova judgment of 15 January 1958). As a consequence, the twenty traders, producers and restaurant owners as well as the victims' representatives dropped their compensation claim against the Italian state, despite the decision of the ECJ. The matter was finally resolved by other means. After negotiations with political representatives who wished to avoid a public prosecution of Italian wine producers the claimants reached an out of court settlement. The Italian state promised action without actually acknowledging its liability.

CASE LAW REFERENCES

Corte d'Appello di Genova judgment of 15 January 1958 (1959) *Il Foro Italiano* I 432; Corte d'Appello di Milano judgment of 30 March 1990; (1990) *Responsabilita Civile e Previdenza* 132.

LITERATURE REFERENCES

D Bellantoni *Trattato di diritto penale degli alimenti* (1994) 341; R Caranta 'La responsabilità della pubblica amministrazione per negligente uso dei poteri di controllo: in margine al caso del vino al metanolo' *Responsabilita Civile e Previdenza* (1991) 761; V Paone 'Nuove disposizioni per la produzione e vendita di prodotti agricoli' (1988) *Il Foro*

Italiano V 97; V Paone 'Il vino al metanolo: ultima tragedia italiana' (1986) *Il Foro Italiano* V 174.

AM

CASE NO. 19 — *Federal Republic of Germany v Council of the European Union* C–359/92

Federal Republic of Germany v Council of the European Union [1994] ECR I–3681

A. Judgment of the ECJ of 9 August 1994

1. Held

1) THE COURT

Dismisses the application.

2) (. . .)

2. Facts of the Case

The Federal Republic of Germany brought an action under the first paragraph of Article 173 (new Article 230) EC Treaty for a declaration that Article 9 of Council Directive 92/59/EC of 29 June 1992 on general product safety (OJ 1992 L228 p 24) is void in so far as it empowers the Commission to adopt, with regard to a product, a decision requiring Member States to take measures from among those listed in Article 6(1)(d) to (h) of the Directive.

Directive 92/59 was adopted under Article 100a (new Article 95(1)) EC Treaty for the purpose of ensuring that consumer products placed on the Internal Market of the Community do not in general present a risk to the consumer under normal conditions of use or, at least, involve only a very low level of risk. Its provisions apply only in so far as more specific Community provisions have not been adopted (Article 1(2) of the Directive). It requires both producers and distributors of products to comply with a general safety requirement. Producers are obliged to place only safe products on the market. They must moreover warn the consumer of the risks attaching to the use of the product and take the necessary measures to identify and avoid such risks. Distributors are required to help to ensure compliance with the general safety requirement (Article 3 of the Directive).

Member States are obliged to adopt the necessary laws, regulations and administrative provisions to ensure compliance with the general safety requirement. In particular, they must establish authorities to check that products placed on the market are safe and confer upon those authorities the necessary powers to take the measures incumbent upon them under the Directive (Article 5). Under Article 6 of the Directive, Member States must adopt provisions enabling them to take, in compliance with the provisions of the Treaty and in particular Articles 30 and 36 (new Articles 28 and 30) thereof, appropriate measures for the purpose of attaining, inter alia, the objectives set out in paragraph 1 of that article. Such measures include those with a view to:

(. . .)

d) subjecting product marketing to prior conditions designed to ensure product safety and requiring that suitable warnings be affixed regarding the risks which the product may present;

e) making arrangements to ensure that persons who might be exposed to a risk from a product are informed in good time and in a suitable manner of the said risk by, inter alia, the publication of special warnings;

f) temporarily prohibiting, for the period required to carry out the various checks, anyone from supplying, offering to supply or exhibiting a product or product batch, whenever there are precise and consistent indications that they are dangerous;

g) prohibiting the placing on the market of a product or product batch which has proved dangerous and establishing the accompanying measures needed to ensure that the ban is complied with;

h) organizing the effective and immediate withdrawal of a dangerous product or product batch already on the market and, if necessary, its destruction under appropriate conditions.

The Directive lays down procedures for notification and exchange of information. Under Article 7, where a Member State takes measures which restrict the placing of a product on the market or require its withdrawal from the market, such as those provided for in Article 6(1)(d) to (h), it must inform the Commission which, after consultations with the parties concerned, has to establish whether or not the measure is justified and inform, as appropriate, the other Member States or the Member State concerned.

Lastly, the Directive contains provisions relating to emergency situations and action at Community level. Article 8 of the Directive provides that, where a Member State adopts emergency measures to prevent, restrict or impose specific conditions on the possible marketing or use of a product presenting serious and immediate risks to the health and safety of consumers, it must immediately inform the Commission, which must ascertain whether that information complies with the provisions of the Directive and forward it to the other Member

States. Those States must inform the Commission of any measures adopted. Article 9 provides as follows:

> If the Commission becomes aware, through notification given by the Member States or through information provided by them, in particular under Article 7 or Article 8, of the existence of a serious and immediate risk from a product to the health and safety of consumers in various Member States and if:
>
> (a) one or more Member States have adopted measures entailing restrictions on the marketing of the product or requiring its withdrawal from the market, such as those provided for in Article 6(1)(d) to (h);
> b) Member States differ on the adoption of measures to deal with the risk in question;
> c) the risk cannot be dealt with, in view of the nature of the safety issue posed by the product and in a manner compatible with the urgency of the case, under the other procedures laid down by the specific Community legislation applicable to the product or category of products concerned; and
> d) the risk can be eliminated effectively only by adopting appropriate measures applicable at Community level, in order to ensure the protection of the health and safety of consumers and the proper functioning of the common market, the Commission, after consulting the Member States and at the request of at least one of them, may adopt a decision, in accordance with the procedure laid down in Article 11, requiring Member States to take temporary measures from among those listed in Article 6(1)(d) to (h).

The procedure provided for in Article 11 of the Directive is variant (b) of Procedure III, as described in Article 2 of Council Decision 87/373/EEC of 13 July 1987 laying down the procedures for the exercise of implementing powers conferred on the Commission (OJ 1987 L197 p 33). During that procedure, the Commission is assisted by the Committee on Product Safety Emergencies, composed of the representatives of the Member States and chaired by a representative of the Commission. It is the duty of that committee to deliver an opinion on the measures proposed by the Commission. The Commission adopts the measures which are in accordance with the Committee's opinion. If the measures proposed are not in accordance with the Committee's opinion, or in the absence of an opinion from the Committee, the Council adopts measures by a qualified majority, on a proposal by the Commission. If the Council does not act within fifteen days of the date on which the proposal was submitted to it, the Commission may adopt the measures proposed, unless the Council has decided against them by a simple majority. Decisions thus adopted are valid for no more than three months, but that period may be prolonged in accordance with the same procedure. Member States must take all necessary measures to implement those decisions within ten days.

3. Extract from the Grounds of the ECJ's Judgment

11. Although the application by the Federal Republic of Germany expressly seeks a declaration that Article 9 of the Directive is void only in so far as it empowers the

Commission to adopt, with regard to a product, a decision requiring Member States to take measures from among those listed in Article 6(1)(d) to (h) of the Directive, its true purpose, given the structure of Article 9, is to obtain the annulment of the article in its entirety.

12. The Federal Republic of Germany bases its application for annulment on two pleas in law. First, it claims that Article 9 of the Directive has no legal base. Second, it claims that the article is contrary to the principle of proportionality. The Council and the Commission contend, for their part, that neither of those two pleas in law is well founded.

The plea in law alleging lack of a legal base.

13. According to the German Government, Article 9 empowers the Commission to apply the Directive to individual cases. It enables the Commission to take decisions replacing those which the national authorities have taken in order to ensure compliance with national legislation transposing the Directive.

14. In its application, the German Government considers that since the Directive was adopted on the basis of Article 100a of the Treaty, it can only derive from Article 100a(5), which empowers the Commission to supervise provisional measures taken by the Member States in accordance with the safeguard clauses which are included in a harmonization measure. The German Government claims that the article does not, however, constitute an adequate legal base, since it allows the Commission only to check whether provisional national measures comply with Community law, but not to adopt measures intended to implement the conclusions which must be drawn, at national level, from that finding.

15. In reply, the Council and the Commission submit that Article 100a(5) of the Treaty does not constitute the legal base for Article 9 of the Directive. In their view, the Directive does not contain any 'safeguard clause' within the meaning of Article 100a(5) of the Treaty, that is to say, any clause authorizing the Member States to adopt provisional measures on one of the non-economic grounds referred to in Article 36 of the Treaty. Consequently, Article 9 does not lay down a 'Community control procedure' for the provisional measures adopted on the basis of such a clause.

16. The Council and the Commission contend that the legal base of Article 9 of the Directive is Article 100a(1) of the Treaty, in conjunction with the third indent of Article 145 thereof. They submit that Article 9 empowers the Commission to adopt 'ad hoc' harmonization measures in the form of decisions which are addressed to Member States, but do not have direct effect with respect to individuals, where emergency measures can be adopted only at Community level and certain conditions are fulfilled.

17. The German Government objects to that argument essentially on the ground that the sole aim of Article 100 *et seq* of the Treaty, and of Article 100a(1) in particular, is the approximation of laws and that those articles do not therefore confer power to apply the law to individual cases in the place of the national authorities, as permitted by Article 9 of the Directive. The German Government further observes that the powers conferred upon the Commission by Article 9 thus exceed those which, in a federal state such as the Federal Republic of Germany, are enjoyed by the Bund in relation to the Länder, since, under the German Basic Law, the implementation of federal laws rests with the Länder. Lastly, the German Government submits that Article 9 cannot be regarded as constituting an implementing power, within the meaning of the third indent of Article 145 of the Treaty, since that article does not embody a substantive power of its own, but merely authorizes the Council to confer implementing powers on the Commission where a legal base exists in primary Community law for the act to be implemented and its implementing measures.

18. It is important to note, in the first place, that Article 100a(5) of the Treaty cannot constitute the legal base for Article 9 of the Directive as, moreover, the parties themselves have recognized.

19. Article 100a(5) of the Treaty provides: 'The harmonization measures . . . shall, in appropriate cases, include a safeguard clause authorizing the Member States to take, for one or more of the non-economic reasons referred to in Article 36, provisional measures subject to a Community control procedure.'

20. That article only concerns supervision, by the Community authorities, of measures taken by the Member States. The purpose of Article 9 of the Directive, however, is not to introduce a control procedure of that kind. It sets out a Community procedure for the coordination of national measures with respect to a product, in order to ensure that it may circulate freely throughout the Community without danger to the consumer.

21. Secondly, the question arises whether Article 100a(1) of the Treaty, supplemented by the third indent of Article 145, constitutes an appropriate legal base for Article 9 of the Directive, as the Council and the Commission contend.

22. As the Court stated in Case C–41/93 (*France v Commission* [1994] ECR I–1829, paragraph 22), for the purposes of implementing the objectives set out in Article 8a of the EEC Treaty (now Article 7a of the EC Treaty), Article 100a(1) of the Treaty empowers the Council to adopt, in accordance with the procedure laid down therein, measures which have as their object the abolition of barriers to trade arising from differences between the provisions laid down by law, regulation or administrative action in Member States.

23. However, the harmonization effected by the Directive is of a particular type, which the Council, by reference to the terms used in the third recital in the preamble to the Directive, describes as 'horizontal' harmonization.

24. According to the fourth recital in the preamble, the Directive establishes at Community level 'a general safety requirement for any product placed on the market that is intended for consumers or likely to be used by consumers'. In accordance with that 'general safety requirement' (see Title II), producers are obliged, first, to place only safe products on the market; second, to provide consumers with the relevant information to enable them to assess the risks inherent in a product throughout the normal or reasonably foreseeable period of its use, where such risks are not immediately obvious without adequate warnings, and to take precautions against those risks; and third, to adopt measures commensurate with the characteristics of the products which they supply, to enable them to be informed of risks which those products might present and to take appropriate action including, if necessary, withdrawing the product in question from the market to avoid those risks. Distributors are required to act with due care in order to help to ensure compliance with the general safety requirement (Article 3 of the Directive).

25. The Directive requires Member States to adopt the necessary laws, regulations and administrative provisions to make producers and distributors comply with their obligations under it in such a way that products placed on the market are safe. In particular, Member States must establish or nominate authorities to monitor the compliance of products with the obligation to place only safe products on the market and arrange for such authorities to have the necessary powers to take the appropriate measures incumbent upon them under the Directive, including the possibility of imposing suitable penalties in the event of failure to comply with the obligations deriving from it (Article 5 of the Directive).

26. Under Article 6 of the Directive, Member States must, for the purposes of Article 5, have the necessary powers, acting in accordance with the degree of risk and in conformity with the Treaty, and in particular with Articles 30 and 36 thereof, to adopt appropriate measures to attain, inter alia, the objectives laid down in Article 6(1)(a) to (h).

27. However, Articles 7 and 8 of the Directive entrust the Commission with the task of supervising measures taken by Member States which are likely to hinder trade.

28. Under Article 7, Member States must inform the Commission of measures which restrict the placing of a product or product batch on the market or require its withdrawal from the market, such as those provided for in Article 6(1)(d) to (h), specifying their reasons for adopting them.

29. Under Article 8, Member States must as a matter of urgency inform the Commission of emergency measures which they have adopted or decided to adopt in order to prevent, restrict or impose specific conditions on the possible marketing or use, within their territory, of a product or product batch by reason of a serious and immediate risk presented by the said product or product batch to the health and safety of consumers. Member States may also pass on to the Commission any information in their possession regarding the existence of a serious and immediate risk before deciding to adopt the measures in question.

30. Under the scheme established by the Directive, it is possible, even likely, that differences may exist between the measures taken by Member States. As the eighteenth recital in the preamble states, such differences may 'entail unacceptable disparities in consumer protection and constitute a barrier to intra-Community trade'.

31. Under that scheme, the nineteenth recital in the preamble to the Directive indicates, it may also be necessary to cope with serious product-safety problems which affect or could affect, in the immediate future, all or a large part of the Community and which, in view of the nature of the safety problem posed by the product and of its urgency, cannot be dealt with effectively under the procedures laid down in the specific rules of Community law applicable to the products or category of products in question.

32. The Community legislature therefore considered it necessary, in order to cope with a serious and immediate risk to the health and safety of consumers, to provide for an adequate mechanism allowing, in the last resort, for the adoption of measures applicable throughout the Community, in the form of decisions addressed to the Member States (see the twentieth recital in the preamble to the Directive).

33. For that purpose, Article 9 of the Directive empowers the Commission, on the basis of the information received, to act in cases where a product placed on the market puts in serious and immediate jeopardy the health and safety of consumers in a number of Member States and those States differ with respect to the measures adopted or planned with regard to that product, that is to say, where such measures do not provide the same level of protection and thereby prevent the product from moving freely within the Community. Article 9 provides that, to the extent that effective protection can be ensured only by action at Community level and no other procedure specifically applicable to the product can be used, the Commission may adopt a decision requiring Member States to take temporary measures from among those listed in Article 6(1)(d) to (h).

34. As is apparent from the eighteenth, nineteenth and twentieth recitals of the preamble to the Directive and from the structure of Article 9, the purpose of that provision is to enable the Commission to adopt, as promptly as possible, temporary measures applicable throughout the Community with respect to a product which presents a serious and immediate risk to the health and safety of consumers, so as to ensure compliance with the objectives of the Directive. The free movement of goods can be secured only if product safety requirements do not differ significantly from one Member State to another. A high level of protection can be achieved only if dangerous products are subject to appropriate measures in all the Member States.

35. Such action must be taken by the Commission in close cooperation with the Member States. For one thing, decisions taken at Community level may be adopted by the Commission only after consulting the Member States and at the request of a Member State. For another, such measures may be adopted by the Commission only if they are in accordance with the opinion of a committee composed of the Member States' representatives and a Commission representative. Otherwise the measure must be adopted by the Council within a specified period. Lastly, those decisions are addressed only to Member States. The twentieth recital in the preamble to the Directive states that such decisions are not of direct application to traders in the Community and must be incorporated in a national measure.

36. Thus, in the circumstances set out in Article 9, action by the Community authorities is justified by the fact that, in the terms used in Article 9(d), 'the risk can be eliminated effectively only by adopting appropriate measures at Community level, in order to ensure the protection of the health and safety of consumers and the proper functioning of the Common Market'.

37. Such action is not contrary to Article 100a(1) of the Treaty. The measures which the Council is empowered to take under that provision are aimed at 'the establishment and functioning of the internal market'. In certain fields, and particularly in that of product safety, the approximation of general laws alone may not be sufficient to ensure the unity of the market. Consequently, the concept of 'measures for the approximation' of legislation must be interpreted as encompassing the Council's power to lay down measures relating to a specific product or class of products and, if necessary, individual measures concerning those products.

38. So far as concerns the argument that the power thus conferred on the Commission goes beyond that which, in a federal state such as the Federal Republic of Germany, is enjoyed by the Bund in relation to the Länder, it must be borne in mind that the rules governing the relationship between the Community and its Member States are not the same as those which link the Bund with the Länder. Furthermore, the measures taken for the implementation of Article 100a of the Treaty are addressed to Member States and not to their constituent entities. Nor do the powers conferred on the Commission by Article 9 of the Directive have any bearing upon the division of powers within the Federal Republic of Germany.

39. Accordingly the legal base of the powers delegated to the Commission by Article 9 of the Directive is Article 100a(1) of the Treaty.

40. Since the German Government does not dispute that such power may accrue to the Commission if its legal base is Article 100a of the Treaty, there is no need to address the question whether the third indent of Article 145 of the Treaty is applicable in this case.

41. It follows from the foregoing that the first plea in law put forward by the Federal Republic of Germany must be rejected.

Breach of the principle of proportionality

42. The German Government claims that Article 9 of the Directive fails to comply with the principle of proportionality in two essential respects. First, the powers given to the Commission are not appropriate for the purpose of ensuring a high level of protection with respect to public health since the adoption of a decision at Community level is no guarantee that the measures taken will be the most suitable. Second, those powers encroach unnecessarily upon the Member States' own powers since the Commission can attain the same objectives by recourse to the infringement procedure under Article 169 of the Treaty and, where appropriate, by making an application to the Court for the adoption of interim measures.

43. The Council and the Commission contend, for their part, that Article 9 of the Directive is not in breach of the principle of proportionality. They submit that action by the Commission, in the situations envisaged by the article, is not only appropriate but also necessary in order to attain the objectives set out in the Directive and, in particular, in order to ensure a high level of protection for consumers whilst maintaining the proper functioning of the internal market. In their view, those objectives cannot be attained by means of the infringement procedure, especially in emergency situations.

44. As the Court has consistently held (see, in particular, Case C–174/89 *Hoche* [1990] ECR I–2681 paragraph 19), the principle of proportionality requires that measures taken by the Community institutions should be appropriate to achieve the objective pursued without going beyond what is necessary to that end.

45. The powers conferred on the Commission by Article 9 are appropriate for the purpose of attaining the objectives pursued by the Directive, that is to say, ensuring a high level of protection for the health and safety of consumers whilst eliminating barriers to trade and distortions of competition arising as a result of disparities between national measures taken in relation to consumer products. The difficulties which might arise if the appropriate measures are determined on a case by case basis cannot lead to the opposite conclusion.

46. Those powers are not excessive in relation to the objectives pursued. Contrary to the assertion made by the German Government, the infringement procedure laid down in Article 169 of the Treaty does not permit the results set out in Article 9 of the Directive to be achieved.

47. In the first place, no obligation can be placed on Member States by means of the infringement procedure to take a specified measure from among those listed in Article 6(1)(d) to (h) of the Directive.

48. Secondly, as the Council and the Commission point out in their observations, even if Member States are required to adopt certain specified measures under the Directive, the Commission would be obliged to bring proceedings for failure to fulfil its obligations against every Member State that had not adopted such measures, inevitably rendering the procedure more cumbersome.

49. Lastly, even if such proceedings were initiated and held by the Court to be well founded, it is not certain that a declaration by the Court to that effect would enable the objectives set out in the Directive to be achieved as effectively as would be the case by a Community harmonization measure.

50. In particular, the infringement procedure would not enable consumer protection to be secured in the shortest possible time. That procedure, which comprises a pre-litigation stage and, where necessary, a contentious stage, inevitably takes a certain amount of time even though, as the German Government points out, the Commission can apply to the Court for the adoption of interim measures. Furthermore, a declaration that a Member State has failed to fulfil its obligations would, in the circumstances envisaged, presuppose a cautious appraisal, scarcely compatible with urgency, of the need to adopt a particular measure, since the Directive merely requires Member States to adopt the measures necessary to compel producers, intermediaries and distributors to place and leave on the market only products which are safe.

51. The second plea in law must therefore be rejected.

52. It follows that the application of the Federal Republic of Germany must be dismissed.

B. Commentary

1. European Law

Initially this case proves somewhat difficult to read. However it serves as a good introduction to some of the fundamental aspects of the law relating to product safety. The core of this area of law is Directive 92/59 on general product safety (OJ 1992 L228/24). This Directive is the culmination of a long line of Community policy to dismantle technical barriers to trade. There are a large number of so-called 'vertical' Directives on the safety of individual products. These were expanded with the general, 'horizontal' Directive 92/59 designed to approximate laws which basically applies to all consumer goods. The horizontal Directive was intended to close the gaps in the law left by the vertical legislation. The Commission is to be granted powers in cases requiring its immediate attention in order to issue uniform emergency measures of general application to the Community.

Directive 92/59 reveals the conflict between the aims of product safety and consumer protection on the one hand, and the completion of the Internal Market on the other. Measures adopted by the Member States designed to implement product safety, in particular prohibitions relating to marketing and duties to warn people on the dangers attaching to the use of individual products, may compromise intra-Community trade. It could also lead to disparities arising in the way individual countries protect the consumer. This becomes even more relevant as the assessment of the dangers presented by a product can vary. In addition, the implications of the decision on the national economy may play a role in the assessment. Directive 92/59 attempts to balance these polarised positions. According to Article 6 of the Directive the Member States are basically responsible for the adoption of measures relating to product safety. They are then duty-bound to notify the Commission of such measures. It will then examine the grounds justifying these measures and finally inform the Member States of its findings (Article 7). Since this procedure can take quite some time, Articles 8 and 9 of Directive 92/59 provide for an accelerated procedure for those products which present serious and immediate risks to the health and safety of consumers. The Member States must immediately inform the Commission of such emergency measures. The Commission will then forward the information to the other Member States (Article 8). According to Article 9 of the Directive (this was the subject of the legal dispute), the Commission has the right under special conditions to oblige Member States to introduce appropriate temporary measures to avert the risk (text from Article 9 is reproduced above in the facts of the case under A2). The conditions include:

1. that one or more Member States have adopted measures (Article 9 (a));

2. that Member States differ on the adoption of measures to deal with the risk in question (b);

3. that the risk cannot be dealt with by means of the ordinary procedure (c);

4. that the risk can be eliminated effectively only by adopting appropriate measures applicable at Community level, in order to ensure the protection of the health and safety of consumers and the proper functioning of the common market (d).

Germany claimed that the power reserved to the Commission was illegal because it had no corresponding legal basis and contravened the principle of proportionality. The ECJ therefore had to pass judgment on the extent of the Community competence to issue measures to complete the Internal Market. The provision in question was Article 95(1) (ex Article 100a) EC Treaty which provided the basis for Directive 92/59 (the wording of this provision is reprinted above in the European law Commentary to ECJ, *Dillenkofer.* Case no 13 in this Casebook). This Article permitted such measures to be adopted by means of a qualified majority vote in Council; this was not the case with Article 94 (ex Article 100) EC Treaty which required unanimity.

The ECJ explained that emergency measures in serious cases of product safety also fell under measures to be adopted under Article 95 (ex Article 100a) EC Treaty which have as their objective 'the establishing and functioning of the Internal Market' (paragraph 37). In a few sentences the judgment dismissed the claim that the Commission's power was disproportionate (paragraphs 45–50). Of particular interest is the fact that the Court rejected the German government's argument that the Commission had a less draconian power at its disposal in the infringement procedure under Article 226 (ex Article 169) EC Treaty. The ECJ considered that infringement proceedings would take too long to ensure the protection of the consumer within the shortest time possible (paragraph 50).

The ECJ therefore confirmed the wide-ranging competence granted to the Commission by Directive 92/59. In this area the ECJ no longer pursues the 'minimum harmonisation' principle which allowed Member States to issue measures relating to consumer protection above the minimum standard required by European law. Directive 92/59 aims at 'horizontal' harmonisation (paragraph 23)—Member States may be prohibited by Community law from exceeding the safety standards proscribed by European law.

As prescribed by Article 16 of Directive 92/59, the Commission has conducted an assessment of the implementation and practical application of the Directive. A report on the main findings of this review has been presented to the European Parliament and the Council (full details available on http://europa.eu.int/comm/dgs/health_consumer/index). As a consequence, the Commission has recently presented a proposal for revising Directive 92/59 (OJ 2000 C337/109) intended to strengthen the power of the Commission to take rapid measures at Community level (see eg Article 13 of the proposal which also permits permanent Community measures to be adopted). In October 2001 the European Parliament endorsed a revised Directive on general product safety which will be published in the OJ in the near future.

LITERATURE REFERENCES

V Constantinesco (1995) *Journal du droit international* 423 (Casenote on *Federal Republic of Germany v Council*); L Gormley (1996) *European Law Review* 63 (Casenote on *Federal Republic of Germany v Council*); G Howells *Consumer Product Safety* (1998); K Mortelmans

(1994) *Sociaal-economische wetgeving* 763 (Casenote on *Federal Republic of Germany v Council*).

HS-N/JJ

2. England & Wales

Before the implementation of Directive 92/59 product safety was regulated by Part II of the Consumer Protection Act 1987. Section 11 of the Act empowers the Secretary of State to introduce safety regulations directed at particular products (eg gas heaters, children's hood cords and babies' dummies). Section 12 makes it a criminal offence to supply goods not complying with these requirements. The Act also gives the Secretary of State power to act quickly and make interim orders using two different means—the Prohibition Notices and the Notices to Warn. These notices are intended to provide emergency solutions to problems posed by specific products or traders. In addition, section 10 of the 1987 Act imposes a general duty to supply only safe goods. The breach of this section is a criminal offence, even in the absence of specific regulations concerning the product:

Section 10. The general safety requirement

2) For the purposes of this section consumer goods fail to comply with the general safety requirement if they are not reasonably safe having regard to all the circumstances, including-

(a) the manner in which, and purposes for which, the goods are being or would be marketed, the get-up of the goods, the use of any mark in relation to the goods and any instructions or warnings which are given or would be given with respect to the keeping, use or consumption of the goods;

(b) any standards of safety published by any person either for goods of a description which applies to the goods in question or for matters relating to goods of that description; and

(c) the existence of any means by which it would have been reasonable (taking into account the cost, likelihood and extent of any improvement) for the goods to have been made safer.

The 1992 Directive clearly follows the policy and the substantive pattern of the 1987 Act, and accordingly its implementation did not require any radical changes. In spite of this, the Government chose to implement the Directive by separate regulations. The General Product Safety Regulations 1994 came into force on 3 October 1994 (statutory instrument 1994/2328). Since then, section 10 of the Act has been 'disapplied' in cases where the safety of a product is covered by the 1994 Regulations and remains in use only for certain, very limited, circumstances (eg where distributors which are not subject to specific product Directives and where the UK implementing regulations only impose obligations on the person who first places the product on the market). Even though the two systems are kept separate in their substantive scope of application, they share core safety standards and enforcement procedures. In particular, Regulation 11 adopts the pre-existing system of enforcement at local level through trading standards officers.

The tension between Europe-wide marketing and local enforcement was, since 1992, a reason of concern for the UK government and led to the Sutherland Report, which made the point that the Internal Market laws would be enforced as part of a network of Community responsibilities. Accordingly, national and local authorities would have Community-wide responsibilities and should accept a duty to co-operate with other such bodies, both through direct contact and via central contact points.

In the 1994 Regulations, the European dimension is demonstrated by the fact that action taken at local level to prohibit or restrict the supply of any product under the Regulations triggers an obligation to notify the Department of Trade and Industry, which passes on the relevant information to the Commission in Brussels. This administrative matter is not specifically mentioned in the Regulations; the UK, however, has actively co-operated in the European Rapid Exchange System: during the years 1993–1998, notifications throughout the Community system totalled 204; thirty-two being reported by the UK. The action brought by the German Republic against the Council, on the other hand, did not raise the interest of UK authorities or commentators.

LITERATURE REFERENCES

Consumer Safety Report by the Secretary of State for the Department of Trade and Industry for the period 1 April 1993–31 March 1998 DTI, November 1998; P Cartwright 'Product Safety and Consumer Protection' (1995) *Modern Law Review* 222; G Howells 'The General Duty to Market Safe Products in the United Kingdom Law' (1994) *Lloyd's Maritime and Commercial Law Quarterly Review*; D Parry 'Product Safety: European Style, An Appraisal' (1995) *Journal of Business Law* 268; 'The Internal Market After 1992: background report' (1993) *European Business Law Review* 116.

PN

3. *Germany*

From the very beginning the Federal Republic resisted the passing of a horizontal Directive but in the event was unable to prevent its adoption on the basis of a majority vote of the Member States. The claim pursued in the ECJ was an attempt to defeat the Commission's jurisdiction in relation to so-called emergency product safety cases (Article 9 of Directive 92/59). The ground for the claim was (apart from the attempt to challenge the loss of state sovereignty) mainly the fear that German safety standards could be compromised by compulsory measures issued by the Commission. Despite the obvious dismay of the Federal Republic, the judgment did not arouse much interest amongst legal writers. Yet the judgment contains a series of criteria which may be of considerable importance to organisational structures in enforcing EC consumer law. In its action Germany compared the allocation of tasks between the *Bund* and the *Länder* within the Federal Republic with the system of jurisdiction provided for in Article 9 of Directive 92/59 (paragraph 38). In support of its case Germany pointed to the fact that the powers granted to the Commission even exceeded the powers granted to the *Bund* over the *Länder*. The ECJ merely remarked that the provisions which regulate the relationship between the Community and the Member States were not the same as those which bind the *Bund* and *Länder*. This argument indicates that in the ECJ's view the interrelationship between the Community and Member States may even be closer than that in a Federal State. The Court of Justice rejected the straightforward transfer of a federal republic state structure. Nevertheless, *Federal Republic of Germany v Council* demonstrates that increasing integration, particularly in the area of law relating to consumer protection, is of benefit to the development of federalist structures in the European Union, even in the enforcement of secondary legislation (*Micklitz*). After considerable delay, the Directive was implemented in Germany by the Law on Product Safety (*Produktsicherheitsgesetz, Bundesgesetzblatt* I 1997, 934).

LITERATURE REFERENCES

Th Klindt *Produktsicherheitsgesetz* (2001); H Micklitz (1994) *Europäische Zeitschrift für Wirtschaftsrecht* 631 (Casenote on *Federal Republic of Germany v Council*).

HS-N

4. France

In France domestic laws relating to product safety apply alongside Community legislation. Together the two sources provide a comprehensive catalogue of preventative measures ensuring the protection of the health and safety of consumers. Some of these provisions apply to all types of products and services. Others have been specially adopted to regulate a certain product or service. Despite the applicability of Community law each state retains its own method of regulation, supervisory bodies and its own procedural law.

In French law general measures on product safety had already been provided by the Law no 83–660 of 21 July 1983, which were integrated into the *Code de la Consommation* under Articles L 221–1 to L 225–1. Article L 221–5 of the *Code de la Consommation* state:

En cas de danger grave ou immédiat, le ministre chargé de la consommation et le ou les ministres intéressés peuvent suspendre par arrêté conjoint, pour une durée n'excédant pas un an, la fabrication, l'importation, l'exportation, la mise sur le marché à titre gratuit ou onéreux d'un produit et faire procéder à son retrait en tous lieux où il se trouve ou à sa destruction lorsque celle-ci constitue le seul moyen de faire cesser le danger. Ils ont également la possibilité d'ordonner la diffusion de mis en garde ou de précaution d'emploi ainsi que la reprise en vue d'un échange ou d'une modification ou d'un remboursement total ou partiel.

Ils peuvent, dans les mêmes conditions, suspendre la prestation d'un service.

Ces produits et ces services peuvent être remis sur le marché lorsqu'ils ont été reconnus conformes à la réglementation en vigueur.

Le ministre chargé de la consommation et, selon le cas, le ou les ministres intéressés entendent sans délai les professionnels concernés et au plus tard quinze jours après qu'une décision de suspension a été prise. Ils entendent également des représentants du comité d'hygiène de sécurité et des conditions de travail, du comité d'entreprises ou, à défaut, les délégués du personnel de l'entreprise intéressée, ainsi que les associations nationales de consommateurs agréées.

Ces arrêtés préciseront les conditions selon lesquelles seront mis à la charge des fabricants, importateurs, distributeurs ou prestataires de services les frais afférents aux dispositions de sécurité à prendre en application des dispositions du présent article.

The application of Article L 221–1 of the *Code de la Consommation* is prohibited by case law if the issue arises after the entry into force of the new law (*Cour d'Appel* Grenoble judgment of 18 December 1995).

France is obliged to inform the Commission if it introduces measures pursuant to Article L 221–5 of the *Code de la Consommation*. However, here there is a difference: Directive 92/59 requires a serious *and* immediate risk to be present, whilst in French law a serious *or* immediate risk is sufficient (*danger grave* ou *immédiat*). This goes to show that French law provides for a higher level of protection because the two requirements are not cumulative. On the whole, French law on product safety provides for a level of protection which has not been significantly changed by Community law. The jurisdiction granted the Commission by Article 9 of Directive 92/59 ensures a uniform system of consumer protection within the Community and in this regard accordingly enhances French law. It is not possible to ascertain the effect the judgment in *Federal Republic of Germany v Council* has had on French law.

CASE LAW REFERENCES

Cour d'Appel de Grenoble judgment of 18 December 1995 *Contrats Concurrence Consommation* December 2000 jurisprudence, no 211.

LITERATURE REFERENCES

V Constantinesco (1995) *Journal du droit international* 423 (Casenote on *Federal Republic of Germany v Council*); M Davis 'La Directive relative à la sécurité générale des produits' (1992) *Revue européenne de droit de la consommation* 132.

BD

5. Italy

Much has been written in Italy about the decision in *Federal Republic of Germany v Council*. For example, it has been argued that the ECJ has failed to provide convincing reasons to justify the Community's passing of the controversial Article 9 of Directive 92/59 (*Carfaggi*). According to this argument, it appears uncertain whether the power to issue urgent measures necessarily guarantees the functioning of the Internal Market or equal protection for consumers. Indeed, according to this opinion the Internal Market could be harmed by Member States' decisions which are at odds with each other. However, Directive 92/59 has taken the possibility of this happening into account. The Directive provides that the assessment of product safety is to be made according to the provisions laid down by the state in which the product was distributed.

According to another opinion, the decision of the ECJ should be justified by virtue of the unique character of the provision in dispute which then gives the Commission a final chance to react to a serious danger presented by a product. The judgment applies the proportionality principle, the scope of which may be perceived in light of the Maastricht Treaty.

Directive 92/59 was transposed into Italian law after one year's delay by the *Decreto Legge* no 115 of 17 March 1995. Whilst other Member States had implemented the Directive by amending existing laws, the Italian legislature largely adopted the text of the Directive word for word. Up to this time there had been no general product safety regulation in Italian law. The *Decreto della Republicca* no 224 of 1988 merely determined liability for defective products. The *Decreto Legge* no 115 of 1995 imposes a general obligation on the manufacturer to ensure 'care and safety'. Responsibility for ensuring adherence to the safety standards is delegated to the Ministries of Trade and Industry, Health, Finance, Transport, Employment and Social Security as well as the Home Office according to the area of responsibility. Within the ambit of their competence the various ministries are able to order that certain products either be made subject to trade restrictions or be taken off the market. Such orders, according to Article 6 no 1 (a) to (h) of *Decreto Legge* no 115 of 1995, which correspond literally with the Directive, must be reported to the Ministry for Trade and Industry, which is then charged with passing the information on to the Commission.

LITERATURE REFERENCES

F Cafaggi 'La responsabilità dell'impresa per prodotti difettosi' in N Lipari (ed) *Diritto Privato Europeo* (1997) 344; L Rossi (1996) *Il Foro Italiano* IV 282 (Casenote on *Federal Republic of Germany v Council*).

AM

CASE NO. 20 — *Commission of the European Community v The United Kingdom of Great Britain and Northern Ireland* C–300/95

Commission of the European Community v The United Kingdom of Great Britain and Northern Ireland [1997] ECR I–2649

A. Judgment of the ECJ of 29 May 1997

1. Held

1. Dismisses the application.

2. (. . .)

2. Facts of the Case

The Commission commenced proceedings under Article 169 (new Article 230) EC Treaty against the United Kingdom for failure to properly implement Directive 85/374 concerning the approximation of laws of the Member States in respect of liability for defective products and the EC Treaty (OJ 1985 L210/29). The Commission accused the UK of not using all means available in order to transpose the Directive correctly, in particular Article 7e. It states:

The Producer is not liable on the basis of the Directive if he can prove that

(. . .)

e) the state of scientific and technical knowledge at the time when he put the product into circulation was not such as to enable the existence of the defect to be discovered.

According to Article 19 of the Directive the Member States had until 30 July 1988 to implement the Directive. The UK transposed Part I of the Directive into law in the Consumer Protection Act 1987. It came into force on 1 March 1988. Section 4(1)(e), implementing Article 7e of the Directive, stated:

> (1) In any civil proceedings by virtue of this Part against any person ('the person proceeded against') in respect of a defect in a product it shall be a defence for him to show-
> [. . .]
>
> (e) that the state of scientific and technical knowledge at the relevant time was not such that a producer of products of the same description as the product in question might be expected to have discovered the defect if it had existed in his products while they were under his control.

The Commission argued that section 4 incorrectly transposed Directive 85/374 and commenced proceedings. It pleaded that the UK had extended the defence in Article 7e beyond what was designed by the Directive and had changed Article 1 of the Directive from the exclusion of liability for developmental risk to one based purely on the producer's negligence.

3. Extract from the Grounds of the ECJ's Judgment

23. In order to determine whether the national implementing provision at issue is clearly contrary to Article 7(e) as the Commission argues, the scope of the Community provision which it purports to implement must first be considered.

24. In order for a producer to incur liability for defective products under Article 4 of the Directive, the victim must prove the damage, the defect and the causal relationship between defect and damage, but not that the producer was at fault. However, in accordance with the principle of fair apportionment of risk between the injured person and the producer set forth in the seventh recital in the preamble to the Directive, Article 7 provides that the producer has a defence if he can prove certain facts exonerating him from liability, including that the 'state of scientific and technical knowledge at the time when he put the product into circulation was not such as to enable the existence of the defect to be discovered' (Article 7(e)).

25. Several observations can be made as to the wording of Article 7(e) of the Directive.

26. First, as the Advocate-General rightly observes in paragraph 20 of his Opinion, since that provision refers to 'scientific and technical knowledge at the time when [the producer] put the product into circulation', Article 7(e) is not specifically directed at the practices and safety standards in use in the industrial sector in which the producer is operating, but, unreservedly, at the state of scientific and technical knowledge, including the most advanced level of such knowledge, at the time when the product in question was put into circulation.

27. Second, the clause providing for the defence in question does not contemplate the state of knowledge of which the producer in question actually or subjectively was or could have been apprised, but the objective state of scientific and technical knowledge of which the producer is presumed to have been informed.

28. However, it is implicit in the wording of Article 7(e) that the relevant scientific and technical knowledge must have been accessible at the time when the product in question was put into circulation.

29. It follows that, in order to have a defence under Article 7(e) of the Directive, the producer of a defective product must prove that the objective state of scientific and technical knowledge, including the most advanced level of such knowledge, at the time when the product in question was put into circulation was not such as to enable the existence of the defect to be discovered. Further, in order for the relevant scientific and technical knowledge to be successfully pleaded as against the producer, that knowledge must have been accessible at the time when the product in question was put into circulation. On this last point, Article 7(e) of the Directive, contrary to what the Commission seems to consider, raises difficulties of interpretation which, in the event of litigation, the national courts will have to resolve, having recourse, if necessary, to Article 177 of the EC Treaty.

30. For the present, it is the heads of claim raised by the Commission in support of its application that have to be considered.

31. In proceedings brought under Article 169 of the Treaty the Commission is required to prove the alleged infringement. The Commission must provide the Court with the information necessary for it to determine whether the infringement is made out and may not rely on any presumption (see, in particular, Case C–62/89 *Commission v France* [1990] ECR I–925 paragraph 37).

32. The Commission takes the view that inasmuch as section 4(1)(e) of the Act refers to what may be expected of a producer of products of the same description as the product in question, its wording clearly conflicts with Article 7(e) of the Directive in that it permits account to be taken of the subjective knowledge of a producer taking reasonable care, having regard to the standard precautions taken in the industrial sector in question.

33. That argument must be rejected in so far as it selectively stresses particular terms used in section 4(1)(e) without demonstrating that the general legal context of the provision at issue fails effectively to secure full application of the Directive. Taking that context into account, the Commission has failed to make out its claim that the result intended by Article 7(e) of the Directive would clearly not be achieved in the domestic legal order.

34. First, section 4(1)(e) of the Act places the burden of proof on the producer wishing to rely on the defence, as Article 7 of the Directive requires.

35. Second, section 4(1)(e) places no restriction on the state and degree of scientific and technical knowledge at the material time which is to be taken into account.

36. Third, its wording as such does not suggest, as the Commission alleges, that the availability of the defence depends on the subjective knowledge of a producer taking reasonable care, having regard to the standard precautions taken in the industrial sector in question.

37. Fourth, the Court has consistently held that the scope of national laws, regulations or administrative provisions must be assessed in the light of the interpretation given to them by national courts (see, in particular, Case C–382/92 *Commission v United Kingdom* [1994] ECR I–2435 paragraph 36). Yet in this case the Commission has not referred in support of its application to any national judicial decision which, in its view, interprets the domestic provision at issue inconsistently with the Directive.

38. Lastly, there is nothing in the material produced to the Court to suggest that the courts in the United Kingdom, if called upon to interpret section 4(1)(e), would not do so in the light of the wording and the purpose of the Directive so as to achieve the result which it has in view and thereby comply with the third paragraph of Article 189 of the Treaty (see, in particular, Case C–91/92 *Faccini Dori v Recreb* [1994] ECR I–3325 paragraph 26). Moreover, section 1(1) of the Act expressly imposes such an obligation on the national courts.

39. It follows that the Commission has failed to make out its allegation that, having regard to its general legal context, especially section 1(1) of the Act, section 4(1)(e) clearly conflicts with Article 7(e) of the Directive. As a result, the application must be dismissed.

B. Commentary

1. European Law

The *Commission v United Kingdom* case is the ECJ's first judgment on Directive 85/374 concerning liability for defective products. The Commission lost its action against the United Kingdom for failure on the latter's part to properly transpose the Directive. The case also clarified the ambiguity which had given rise to a plethora of interpretations to one aspect of the Directive in the past. Directive 85/374 basically imposes strict liability on the producer. According to Article 4, the injured party has only to prove the damage, defect and causal connection between the two. The concept of fault is absent from the Directive. Doubts about this important aspect were raised in the proceedings concerning the disputed exception operating to the benefit of the producer in Article 7(e) of the Directive. According to this provision the producer is not liable if he furnishes evidence that:

> the state of scientific and technical knowledge at the time when he put the product into circulation was not such as to enable the existence of the defect to be discovered.

The United Kingdom had worded the measure transposing this provision in such a way that it apparently required the consumer having to show that the producer was negligent. Section 4(1)(e) of the Consumer Protection Act 1987 states:

> (1) In any civil proceedings by virtue of this Part against any person ('the person proceeded against') in respect of a defect in a product it shall be a defence for him to show-
> [. . .]

> (e) that the state of scientific and technical knowledge at the relevant time was not such that a producer of products of the same description as the product in question might be expected to have discovered the defect if it had existed in his products while they were under his control.

The Commission argued that this provision did not correctly transpose the strict liability provided for by the Directive in that it transformed the exclusion of liability for developmental risk into a liability founded purely on negligence on the part of the producer.

In its judgment the ECJ first of all interpreted Article 7(e) of Directive 85/834 in such a way that liability did not depend on the fault of the producer. Thus far the Court's decision corresponded to the Commission's opinion on the law. The judgment emphasised three particular aspects:

> 1. The provision does not refer to the *usual* safety procedures and standards but without restriction to the state of scientific and technical knowledge at the time when the producer put the product into circulation. Therefore the most advanced level of science and technology is implied (paragraph 26).

> 2. It does not depend on what the producer actually knew or could have known, but rather on the objective state of scientific and technical knowledge which the producer is considered to be informed of (paragraph. 27).

> 3. The wording of Article 7(e) refers solely to the relevant scientific and technical knowledge at the time the product was brought into circulation (paragraph 28).

The Court dismissed the claim because the Commission failed to prove that the Directive had been clearly infringed and in particular, that the courts in the United Kingdom would fail to construe the relevant provisions of the transposing measure in accordance with the Directive. In so deciding, the ECJ cited Section 1(1) of the Consumer Protection Act 1987, which states:

> This Part shall have effect for the purpose of making such provision as is necessary in order to comply with the product liability Directive and shall be construed accordingly.

Even the Commission admitted that this provision constituted a 'very important point of reference for the national courts' (paragraph 18 of the judgment). The ECJ therefore relied on the United Kingdom courts to interpret the provision in accordance with the Directive. At the same time however it made explicit reference to the possibility or obligation to make a reference for a preliminary ruling under Article 234 (ex Article 177) EC Treaty (paragraph 29).

The ECJ's interpretation of Directive 85/374 shows a readiness to achieve a high level of consumer protection. The ECJ has clearly opposed moves to introduce a fault based liability through the back door by means of the exemption provisions for developmental risks in Article 7(e) of the Directive. When coming to its decisions the Court is guided by the aim to fairly apportion the risk presented by the product between the producer and the injured party (paragraph 24). It does not depend on the producer being at fault. According to Article 7(e) of Directive 85/374 the exculpation of the producer ceases to apply in the case where, anywhere in the world, according to the highest possible state of science and technology, the fault could have been established.

On a different note, the ECJ revealed in this judgment a certain reserve on the part of the Community in its dealings with the Member States. Even the wording of the Directive which, in a law designed to transpose Community legislation at the very least is ambiguous, does not immediately lead to prosecution for breach of Community law, as long as the possibility exists that the domestic courts construe the provision in accordance with the Directive. The ECJ once again merely pointed out to the domestic courts that in their interpretation of domestic laws they were bound to comply with Community law and where necessary consider whether to make a preliminary reference to the ECJ. The judgment also demonstrates how useful it may be to refer to authoritative Community law in domestic cases.

Despite this, it is doubtful whether Directive 85/374 has important consequences for consumer protection. The ECJ pointed out in its judgment that the Commission was unable to cite one single decision of a UK court in support of its opinion. There appears to be little national case law concerning this Directive and the laws transposing it (some examples are given in the commentaries to individual countries). It is clear, that in some countries the Directive has been of little practical importance up to now. Only time will tell whether the latest amendment to Directive 85/374 (Directive 1999/34, OJ 1999 L141/20) concerning, inter alia, defects caused by 'primary agricultural products' will have any noticeable effect. But, as a recent case illustrates, the Directive may improve the position of the consumer who undergoes an operation in a hospital (ECJ *Veedfald* Case C–203/99).

LITERATURE REFERENCES

C Hodges 'Development Risk: some Unanswered Questions' (1998) *Modern Law Review* 560; M Mok 'Omzetting richtlijn productaansprakelijkheid' (1997) *TVVS ondernemingsrecht en rechtspersonen* 259; A Penneau (1998) *Recueil Dalloz Sirey* Jurisprudence, 490 (Casenote on *Commission v United Kingdom*).

HS-N/JJ

2. England & Wales

The product liability Directive was implemented in the UK by Part I of the Consumer Protection Act 1987 which came into force on 1 March 1988. Until that time, the UK had dealt with product liability in two ways: the general principles of tort law (entailing a fault based system of liability); and the law of contract (to the extent permitted by the privity doctrine).

From the outset, concern was expressed in the academic world and in Parliament that the Act did not properly implement the Directive: during its enactment, the House of Lords made an amendment to section 4(1)(e) of the Act in order to bring it in line with the wording of Article 7(e) of the Directive. This amendment, however, was reversed in the House of Commons in response to the pressure by industry.

The fact that the Consumer Protection Act does not reproduce *verbatim* the text of the Directive led the Commission to allege, in their first letter before action, six grounds of infringement against the UK. However, in view of the UK's response and of section 1(1) of the Act under which the relevant provisions are to be construed in accordance with the Directive the Commission only pursued one of these grounds.

The UK put forward two arguments in the course of the proceedings: first, in the absence of any domestic judicial interpretation of section 4(1)(e) of the Act, the Commission could not claim that it was incompatible with Article 7(e); and secondly, the UK considered that the only sensible interpretation of the wording of Article 7(e) (reproduced by section 4(1)(e) of the Act) is that the capacity of the producer in question (or of producers of similar products) constitutes an objective, abstract notion referring not to what the producer knew or did not know, but to what he should and/or could have known in the light of the scientific and technical knowledge available at the time.

The judgment triggered different reactions in the UK academic environment. Some commentators have argued that, by referring the test imposed by Article 7(e) to the 'objective state of accessible scientific knowledge at its most advanced level', the ECJ has stricken a fair balance between the interests of the consumer and the attribution of a fair degree of risk to the producer and has provided national courts ample material on the scope and interpretation of the Directive (*O'Donoghue*). Other commentators, on the other hand, have argued that such a test is not practicable without including a requirement of reasonableness in relation to both the state of knowledge and to discoverability (*Hodges*). Finally, others have indicated as the main difficulty, unresolved by the Court, the definition of the meaning of 'state': the choice would be between requiring the knowledge leading to the defect to be available as a whole or to be available in its component parts with the logical or empirical connection remaining to be made. Accordingly, the best solution to redress the failure of the Directive would be to remove the development risk defence completely (*Mildred-Howells*).

LITERATURE REFERENCES

N Newdick 'The Development Risk Defence and the Consumer Protection Act 1987' (1988) *Cambridge Law Journal* 455; C Hodges 'Development Risk: some Unanswered Questions' and M Mildred/G Howells Comment on 'Development Risk: Unanswered Questions' (1998) *Modern Law Review* 560–570 and 570–573; R O'Donoghue *Commission v UK*: Wasted Opportunity or Pyrric Victory?' *European Current Law* November 1997 ix–xii; J Stapleton *Product Liability* (1994); Miller *Product Liability and Safety Encyclopedia* (1999) III 122–127.

PN

3. Germany

In Germany, Directive 85/374 was belatedly transposed by the Law on Product Liability (*Produkthaftungsgesetz, Bundesgesetzblatt* I 1989 2198, as amended by *Bundesgesetzblatt* I 2000 1478) about one and half years after the period of implementation had expired. The Law on Product Liability supplements the general law on tort which is regulated in the Civil Code (*Bürgerliches Gesetzbuch* §§ 823 to 853). On occasion, however, Directive 85/374 has also been cited in order to interpret the general law on tort (eg *Bundesgerichtshof* (Federal Court of Justice), judgment of 19 November 1991). The Federal Republic, like the United Kingdom, made use of the option to exclude liability for developmental risks. Paragraph 1(2) no 5 of the Law on Product Liability states:

Die Ersatzpflicht des Herstellers ist ausgeschlossen, wenn [. . .]

5. der Fehler nach dem Stand der Wissenschaft und Technik in dem Zeitpunkt, in dem der Hersteller das Produkt in den Verkehr brachte, nicht erkannt werden konnte.

According to Directive 85/374, a claim of damages which is contained in the Law on Product Liability is difficult to put into the categories which are laid down by the German law of tort. German legal writers are divided as to whether the liability is to be categorised as strict, as no-fault liability for an objective wrong doing or a hybrid liability arising from fault and wrong doing to be determined by the nature of the wrong committed (see *Staudinger/Oechsler*). Moreover, from the exclusion of liability for development risks contained in § 1(2) no 5 of the Law on Product Liability, it has sometimes been concluded that liability is being imposed for a suspected wrongdoing. The judgment of the ECJ in *Commission v the United Kingdom* however resists the adoption of fault-based liability. Remarkably, this judgment has had no discernible influence on the debate.

The only judgment of the *Bundesgerichtshof* thus far on development risk concerned an exploding mineral water bottle (judgment of 9 May 1995). The lower courts had ascertained that despite all reasonable measures the exploding bottle resulted from an unavoidable fault in the production process. Therefore the producer was not at fault. The *Bundesgerichtshof* confirmed the imposition of liability according to the Law on Product Liability. In particular, liability could not be excluded on the basis of a development risk as laid down in § 1(2) no 5. This provision only applied to faults in construction and not in production. Paragraph 1(2) no 5 does not exclude liability for faults in manufacturing.

However, it is difficult to understand the grounds on which the *Bundesgerichtshof* declined to refer the case to the ECJ. Among the reasons given was the argument that a reference need only be submitted if the interpretation of the rule of Community law is disputed in case law or in legal writings or if the domestic court intends to distinguish the case from the case law of the ECJ. These conditions had not been fulfilled in this case. It appears from its submissions that the *Bundesgerichtshof* wished to apply the *acte clair* doctrine. According to this doctrine a request for a preliminary ruling from the ECJ is not necessary if the answer to the legal question is clear and immediately apparent. However, the ECJ has set narrow limits within which this doctrine may be applied. A court of last instance may only decline to request a preliminary ruling if the correct application of Community law is so apparent that 'so obvious as to leave no scope for any reasonable doubt as to the manner in which the question raised is to be resolved' (*CILFIT* [1982] ECR 3415 paragraph 16). The German *Bundesverfassungsgericht* (Federal Constitutional Court ruling of 9 January 2001) has recently clarified under which circumstances German courts are obliged to make a reference to the ECJ for a preliminary ruling. In the light of the criteria developed by the *Bundesverfassungsgericht*, the *Bundesgerichtshof* should probably have referred the mineral water bottle case to the ECJ.

CASE LAW REFERENCES

Bundesgerichtshof judgment of 19 November 1991 *Entscheidungen des Bundesgerichtshofs in Zivilsachen* Volume 116 104; Bundesgerichtshof judgment of 9 May 1995 (1995) *Neue Juristische Wochenschrift* 2162; Bundesverfassungsgericht ruling of 9 January 2001 (2001) *Neue Juristische Wochenschrift* 1267.

LITERATURE REFERENCES

J Oechsler *Staudingers Kommentar zum Bürgerlichen Gesetzbuch, Produkthaftungsgesetz, Einleitung*, no 27–42; § 1 no 110–130; A Staudinger 'Zur Novellierung des Produkthaftungsgesetzes' (2001) *Neue Juristische Wochenschrift* 275.

HS-N

4. France

It took ten years for France to implement Directive 85/374 in Law no 98–389 of 19 May 1998. Before implementation of the Directive the French courts had tried on many occasions to achieve its aims by construing the general law on tort in accordance with the Directive (judgments of the *Cour de Cassation* of 17 January 1995 and 28 April 1998). According to Law no 98–389 a new title IV entitled '*Des différents manières dont on acquiert la propriété*' was added to the third book of the *Code civil* under the heading '*De la responsabilité du fait des produits défectueux*' which contains Articles 1386–1 to 1386–18. Article 1386–11 states:

> Le producteur est responsable de plein droit à moins qu'il ne prouve:
>
> (. . .)
>
> 4° Que l'état des connaissances scientifiques et techniques, au moment où il a mis le produit en circulation, n'a pas permis de déceler l'existence du défaut;

This wording is an almost literal transposition of the Directive. Nevertheless, as far as consumer protection is concerned, this exclusion of liability for development risk represents a retreat in comparison with the previous domestic law. In general, French courts had rejected clauses excluding liability for development risks (*Cour de Cassation, Sang contaminé* judgments of 12 April 1995, upheld in the judgments of 9 July 1996). The French government had vehemently opposed an exclusion of liability for development risk at the time Directive 85/374 was being debated in the Council. Only during parliamentary debates on French legislation to transpose the Directive was the exclusion of liability introduced following pressure from the lobby representing various economic interests. In France, the transposition of Directive 85/374 therefore led to a reduction in the level of consumer protection.

CASE LAW REFERENCES

Cour de Cassation 1ère chambre civile judgment of 17 January 1995 (1995) *Recueil Dalloz Sirey* Jurisprudence 350; Cour de Cassation 1ère chambre civile judgment of 12 April 1995 (*Sang contaminé*) *Juris-classeur périodique—La semaine juridique* édition générale 1995 II 22467; Cour de Cassation 1ère chambre civile judgment of 9 July 1996 (1996) *Recueil Dalloz Sirey* Jurisprudence 610; Cour de Cassation 1ère chambre civile decision of 28 April 1998 *Juris-classeur périodique—La semaine juridique* édition générale 1998 850.

LITERATURE REFERENCES

A Penneau (1998) *Recueil Dalloz Sirey* Jurisprudence 490 (Casenote on *Commission v UK*); G Viney 'L'introduction en droit français de la Directive européenne du 25 juillet 1985' (1998) *Recueil Dalloz Sirey* Chronique 291; G Raymond 'Premières vues sur la loi no 98–389 du 19 mai 1998 relative à la responsabilité du fait des produits défectueux' (1998) *Contrats Concurrence Consommation* chronique no 16; E Fouassier 'La responsabilité du fait des produits défectueux s'étend-elle au prejudice moral?' *Petites Affiches* no 9, January 1999 17.

BD

5. Italy

Very little has been written in Italy about the decision in the case *Commission v United Kingdom*. It has been argued that the result reached by the ECJ, that section 4(1)(e) of the Consumer Protection Act 1987 complies with Directive 85/374 was predictable (*Ponzanelli*). In Italy, Directive 85/374 was implemented by *Decreto Presidente della* Repubblica no. 224 of 24 May 1988. Its title states:

> Attuazione della Direttiva CEE n 85/374 relativa al ravvicinamento delle disposizioni legislative regolamentari ed amministrative degli Stati membri in materia di Responsabilita' per danno da prodotti difettosi.

This *Decreto* introduced strict liability (*responsabilita senza colpa*) for defective products. Even before this the principle of strict liability had been acknowledged by some Italian courts (see especially *Corte di Cassazione, Saiwa* judgment of 25 May 1964) using the general law of tort (Article 2043 *Codice civile*).

The prerequisites for product liability derive from Article 1 in conjunction with Article 6 of *Decreto Presidente della Repubblica* no. 224 of 1988. Article 1 defines the manufacturer's liability for damage which is caused by a defective product. Article 6 enumerates those instances where liability may be excluded. For example, letter 'e' of the Article declares that liability is excluded if:

> lo stato delle conoscenze scientifiche e tecniche, al momento in cui il produttore ha messo in circolazione il prodotto, non permetteva ancora di considerare il prodotto come difettoso.

Italy therefore chose to exercise the option provided for in the Directive to exclude liability for risks incurred in product development. A commission which had been set up by the Italian Ministry of Justice decided against imposing liability on the manufacturer for development risks because applying a strict product liability in cases of unforeseeable risk would have primarily had an insurance purpose, not consumer protection.

Article 6 letter 'e' of *Decreto Presidente della Repubblica* no 224 of 1988 repeats Article 7 letter 'e' of Directive 85/374 with one small exception. The Italian law states that: '*lo stato delle conoscenze scientifiche e tecniche (. . .) non permetteva ancora di considerare il prodotto come difettoso*' ('the level of science and technology does not allow the product to be regarded as defective'), whilst the Directive states that '*non permetteva di scoprire l'esistenza del difetto*' (literally: 'does not make it possible to detect the presence of a defect'; the German version of the Directive translates: 'that it was not possible to detect the defect present'). The Commission complained about this discrepancy but declined to pursue the matter further. In contrast to the United Kingdom, an action for breach of Community law was not commenced against Italy.

The interpretation of the whole provision depends on the meaning of the expression 'level of science and technology'. It is accepted amongst Italian writers that this term applies to both experimental and non-experimental studies (*Alpa, Ponzanelli*). The level of science and technology can be ascertained according to the majority opinion of scientists or even according to minority opinions, provided they are well founded. Italian legal writers adopt the latter point of view. There have hitherto been only a few judgments relating to the new product liability law. For example, judgments of the *Tribunale* Milan of 13 April 1995 and the *Tribunale di Monza* of 20 July 1993 have been published. However, neither tackle the question of development risks.

CASE LAW REFERENCES

Corte di Cassazione *Saiwa* judgment of 25 May 1964 (1965) *Il Foro Italiano* I 2098; Tribunale di Monza judgment of 20 July 1993 (1994) *Il Foro Italiano* I 251; Tribunale di Milano judgment of 13 April 1995 (1996) *Danno e Responsabilità* 381; Corte di Cassazione judgment of 21 January 2000 no 639 (2000) *Massimano*.

LITERATURE REFERENCES

G Alpa 'La responsabilità del produttore nelle proposte della dottrina e nei modelli legislativi' (1991) *Scritti in onore di Angelo Falzea* 211; G Alpa 'L'attuazione della direttiva comunitaria sulla responsabilità el produttore, tecniche e modelli a confronto' (1988) *Contratto e Impresa* 343; M Bin 'L'esclusione della responsabilità' *La responsabilità del produttore. Trattato di Diritto commerciale e di diritto pubblico dell'economia* (1994) 423; G Ponzanelli 'Regno Unito, Corte di giustizia ed eccezioni allo state of art' (1997) Il Foro Italiano IV 388; G Ponzanelli (1996) Danno e Responsabilità 381 (Casenote on Tribunale di Milano judgment of 13 April 1995); Istituto Internzionale per la promozione della cultura arbitrale, (a cura di), Lo sviluppo della disciplina della responsabilità del produttore Contratti 1999 1181; A Oddo 'Responsabilità del produttore e direttiva n 85/374/CEE: lo stato delle conoscenze scienfiche e tecniche quale causa di esclusione della responsabilità nella interpretazione della Corte di Giustizia' (1998) *Diritto communitario e degli Scambi Internazionale* 367; U Carnevali 'Responsabilità del produttore' *Enciclopedia del diritto*, Agg. II 1998 936; M Franzoni 'Diece anni di repsonsabilità del produttore' (1998) *Danno e Responsabilità* 823; A Caiola 'L'evoluzione dell giurisprudenza italiana in material di responsabilità per danni da produtti difettosi' (1993) *Diritte communitario e degli Scambi Internazionale* 639.

AM

6. Austria

Whilst there is scarcely any published case law on legislation transposing Directive 85/374 in some countries, Austria already has a number of judgments from the higher courts in this area. This is because of the actions of consumer pressure groups. Thus, the *Oberster Gerichtshof* (Supreme Court) has already decided three cases concerning exploding drink bottles (judgments of 30 July 1992, 1 July 1993 and 8 April 1997).

Austria had voluntarily put Directive 85/374 into effect by the enactment of the Law on Product Liability (*Produkthaftungsgesetz, PHG, Bundesgesetz* of 21 January 1988 no 99) even before it became a member of the European Community. For a long time it was unclear the extent to which the *PHG* should be interpreted in accordance with the Directive. The *Oberster Gerichtshof* has now stressed that the statute must be interpreted in accordance with the Directive, at least in cases of injury which have occurred since Austria's accession to the Community legal order on 1 January 1995 (judgment of 26 May 1997).

The exclusion of liability for development risk contained in Article 7(e) of the Directive has been transposed by § 8(2) *PHG*. However, the wording derogates somewhat from the provision in the Directive. While the Directive states 'the existence of the defect [was not able to be] . . . discovered', § 8(2) requires that 'the properties of the product [. . .] were not able to be identified as being faulty'. As a consequence of this the *Oberster Gerichtshof* has been guided in making its decisions by asking whether the danger presented by a particular property of the product was identifiable or not at the time it was put into circulation (ruling of 28 June 1995; judgments of 8 April and 16 of April 1997). It is however quite possible that a certain property of the product was clearly identifiable as constituting a danger but that when measured against the highest level of scientific and technological knowledge demonstrated the best safety precautions possible and thereby could not be identified as faulty within the meaning of the Directive. As a result, the *Oberster Gerichtshof* has completely refused to allow liability to be excluded on the basis of developmental risk in the case of products which by their very nature are dangerous (eg, electric conductors (judgment of 16 April 1997)).

In respect of the Directive this means an improvement in the legal position of the consumer and a greater burden on the producer. This national law cannot be challenged on grounds of Community law. Article 15(1)(b) of Directive 95/374 expressly grants Member States the possibility of not allowing the defence of development risk.

A different question is whether the *Oberster Gerichtshof's* interpretation does justice to the wording of § 8(2) *PHG* which regards the identification of a 'faulty' (as opposed to a 'dangerous') property of the product as being decisive.

CASE LAW REFERENCES

Oberster Gerichtshof *Coca-Cola-Flasche* judgment of 30 July 1992 (1993) *Juristische Blätter* 524; Oberster Gerichtshof *Limonadenflasche* judgment of 1 July 1993 (1994) *Juristische Blätter* 193; Oberster Gerichtshof *Hubarbeitsbühne* judgment of 28 June 1995 (1996) *Juristische Blätter* 188; Oberster Gerichtshof *Mineralwasserflasche* judgment of 8 April 1997 (1998) *Zeitschrift für Verkehrsrecht* 19; Oberster Gerichtshof *Stromleitung* judgment of 16 April 1997 (1997) *Juristische Blätter* 739; Oberster Gerichtshof *Trampolinanlage* judgment of 26 May 1997 (1997) *Juristische Blätter* 779.

LITERATURE REFERENCES

P Madl/P Kelly/R Attree (eds) *European Product Liabilities* (1997) 39; W Posch/M Schwimann (eds) *Praxiskommentar zum ABGB*, Volume 8 Haftpflichtgesetze (1997) 375.

AE